Understandi

Understanding Jesus
Five Ways to Spiritual Enlightenment

Peter S. Williams

Paternoster:
thinking faith

17 16 15 14 13 12 11 7 6 5 4 3 2 1

This edition first published 2011 by Paternoster
Paternoster is an imprint of Authentic Media Limited
Presley Way, Crownhill, Milton Keynes, MK8 0ES
www.authenticmedia.co.uk

British Library Cataloguing in Publication Data

A catalogue record for this book is available from the
British Library

ISBN-13: 978-1-84227-739-3

Unless otherwise specified all Scripture quotations are taken from the Holy
Bible, Today's New International Version™ TNIV®. Copyright © 2001, 2005 by
International Bible Society®. All rights reserved worldwide.

[Other versions cited: AV, CEV, ESV, NIV, NLT, RSV]

[Abbreviations used in footnotes: *Ann Intern Med* (*Annals of Internal Medicine*);
BARev (*Biblical Archaeology Review*); JAMA (*Journal of the American Medical
Association*); NTTS (New Testament Tools and Studies series); *SMJ* (*Southern
Medical Journal*); TJ (*Trinity Journal*)]

The viability of all web links was checked 7–25 September 2010.

Cover design by Paul Airy at DesignLeft (www.designleft.co.uk)
Printed and bound by CPI Group (UK) Ltd, Croydon, CR0 4YY

This book is dedicated to Rob J. Stroud
and to Transatlantic
for their sublime album *The Whirlwind* (Insideout, 2009)

Contents

Rationalists, free thinkers, and atheists all rely for their philosophies on reason and evidence rather than superstition or blind faith. This can lead to some unexpected conclusions.

Editorial, *New Humanist*, September–October 2010

Author's Preface

The historical quest for the historical Jesus has ended; the interdisciplinary quest for the historical Jesus has just begun.

Bernard Brandon Scott[1]

As a Christian philosopher, I've had a long-standing ambition to write a book about Jesus. James K. Beilby and Paul Rhodes Eddy observe that 'it is no longer merely New Testament scholars and historians who are wading into the rushing waters of the quest [for the historical Jesus], but an entire cadre of interdisciplinary explorers, each bringing their own distinctive disciplinary methods, tools and insights to the historical study of Jesus and the Gospels.'[2] In particular, they note that 'in recent times one can find a variety of philosophers and philosophical theologians weighing in on relevant matters.'[3] I'm thankful to Paternoster Press for giving me this opportunity to apply some contemporary philosophical methods, tools and insights to the interdisciplinary study of the *logos* made flesh.

I'd like to register my thanks to everyone who has supported my ministry over the years through gifts of prayer, money, encouragement and opportunities to exercise my calling. I'd like to offer particular thanks to: the University of Central Lancashire Christian Union for inviting me to lecture on 'Understanding Jesus' in 2009; everyone involved with the first three iterations of the 'Reasonable Faith?' course at Highfield Church, Southampton; my church home-group (especially Dr Claire Swabey for her mathematical assistance); the Tyndale Fellowship; my colleagues at the Damaris Trust (www.damaris.org) and at Gimlekollen School of Journalism and Communication, Kristiansand, Norway (www.mediehogskolen.no); Chris Knight; Rob Stroud and the 'Tippling Philosophers' of Fareham; Dr Robin Parry, for his warmth towards my original pitch, and to Dr Mike Parsons and the team at Paternoster (including my copy editor Mollie Barker) for making it a reality.

Responsibility for any infelicitous content naturally remains with me, for as Stuart C. Hackett once wrote: 'I am after all a merely finite thinker wielding a weapon of objective rationality which I suppose clearly to possess a far greater adequacy than attaches to any limited and effective use I may make of it.'[4]

Peter S. Williams
Assistant Professor in Communication and Worldviews
Gimlekollen School of Journalism and Communication, Norway

Southampton, September 2010

1

Five Ways to Understanding Jesus

'Have courage to use your own understanding' – that is the motto
of enlightenment.

Immanuel Kant[1]

The Roman emperor Trajan (AD 98–117) was paranoid about
private clubs nurturing political opposition, so he 'pronounced an
outright ban on all such organizations ... his suspicion of "secret"
clubs went to such lengths that he banned even voluntary fire
brigades!'[2] Another group caught up in Trajan's paranoia were
adherents of a young, but fast-growing, religious movement:

> a rabble of profane conspiracy. Their alliance consists in meet-
> ings at night with solemn rituals and inhuman revelries ... They
> despise temples as if they were tombs. They disparage the gods
> and ridicule our sacred rites ... Just like a rank growth of weeds,
> the abominable haunts where this impious confederacy meet are
> multiplying all over the world.[3]

Despite nightmarish atrocities committed against them by the
emperor Nero (AD 37–68), these conspirators persisted in the
laughable, scandalous practice of worshipping an ignominious
criminal called 'Yeshu'. He'd claimed to be the Jewish *Meshiach*
(that is, 'Messiah', meaning 'anointed one') but was subsequently crucified by the authorities. Roman lawyer Minucius
Felix reported the received opinion about this strange religious
movement: 'To venerate an executed criminal and ... the wooden
cross on which he was executed is to erect altars which benefit ...
depraved wretches.'[4]

'Yeshu' is the shortened form of 'Yeshua' (i.e. Joshua). In Greek the name is rendered *Iēsous*, which in English becomes 'Jesus'. Likewise, *Meshiach* is rendered *ho christos* in Greek, which in English becomes 'the Christ'. Although the original worshippers of *Iēsous christos* (Jesus Christ) described themselves as 'followers of the Way' (cf. John 14:6; Acts 22:4), the public at large dubbed them 'Christians' (cf. Acts 11:26).

Worries about the growth of the criminal-worshipping 'Christians', combined with some salacious rumours, led Trajan to outlaw Christianity. After all, the word on the street said Christians were cannibals! Leigh Churchill explains:

> The bizarre rumour of cannibalism seemed plausible to many … who were misled by what seemed, to them, one of the most unusual activities of the early church. In ancient pagan society unwanted babies, particularly handicapped infants, were often thrown into the streets to die. This practice … was considered quite acceptable – even by leading pagan philosophers and moralists. The church, of course, vigorously opposed such conduct, and Christians across the empire became known for rescuing and adopting such infants.[5]

Some said Christians actually took abandoned babies to devour in secret rites, a misunderstanding or misrepresentation of the Christian practice of consuming bread and wine as the metaphorical 'flesh and blood' of Jesus.

As a consequence of Trajan's paranoia, and of rumours such as those about cannibalism, the city of Antioch instigated a crackdown on illegal clubs c. AD 107. One of those arrested was the city's Christian leader (or 'bishop'), Ignatius. Hauled before the local governor, 'when he refused to deny Christ he was sentenced to be transported to Rome to be thrown to the lions in the amphitheatre.'[6] According to the early church historian Eusebius, Ignatius was martyred in AD 108.

The idea behind sending Ignatius to Rome was 'to spread the fear of a similar fate to Christians all along the route of the martyr's last journey.'[7] However, Ignatius actually became a source of encouragement to Christians, writing several letters explaining why he was willing to be executed for trusting Jesus: 'We still possess these letters, seven in all, and they are among the most important writings of the early church.'[8]

For example, in his letter to the Ephesians, Ignatius writes about 'our God, Jesus'[9] as a spiritual physician who is 'fleshly and spiritual … God in man, true life in death …'[10] He recounts how 'God was displayed in human form to bring "newness of life" [cf. Romans 6:4] with reference to the new man, Jesus Christ, which consists in faith towards him and love towards him, in his passion and resurrection … our antidote to ensure that we shall not die but live in Jesus Christ forever.'[11] Clearly, it was his confidence in a resurrected life through faith in Jesus that lay behind Ignatius' willingness to suffer the death penalty.

Writing to the Trallians, Ignatius encouraged them about 'Jesus Christ, who died for us that you might escape death through faith in his death', and entreating them to ignore those who denied Jesus' humanity: 'Turn a deaf ear to any speaker who avoids mention of Jesus Christ, who was of David's line, born of Mary, who was truly born, ate and drank; was truly persecuted under Pontius Pilate, truly crucified and died … who also was truly raised from the dead, the Father having raised him, who in like manner will raise us who believe in him.'[12]

Ignatius told the Smyrneans of his:

> full conviction with respect to our Lord that he is genuinely of David's line according to the flesh, son of God according to the divine will and power, really born of a virgin and baptized by John … really nailed up in the flesh for us in the time of Pontius Pilate and the Tetrarchy of Herod … that he might 'raise up a standard' for all ages through his resurrection … For he suffered all this on our account, that we might be saved. And he really suffered, as he really raised himself. Some unbelievers say he suffered in appearance only. Not so … For I know and believe that even after his resurrection he was in a physical body; and when he came to Peter and his companions he said, 'Take hold and feel me, and see that I am not a bodiless phantom.' [cf. Luke 24:39] And immediately they touched him and believed, when they had contact with his flesh and blood. Therefore also they despised death and proved superior to death.[13]

It's worth emphasizing that the pressing temptation for those attracted to a Jesus-centred spirituality in the first decade of the second century wasn't to deny Jesus' divinity, but to deny his humanity: 'The early church struggled hard to assert the full humanity of Christ against the "modern" and secular ethos that wanted to see him as a wholly divine figure, untouched by the world. The great heretics of the time, Arius, Apollinarius, Nestorius, and Eutyches, all proclaimed a divine Christ.'[14] It's also worth noting that in countering this temptation Ignatius appeals *to the historical testimony of the first Christians concerning the Jesus they knew in the flesh.*

The one personal letter written by Ignatius on his final journey was to Polycarp (c. AD 70–c. 155),[15] a man who was to be a martyr himself, and who'd been a disciple (i.e. student) of one of Jesus' own disciples (it's unclear whether this was John the apostle or John the Elder). Irenaeus (who was in turn Polycarp's disciple) reports that his teacher 'was not only instructed by apostles, and conversed with many who had seen Christ, but was also by apostles in Asia appointed bishop in the church in Smyrna … [He] always taught the things he had learned from the apostles …'[16] In his *Letter to Florinus* (preserved by Eusebius) Irenaeus declared:

> I distinctly recall … the very place where the blessed Polycarp used to sit as he discoursed … how he would tell of his conversations with John and with the others who had seen the Lord, how he would relate their words from memory; and what the things were which he had heard from them concerning the Lord, his mighty works and his teaching, Polycarp, as having received them from the eyewitnesses of the life of the Logos, would declare.[17]

Polycarp was also friends with Papias (c. AD 70–130), who'd learnt about Jesus from 'Aristion, the Elder John, and the [four] daughters of Philip the evangelist.'[18] In a surviving passage from his book *The Exposition of the Oracles of the Lord*, Papias explains:

> If, then, any one who had attended on the elders came, I asked minutely after their sayings – what Andrew or Peter said, or what was said by Philip, or by Thomas, or by James, or by John, or by Matthew, or by any other of the Lord's disciples: which things

Aristion and the presbyter John, the disciples of the Lord, say. For I imagined that what was to be got from books was not so profitable to me as what came from the living and abiding voice.[19]

Ignatius was himself 'the disciple of John the apostle'[20] (the Greek *apostolos* means 'one sent forth as a messenger' and was a term used of Jesus' closest disciples), and both Eusebius (c. AD 263–339)[21] and Theodoret of Cyrrhus[22] (c. AD 393–c. 457) state that it was the apostle Peter who appointed Ignatius to the position of bishop.

Ignatius was willing to stake his whole life, and had the courage to suffer a grisly and avoidable death, on the basis of his confidence in what Edwin M. Yamauchi calls 'the historic underpinnings of Christianity'.[23] For Ignatius, those historical underpinnings weren't primarily the written testimony of what we now call the New Testament (NT), although 'it can … be determined with certainty that he knew the Gospel of Matthew and four Pauline epistles: 1 Corinthians, Ephesians and 1 and 2 Timothy.'[24] It was, rather, 'the living and abiding voice' of testimony to the life, death and resurrection of Jesus provided by those known to Ignatius who had themselves known Jesus in the flesh (e.g. Peter and John), and by those who knew those who had done so (e.g. Polycarp and Papias). The multiple attestation of these 'living and abiding' voices clearly explains why Ignatius had the confidence to write as he did to the Christians in his final destination, Rome: 'Let all come, fire and cross and conflicts with beasts, hacking, cutting, wrenching of bones, chopping of limbs, the crushing of my body … Only let me attain Jesus Christ … an imitator of the passion of my God …'[25]

Continuing Persecution

Remember those earlier days after you had received the light, when you endured in a great conflict full of suffering.

(Hebrews 10:32)

Seeing that the execution of Christians like Ignatius was having quite the reverse of the desired effect, Trajan shifted to a 'don't ask, don't tell' policy. This shift appears to have sown some admin-istrative confusion. In c. AD 112 Pliny the Younger, governor of Bithynia in Asia Minor, wrote to Trajan asking for guidance on how to deal with Christians. His letter is worth quoting at some length:

> whether repentance entitles them to a pardon; or if a man has been once a Christian, it avails nothing to desist from his error; whether the very profession of Christianity, unattended with any criminal act, or only the crimes themselves inherent in the profession are punishable; on all these points I am in great doubt. In the mean-while, the method I have observed towards those who have been brought before me as Christians is this: I asked them whether they were Christians; if they admitted it, I repeated the question twice, and threatened them with punishment; if they persisted, I ordered them to be at once punished: for … inflexible obstinacy certainly deserved correction … But this crime spreading (as is usually the case) while it was actually under prosecution, several instances of the same nature occurred. An anonymous information was laid before me containing a charge against several persons, who upon examination denied they were Christians, or had ever been so. They repeated after me an invocation to the gods, and offered reli-gious rites with wine and incense before your statue … and even reviled the name of Christ: whereas there is no forcing, it is said, those who are really Christians into any of these compliances: I thought it proper, therefore, to discharge them. Some among those who were accused by a witness in person at first confessed them-selves Christians, but immediately after denied it; the rest owned indeed that they had been of that number formerly, but had now (some above three, others more, and a few above twenty years ago) renounced that error … They affirmed the whole of their guilt, or their error, was, that they met on a stated day before it was light, and addressed a form of prayer to Christ, as to a divinity, binding themselves by a solemn oath, not for the purposes of any wicked design, but never to commit any fraud, theft, or adultery, never to falsify their word, nor deny a trust when they should be called upon to deliver it up; after which it was their custom to separate, and then reassemble, to eat in common a harmless meal. From this custom, however, they desisted after the publication of my edict,

by which, according to your commands, I forbade the meeting of any assemblies. After receiving this account, I judged it so much the more necessary to endeavor to extort the real truth, by putting two female slaves to the torture, who were said to officiate in their religious rites: but all I could discover was evidence of an absurd and extravagant superstition. I deemed it expedient, therefore … to consult you. For it appears to be a matter highly deserving your consideration, more especially as great numbers must be involved in the danger of these prosecutions, which have already extended, and are still likely to extend, to persons of all ranks and ages.[26]

Trajan's reply was comparatively brief:

You have adopted the right course … It is not possible to lay down any general rule for all such cases. Do not go out of your way to look for them. If indeed they should be brought before you, and the crime is proved, they must be punished; with the restriction, however, that where the party denies he is a Christian, and shall make it evident that he is not, by invoking our gods, let him (notwithstanding any former suspicion) be pardoned upon his repentance. Anonymous informations ought not to be received in any sort of prosecution. It is introducing a very dangerous precedent, and is quite foreign to the spirit of our age.[27]

As Gary R. Habermas comments: 'These conditions imposed by Emperor Trajan give us some insight into early official Roman views about Christianity … The spread of Christianity unfortunately involved persecution fairly early in its history.'[28] So why were the likes of Ignatius and Polycarp willing to exchange their lives for a profession of faith in Jesus? The answer is that their 'faith' *wasn't a matter of 'blind trust'*, but a response to what they believed they *knew* to be true *on an appropriate basis of evidence.*

Doubting Dawkins

> One of the most notable phenomena in critical research today is the re-emergence of the historical Jesus from the mists of critical uncertainty.
>
> Stephen Neill[29]

If anyone represents 'the spirit of our age' when it comes to investigating the charges against Christians and portraying faith in Jesus as an 'absurd and extravagant superstition', it is surely Richard Dawkins. Professor Dawkins sees Christians as 'dyed-in-the-wool faith-heads [who] are immune to argument'[30] because their faith is by definition a matter of 'blind trust, in the absence of evidence, even in the teeth of evidence.'[31] Indeed, according to Dawkins's best-selling book *The God Delusion*: 'it is even possible to mount a serious, though not widely supported, historical case that Jesus never lived at all, as has been done by, among others, Professor G.A. Wells of the University of London …'[32] Fellow neo-atheist Victor J. Stenger boldly asserts: 'A number of scholars have made the case for the non-historicity of Jesus, and their conclusions are convincing.'[33] Luke Timothy Johnson, professor of New Testament and Christian origins at Emory University, doesn't agree:

> Even the most critical historian can confidently assert that a Jew named Jesus worked as a teacher and wonder-worker in Palestine during the reign of Tiberius, was executed by crucifixion under the prefect Pontius Pilate, and continued to have followers after his death … the evidence is sufficient to support a substantial number of historical assertions concerning Jesus with a high degree of probability. We not only know that Jesus existed as something more than a fictional character – the sheer production of ancient literature interpreting him and referring to him suffices to show that – but we can have confidence about such fundamental issues as the time and place of his activity and the manner of his death, as well as some clues as to the character of his activity.[34]

Jewish New Testament scholar Geza Vermes likewise begs to differ: 'Jesus was a real historical person. In my opinion, the difficulties arising from the denial of his existence, still vociferously maintained in small circles of rationalist "dogmatists", far exceed those deriving from its acceptance.'[35] According to historian Paul L. Maier: 'there is more evidence that Jesus of Nazareth certainly lived than for most famous figures of the ancient past.'[36] As Graham Stanton, Lady Margaret's professor of divinity in the University of Cambridge, comments:

> the early Christians' opponents *all* accepted that Jesus existed, taught, had disciples, worked miracles, and was put to death on a Roman cross. As in our day, debate and disagreement centred largely not on the story but on the significance of Jesus. Today nearly all historians, whether Christians or not, accept that Jesus existed and that the gospels contain plenty of valuable evidence which has to be weighed and assessed critically.[37]

Dawkins doesn't endorse the fringe position advocated by Stenger (professor emeritus of physics and astronomy, University of Hawaii; adjunct professor of philosophy, University of Colorado) and Wells (professor emeritus of German at Birkbeck College, London). Dawkins admits that 'Jesus probably existed ...'[38] Nevertheless, this admission is so mealy-mouthed that it seems calculated to plant doubt in the uninformed reader's mind. Indeed, Dawkins embraces an extreme scepticism about the historical Jesus that is almost as far out as that displayed by Stenger and Wells:

> Ever since the nineteenth century, scholarly theologians have made an overwhelming case that the gospels are not reliable accounts of what happened in the history of the real world. All were written long after the death of Jesus, and also after the epistles of Paul, which mention almost none of the alleged facts of Jesus' life. All were then copied and recopied, through many different 'Chinese Whisper generations' ... The four gospels that made it into the official canon were chosen, more or less arbitrarily, out of a larger sample of at least a dozen ... Nobody knows who the four evangelists were, but they almost certainly never met Jesus personally. Much of what they wrote was in no sense an honest attempt at history. But was simply rehashed from the Old Testament, because the gospel makers were devoutly convinced that the life of Jesus

must fulfill Old Testament prophecies ... Although Jesus probably existed, reputable Bible scholars do not in general regard the
New Testament (and obviously not the Old Testament) as reliable
records of what actually happened in history, and I shall not consider the Bible further as evidence for any kind of deity ... The
only difference between *The Da Vinci Code* and the gospels is that
the gospels are ancient fiction while *The Da Vinci Code* is modern
fiction.[39]

This really will not do, for as N.T. Wright comments: 'One of the
great gains of New Testament scholarship in the last generation
has been to re-establish that the canonical gospels certainly were
intended, and certainly are to be read, within the framework of
ancient biographical writing.'[40] Since Dawkins denies that theology is a proper subject,[41] it's interesting to see him appealing to the
authority of 'scholarly theologians' (by which he seems to mean
any theologian who agrees with him)! It's even more enlightening to ponder his reference to theology 'since the nineteenth
century', for Dawkins' scepticism about Jesus is clearly stuck in
what scholarly theologians call (with some exaggeration) the early
twentieth-century 'no quest' period of historical Jesus research, a
period associated with Albert Schweitzer and Rudolf Bultmann.
Thomas R. Yoder Neufeld, professor of religious studies at the
University of Waterloo, Ontario, reviews the shifting history of
the quest for the historical Jesus:

> The first to attempt a historical investigation of Jesus was Hermann
> Samuel Reimarus, whose fragmentary work *The Aims of Jesus and
> His Disciples* was published posthumously in 1778 ... the church's
> official portrait of Jesus was largely ignored in favour of one of
> Jesus as teacher of ethics ... The first quest came to an end with
> the German publication in 1906 of *The Quest for the Historical Jesus:
> A Critical Study of Its Progress from Reimarus to Wrede* by ... Albert
> Schweitzer ... Schweitzer's dismissal of the 'lives of Jesus' up to
> that point was joined by a very thoroughgoing skepticism that
> the gospels ... would divulge much of anything historically reli-
> able about Jesus. Schweitzer's work ushered in a time of severe
> skepticism among many scholars regarding the New Testament
> as a historical source for Jesus. The name most often identified

with this radical historical skepticism is Rudolf Bultmann ... He wedded his historical skepticism with an existentialist theological approach where what truly matters is the authentic 'decision of faith', not whether one can verify something historically ... Several of Bultmann's students broke rank and began what has come to be known as the new quest or second quest for the historical Jesus. These scholars recognized that the gospels make access to Jesus difficult, but they insisted that ... they do provide access ... A so-called third quest has emerged on the scene in the last few decades, marked by renewed interest in the Jewish matrix of Jesus's life, identity, and teachings, as well as renewed debate over the historical value of the gospels and extrabiblical writings.[42]

Dawkins fails to offer any sense of the historical context or current standing amongst scholarly theologians of his Bultmann-esque scepticism about Jesus in *The God Delusion*, but as Professor Habermas writes: 'at the present, there has been a somewhat positive assessment of attempts to understand Jesus in historical terms.'[43] Craig L. Blomberg, distinguished professor of New Testament at Denver Seminary, states that 'the so-called Third Quest for the historical Jesus over the past quarter-century has for the most part been proving more and more optimistic about how much we can know about the founder of Christianity.'[44] William Lane Craig, research professor of philosophy at Talbot School of Theology (a scholar who holds doctorates in *both* philosophy and theology) confirms that contemporary 'biblical criticism has embarked upon a renewed quest for the historical Jesus which treats the Gospels seriously as valuable historical sources for the life of Jesus and has confirmed the main lines of the portrait of Jesus painted in the Gospels.'[45] Darrell L. Bock, research professor in New Testament studies at Dallas Theological Seminary, reports that 'those who participate in the third quest have tended to see far more historicity in the Gospels than either of the previous quests, showing a renewed respect for the general historical character of the Gospels.'[46] Bock notes this doesn't mean that 'the third quest has reached a consensus or that it is fundamentally conservative',[47] but it puts Dawkins' 'no quest' stance in perspective.

Even putting all discussion of the NT to one side, Dawkins' critique of 'the historic underpinnings of Christianity' misses the fact that the faith of martyrs like Ignatius and Polycarp wasn't primarily grounded in written documents, but in 'the living and abiding voice' of *eyewitnesses whom they knew personally*. Indeed, several of the first century eyewitnesses were themselves martyred for their beliefs about Jesus! For example, Eusebius 'records the martyrdoms of Peter (crucified upside down), Paul (beheaded), James the brother of Jesus (stoned and clubbed), and James the brother of John (killed by the sword).'[48] The martyrdom of James the brother of Jesus is mentioned by Josephus in his *Antiquities*; whilst Paul's martyrdom is multiply attested by Clement of Rome, Polycarp, Tertullian and Origen.

I am *not* making a general claim to the effect that martyrdom proves the truth of the cause for which one dies. It's obvious that jihadist suicide bombers do nothing to recommend the reality of the deity in whose name they murder. However, willingness *to be murdered* on the basis of one's adherence to the truth of an empirical claim (such as that Jesus rose from the dead) when one is in a good position to know the truth or falsity of that claim, surely says something truth conducive; for such a willingness to die speaks not only to the sincerity of the martyr, but to the confidence they have in both the significance and reliability of the empirical claim in question. Hence, the particular kind of martyrdom suffered by the early Christians constitutes an implicit form of historical testimony.

The real history-denier

Dawkins' hyper-scepticism about Jesus is ironic in light of his complaints about people who raise doubts concerning the neo-Darwinian theory of evolution. Introducing his case for evolution as a sufficient explanation for biological complexity in *The Greatest Show on Earth* (Bantam Press, 2009), Dawkins asks the reader to:

> Imagine that you are a teacher of Roman history and Latin language ... Yet you find your precious time continually preyed upon, and your class's attention distracted, by a baying pack of ignoramuses ... who, with strong political and especially financial support, scurry about tirelessly attempting to persuade your unfortunate pupils that the Romans never existed. There never was a Roman

Empire ... Spanish, Italian, French, Portuguese, Catalan, Occitan, Romanish: all these languages and their constituent dialects sprang spontaneously into being, and owe nothing to any predecessor such as Latin ... [Or] imagine you are a teacher of more recent history, and your lessons on twentieth-century Europe are boycotted, heckled or otherwise disrupted by well-organized, well-financed and politically muscular groups of Holocaust-deniers.[49]

Dawkins draws an analogy between these hard-pressed teachers and 'the plight of science teachers today'[50] in the face of mounting opposition to the neo-Darwinian theory of evolution.[51] While Dawkins does at least note that there are 'thoughtful and rational churchmen and women'[52] who accept evolution (belief in evolution is, after all, compatible with belief in the *doctrine* of creation),[53] it is interesting to observe that he tendentiously confuses all dissent with a specifically 'young earth' *model* of creation: 'I shall be using the name "history deniers" for those who deny evolution: who believe that the world's age is measured in thousands of years rather than thousands of millions of years, and who believe humans walked with dinosaurs.'[54] While I join with Dawkins in rejecting Young Earth creationism, I think it's rhetorically overblown to compare those who do accept it with holocaust deniers, as Dawkins does here. Moreover, by writing both Old Earth creationism[55] and Intelligent Design Theory[56] out of the history of ideas, Dawkins lays the groundwork for a false dilemma: *either* accept the theory of evolution *in toto* (lock, stock and both smoking barrels) *or* endorse a 'young earth' creationist viewpoint. Of course, irrespective of one's religious beliefs, one might reject this false dilemma by doing neither.[57] Likewise, when it comes to a rational consideration of Jesus, one does *not* face a dilemma between accepting *either* the radically sceptical viewpoint of Dawkins and the 'new atheists' *or* the supposedly naïve belief of Dawkins' hypothetical 'person in the pew ... an uneducated churchgoer'.[58] Once again, one might do neither.

When it comes to the historical Jesus (a subject that is after all part of Roman history) it's actually Dawkins and other 'new atheists' who are *literally* the history deniers (although let me hasten to add that I do *not*, in the use of this phrase, mean to tar Dawkins *et al.* with an immoral taint analogous to holocaust denial). We could very well ask Dawkins to imagine that he is an ancient historian who finds his precious time continually preyed upon, and his class's attention distracted, by a baying pack of ignoramuses who, with strong financial support, scurry about tirelessly attempting to persuade his unfortunate pupils that Jesus never existed, or that even though he probably existed, nothing can be known about him on the basis of the available evidence! Mark Allan Powell, associate professor of New Testament at Trinity Lutheran Seminary, pulls no punches regarding this sort of thing: 'A hundred and fifty years ago a fairly well respected scholar named Bruno Bauer maintained that the historical person Jesus never existed. Anyone who says that today – in the academic world at least – gets grouped with ... the scientific holdouts who want to believe the world is flat.'[59] The verdict on Dawkins' shoddy NT scholarship delivered by Paul Barnett (visiting fellow in ancient history at Macquarie University in Australia and a teaching fellow at Regent College, Vancouver) is worth taking seriously:

> Dawkins ... refers to the anecdotes about the boy Jesus in the Gospel of Thomas that he confuses with the *Infancy Story of Thomas* ... Worse, Dawkins attributes the story of the Magi to the Gospel of Luke, when it actually appears in the Gospel of Matthew ... Dawkins reveals his ignorance in ascribing tribal harshness ('outgroup hostility') to Jesus, as in Old Testament attitudes to non-Jews. But Jesus' friendship with 'sinners' and social outcasts is one of the most secure historical details about him. Finally, Dawkins shows amazing ignorance in asserting the Gospels were as much works of fiction as Dan Brown's *Da Vinci Code*. Bible scholars of all stripes, to the contrary, have reached a consensus in viewing the Gospels as identifiable historical biographies.[60]

Seeking Enlightenment

> I have come into the world as a light, so that no one who believes in me should stay in darkness.
>
> Jesus (John 12:46)

Secular humanist Mark Vernon introduces 'the Enlightenment' as an intellectual movement:

> In the first half of the eighteenth century, the title pages of several German philosophy books appeared to share a common design. The sun was shown shining through departing clouds. To ensure the message was not missed a caption might spell it out, reading something along the lines of 'light dispelling darkness'. In short, these books carried a philosophy that saw itself as enlightening – or as of a period of Enlightenment, or *Aufklärung* as it is in German. The power behind this enlightenment was reason.[61]

'Enlightenment' is a metaphorical concept that draws upon the experience of darkness replaced by reality-revealing light, a metaphor often associated with spirituality. To have an 'enlightening' experience is to be freed from a prior state of ignorance by a life-changing insight into reality. Hence the author of the NT letter to the Hebrews refers to Christians as 'those who have once been enlightened, who have tasted the heavenly gift, who have shared in the Holy Spirit, who have tasted the goodness of the word of God ...' (Hebrews 6:4–5) The author of Ephesians likewise prays 'that the God of our Lord Jesus Christ, the glorious Father, may give you the Spirit of wisdom and revelation, so that you may know him better. I pray that the eyes of your heart may be enlightened in order that you may know the hope to which he has called you ...' (Ephesians 1:17–18)

The first-century 'Gospel according to John' famously uses enlightenment imagery to introduce Jesus:

> In the beginning was the Word [*Logos*], and the Word was with God, and the Word was God. He was with God in the beginning. Through him all things were made; without him nothing was made that has been made. In him was life, and that life was the light of all people. The light shines in the darkness, and the darkness has not [understood] it.
>
> There was a man sent from God whose name was John [the Baptist]. He came as a witness to testify concerning that light, so that through him all might believe. He himself was not the light; he came only as a witness to the light.

> The true light that gives light to everyone was coming into the world. He was in the world, and though the world was made through him, the world did not recognize him. He came to that which was his own [i.e. Israel], but his own did not receive him. Yet to all who did receive him, to those who believed in his name, he gave the right to become children of God – children born not of natural descent, nor of human decision or a husband's will, but born of God.
>
> The Word became flesh and made his dwelling among us. We have seen his glory [i.e. beauty], the glory of the one and only [Son], who came from the Father, full of grace and truth (John 1:1–14).

Logos is a term from Greek philosophy that means something like 'the rational principle behind reality'. The claim made by John is that in Jesus the ultimate, rational principle behind reality has revealed itself as a personal being characterized by truth, goodness, beauty and a desire for loving, familial relationship with human beings. Jesus is thus 'the light of the world' (John 8:12) both in that his incarnation ('enfleshment') brings us enlightenment *about God* and in that he desires to transform us by facilitating a revolution in our relationship *with God* through faith in him: 'I am the light of the world. Whoever follows me will never walk in darkness, but will have the light of life' (John 8:12).

Immanuel Kant (1724–1804) has been called 'the paradigmatic philosopher of the European Enlightenment'.[62] In an essay published in the December 1784 edition of the *Berlinische Monatsschrift* (*Berlin Monthly*) Kant defined what he meant by '*Aufklärung*' (the word derives from *auf*, meaning 'up' and *klären*, meaning 'to clear', from the Latin *clarus*):

> Enlightenment [*Aufklärung*] is man's emergence from his self-imposed immaturity. Immaturity is the inability to use one's understanding without guidance from another. This immaturity is self-imposed when its cause lies not in lack of understanding, but in lack of resolve and courage to use it without guidance from another. *Sapere Aude!* [Dare to know!] 'Have courage to use your own understanding!' – that is the motto of enlightenment.[63]

Atheist philosopher Daniel Dennett accuses all religion of failing to live up to this Enlightenment ideal:

If religion isn't the greatest threat to rationality and scientific progress, what is? ... [Religion] doesn't just disable, it honours the disability. People are revered for their capacity to live in a dream world, to shield their minds from factual knowledge and make the major decisions in their lives by consulting voices in their heads that they call forth by rituals designed to intoxicate them ... This imperviousness to reason is, I think, the property that we should most fear in religion. Other institutions or traditions may encourage a certain amount of irrationality ... but only religion demands it as a sacred duty.[64]

It would be easy to assume that this description must be accurate. If it is, there's something oxymoronic about a book such as this, which offers an examination of the defining element of Christianity – namely, its understanding of Jesus – which purports to be both orthodox and rational. However, to uncritically accept Dennett's well-poisoning description of religion would be to acquiesce in precisely the sort of 'self-imposed immaturity' condemned by Kant. After all, there would appear to be something of 'imperviousness to reason' about Dennett's critique given Terry Eagleton's observation that 'the Enlightenment was deeply shaped by values which stemmed from the Christian tradition.'[65] Indeed, many of the Enlightenment's leading intellectuals were Christians, or at least theists (e.g. George Berkeley, Immanuel Kant, Gottfried Leibniz, John Locke, Isaac Newton, Thomas Reid). According to historian Helena Rosenblatt:

The term 'Christian Enlightenment' no longer raises eyebrows; but this is a relatively recent phenomenon. A widespread consensus used to exist that the very essence of the Enlightenment – what made the Enlightenment 'enlightened' – was its attack on religion ... Peter Gay described the Enlightenment as a 'war on Christianity'. Many scholars before and after agreed with this point of view. They described the Enlightenment as being – by its very nature – anti-Christian, anti-Church and even anti-religious. We now know, however, that the relationship between Christianity and the Enlightenment was far more complex and interesting. We realize that these previous interpretations were overly focused on France, and erroneously tended to posit a single Enlightenment.

Over the past few years, scholars have been 'pluralizing' the Enlightenment, the result being that we now see it not so much as a unified and Francophone phenomenon, but rather as a 'family of discourses' with many regional and national variations across Europe and in America. It has become clear that earlier interpretations were based on an impoverished view of religious traditions and perhaps even an outright disdain for them.[66]

Moreover, consider the fact that philosopher Antony Flew refers to the apostle Paul as 'a first-class intellectual'[67] with 'an outstanding philosophical mind.'[68] Paul was 'a highly educated man'[69] who was 'well acquainted with pagan "high culture" ...'[70] He was 'a Tarsian from Cilicia [cf. Acts 9:30; 21:39; 22:3] ... a centre of Hellenistic culture, claiming to rival Athens and Alexandria in its fame for learning. Paul was a child of two cultures. While his Jewish spiritual heritage was the most formative influence, he also knew the ways of the Hellenistic world.'[71] Theologian J. Daryl Charles describes the apostle as 'knowledgeable, dialectical, well read, relevant, and rhetorically skilful.'[72] It should come as no surprise, then, to read Paul telling Christians to 'stop thinking like children. In regard to evil be infants, but in your thinking be adults' (1 Corinthians 14:20). Again, it was Paul who formulated a famous analogy that could rival Kant's own definition of Enlightenment: 'When I was a child, I talked like a child, I thought like a child, I reasoned like a child. When I became a man, I put the ways of childhood behind me' (1 Corinthians 13:11).

Paul described his own ministry in terms of 'defending and confirming the gospel' (Philippians 1:7). The first-century book of Acts repeatedly describes Paul's standard evangelistic practice as *rational* and *evidence-based*:

> The key word that describes Paul's activity is that he 'reasoned' with people. So, in the Jewish synagogue, 'according to his custom, he reasoned with them from the Scriptures' (Acts 17:2). In Athens he not only 'reasoned' with Jews and Gentiles in the synagogue but also 'reasoned' in the market place with whoever was there (Acts 17:17). He did the same in Corinth, 'reasoning' with Jews and Greeks (Acts 18:4). Later in Ephesus, he spent three months 'reasoning' in the synagogue, then for two years in a secular hall 'reasoning

daily' (Acts 19:9–10). He adopted the same approach wherever he went. The Greek word for 'reason' means dialogue. Instead of giving sermons six foot above contradiction, Paul engaged in a two-way exchange. With the Jews, he discussed the meaning of the Old Testament writings. With the philosophers, he discussed their beliefs, challenging their assumptions … Other words fill out the picture. This 'dialogue' involved 'explaining', 'giving evidence', 'proclaiming' and 'persuading' (Acts 17:3–4). With the philosophers, he was 'disputing' (Acts 17:18). In Corinth, he was 'trying to persuade' Jews and Greeks (Acts 18:4). In Ephesus he was 'arguing persuasively about the kingdom of God' (Acts 19:8). Paul was 'discussing' with Felix the Governor (Acts 24:25), while King Agrippa thought Paul was trying to 'persuade' him to become a Christian. In Rome he was 'explaining', 'testifying' and 'trying to convince them about Jesus' (Acts 28:23).[73]

None of this fits Dennett's disdainful generalization about religion being an intellectual disability.

Kant wryly observed: 'It is so easy to be immature. If I have a book to serve as my understanding, a pastor to serve as my conscience, a physician to determine my diet for me, and so on, I need not exert myself at all. I need not think, if only I can pay: others will readily undertake the irksome work for me.'[74]

Kant wasn't against using books in the process of forming one's understanding. After all, he wrote several himself! Rather, he was against treating any book as a way of simply outsourcing the 'irksome' task of *arriving at one's own understanding*. The enlightenment proclaimed by John's gospel may be one in which the initiative rests within the ultimate rationality himself (the *logos*), but this no more enforces or excuses a self-imposed rational immaturity than does Kant's own proclamation of enlightenment. As Mark Vernon observes:

> Simplistically, it might be thought that religion is key [to Kant's discussion of Enlightenment] because it entails submitting to an authority other than yourself – that is, it is a quintessential case of the immaturity that Enlightenment urges us to discard. However, Kant was not against religion per se. In fact, it turns out that religion was essential to his understanding of morality. Rather, it is the

relationship between the two that lies at the heart of his concerns. For what Enlightenment requires – at least according to Kant – is a more sophisticated attitude towards religion, not an automatic and therefore adolescent-like rejection.[75]

It isn't submission to authority *per se* that goes against the spirit of the Enlightenment, but *thoughtless submission*. After all, failure to submit to the authority of truth is itself a sign of intellectual immaturity. Kant viewed Christianity as 'a complete religion, which can be presented to all men comprehensibly and convincingly through their own reason.'[76] Hence I trust readers will forgive me if I invite them to undertake a journey that the 'immature' would doubtless find 'irksome'. In particular, we must have the maturity to see through the sort of rationally vacuous hyper-scepticism offered by the likes of Dawkins and Dennett. We need to be even-handed in our scepticism, and to exert ourselves in studying the Jesus phenomenon from first principles.

Like the apostle Paul, I have no desire to abrogate, and every desire to encourage, what Kant called 'each person's calling to think for himself.'[77] Far from wanting readers to 'shield their minds from factual knowledge', I want them to have an open mind towards a knowledge of the relevant facts. Far from demanding 'irrationality … as a sacred duty',[78] I am going to demand rationality as a sacred duty. In light of Dennett's comments, alcohol should only be consumed at the reader's discretion! In sum, my intent is to provide readers interested in understanding Jesus with a set of relevant data, established through the application of sound methodological principles, and a set of rational arguments in support of a Christian interpretation of that data. Like Paul, I fully expect and encourage readers to enter into dialogue with this material and to make up their own minds about the truth claims I make and the cogency or otherwise of the arguments I will present. I am committed to this methodology because, *contra* Dennett's misrepresentations, Christian philosopher Tom Price hits the nail on the head when he points out that 'faith loves logic … because real, authentic faith cares about real things like integrity, and honesty. And it would be pretty odd for a faith to extol these virtues, but require the opposite of them for its initial impulse or conception.'[79]

Understanding spirituality

> When the people heard this, they were cut to the heart and said to
> Peter and the other apostles, 'Brothers, what shall we do?'
>
> (Acts 2:37)

The word 'philosophy' comes from two ancient Greek terms: 'philo' meaning 'brotherly love', and 'sophia' meaning 'wisdom'. Philosophy is literally *philo-sophia*, the brotherly love of wisdom. Hence Thomas V. Morris writes that 'philosophy is the love of wisdom, along with an unending desire to find it, understand it, put it into action and pass it on to others.'[80] As such, it seems to me that *philosophy is an inherently spiritual activity*. Paul Copan affirms that 'the quest for wisdom isn't merely intellectual fact-gathering; it's also a *virtuous* and *spiritual* endeavour, requiring certain attitudes and character qualities.'[81] According to physicist-turned-theologian John Polkinghorne, the essence of rationality 'lies in a seeking to conform our thinking to the nature of the object of our thought.'[82] Philosophy is a spiritual quest for the true understanding (i.e. enlightenment) that comes from humbly *standing under the authority of the truth* to be that which determines what we should believe about reality, what attitudes we should adopt towards reality, and what actions we should take in reality. Indeed, a spirituality just is *a way of relating to reality* – to ourselves, to each other, to the world around us and (most importantly) to ultimate reality – *via our worldview beliefs, concomitant attitudes and subsequent behaviour.*

Different spiritualities embody different answers to the question of how people can best relate to reality (or how they *ought* to relate to reality). Spiritualities make distinctive and mutually contradictory knowledge claims that cannot all be true. While people may be created equal, ideas, attitudes and actions are not. Some ideas are true, but others are false. Some attitudes are beautiful, but others are ugly. Some actions are good, but others are evil. It is therefore crucial that we take an enlightened, questioning, sceptical attitude towards spirituality, so as to actively distinguish the beautiful from the ugly, the good from the bad and the true from the false: 'Test everything. Hold on to the good' (1 Thessalonians 5:21 [NIV]).

Spirituality and worldview

The answers we give to fundamental worldview questions determine the broad form of our spirituality: *Our worldview is the
foundation of our spirituality*. What we believe about the answers
to the fundamental questions affects our attitudes, decisions and
actions in life. As Charles Colson and Nancy Pearcey explain:
'Our choices are shaped by what we believe is real and true, right
and wrong, good and beautiful. Our choices are shaped by our
worldview … a person's worldview is intensely practical … so
understanding worldviews is extremely important to how we live
… our lives are defined by our ultimate beliefs more sharply than
by any other factor.'[83]

What we think is and isn't true about reality affects what attitudes we take towards reality and what practices we think our
spirituality should include:

• Our worldview *beliefs* ground our spiritual *attitudes* and thereby
  sustain our spiritual *actions*

This understanding of spirituality correlates with the schema
undergirding Cognitive Behavioural Therapy:

> CBT can help you to make sense of overwhelming problems by
> breaking them down into smaller parts … These parts are: A
> Situation – a problem, event or difficult situation. From this can
> follow: Thoughts, Emotions, Physical feelings, Actions. Each of
> these areas can affect the others. How you think about a problem
> can affect how you feel physically and emotionally. It can also alter
> what you do about it.[84]

As Glen Schultz puts it: 'At the foundation of a person's life, we
find his beliefs. These beliefs shape his values, and his values drive
his actions.'[85] What Bill Smith says of Christian spirituality actually goes for *all* spiritualities: 'spirituality is holistic in the truest
sense. It encompasses reason and feeling … we need to proclaim
and live a [spirituality] that integrates the mind (orthodoxy), the
heart (orthopathy) and the hands (orthopraxy).'[86] All spiritualities
(including atheistic spiritualities) can be analyzed in terms of this
three-part structure:

Spirituality

Practices (Orthopraxy: Actions)
↑
Attitudes (Orthopathy: Attitudes)
↑
Worldview (Orthodoxy: Beliefs)

Figure 1

This discussion will have a familiar ring to anyone acquainted with Jesus' teaching about the requirement to 'Love the Lord your God with all your heart [i.e. your will, your attitudes] … and with all your mind [including your worldview], and with all your strength [i.e. your actions]' (Mark 12:30,33; cf. Deuteronomy 6:5). Jesus calls upon people to build their lives upon a strong belief in a specific God (as revealed in and through his own person). Jesus' God-centred principal commandment, which establishes the contours of Christian spirituality, is immediately and organically followed by the command to 'love your neighbor as yourself' (Mark 12:31, cf. Leviticus 19:18).[87] The following diagram therefore represents the central content of Christian spirituality, as defined by Jesus:

Christian **Spirituality** = *Love God, and thus your neighbour, with all your:*

Practices (Orthopraxy: Actions – 'strength')
↑
Attitudes (Orthopathy: Attitudes – 'heart')
↑
Worldview (Orthodoxy: Beliefs – 'mind')

Figure 2

As Douglas Groothuis warns: 'Christianity makes claims on the entire personality; accepting it as true is not a matter of mere intellectual assent, but of embarking on a new venture in life.'[88]

The organically tripartite structure of Christian spirituality as involving mind, heart and strength, and as being founded upon a love that naturally leads to community, is seen in the apostle Paul's letter to the Colossians:

And *above all these put on love, which binds everything together in perfect harmony.* And *let the peace of Christ rule in your hearts* ['all your heart'], to which indeed you were called in one body. And be thankful. *Let the word of Christ dwell in you richly, teaching and admonishing one another in all wisdom* ['all your mind'], singing psalms and hymns and spiritual songs, with thankfulness in your hearts to God. And *whatever you do* ['all your strength'], in word or deed, do everything in the name of the Lord Jesus, giving thanks to God the Father through him (Colossians 3:14–17 [ESV], my italics).

The same structure underpins the command to Christians in 1 Peter 3:15:

In your *hearts* [a matter of both mind and attitude] set apart Christ as Lord and always be prepared to give [i.e. this is something one must be prepared to *do*] an answer [*apologia* – a rational defence] to everyone who asks you to give the reason [nothing here about 'blind faith'!] for the *hope* that you have [i.e. in your heart]. But do this [action] with [the attitudes of] gentleness and respect. ([NIV], my italics)

This verse is the origin of the term 'apologetics', and it defines the intent of this book. In an age where many portray faith as a matter of blind rather than insightful trust, this is a point well worth emphasising. As Norman L. Geisler and Patrick Zukeran explain, Jesus' own enlightened approach to spirituality underlies that displayed by disciples such as Peter and Paul:

Apologetics comes from the Greek word *apologia*, which means a defense ... Jesus was continually confronted with the need to defend his claims to be the Messiah, the Son of God. So by definition, he was an apologist ... Those who oppose apologetics in favor of a leap of faith without evidence will be disappointed in Jesus ... Everywhere Jesus demonstrates a willingness to provide evidence for what he taught to every sincere seeker. Indeed, the Law and the Prophets, which Jesus came to fulfil (Matt. 5:17), inform us of a God who says, 'Come now, let us reason together' (Isa. 1:18), and exhorts us to test false prophets (Deut. 13:1–5; 18:14–22). And those who were taught by Jesus exhort us to 'give the reason for our faith'

(1 Peter 3:15) and not to make *a leap of faith in the dark* but rather to take a step of faith in the light – in the light of the evidence he has provided in nature (Rom. 1:19–20), in our hearts (Rom. 2:12–15), and in history (Acts 17:30–31) … In making his case, Jesus gives reasons and evidence for his claims. He does not expect his listeners simply to believe or make a blind leap of faith … Jesus is an evidentialist, not a fideist, in that he believes in the use of evidence to convince others of the truth of his claims.[89]

Spirituality as faith and works

The NT letter of James argues that true faith (i.e. insightful, trusting belief) naturally results in faith-filled actions (i.e. works):

> What good is it, my brothers, if a man claims to have faith but has no deeds? Can such faith save him? Suppose a brother or sister is without clothes and daily food. If one of you says to him, 'Go, I wish you well; keep warm and well fed,' but does nothing about his physical needs, what good is it? In the same way, faith by itself, if it is not accompanied by action, is dead.
>
> But someone will say, 'You have faith; I have deeds.'
>
> Show me your faith without deeds, and I will show you my faith by what I do. You believe that there is one God. Good! Even the demons believe that – and shudder (James 2:14–19).

Spirituality as Faith and Works

Works = resulting **Practices**
↑
Faith = **Worldview** plus attendant **Attitudes**

Figure 3

Any spirituality can be understood in terms of attitudes based upon worldview beliefs (i.e. 'faith') that in their turn result in various actions (i.e. 'works'). As philosopher C.E.M. Joad argued:

> action always presupposes an attitude of mind from which it springs, an attitude which, explicit when the action is first embarked upon, is unconscious by the time it has become an habitual and well established course of conduct. When I act in a certain manner

towards anything, I recognize by implication that it possesses those characteristics which make my conduct appropriate. So, too, when my action is in regard to God ... If I cannot find good grounds for my beliefs, I shall certainly not persuade myself to act in conformity to them; thus, if I do not accept the attribution of personality to God I shall not succeed in inducing myself to act towards him as if he were a person; that is, I shall not seek to know and to love him, or to pray to him. Thought, in other words, precedes action in the religious as well as other spheres, and the practical significance of the precepts of religion is not separable from the theoretical content from which they derive. It is, then, because my intellect is on the whole convinced that I made such shift as I can to live conformably with its dictates ... intellect, faith, will and desire ... co-operate to produce religious belief and the endeavour to act conformably with it.[90]

That is, spiritual practices are not only the *result of* our spiritual beliefs and their attendant attitudes, but also constitute additional *openings to* the object of faith (whether real or imagined), openings that reinforce our initial beliefs and attitudes. Spiritual practices are not just the natural, practical outworking *of* faith, but also positive aids *to* faith. Spiritual practices are part of a spiritual 'positive feedback loop' (this is obvious enough when one thinks of practices such as prayer; but spiritual practice encompasses the whole of life *insofar as it is lived out of our spiritual beliefs and attitudes*). Our attitudes not only reflect what we believe; they can also restrict the range of truth-claims we will even actively consider for belief. In light of this fact, it would be appropriate to represent spirituality as a dynamic loop:

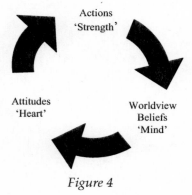

Actions
'Strength'

Attitudes
'Heart'

Worldview
Beliefs
'Mind'

Figure 4

Given the self-reinforcing nature of all spiritualities, it is fortunate that Christian spirituality demands adherence to beliefs, attitudes and actions that mitigate the universal tendency towards epistemic 'selective attention' (cf. 1 Thessalonians 5:21; 1 Corinthians 13:11; 14:20).

A Trinity of trinities

The three elements of spirituality organically correlate with the three 'transcendental values' of classical philosophy (truth, goodness and beauty) that John saw as exemplified in Jesus.[91] They also correlate with the three elements of classical rhetoric. Now, as Phillip E. Johnson laments:

> The meaning of the term 'rhetoric' has been distorted in our time by some unfortunate associations. When we dismiss some politician's speech as 'mere rhetoric,' we mean that it contains nothing but bombast. People today need to be reminded that rhetoric is actually a noble art which has been the subject of serious study since the time of Aristotle and before. Put simply, rhetoric is the art of framing an argument so that it can be appreciated by an audience, even one which is relatively uneducated in the subject or predisposed not to appreciate it.[92]

Aristotle defined rhetoric as:

- 'the power to observe the persuasiveness of which any particular manner admits.'[93]

In practice, rhetoric encompasses the principles of how best to communicate such objective observations to an audience: 'For a speech is composed of three factors – the speaker, the subject and the listener – and it is to the last of these that its purpose is related.'[94] Aristotle explains that rhetoric encompasses three interrelated areas: 'Of those proofs that are furnished through the speech there are three kinds. Some reside in the *character* of the speaker, some in a certain *disposition* of the audience and some in the *speech* itself, through its demonstrating or seeming to demonstrate.'[95]

These three aspects of rhetoric are traditionally referred to by the Greek terms *ethos, pathos* and *logos*:

- **Ethos** – how the character and credibility of a speaker influences people to consider them to be believable (cf. Galatians 5:22)
- **Pathos** – the use of affective appeals (e.g. through storytelling, or otherwise presenting the topic in a way that evokes strong affections in the audience)
- **Logos** – the use of reason to construct arguments

Thus we can relate the three elements of spirituality to the three transcendental values and the three elements of rhetoric:

Spirituality	Judged by	Transcendental Values	Communicated through	Classical Rhetoric
Actions	Judged by	Goodness	Communicated through	*Ethos*
↑ Attitudes	Judged by	Beauty	Communicated through	*Pathos*
↑ Beliefs	Judged by	Truth	Communicated through	*Logos*

Figure 5

I find the etymology of 'philosophy' interesting in light of Paul's claim that Jesus is the person 'in whom are hidden all the treasures of wisdom and knowledge' (Colossians 2:2–3). As Paul K. Moser argues: 'if it is the job of philosophy to understand, explore, and expand upon knowledge in the realm of ultimate truth … and if God is the locus of such truth, then philosophers (knowingly or not) pursue divine truth.'[96] A true philosopher is someone who seeks to know and defend the true, the good and the beautiful by thinking wisely and arguing well (i.e. using good rhetoric). As medieval philosopher-theologian Thomas Aquinas wrote: 'the twofold office of the wise man [is] to mediate and speak forth ... truth ... and to refute the opposing error.'[97] In this book I invite you to join me on a philosophical exploration of the Christian claim that Jesus' entry into space-time was the true enlightenment through which the light of the world offers to enfold humanity into the loving embrace of true spirituality.

The New Theism

I spend a great deal of time thinking, publishing and debating about one of the most fundamental of all questions: What is the nature of 'ultimate reality'? Is ours a mind-first reality or a matter-first reality? In vernacular terms, is there, or is there not, a God? I am convinced, to borrow the title of the 'last will and testament'[98] by philosopher Antony Flew (1923–2010), that *There Is a God*. Flew, 'a legendary British philosopher and atheist [who was] an icon and champion for unbelievers for decades',[99] publically renounced atheism in 2004 after coming to the conclusion that 'the case for an Aristotelian God who has the characteristics of power and also intelligence, is now much stronger than it ever was before.'[100] Interestingly, Flew stated that 'the most impressive arguments for God's existence are those that are supported by recent scientific discoveries ...'[101]

Flew's conclusion is at odds with the headline-grabbing but philosophically naïve assertion by physicist Stephen Hawking that 'because there is a law such as gravity, the Universe can and will create itself from nothing,'[102] and hence that 'God did not create [the] Universe.'[103] Hawking opines that while fundamental questions about reality and the need for a creator thereof have traditionally been issues for philosophers, 'philosophy is dead' because 'philosophy has not kept up with modern developments in science, particularly physics. Scientists have become the bearers of the torch of discovery in our quest for knowledge.'[104] Of course, it was precisely keeping up 'with modern developments in science' that Flew testified contributed to his change of mind about God! Professor Chris Isham, a philosopher and theoretical physicist at Imperial College London, is unimpressed by Hawking's obituary for philosophy: 'I groaned when I read this. Stephen's always saying this sort of thing ... but I suspect he's never read a philosophy book in his life.'[105] Oxford University mathematician and philosopher of science Professor John Lennox makes the obvious but devastating response to Hawking's philosophical pronouncement:

> I find this an astonishing statement ... leaving aside the scientistic hubris of it, it constitutes wonderful evidence that at least one scientist – Hawking himself – has not only 'not kept up with' philosophy, he does not appear to understand the first thing about it, nor its commitment to the elementary rules of logical analysis; because, of course, his statement 'philosophy is dead' ... is itself a statement of philosophy! Hawking is not avoiding the metaphysics that he despises; it's a classic example, therefore, of logical incoherence.[106]

As Professor George Ellis, president of the International Society for Science and Religion argues, 'Philosophy is not dead. Every point of view is imbued with philosophy. Why is science worth doing? The answer is philosophical ... Science can't answer that question about itself.'[107]

On the one hand, one needn't know anything about cosmology to see that it's logically impossible for anything to literally 'create itself from nothing', since things can only have causal effects if they exist and 'nothing' is by definition *the absence of anything capable of doing anything whatsoever*. As theologian and Archbishop of Canterbury Dr Rowan Williams dryly observed in response to Hawking: 'Physical laws ... are about the regular relations between actual realities. I cannot see how they explain the bare fact that there is any reality at all.'[108] On the other hand, for many contemporary scientists and scientifically informed philosophers (*contra* Hawking, they do exist!) the discoveries of modern science have actually served to *strengthen* the case for theism.[109]

I enthusiastically endorse philosopher Robert C. Koons' affirmation that 'the evidence for theism has never been so clear and so strong as it is now.'[110] Of course, one may observe with

Edward Feser that 'atheist chic is now, out of the blue as it were, the stuff of best sellers, celebrity endorsements, and suburban reading groups.'[111] However, the irrationality of the 'new atheism' only serves to demonstrate the intellectual bankruptcy of the matter-first worldview: 'their books stand out for their manifest ignorance of [the theistic tradition] and for the breathtaking shallowness of their philosophical analysis of religious matters.'[112] As Michael Ruse muses: 'It is not that the atheists are having a field day because of the brilliance and novelty of their thinking. Frankly – and I speak here as a non-believer myself, pretty atheistic about Christianity and skeptical about all theological claims – the material being churned out is second rate. And that is a euphemism for "downright awful."'[113] In my opinion, Paul Copan is right to complain that 'the new atheists are remarkably out of touch with [contemporary] sophisticated theistic arguments for God's existence.'[114] For a critique of the 'new atheism' I draw readers' attention to my book *A Sceptic's Guide to Atheism: God Is Not Dead* (Paternoster, 2009).[115]

The waning of naturalism

Gary R. Habermas observes that while 'philosophical naturalism of various stripes holds sway in intellectual circles … there are signs at present that the naturalistic fortress is crumbling.'[116] The matter-first worldview of 'metaphysical naturalism' has been the subject of a growing chorus of high-calibre intellectual criticism in recent years. As Robert C. Koons and George Bealer comment in introducing *The Waning of Materialism* (Oxford University Press, 2010):

> materialism is waning in a number of significant respects – one of which is the ever-growing number of major philosophers who reject materialism or at least have strong sympathies with anti-materialist views … Over the last fifty or so years, materialism has been challenged by a daunting list of arguments … This seems to be reflected in the attitudes of many contemporary philosophers of mind. A growing number – among them prominent philosophers who once had strong materialist sympathies – have come to the conclusion that at least some of the arguments against materialism cannot be overcome.[117]

Nor are the problems with naturalism restricted to the test case of consciousness. As today's leading philosopher of religion, Alvin Plantinga opines: 'despite the smug and arrogant tone of the so-called New Atheists ... naturalism is in philosophical hot water ... on several counts.'[118] Here I agree with philosopher David Baggett:

> naturalism encounters some severe difficulties ... It fares poorly in accounting for qualia, consciousness, the emergence of life and the start of the universe. It lacks resources in accounting for human reason itself ... I think naturalism is especially vulnerable when it comes to accounting for such realities as moral regret, moral obligations, moral rights and moral freedom, all of which make considerably more sense from a theistic viewpoint.[119]

An outstanding collection of papers critiquing metaphysical naturalism is *Naturalism: A Critical Analysis* (Routledge, 2001), edited by William Lane Craig and J.P. Moreland. For an insight into just how intellectually robust the positive case for theism has become within contemporary philosophy (including arguments that interact with contemporary scientific cosmology), one need only consult the monumental *Blackwell Companion to Natural Theology* (Blackwell, 2009), likewise edited by Craig and Moreland.[120]

Satisfying Hume's Sentiment

It is somewhat ironic that many atheists look to the Scottish Enlightenment philosopher David Hume (1711–76) as an intellectual forebear, for as John Perry and Michael Bratman report:

> the mature Hume was a theist, albeit of a vague and weak-kneed sort. He seems to have been convinced by the argument from design of the proposition 'That the cause or causes of order in the universe probably bear some remote analogy to human intelligence.' But he was also convinced that the argument does not permit this undefined intelligence to be given further shape or specificity.[121]

As Hume wrote in his *Natural History of Religion*:

> The whole frame of nature bespeaks an intelligent author; and no rational enquirer can, after serious reflection, suspend his belief a moment with regard to the primary principles of genuine Theism ... All things of the universe are evidently of a piece. Every thing is adjusted to every thing. One design prevails throughout the whole. And this uniformity leads the mind to acknowledge one author.[122]

Many people empathize with Hume's vague belief in some sort of a divine author whilst remaining reticent about embracing the sort of theological specificity that comes with embracing any particular religious tradition. Indeed, Flew qualified his intellectual conversion to theism in precisely such terms: 'I do not accept any claim of divine revelation though I would be happy to study any such claim (and continue to do so in the case of Christianity).'[123] However, having arrived at belief in God, Flew observed that while he had previously 'taken issue with many of the claims of divine revelation'[124] his changed position was 'more open to at least certain of these claims'[125] for the simple reason that 'you cannot limit the possibilities of omnipotence except to produce the logically impossible. Everything else is open to omnipotence.'[126] Flew even singled out Christianity for consideration because 'the claim concerning the resurrection is more impressive than any by the religious competition' and because 'the claim that God was incarnate in Jesus Christ is unique.'[127]

Flew was a noted exponent of Hume's thought, so it's not surprising to find a similar sentiment expressed by Hume through the voice of Philo in his *Dialogues Concerning Natural Religion*:

> The most natural sentiment, which a well-disposed mind will feel on this occasion, is a longing desire and expectation, that Heaven would be pleased to dissipate, at least alleviate, this profound ignorance, by affording some more particular revelation to mankind, and making discoveries of the nature, attributes, and operations of the divine object of our faith.[128]

This book argues that the person at the centre of the Christian revelation claim which so intrigued Flew is in fact the fulfilment of

Hume's 'most natural sentiment' that longed for a bridge between the general acknowledgement of 'an intelligent author' of nature on the one hand and 'some more particular revelation to mankind [concerning] the nature, attributes, and operations of the divine' on the other.

An examination of Jesus serves double duty, both in offering evidence for the existence of God and in offering greater specificity to the concept of divinity than almost any other argument (or set of arguments) within the field of natural theology. Readers who begin this exploration alongside the likes of Hume and Flew may view the case that I offer as having the primary goal of bringing specificity to a pre-existing vague theism and the secondary goal of reinforcing a belief in God in the process.

An interdisciplinary study

Our subject is by nature interdisciplinary. It will, for example, involve consideration of the presuppositions, methods and results of historical investigation. This interdisciplinary study brings advantages for those who would otherwise find consideration of an essentially metaphysical question about the nature of ultimate reality too abstract. As atheist Bradley Monton observes: 'a key part of Christian doctrine is that God became flesh in the form of Jesus Christ, and that Christ acted in the world in such a way that we can get evidence of his existence, and of his divinity.'[129] Christianity is the only religion to make the claim that God has revealed himself to humanity, not merely though the prophets and/or the Scriptures and/or this or that miraculous event, but, if I may be permitted a somewhat awkward turn of phrase, by revealing himself *in person, in a person*!

There are, of course, a host of *metaphysical* issues that attend such a claim. The early Christians put much intellectual effort into preserving, clarifying and codifying their understanding of Jesus' simultaneous humanity and divinity. The early extra-biblical creeds exhibit a fascinating theological development of the essential historical data concerning the nature of Jesus and the God he claimed to reveal. Recent decades have seen a renaissance of work in the field of philosophical theology aimed at clarifying a coherent Christian understanding of the incarnation and the related doctrine of God's nature as three divine persons in one divine being (the doctrine of 'the Trinity'), and, as philosopher Peter van Inwagen affirms, 'these doctrines can be formulated in a way that allows no formal contradiction to be deduced from them.'[130] These are very deep waters into which we cannot stray here, except to note with Peter Kreeft that:

> The idea that God is only one Person *and* is three Persons would be a logical contradiction. But that is not Christianity. And the idea that God has only one nature *and* has three natures would be a contradiction. But that is not Christianity. And the idea that God is one God with one nature in three Persons is *not* a contradiction. And that is Christianity. The idea that Jesus is only one Person *and* is two Persons would be a logical contradiction. And the idea that Jesus has only one nature *and* has two natures would be a logical contradiction. But the idea that Jesus is only one Person but has two natures is not a logical contradiction. And that is Christianity.[131]

Readers wishing to delve further into the metaphysics of the incarnation and the Trinity should consider Richard Swinburne's *Is Jesus God?* (Oxford University Press, 2009).[132]

Belief that before belief in

A Christian understanding of Jesus claims that Jesus had certain specific ideas about spirituality and about the role the God of Israel wanted him to play in offering spiritual enlightenment to humanity, ideas that were grounded in his self-understanding as the Jewish Messiah. A Christian understanding of Jesus claims to have a sufficiently reliable access to Jesus' self-understanding to make it possible for us to understand him in the same way. Of course, Christians don't merely claim that it is *possible* to understand Jesus in the same way that Jesus understood himself; they claim that this is how we *should* understand Jesus, *because such an understanding of Jesus is both true and rationally compelling*. Moreover, Christians claim that the right response to understanding Jesus as they do in an *intellectual* sense is to understand him in a more holistic *spiritual* sense as well. That is, the Christian is one who

combines the belief *that* Jesus is Messiah with a whole-life commitment of trust (faith) *in* Jesus.

Philosophers distinguish between having a belief *that* (or *about*)
something and having a belief *in* something. In order to have a
belief *in* something one must have a belief *that* concerning the
object of one's belief. For example, it's obviously impossible to
believe *in* God if one does not believe *that* God exists. Another
way of saying that you believe *in* something is to say that you have
faith – or trust – in it. Moreover, it should also be clear that since
faith – or trust – is a matter of belief *in*, there's nothing intrinsic
about faith that undermines or detracts from any rational responsibilities that attach to the belief *that* the object of one's faith – or
trust – is real. Neither is there anything intrinsic to the nature of
faith that undermines or detracts from any rational responsibilities that attach to having trust *in* the object of one's faith. As the
command of 1 Peter 3:15 indicates, having trust is clearly compatible with having every reason to believe that the object of one's
trust is trustworthy.

Specifying spirituality

We can plot beliefs on a spectrum with axes measuring *strength*
(from certain belief to certain disbelief) and *content* (from vague
to specific).[133] Hence beliefs (whether positive or negative) can be
simultaneously more or less vague and more or less certain com-
ponents of our spirituality:

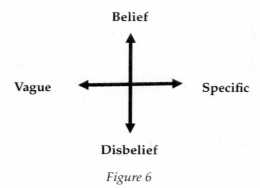

Figure 6

As a Christian I have some pretty specific belief about God and his self-revelation through Jesus, both in history and in my own life. I believe *that* these ideas are true; and I combine this belief *that* with a belief *in* the Christian God, an act of rationally motivated existential trust that Christians call 'faith'.

A worldview with no mysteries would rightly raise suspicions of being a human invention. My beliefs about God are not so specific that I think I *comprehend* the nature of God or his interactions with creation. Christians have always held that 'we see through a glass, darkly' (1 Corinthians 13:12 [AV]). Nevertheless, I have beliefs that are *specific enough* for a rational assessment of their truth to be possible. Considered as a worldview, Christianity meets philosopher Gordon R. Lewis' criterion that 'proposed explanations … must be defined with sufficient clarity that others may know what is being proposed'.[134] As Richard Purtill comments:

> Some Christians who were trying to emphasize God's greatness have, indeed, talked as if we could understand nothing about God, and if this were true, our belief could have no content. But the case is, of course, that some things in the Christian message we understand immediately and easily, some things we come increasingly to understand as we try to live by them, and others remain dark to us in varying degrees. After all, there is nothing surprising in this. We have the same experience in reading a great philosopher or in getting to know a human being. The only things we can *completely* understand are very simple and abstract things like the laws of mechanics, or systems that have been invented by our own minds. But any real thing, even something as simple as a fish or an onion, is at least partly mysterious to us. Any completely comprehensible revelation would be immediately suspicious and probably man-made.[135]

Nor are my beliefs about God so firm that they occupy the 'certain' tip of the 'belief' axis. I don't claim to know that Christian spirituality is true with the same degree of certainty that I know I exist (i.e. Descartes' 'I think, therefore I am'), or that the law of non-contradiction is true (just try denying it!). Rather, I merely claim to have a *sufficient* degree of certainty to make belief (both belief *that* and belief *in*) the most rational course of action.

An Accumulation of Ways to Understanding Jesus

The medieval philosopher Thomas Aquinas famously offered five 'ways' to understanding the reality of God.[136] Against the radical scepticism evinced by Dawkins, but without inviting readers to embrace the blind faith he falsely attributes to Christians, this book will present five 'ways' that together form a cumulative argument for understanding Jesus as orthodox Christians understand him. Each of the five 'ways' I will present is a restatement of an argument given by Jesus and/or his first-century followers in support of Jesus' own claims.

A cumulative argument is an argument – like those often presented by historians, scientists, or lawyers – that depends upon an accumulation of evidences and/or arguments, which jointly point to the same conclusion. In considering a cumulative argument, Flew cautions, 'We [must] insist upon a sometimes tricky distinction: between, on the one hand, the valid principle of the accumulation of evidence, where every item has at least some weight in its own right; and, on the other hand, the Ten-leaky-buckets-tactic, applied to arguments none of which hold water at all.'[137] If each of the arguments in a cumulative case has 'some weight in its own right', then even if each argument considered individually lacks sufficient 'weight' to tip the scales of reason in favour of the hypothesis being advanced, the accumulation of such arguments *taken together* may nevertheless be enough to tip the scales.

However, where one ends up, after considering a cumulative argument, doesn't depend wholly upon one's judgement about how strong the argument is. It also depends, in part, upon the strength of one's initial scepticism towards the hypothesis being advanced. It would obviously take stronger evidence to convince someone who brings to their study of Jesus a prior commitment to a naturalistic worldview than someone who begins their investigation as an agnostic or a philosophical theist. As scientists John Polkinghorne and Nicholas Beale write: 'judgments about the historicity of the resurrection are inevitably caught up in whether people think that the prior probability of the existence of God is significant. If it is negligible, then the resurrection [is highly unlikely to] have happened. If God exists, as we believe, the evidence is pretty strong.'[138]

Richard Dawkins uses the idea of 'a spectrum of probabilities'[139] along which we can place 'human judgments about the existence of God … between two extremes of opposite certainty'.[140] He notes that such a spectrum 'is continuous'[141] but that it can be represented by 'milestones along the way'.[142] Dawkins provides a seven-point scale, but because it is standard for probability calculus we will use a ten-point spectrum of epistemological probability (i.e. how likely we judge something to be) where 0 equals the judgement that a proposition is an impossibility (i.e. it is logically incoherent), 1 equals the judgement that a proposition is necessarily true, and 0.5 equals the judgement that a proposition is just as likely to be true as not.[143]

Dawkins reckons that 'reason alone could not propel one to total conviction that anything [coherent] definitely does not exist'[144] and says that he'd 'be surprised to meet many people'[145] in the category of absolutely certain disbelief in God (Christopher Hitchens likewise avers that God's existence 'cannot be disproved'[146]). So, suppose one has a prior belief that metaphysical naturalism is very likely true and, conversely, that God probably does not exist and hence that the Christian understanding of Jesus is very likely to be false. One might register one's initial position with respect to the proposition that 'the Christian understanding of Jesus is true' as 0.1. One then examines the first of the five 'ways' presented herein, and one thinks the argument has some weight. Perhaps one thinks the 'first way' raises the probability of a Christian understanding of Jesus by a mere 0.05 on our scale. The 'first way' has, as it were, soaked up a small proportion (5%) of one's pool of initial scepticism. The important thing to note is that, when one comes to considering the 'second way', one has a slightly shallower pool of prior scepticism than before, *and so on*. Hence, if each argument in a cumulative case carries some weight, then (if one doesn't begin with a categorical commitment to an unfalsifiable naturalism) each argument soaks up some of one's prior scepticism, and it *may* be that after considering each element in a cumulative case, one's prior scepticism hasn't merely been soaked up, but has been counterbalanced.

The following chart illustrates the effect a cumulative case for a Christian understanding of Jesus might have upon an atheist (diamond), an agnostic (square) and a theist (triangle), all of whom begin with different degrees of initial scepticism about the Christian understanding of Jesus, but all of whom assign the same weight to each argument in the cumulative case under consideration:

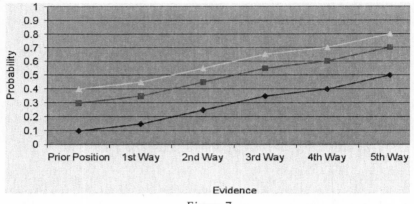

Figure 7

Of course, cumulative arguments aren't concerned with the mere *addition* of evidences, but with the *combination* of evidences. The accumulation of evidence in a cumulative case forms an evolving context of interpretation, a context within which one piece of evidence may be seen to relate to another in a mutually reinforcing manner, such that the overall strength of a cumulative argument can transcend the merely linear sum of its evidential parts:

> since components of a cumulative case argument can strengthen or, less happily, weaken one another, the opponent of a cumulative case argument must not improperly 'divide and rule' by treating the arguments separately … Considering individual component arguments in isolation may help clarify each component argument in itself, but such isolation may crucially distort the overall nature, structure, and strength of the combined argument.[147]

As philosophers Timothy and Linda McGrew caution:

> Cumulative case arguments … draw on many details and often require, for their full appreciation, more than a passing acquaintance with multiple disciplines. Beyond this, there is the sheer

cognitive difficulty of appreciating the evidential impact of multiple pieces of evidence on a single point; we are apt to focus on two or three considerations and discount the rest. Finally, the pieces of evidence must themselves be not only considered in isolation but coordinated, that is, considered in connection with each other. This coordination requires good judgment.[148]

Bearing these caveats in mind, readers may like to use the blank chart in Figure 8 (or a photocopy thereof) to record their own prior assessment of the probability that a Christian understanding of Jesus is true (something that will primarily be determined by their prior assessment of the probability that theism is true), and to keep track of the evolving degree, if any, to which the following cumulative case affects that scepticism as we investigate the five 'ways' to understanding Jesus.

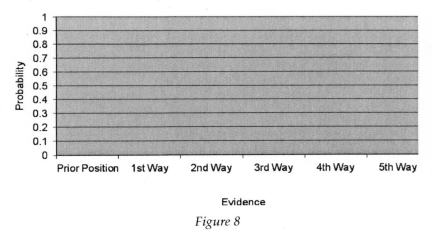

Figure 8

The Way Ahead

In the spirit of the Enlightenment, and before we examine the five 'ways' to understanding Jesus, we will turn to examining the relevant historical sources. I will argue, in answer to a series of standard historical questions, that the NT should be recognized as *a generally reliable source of historical information about what really happened in history.*

Recommended Resources

Websites

Last Seminary – Papers against Naturalism http://www.lastseminary. com/against-naturalism.
— Philosophy of Religion Articles http://www.lastseminary.com/ philosophy-of-religion-article.

Video

Benson, Bruce. 'Renaissance of Christian Belief' http://www.public christianity.com/Videos/renaissance_christian_belief.html.
Craig, William Lane. 'Why Does Anything at All Exist?' http://rfmedia. org/av/video/why-does-anything-at-all-exist-wake-forest/.
— 'Dawkins and the Arguments for Theism' http://www.apologetics. blip.tv/file/3567925/.
God – New Evidence http://www.focus.org.uk/?page_id=101.
Koons, Robert C. 'Science and Belief in God' http://www.vimeo. com/9196750.
Lennox, John. 'Stephen Hawking and God: A Response' http://www.john lennox.org/index.php/en/resource/stephen_hawking_and_god/.
Ward, Keith. 'Philosophy and the New Atheism' http://www.public christianity.com/ward.html.

Audio

Craig, William Lane. 'Response to Richard Dawkins' Book *The God Delusion*' http://www.rfmedia.org/RF_audio_video/Other_clips/ UF-Responding-to-Dawkins-The-God-Delusion/UF_Bill_Craig_s_ Response_to_The_God_Delusion.mp3.
— 'The Arguments for God's Existence and Critique of the New Atheists' http://www.rfmedia.org/av/audio/gracepoint-gods-existence-and-critique-of-new-atheists/.
— 'Has Science Made it Impossible to Believe in God?' http://www. rfmedia.org/RF_audio_video/Other_clips/A97TAMU01.mp3.
— 'Greg Koukl Interviews William Lane Craig about Hawking's New Book' http://www.rfmedia.org/av/audio/stephen-hawkings-new-book-str-interview/.

— 'Questions for Stephen Hawking' http://www.reasonablefaith.org/site/News2?page=NewsArticle&id=5887.

— 'Lawrence Krauss on Creation out of Nothing' http://www.reasonable faith.org/site/News2?page=NewsArticle&id=5887.

— vs. Lewis Wolpert. 'Is God a Delusion?' http://www.brianauten.com/Apologetics/craig-wolpert-debate.mp3.

Koons, Robert C. 'Science and Belief in God' http://www.veritas.org/Media.aspx#/v/535.

Williams, Peter S. 'Arguments for Theism' http://www.damaris.org/cm/podcasts/359.

— 'A Sceptic's Guide to the New Atheism' http://www.damaris.org/cm/podcasts/355.

— 'Book Launch: A Sceptic's Guide to Atheism' http://www.cis.org.uk/upload/peter_williams_sceptics.mp3.

— 'Evidence for Jesus from the Early Church Fathers' http://www.damaris.org/cm/podcasts/309.

— 'Introduction to Apologetics' http://www.damaris.org/cm/podcasts/360.

— 'Apologizing for a Reasonable Faith?' http://www.damaris.org/cm/podcasts/281.

— '1 Peter 3:15 – Apologetics: What, Where, When, Who, How and Why?' http://www.damaris.org/cm/podcasts/261.

— 'Apologetics in 3D' http://www.damaris.org/cm/podcasts/248.

— vs. Peter Cave. 'Is Belief in God Reasonable?' http://www.damaris.org/cm/podcasts/364.

Online papers

Barnett, Paul. 'Did Jesus Exist? Early Non-Christian References' http://www.lastseminary.com/sources-outside-the-new-testam/.

Craig, William Lane. 'God Is Not Dead Yet' http://www.reasonablefaith.org/site/News2?page=NewsArticle&id=6647.

— 'The New Atheists and Five Arguments for God' http://www.reasonable faith.org/site/News2?page=NewsArticle&id=8088.

— 'What Is the Relationship between Science and Religion?' http://www.reasonablefaith.org/site/News2?page=NewsArticle&id=5355.

Habermas, Gary R. 'A Summary Critique: Questioning the Existence of Jesus' http://www.garyhabermas.com/articles/crj_summary critique/crj_summarycritique.htm.

Hazen, Craig J. 'My Pilgrimage from Atheism to Theism: An Exclusive Interview with Former British Atheist Professor Antony Flew' http://www.biola.edu/antonyflew/.

May, Peter. 'Testing the Golden Rule' http://www.bethinking.org/bible-jesus/introductory/testing-the-golden-rule.htm.

Penrose, Roger. 'The Grand Design: Review' http://www.ft.com/cms/s/2/bdf3ae28-b6e9-11df-b3dd-00144feabdc0.html.

Plantinga, Alvin. 'The Dawkins Confusion' http://www.christianitytoday.com/bc/2007/002/1.21.html.

Roberts, Mark D. 'Did Jesus Even Exist?' http://www.markdroberts.typepad.com/markdroberts/2007/11/did-jesus-even-.html.

Williams, Peter S. 'The Big Bad Wolf, Theism and the Foundations of Intelligent Design Theory: A Review of Richard Dawkins' *The God Delusion*' http://www.epsociety.org/library/articles.asp?pid=53.

— 'The Emperor's New Clothes: Pointing the Finger at Dawkins' Atheism', *Think* (Spring 2010): pp. 29–33 http://www.journals.cambridge.org/action/displayFulltext?type=1&pdftype=1&fid=7191812&jid=THI&volumeId=9&issueId=24&aid=7191804.

Books

Berlinski, David. *The Devil's Delusion: Atheism and Its Scientific Pretensions* (New York: Crown Forum, 2008).

Bettenson, Henry, ed. *The Early Christian Fathers* (OUP, 1969).

Carter, Joe and John Coleman. *How to Argue Like Jesus: Learning Persuasion from History's Greatest Communicator* (Wheaton, IL: Crossway, 2009).

Churchill, Leigh. *The Blood of Martyrs: The History of the Christian Church from Pentecost to the Age of Theodosius* (Carlisle: Paternoster, 2005).

Copan, Paul and Paul K. Moser, eds. *The Rationality of Theism* (London: Routledge, 2003).

Craig, William Lane, ed. *Philosophy of Religion: A Reader and Guide* (Edinburgh University Press, 2002).

— and Chad Meister, eds. *God Is Good, God Is Great: Why Believing in God Is Reasonable and Responsible* (Downers Grove, IL: IVP, 2009).

— and J.P. Moreland, eds. *The Blackwell Companion to Natural Theology* (Oxford: Wiley-Blackwell, 2009).

— eds. *Naturalism: A Critical Analysis* (London: Routledge, 2001).

Davies, Brian. *An Introduction to the Philosophy of Religion* (OUP, 3rd edn, 2004).

Evans, C. Stephen and R. Zachary Manis. *Philosophy of Religion: Thinking about Faith* (Downers Grove, IL: IVP, 2nd rev. edn, 2009).

Flew, Antony and Roy Abraham Varghese. *There Is a God* (London: HarperOne, 2009).

Ganssle, Gregory E. *A Reasonable God: Engaging the New Face of Atheism* (Baylor University Press, 2009).

Goetz, Stewart and Charles Taliaferro. *Naturalism* (Grand Rapids, MI: Eerdmans, 2008).

Groothuis, Douglas. *Truth Decay: Defending Christianity against the Challenges of Postmodernism* (Downers Grove, IL: IVP, 2000).

Hackett, Stuart C. *The Reconstruction of the Christian Revelation Claim: A Philosophical and Critical Apologetic* (Eugene, OR: Wipf & Stock, 2008).

Hasker, William. *The Emergent Self* (Cornell University Press, 1999).

Koons, Robert C. and George Bealer, eds. *The Waning of Materialism* (Oxford University Press, 2010).

Lennox, John C. *God's Undertaker: Has Science Buried God?* second edition (Oxford: Lion, 2009).

Meister, Chad V. *Building Belief: Constructing Faith from the Ground Up* (Eugene, OR: Wipf & Stock, 2009).

Menuge, Angus. *Agents under Fire: Materialism and the Rationality of Science* (Oxford: Rowman & Littlefield, 2004).

Moreland, J.P. *Consciousness and the Existence of God: A Theistic Argument* (London: Routledge, 2008).

— *Scaling the Secular City: A Defense of Christianity* (Grand Rapids, MI: Baker, 1987).

— and William Lane Craig. *Philosophical Foundations for a Christian Worldview* (Downers Grove, IL: IVP, 2003).

— and Kai Nielsen. *Does God Exist? The Debate between Theists and Atheists* (New York: Prometheus, 1993).

Morris, Thomas V. *The Logic of God Incarnate* (Eugene, OR: Wipf & Stock, 2001).

Murray, Michael J. and Michael Rea, *An Introduction to the Philosophy of Religion* (CUP, 2008).

Plantinga, Alvin. *Warranted Christian Belief* (OUP, 2000).

— and Michael Tooley, *Knowledge of God* (Oxford: Blackwell, 2008).

Reppert, Victor. *C.S. Lewis' Dangerous Idea: In Defense of the Argument from Reason* (Downers Grove, IL: IVP, 2003).

Reynolds, John Mark. *When Athens Met Jerusalem: An Introduction to Classical and Christian Thought* (Downers Grove, IL: IVP Academic, 2009).

Sennett, James F. and Douglas Groothuis, eds. *In Defense of Natural Theology* (Downers Grove, IL: IVP, 2005).

Smart, J.J.C. and J.J. Haldane. *Atheism and Theism* (Oxford: Blackwell, 2nd edn, 2003).

Spitzer, Robert J. *New Proofs for the Existence of God: Contributions Of Contemporary Physics and Philosophy* (Grand Rapids, MI: Eerdmans, 2010).

Swinburne, Richard. *Was Jesus God?* (OUP, 2008).

Taliaferro, Charles. *Philosophy of Religion* (Oxford: OneWorld, 2009).

Wallace, Stan W., ed. *Does God Exist? The Craig–Flew Debate* (Aldershot: Ashgate, 2003).

Ward, Keith. *Why There Almost Certainly Is a God* (Oxford: Lion, 2008).

— *God, Chance and Necessity* (Oxford: OneWorld, 1996).

Willard, Dallas. *Knowing Christ Today: Why We Can Trust Spiritual Knowledge* (London: HarperOne, 2009).

Williams, Peter S. *A Sceptic's Guide to Atheism: God Is Not Dead* (Carlisle: Paternoster, 2009).

— *I Wish I Could Believe in Meaning: A Response to Nihilism* (Southampton: Damaris, 2004).

Zacharias, Ravi. *Can Man Live without God?* (Milton Keynes: W Publishing Group, 2004).

2

Trusting the Biblical Testimony to the Historical Jesus

> The Gospels are testimony. This does not mean that they are testimony *rather than* history. It means that the kind of historiography they are is testimony.
>
> Richard Bauckham[1]

The New Testament (NT) letter 2 Peter declares: 'we did not follow cleverly devised stories when we told you about the coming of our Lord Jesus Christ in power, but we were eyewitnesses of his majesty' (2 Peter 1:16). The letter of 1 John states: 'That which was from the beginning, which we have heard, which we have seen with our eyes, which we have looked at and our hands have touched – this we proclaim concerning the Word of life' (1 John 1:1–2). Craig J. Hazen comments:

> having myself done a doctorate in religious studies and having had an opportunity to study and compare most of the sacred texts of the great religious traditions, I find these kinds of passages in the New Testament utterly compelling. You simply do not find this kind of empirical, verificationist language in the Bhagavad-Gita, the Granth, the Tripitaka, or the Qur'an. The writers of the New Testament were obsessed with this kind of language because something astonishing had happened right in their midst, in broad daylight for all to see … this kind of language sets the New Testament apart as a unique type of religious literature – spiritually edifying *and empirically testable*.[2]

Of course, the fact that something is empirically testable doesn't mean that one must test it before one can rationally trust it. I can empirically test your testimony that we've run out of milk, but I needn't do so for my act of adding 'milk' to the shopping list to be rational. As Richard Bauckham observes: 'testimony should not be treated as credible only to the extent that it can be independently verified ... Trusting testimony is not an irrational act of faith that leaves critical rationality aside ...'[3] Nevertheless, the NT use of verificationist language opens up the possibility of independent verification. These approaches are complementary; so let's investigate the epistemology of 'trusting testimony' and apply it to the NT, before putting that testimony to the test of independent confirmation.

Understanding Testimony

> The Gospels are prima facie evidence for what the historical Jesus said and did.
>
> David Wenham and Steve Walton[4]

Philosopher Robert Audi observes that 'when philosophers speak of testimony, they usually have in mind not the formal reporting of the court witness ... but virtually any instance of someone's telling somebody something ...'[5] Audi observes that:

> what we think of as 'our knowledge,' in an overall sense, would collapse if the contribution to it made by testimony were eliminated: what remained would be at best fragmentary. Testimony is in this respect globally essential for human knowledge ... one simply could not develop a body of knowledge at all apart from the instruction one receives in childhood, in which testimony is central.[6]

Audi defines testimony-based belief as: 'the kind of belief that arises naturally, non-inferentially, and usually unselfconsciously in response to what someone says to us. I ask you the time; you tell me it is nine o'clock; and straightaway I believe this on the basis of your saying it.'[7] As Thomas Reid argued:

It is evident that, in the matter of testimony, the balance of human judgement is by nature inclined to the side of belief; and turns to that side of itself when there is nothing put into the opposite scale. If it were not so, no proposition that is uttered in discourse would be believed, until it was examined and tried by reason; and most men would be unable to find reasons for believing the thousandth part of what is told to them.[8]

Reid dubbed the primacy of trust in matters concerning testimony, sense perception and the like, the *principle of credulity*: 'a disposition to confide in the veracity of others, and to believe what they tell us.'[9] Contemporary Oxford philosopher Richard Swinburne elaborates upon Reid's discussion, distinguishing between the 'principle of credulity' and the 'principle of testimony':

It is indeed a basic principle of rational belief – which I call the Principle of Credulity – that what seems to you to be so on the basis of experience, probably is so – in the absence of counter-evidence … And it is also a basic principle of rational belief which I call the Principle of Testimony, that what people tell you is probably true – in the absence of counter-evidence.[10]

As Iain W. Provan observes:

we generally regard it as a sign of emotional or mental imbalance if people ordinarily inhabit a culture of distrust in testimony at the level of principle, and most of us outside mental institutions do not inhabit such a universe … we recognize that healthy people generally place trust in the testimony of others, reserving suspicion for those who give grounds for it. In everyday life, then, the exercise of a thoroughgoing 'hermeneutic of suspicion' with regard to testimony is considered no more sensible than the exercise of blind faith in terms of our apprehension of reality in general. Nor should either approach be considered sensible in terms of our apprehension of *past* reality in particular.[11]

Whilst stipulating that testimony-based belief is 'never inferential',[12] Audi is at pains to note that this 'is not to imply that it is "uncritical" or even manifests a degree of credulity incompatible with a critical habit of mind.'[13] Even if only subconsciously, we rightly sieve the testimony we receive for signs of untrustworthiness: 'Even active monitoring of testimony is possible without making inferences: if nothing is noticed that requires raising questions or drawing inferences, no questioning or inference need arise even from attentive monitoring by a critical listener.'[14] Thus it can be rational, and fully compatible with 'a critical habit of mind', to adopt a belief purely on the non-inferential basis of testimony.

Testimony-based belief carries *prima facie* (literally 'on the face of it') justification. As John Warwick Montgomery writes, summarizing Aristotle's dictum: 'The benefit of the doubt is to be given to the document itself, and not arrogated by the critic to himself.'[15] In the same vein theologian Hugh Montefiore sets out 'the criterion of historical presumption: a saying or story is likely to be authentic unless there are good reasons for thinking otherwise.'[16]

Philosopher Peter Graham distinguishes between *pro tanto* and *on balance* forms of *prima facie* justification. This amounts to distinguishing between there being *some* evidence and *enough* evidence for any given claim: 'A *pro tanto* justification is a consideration in favour of a certain belief … A *pro tanto* justification may only justify the belief to a certain *degree* …'[17] Thus, even if one doesn't think that testimony concerning some proposition P provides *prima facie on-balance* justification that's *enough* to warrant belief, one might nevertheless think that it provides *prima facie pro tanto* justification. This *pro tanto* justification might be combined with additional *pro tanto* justifications and/or additional non-testimonial justification, to render the belief in question justified *on balance*. In the latter case, one's belief would have *prima facie* justification *partially* on the basis of testimony.

Audi highlights another use of testimony in rational belief-formation, noting that if:

> I believe something on the basis of *premises* supporting your testimony, as where the content seems implausible by itself but I judge you to be both highly competent and unassailably sincere, and for that reason I believe what you say … this is not belief or knowledge on the *basis* of your testimony. My basis is a combination of your testimony and my beliefs about you.[18]

This raises the question of whether a belief based in whole or part upon the *subconscious* awareness of such 'premises' (i.e. grounds for trust) should be classified as a testimony-based belief, or as belief based upon 'a combination of your testimony and my beliefs about you.' Perhaps if one is aware of having subconscious grounds for trust – i.e. one has a 'hunch' or 'gut feeling' of reliability that one does not, and perhaps cannot, consciously articulate – this might still be classified as a testimony-based belief; whereas, if one can and does consciously articulate one's grounds for trust, then one's belief clearly isn't 'testimony-based' in Audi's sense.

In sum, there's a spectrum of testimonial warrant: beliefs can be *prima facie* justified either entirely (i.e. *on balance*) or partially (i.e. *pro tanto*) on the non-inferential basis of testimony. Furthermore, even if a belief isn't justified (whether entirely or partially) on the basis of testimony, testimony can still feature among the rational grounds for a belief when taken in combination (either subconsciously or consciously) with premises that provide inferential support for its reliability. Hence on-balance *prima facie* justification constitutes a spectrum, from belief formed wholly on the non-inferential basis of testimony, to belief formed only on the basis of testimony in conscious conjunction with supporting premises.

Feeling what we know

As a feature both of the 'attentive monitoring' that can accompany testimony-based belief, and of the subconscious recognition of testimony-supporting premises, it's worth pondering the role of feelings in our acceptance of testimony. Not only can we know our own feelings, we can feel or intuit our own acts of knowing. Sometimes we know more than we can say or even explain how we know, and feelings can alert us to this. Recent scientific research bears out the wisdom of trusting our intuition in such matters.

For example, researchers at Washington University in St Louis have identified an area of the brain (called the anterior cingulate cortex) that 'may help us unconsciously pick up warning signs and steer clear of danger.'[19] Consider the example of a woman walking home at night who realizes she is feeling afraid. In point of fact, she has a feeling *about a certain state of affairs*. Her 'feeling' includes qualities of *belief* and *intentionality* in that it is about her personal safety relative to her current situation. Assuming we're talking about something more akin to a vague sense of unease and wariness than to an obviously disproportionate full-blown fight-or-flight response, it's reasonable for a woman in this situation to take the fact that she feels frightened as adequate grounds (via the principle of credulity) for believing that she is in danger. Her fear might be justifiable in terms of various beliefs that she has (e.g. the local paper recently reported several attacks upon lone women in this area). However, just because she *could* reason her way explicitly to the conclusion that she is in danger doesn't mean that she *must* go through the logical motions in order to rationally believe that she is in jeopardy. Indeed, the rationality of her fear wouldn't be undermined by a mere inability on her part to explicitly reason her way to the same conclusion. For the rationality of her fear to be threatened, it would have to be the case that she could reason her way *to the opposite conclusion*, and *with a level of confidence sufficient to overwhelm the rationality of her feeling-based belief*. In the absence of sufficient reasons for doubt, though, she is justified in trusting her feelings.

Again, consider research into the phenomena of 'blind sight'. Scientists at Rice University in Houston, Texas, used an electro-magnetic device to temporarily shut down the primary visual cortex in sighted volunteers, before presenting them with a series of images:

> they were asked to say whether a bar was horizontal or vertical. They were also asked to say how confident they felt about their decision … If people were blindfolded and simply guessed, chance alone would suggest they would get half right. But during the tests, volunteers typically got around three quarters correct. Some said they were simply guessing. But others said they had a 'feeling' of seeing something, despite having no conscious idea of what it was. This was backed up by their confidence scores. Those who felt more sure of themselves got more answers right.[20]

Researchers hypothesized that, after disruption to the primary visual pathways, other pathways were functioning to provide this 'blind sight', something previously observed in certain blind people: 'One 52-year-old doctor who had lost his sight after two strokes was even able to detect different emotions on faces. This suggested to scientists there must be other connections in the brain that allow unconscious sight.'[21] The most accurate blinded volunteers were those who went on the basis of their 'feelings'. Far from excluding knowledge, having a feeling, hunch or intuition can actually function *as the rational conduit of cognisance.*

Scientists at the University of Iowa undertook a study in which volunteers played a gambling game. Participants were presented with four packs of cards, two blue and two red. Each card they turned over would either win or lose them money. They were tasked with trying to maximize their winnings. What the participants weren't told was that while the blue packs offered a steady diet of modest rewards and penalties, the red packs offered both high wins *and losses.* The scientists wanted to see how long it took people to figure out the difference between the packs. They found that after turning over about fifty cards, most people start developing a hunch about what's going on. After turning over about eighty cards, most people have figured out the game and can explain why picking the red decks is a bad idea. The significant point here is that people had a *hunch* about the red cards *before* they had an explicit understanding about why the red decks were a worse bet:

> But the Iowa scientists did something else, and this is where the strange part of the experiment begins. They hooked each gambler up to a machine that measured the activity of the sweat glands below the skin in the palms of their hands. Like most of our sweat glands, those in our palms respond to stress as well as temperature … What the Iowa scientists found is that gamblers started generating stress responses to the red decks by the tenth card, forty cards before they were able to say they had a hunch about what was wrong with those two decks. More importantly, right around the time their palms started sweating, their behaviour began to change as well. They started favouring the blue cards and taking fewer and fewer cards from the red decks. In other words, the gamblers figured the game out before they realized they had figured the game out.[22]

In his fascinating book *Blink: The Power of Thinking without Thinking* (Penguin, 2005) Malcolm Gladwell hypothesizes that such results are achieved by the use of the technique of 'thin slicing', where focusing on a small amount of salient data is sufficient for making accurate assessments and predictions of patterns by 'the adaptive unconscious.'[23] This is a cognitive faculty we all have, but which appears in a fine-tuned form in the professional 'gut instincts' of the expert.

A Translator's Testimony

J.B. Phillips (1906–82) was a scholar and Anglican clergyman who spent twenty-five years single-handedly translating the NT into English.[24] 'Few people have had such a close and constant contact with the New Testament as I have,' wrote Phillips. 'I say this in no spirit of conceit; it is a matter of simple fact.'[25] Phillips recorded his professional impression that 'the New Testament, given a fair hearing, does not need me or anyone else to defend it. It has the proper ring for anyone who has not lost his ear for truth.'[26] Phillip's 'hunch' that the NT is trustworthy is surely no less warranted than the 'hunch' of the person who, during the course of a game of cards, begins to feel that the blue decks are a better bet than the red decks. Closing his book *Ring of Truth: A Translator's Testimony* (Lakeland, 1984), Phillips delved deeper into his 'hunch':

> In the whole task of translating the New Testament I never for one moment, however provoked and challenged I might be, felt that I was being swept away into a world of spookiness, witchcraft and magical powers such as abound in the books rejected from the New Testament. It was the sustained down-to-earth faith of the New Testament writers which conveyed to me that inexpressible sense of the genuine and the authentic ... we 'of the cloth' learn to recognize the phoney begging letter, the bogus testimonial and the false front put up by men and women, so often in pathetic self-defence. This ability to discriminate does not desert us when we move into the field of what man has written. We acquire a 'nose' for the fake and the imitation even though it may deceive the inexpert. It is my

serious conclusion that we have here in the New Testament, words that bear the hall-mark of reality and the ring of truth.[27]

Thus Phillips took his trust in the NT to be justified on-balance by a combination of critically monitored non-inferential *pro tanto* justification on the basis of testimony and justification from testimony conjoined with subconscious premises.

We shouldn't ignore the role that intuition (especially the intuition of experts) can play in the rationality of belief in the testimony of the NT. For example, lawyer Roy Williams' assessment of the gospels appears to range across the spectrum of testimonial warrant: 'When I read the Gospels, the overall effect is one of verisimilitude. In particular, the character of Jesus ... seems to me too singular, and yet at the same time too "real", to have been capable of having been wholly or even mainly invented.'[28] Even if our own reading of the NT fails to stir within us an intuition that chimes with Phillips' 'ring of truth' and Williams' 'verisimilitude', we shouldn't ignore the intuitive testimony of other readers, especially if they have a relevant expertise. By the 'principle of testimony', an expert's intuition constitutes evidence that we must take into account in forming our own judgement. As philosopher Elizabeth Fricker comments: 'it is rational to defer to another's apparently sincere testimony on some topic P just if I recognize that she is better placed than me to judge whether P (and I am aware of no significant contrary testimony regarding P).'[29]

A Critic's Criticism

> As a literary historian, I am perfectly convinced that whatever else the Gospels are they are not legends. I have read a great deal of legend and I am quite clear that they are not the same sort of thing.
>
> C.S. Lewis[30]

C.S. Lewis is well known as a Christian author and apologist. After studying and teaching at Oxford, he became the first professor of Medieval and Renaissance English at the University of Cambridge. While Lewis had a background in philosophy, his professional expertise was in literary studies. In an invited lecture to theological students at Westcott House, Cambridge, Lewis famously rebuffed the views of certain scholars who held that the gospels were legends:

> Whatever these men may be as Biblical critics, I distrust them as critics. They seem to me to lack literary judgement ... A man who has spent his youth and manhood in the minute study of the New Testament texts and of other people's studies of them, whose literary experience of those texts lacks any standard of comparison such as can only grow from a wide and deep and genial experience of literature in general, is, I should think, very likely to miss the obvious things about them. If he tells me that something in the Gospel is legend or romance, I want to know how many legends and romances he has read, how well his palate is trained in detecting them by the flavour; not how many years he has spent on that Gospel ... turn to *John*. Read the dialogues: that with the Samaritan woman at the well, or that which follows the healing of the man born blind. Look at the pictures: Jesus (if I may use the word) doodling with his finger in the dust ... I have been reading poems, romances, vision-literature, legends, myths all my life. I know what they are like. I know that not one of them is like this.[31]

Lewis went on to argue:

> Of this text there are only two possible views. Either this is reportage – though it may no doubt contain errors – pretty close up to the facts; nearly as close as Boswell. Or else, some unknown writer ... without known predecessors or successors, suddenly anticipated the whole technique of modern, novelistic, realistic narrative. If it is untrue, it must be narrative of that kind. The reader who doesn't see this has simply not learned to read.[32]

While a few neo-atheists agree with Victor J. Stenger's assertion that 'most of the Bible [is] fiction',[33] it's worth recalling that 'There is a broad consensus today that the Gospels are a Jewish-Christian form of the well known Graeco-Roman literary genre of *Bios* or Biography.'[34] As William Lane Craig comments: 'radical critics still get a free pass from the press today for their sensational assertions, but they are being increasingly marginalized within the academy, as scholarship has come to a new appreciation of the historical reliability of the New Testament documents.'[35] To better understand the scholarly marginalization of the sort of scepticism displayed by the neo-atheists towards the gospels, we turn from the epistemology of trusting testimony to the testimony of standard historiography.

The Chain of Testimony

> The New Testament is a basically reliable source of information about the life of Jesus.
>
> Richard Swinburne[36]

Philosopher Ernest Sosa writes that:

> Testimonial knowledge is a collaborative accomplishment involving one's informational sources across time. Consider what is required: the gathering, retaining, transmitting, and receiving of information, with pertinent controls applied each step of the way ... Think of the documents consulted by a historian, of those responsible for their production, for their preservation and transmission unaltered, and so on.[37]

When assessing written testimony at a conscious level, historians want to know the strength of various 'links' in the 'chain of testimony' that stretches from the facts about which a source purports to inform us, through the source and the composition of their testimony, to the contemporary reception thereof. There are four links in the chain of testimony that demand examination:

Link 1) Between the reported events and the reporting source
   Link 2) Between the reporting source and the writing down of their testimony
      Link 3) Between the original written report (the 'autograph') and the surviving copies
         Link 4) Between the autograph and the text we can reconstruct today from surviving copies

In each case, the *stronger* the link, the better. The first two links in the chain of testimony concern the *origins of the testimony*, whereas the last two links concern the *transmission of the testimony*. Let's test the gospels by these criteria.

The Origins of the Gospel Testimonies

Discussing the supposed paucity of historical evidence for Jesus, Richard Dawkins patronisingly opines: 'The fact that something is written down is persuasive to people not used to asking questions like: "Who wrote it, and when?"'[38] There follows his notorious remark about how 'Ever since the nineteenth century, scholarly theologians have made an overwhelming case that the gospels are not reliable accounts of what happened in the history of the real world.'[39] However, the continued scholarly pursuit of answers to questions like 'Who wrote it, and when?' has actually led to a far greater receptivity towards the NT gospels as generally 'reliable accounts of what happened' on the part of modern scholars in the so-called 'third quest' for the historical Jesus.

Link 1

The Greek term *euangelion* – which means 'good news' and is translated by the English term 'gospel' – wasn't used to describe written accounts of Jesus' ministry until the middle of the second century. Originally 'they were called narratives and memoirs. A narrative tells a story; a memoir is a narrative composed from personal experience ... The four Gospels are biographical memoirs.'[40] Mark L. Strauss discerns 'four main stages in the development of the Gospels':[41]

Stage 1: The historical Jesus (Jesus died in AD 30 or 33)
Stage 2: The period of oral history, when the teaching of and stories about Jesus were preserved primarily in the oral memory of the eyewitnesses and of the wider Christian community
Stage 3: The period of written sources, when collections of sayings and other material were collected
Stage 4: The writing of the gospels

Strauss notes how Luke's gospel prologue refers to all four stages:

> Many have undertaken to draw up an account [stage 3] of the things that have been fulfilled among us [stage 1], just as they were handed down to us by those who from the first were eyewitnesses and servants of the word [stage 2]. With this in mind, since I myself have carefully investigated everything from the beginning, I too decided to write an orderly account for you, most excellent Theophilus [stage 4] (Luke 1:1–3).

All four stages should be pictured as overlapping to some degree.

According to the scholarly consensus, Mark was the first published gospel, and hence 'the gospel with the highest claims to be accepted as a reliable historical source.'[42] Mark was followed by Matthew and Luke, who incorporated much of Mark into their accounts. These three gospels are called the 'synoptic' gospels:

> scholars today hold the view that Matthew and Luke both used (1) The Gospel of Mark, (2) a source or sources which Matthew and Luke had in common, conveniently referred to as Q [an abbreviation of the German *Quelle*, 'source'], and (3) unique material which each had in hand, conveniently designated as M (Matthew's unique material) and L (Luke's unique material).[43]

The synoptic gospels were followed by John's non-synoptic gospel, which offers an independent but complementary picture of Jesus. According to Norman L. Geisler: 'John uses independent sources of his own that can be traced on linguistic grounds to between A.D. 30 and 66 ...'[44] Craig L. Blomberg notes 'John's use of a "sign's source," often dated to the 60s, for his distinctive miracle stories ...'[45] John Dickson, a senior research fellow of the Department of Ancient History, Macquarie University (Sydney), explains that 'many scholars ... detect an earlier source within the Gospel of John. They call it the Signs Source or SQ for short (SQ stands for *Semeia Quelle*: the Greek word for 'signs' with the German word for 'source'). SQ appears to have been a collection of seven miracle stories or signs highlighting Jesus' status as Messiah.'[46]

The four gospels thus provide access to *at least five independent sources of information about Jesus* that take us back to the time of written sources and oral history. Paul Barnett notes that '"Q" texts are cited or echoed in letters of Paul written in the mid-fifties.'[47] Likewise, D.C. Allison 'concludes that Paul knew material from Mark, material common to Luke and Matthew ("Q"), material unique to Luke ("L"), and perhaps material unique to Matthew ("M").'[48] Thus, at least elements of Q, L and M existed *within twenty years of the historical Jesus.*

Discussing research into oral cultures, theologians Gregory A. Boyd and Paul Rhodes Eddy comment:

> the case for accepting the early church tradition regarding the authorship and relatively early dating of the four Gospels is stronger than many suppose. But ... not too much hangs on this ... even if we grant that the Gospels were written between AD 70 and 100, as many scholars maintain, and even if we grant that we don't know who wrote these books, this still doesn't warrant the conclusion that these authors were not in a position to pass on reliable history.[49]

Oral cultures:

> are invested in accurately preserving the memory of events that shape their communal identity ... while tradents entrusted with the task of retelling a community's oral traditions are allowed creative flexibility in how they express traditional material, the community as a whole typically assumes responsibility to ensure that the tradent's creative performance doesn't alter the substance of the tradition he or she is passing on. So it is, as many orality specialists now argue, that orally dominant communities typically evidence the ability to reliably transmit historical material for long periods of time – in some cases, for centuries.[50]

Studies of oral traditions reveal a characteristic balance between form and freedom. The narrator (or 'tradent') 'is granted a certain amount of creativity and flexibility in how he or she presents the traditional material, but there are also strong constraints when it comes to altering the core content of traditional material ... if the narrator alters the material too much, the community objects and corrects him or her in the midst of the performance.'[51] Comparing the gospels, we notice the same balance:

> The order of events and wording of Jesus' sayings, for example, often varies from Gospel to Gospel, though the basic content and broad narrative framework is similar. In light of the new discoveries in orality studies, this suggests that we should view the Gospels as written versions – or 'textualizations' – of the oral performances that would have been so common among the early Christian communities ... this suggests that the oral traditions about Jesus that lie behind the Gospels – including their overall narrative framework of his life – are solidly rooted in history.[52]

As Richard Bauckham argues: 'Gospel traditions did not, for the most part, circulate anonymously but in the name of the eyewitnesses to whom they were due ... in imagining how the traditions reached the Gospel writers, not oral tradition but eyewitness testimony should be our principle model.'[53] In other words, the gospels aren't based upon *oral traditions* (something technically characterized by the oral transmission of information over at least a generation) but upon contemporary, eyewitness, *oral history*. Taking these points into consideration:

> it should be clear that, whoever they were and whenever they wrote, we have good reasons to accept that the Gospel authors were in a position to transmit reliable reports about Jesus. Unless we arbitrarily assume that the early Christian communities were remarkably atypical for orally dominant communities, the sheer fact that the Gospel authors wrote as tradents of an early church tradition should incline us to accept this much.[54]

After all, 'historians frequently trust authors who wrote about events that preceded them by greater spans of time than forty to sixty years and who were not directly connected to the events they wrote about via a community's orally transmitted history.'[55]

Moreover, 'A broad range of studies – from ancient Greece to nineteenth-century Serbo-Croatia to contemporary Africa – have all confirmed that orally orientated historical traditions (both oral and written in medium) ... within roughly 80 to 150 years of the event recorded – tend to be quite reliable.'[56] However, 'The picture of Jesus in the New Testament was established well within that length of time.'[57] Hence we can rest assured with William P. Alston that 'the Gospels embody items from the tradition that stretches to them from Jesus himself during his life on earth, and in such a way that it is sufficiently free from distortion to present an accurate account ... '[58] As Paul Copan argues:

> Given (1) the importance of memorization and oral tradition in first-century Palestine, (2) the practice of (occasionally) writing down and preserving the teachings of rabbis by their disciples, (3) the fact that the vast majority of Jesus' teaching was in poetic (and easily memorable) form, (4) the importance and revered status of religious traditions in Palestine, and (5) the presence of apostolic authority in Jerusalem to ensure the accurate transmission of tradition (and to check potential heresy), we have good reason to believe that the material in the Gospels was carefully and correctly set down.[59]

Finally, it's worth noting with philosopher Stephen T. Davis that there are powerful arguments against the idea that the gospel writers felt free to invent their content:

> First, had the early Christians engaged in such a practice, it is highly probable that sayings would have been placed in the mouth of Jesus that were relevant to the central concerns and controversies of the church in the second half of the first century. But notice that there are no sayings of Jesus in the canonical gospels that are directly relevant to such burning issues in the late-first-century church as the proper use of spiritual gifts, whether male Gentile converts were obliged to be circumcised, whether Christians should divorce their non-Christian spouses, the proper practice of the Lord's supper, how churches ought to be governed, etc. Second, notice that the church preserved and passed on 'difficult' sayings of Jesus – sayings that it would have been convenient for the church to forget – for example, sayings about the human failings of some of the church's greatest leaders (e.g. Peter, in Mark 14:66–72) ... these arguments show, I believe, the respect that the

church had for the actual teachings of Jesus – I believe they were reliably preserved and passed on rather than amended or even made up.[60]

Eyewitnesses' testimony

J.P. Moreland states that 'a strong case could be made for the fact that much of the New Testament, including the Gospels and the sources behind them, was written by eyewitnesses.'[61] Some of these eyewitnesses were martyred for refusing to renounce their claims, a fact which speaks to their *sincerity* if not their accuracy. As Boyd and Eddy argue:

> Orality specialists now realize that, while the community plays a significant role in preserving the accuracy of an oral tradition … oral communities typically designate individual tradents … to be the primary and official transmitters of the tradition. When an individual was an eyewitness to events that have become part of a community's oral historical traditions, he or she is often recognized as a crucial link in the communal preservation of that tradition … this discovery of the crucial role of individual tradents suggests that we can no longer conceive of the traditional material about Jesus being transmitted in the early church *apart from the strong influence of original eyewitnesses*. This renders it virtually impossible to conceive of the oral traditions in the early church veering too far from the historical events observed by eyewitnesses.[62]

In *Jesus and the Eyewitnesses: The Gospels as Eyewitness Testimony* (Eerdmans, 2006), Richard Bauckham argues that the presence of various named characters in the synoptic gospels is best explained by the hypothesis that these characters were the eyewitness tradents of the tradition to which their names are attached: 'many of these named characters were eyewitnesses who not only originated the traditions to which their names are attached but also continued to tell these stories as authoritative guarantors of their traditions.'[63]

Authoritative authors

According to Dawkins: 'Nobody knows who the four evangelists were, but they almost certainly never met Jesus.'[64] However,

Mark D. Roberts reports that 'in recent years many have come to believe that the first and fourth Gospels reflect the memory and the perspective of Jesus' own disciples, both Matthew and John … Matthew and John may not have been the ones who finally put pen to papyrus, but they, their memory, and their authority stand behind the Gospels that bear their names.'[65] According to Craig L. Blomberg, 'a good case can still be made for Matthew, Mark, Luke, and John as the authors of the Gospels that have traditionally been attributed to them.'[66] Timothy Paul Jones argues that there is:

> no compelling reason to reject the ancient oral traditions that connected the New Testament Gospels to Matthew, Mark, Luke and John. Given the evidence that's available, no one can be certain who wrote these books … still, the best evidence that we possess suggests that the sources for the four Gospels were a tax collector named Matthew, Simon Peter's translator Mark, the physician Luke and a fisherman named John.[67]

R.T. France reports:

> Luke, the doctor who was a companion of Paul (Colossians 4:14; 2 Timothy 4:11; Philemon 24) is the most widely accepted, as the author of both the third gospel and its sequel, the Acts of the Apostles. Mark, similarly a colleague of Paul (Acts 12:25; 15:37–41; Colossians 4:10; 2 Timothy 4:11; Philemon 24), but also, if the same Mark is intended, a companion of Peter (1 Peter 5:13), is accepted by many as at least a possible author of the second gospel … There are in fact weighty defenders today of the traditional authorship of all four gospels … I find all four traditional ascriptions at least plausible.[68]

Christians probably wouldn't attribute gospels to such peripheral characters as Mark, Luke, and even Matthew, if they didn't write them: 'Mark and Luke, after all, were not among Jesus' twelve apostles … Though an apostle, Matthew is best known for … his unscrupulous past as a [tax-collector].'[69] By contrast with the canonical gospels, 'the later second- through fifth-century apocryphal Gospels and Acts are all (falsely) ascribed to highly reputable, influential early Christians to try to make them appear as authoritative and credible as possible.'[70]

Link 2

The evidence considered thus far indicates that the first-century, New Testament gospels stem from sources in a spatio-temporal position to make good upon their apparently sincere intention to testify about the events of Jesus' life with a reasonable degree of accuracy. But what about the link between these first-century sources and the composition of the written gospel autographs? William Lane Craig notes how 'all historians agree that the gospels were written down and circulated during the first generation after the event.'[71] Indeed, 'The rough consensus seems to be some time between AD 60 and AD 90, though both earlier and later dates have been proposed.'[72] This table lists the range of 'conservative' and 'liberal' dates proposed for the writing of the gospel autographs:

Gospel	'Conservative' Dating AD	'Liberal' Dating AD
Mark	late 40s–early 60s	60–75
Matthew	late 40s–early 60s	65–85
Luke	mid-50s–early 60s	65–95
John	mid-60s–95	75–100

Figure 9

'Liberal' scholars place Mark *within c. 40 years of Jesus' death*. More 'conservative' scholars date all the synoptic gospels *within c. 30 years of Jesus' death*, placing Mark *within c. 20 years of Jesus' death*. According to F.F. Bruce, 'even with the later dates, the situation is encouraging from the historian's point of view, for the first three Gospels were written at a time when many were alive who could remember the things that Jesus said and did, and some at least would still be alive when the fourth Gospel was written.'[73] However, as Moreland notes, 'in recent years, there has been a trend in New Testament studies towards dating the Gospels earlier.'[74] For example, James G. Crossley, of the Department of Biblical Studies at the University of Sheffield and co-chair of the Jesus Seminar for the British New Testament Conference, argues that Mark was written *between the mid-30s and mid-40s AD*. As

Carsten Peter Thiede reports: 'those who argue for early dates of authentic Gospels as sources of information about an historical Jesus ... are no longer the conservative or fundamentalist outsiders.'[75]

Genesis of the four-fold gospel

> The fourfold gospel witness to Christ was in circulation within one generation, following the first generation after Jesus. In terms of the documentation of key figures in antiquity, this is a phenomenon almost without parallel.
>
> Paul Barnett[76]

It is impossible to know for sure when the gospels were written (apart from the AD 30–100 timeframe): 'The Gospels do not say when they were written and there is no unambiguous external evidence.'[77] Nevertheless, scholars offer reconstructions for the historical genesis of the gospels, and the following strikes me as the most plausible.

Paul Barnett argues that in the early church four overlapping mission groups emerged by the 40s AD 'led by Peter, James, John, and Paul',[78] and that each mission group is associated with 'one gospel and one or more letters'[79] that were gathered into the NT during the second century (having been recognized as authentic by the first-century Christian community). This hypothesis 'explains the dissemination of Christian belief as well as the origin and purpose of the greater part of the NT.'[80]

Mission Group Leader	Mission Group Literature
Peter	1 Peter, 2 Peter, Gospel of Mark
James	Letter of James, Gospel of Matthew
Paul	Paul's letters, Gospel of Luke, Acts
John	Gospel of John, 1 John, Revelation

Figure 10

Let's consider the origins of each of the four gospels in historical order.

The Gospel according to Mark

Concerning the origins of Mark, Craig L. Blomberg notes that 'the oldest and most important testimony, from very early in the second century and recorded by Eusebius in the early 300s, is that of Papias'[81] who cites the apostle John as having taught that:

> Mark became Peter's interpreter and wrote accurately all that he remembered, not indeed, in order, of the things said or done by the Lord. For he had heard not the Lord, nor had he followed him, but later on, as I said, followed Peter, who used to give teaching as necessity demanded but not making, as it were, an arrangement of the Lord's oracles, so that Mark did nothing wrong in writing down single points as he remembered them. For to one thing he gave attention, to leave out nothing of what he had heard and to make no false statement in them.[82]

Blomberg comments: 'Given that Mark was not one of the Twelve [apostles] but a relatively obscure character with a mixed record of ministry during his lifetime, it is unlikely that anyone unfamiliar with the true author of this Gospel but desiring to credit it to an authoritative witness would have selected Mark as his man.'[83] As Harvard law professor Simon Greenleaf observed:

> Peter's agency in the narrative of Mark is asserted by all ancient writers, and is confirmed by the fact that his humility is conspicuous in every part of it, where anything is or might be related to him; his weaknesses and fall being fully exposed, while things which might redound to his honor, are either omitted or but slightly mentioned; that scarcely any transaction of Jesus is related, at which Peter was not present, and that all are related with that circumstantial minuteness which belongs to the testimony of an eye-witness.[84]

David Wenham and Steve Walton report that: 'This remains a widely held view in scholarship [as it] offers a plausible explanation for many incidental details in the Gospel. It also fits well with Mark's reports of occasions when only Peter and a few others were present (e.g. 1:16–20, 29–31; 9:2–8; 14:27–31), and the frequent mentions of Peter's failures and mistakes (e.g. 8:32f.; 9:5f.;

10:28–31; 14:29–31, 66–72).'[85] As for Mark, he 'is generally identified with the young man who fled, leaving behind his tunic, on the occasion of the arrest of Jesus. He was a native of Jerusalem – the disciples met in his mother's house – and he had been a companion of Paul.'[86]

Carsten Peter Thiede notes that early Christian writers Papias, Eusebius and Jerome 'supply valuable information from first-generation eyewitness accounts (Papias) and from massive archival material ... that Peter first visited Rome in the second year of the Emperor Claudius who ruled from AD 41–54. With him was Mark, sometimes called John Mark, or John, in the New Testament.'[87] Peter's escape from the prison of Herod Agrippa I and his fleeting visit thereafter to the home of Mark's mother in Jerusalem (cf. Acts 12)[88] must have happened in AD 41 or 42: 'then, Luke simply says: "And he left for another place." If Papias, Eusebius and Jerome are correct, then the final destination of this journey must have been Rome.'[89] This fits the fact that the phrase 'to another place' is found in the Septuagint Greek version of the Old Testament, where it refers to Babylon, the mantle of which had figuratively fallen on Rome by NT times (cf. Revelation 17:5, an identification also made by Roman writers such as Plautus). Indeed, this identification is made explicit at the end of Peter's first letter written in Rome: 'She who is in Babylon, chosen together with you, sends you her greetings and so does my son Mark.' Luke is thus obliquely referring to Peter's destination:

> So Rome it was for Peter. And Mark probably went with him straightaway. That he was with Peter in Rome at some stage at least is clearly stated in 1 Peter 5:13 ... But all other early sources also confirm that he was present when Peter preached the gospel to the Romans. And Peter could have spent at least two, perhaps three, years in the city during his first stay. When Herod Agrippa died in AD 44, the man who had put him into prison back in Jerusalem could no longer endanger his safety ... Therefore, in AD 44 at the earliest, Peter could have left Rome to return to Jerusalem ... One way or another, he was back in Jerusalem in time for the apostolic council mentioned in Acts 15:1–29 ... And this council can be dated to about AD 48.[90]

Thiede hypothesizes that 'soon ... after the "exodus" of Peter from Rome – a term used by the second-century author Irenaeus in his brief report about the four Gospels, and all too often mistranslated as "death" instead of "departure" – the Christians would have asked Mark to write down ... what Peter had taught him about the life and sayings of Jesus.'[91] This would seem to be a natural reaction to the departure of the community's primary tradent of the oral history about Jesus. Maurice Casey argues that much of Mark is easily retrojected back into Aramaic: 'Casey's insights favour the suggestion of Bauckham that Mark translated Peter's Aramaic recollections into his Gospel. Peter spoke in Aramaic and perhaps some wooden Greek, remembering various things Jesus did and said, and Mark wrote it down in better Greek.'[92]

Mark's product, however, would only have been the *first draft* of what was to become his gospel; for Thiede constructs his theory to solve a paradox arising from the writings of Clement of Alexandria (c. AD 150–214) who:

> wrote twice about the reception given to Mark's Gospel. Both state-ments are quoted by the historian Eusebius of Caeserea, and they appear to contradict each other. In one report, having told how the Roman Christians asked Mark to write down Peter's preach-ing after his departure, he says 'When the matter came to Peter's knowledge, he neither expressly hindered it nor actively encour-aged it.' But in another report, Clement states ... that Peter was pleased at the zeal of the Roman Christians and ratified the Gospel for study in the churches.[93]

Thiede's reconstruction resolves this paradox: 'Clement, quoted by Eusebius in different contexts, describes a development. The first stage describes the collection of the material, the com-position of a first version of the Gospel. The second stage is the refined version, the finished product, proofread perhaps by Peter himself.'[94] Hence:

> Mark ... could have started to write his Gospel ... in AD 44 at the earliest. In about AD 46, he is back in Jerusalem from where he joins Paul and Barnabas on a journey to Antioch (Acts 12:25). Since our sources are adamant that the Gospel was written before Mark left

Rome, sheer mathematical logic leads to the conclusion that it was written between AD 44 and AD 46.[95]

John A.T. Robinson likewise suggests that 'the first draft of Mark's gospel could be as early as 45 AD.'[96] By assuming that what Mark had completed c. AD 45–6 was only a first draft, we illuminate an incident recorded by Luke in Acts 13:13, where Mark suddenly leaves his cousin Barnabas and Paul in the lurch and returns to Jerusalem. When Barnabas later suggests taking Mark on a second journey, Paul refuses 'because he had deserted them in Pamphylia and had not continued with them in the work' (Acts 15:37–38) even though Barnabas defends Mark: 'They had such a sharp disagreement that they parted company. Barnabas took Mark and sailed for Cyprus' (Acts 15:39). So why did Mark leave Paul and Barnabas in the lurch on their first journey, and why was Barnabas happy to go it alone with Mark on that second occasion? Perhaps Mark:

> left them and returned to Jerusalem because he had heard that Peter had returned there. For Mark … this would have been the long-awaited chance to show his work to the man on whose preaching it was based. And here, at this meeting or soon after, the second stage of the completion of the Gospel may have begun – the drafting of the one which was to meet with Peter's approval, the one ratified by him for copying and distribution …[97]

According to this reconstruction, Mark began writing his gospel, based upon Peter's teaching, in Rome c. AD 44. His first draft was subsequently modified under the supervision of Peter in Jerusalem c. AD 46. Perhaps it was at this stage that Mark married his record of Peter's oral history about Jesus' teaching and deeds to our earliest narrative account of Jesus' passion:

> The story of Jesus' suffering and death, commonly called the passion story, was probably not originally written by Mark. Rather Mark used a source for this narrative. Mark is the earliest gospel, and his source must be even earlier still. In fact, Rudolf Pesch, a German expert on Mark, says the passion source must go back to at least AD 37.[98]

Peter approved Mark's completed gospel for copying and distribution amongst the Christians in Rome. Plausibly, this took place after Peter and Mark had returned to Rome following the Jerusalem council of AD 48. Thus the completed gospel was probably in circulation by AD 49 (interestingly, this was the year the emperor Claudius expelled Jews from Rome on account of a dispute over 'Chrestus', i.e. Christ. Might this dispute have been sparked by the publication of the first gospel?).

The Gospel according to Matthew

Following Peter's initial departure for Rome in AD 44, 'the leadership of the Jerusalem church passed to James, the Lord's brother …'[99]; which brings us to Barnett's second missionary group, associated with the Gospel of Matthew. Matthew's gospel was probably written after Mark, sometime between the mid 50s and early 60s AD. However, Boyd and Eddy note that 'Papias – a man who seems to have been in direct contact with the apostle John – mentions that Matthew was a designated note-taker among the earliest disciples.'[100] Michael Green argues that:

> Probably the name Matthew became associated with this Gospel because it embodies a lot of special material that the apostle Matthew gathered. This was a collection of the many sayings of Jesus, absent from Mark, which also appear in Luke. Scholars call this the 'Q' material, and it is clearly very ancient. Probably Matthew the apostle assembled 'Q', the teachings of his master, Jesus, and quite possibly during his ministry. He certainly had ample opportunity to do this, as he followed Jesus for those three years. And as a tax-gatherer he must have had the writing skills and probably shorthand as well, which was well known in the ancient world.[101]

Grappling with comments from Irenaeus and Papias about Matthew writing in Hebrew (the gospel we have is in Greek), Barnett likewise hypothesizes:

> One possible solution is that Matthew originally wrote Q … in Hebrew. In this case, Matthew, or some other writer unknown to us, subsequently translated these 'Hebrew oracles' into Greek and

combined them with Mark and the other source(s), thus completing the Gospel in its present form ... What can be stated is that the Gospel was in use at least by the eighties and that the author made use of the three sources Mark, Q and M.[102]

Strauss similarly suggests: 'Perhaps Matthew wrote an original Gospel (or a collection of Jesus' sayings: Q?) in Aramaic or Hebrew. He could have later published a Greek edition of this Gospel (not a translation but a new edition). As a tax collector, Matthew no doubt would have been proficient in both Aramaic and Greek.'[103] This hypothesis comports with the explanation offered by James D.G. Dunn for the twin facts of Q's 'marked Galilean character' and 'lack of a passion narrative'; namely, that *the Q material first emerged in Galilee and was given its lasting shape there prior to Jesus' death in Jerusalem.*'[104] Dunn thinks that 'Matthew, the tax collector, is the most obvious candidate for the role of a literary disciple (one who could read and write), who, conceivably, could have taken notes during Jesus' preaching and teaching sessions.'[105] Timothy Paul Jones explains that 'tax collectors carried *pinakes*, hinged wooden tablets with beeswax coating on each panel. Tax collectors etched notes in the wax using styluses; these notes could be translated later and rewritten on papyrus.'[106] Hence Thiede concludes: 'Matthew, the shorthand-writing tax and customs official, was the ideal man to safeguard the beginnings of a literary tradition; but Mark, following the oral message of Peter, was the first to write a complete, fully developed Gospel ... Matthew was both the first and the second Christian writer.'[107]

The Gospel according to Luke

Dunn praises Luke as 'one of the most reliable historians of his age, whose account can be credited with a high degree of trustworthiness.'[108] Luke 'had extensive associations with Paul [the leader of our third missionary group], considerable contact with Mark, and opportunity to meet Peter (in Rome – 2 Tim 4:11; 1 Peter 5:13).'[109] It also seems likely that 'L' consists of multiple oral sources. Moreover, it's not the early 60s dating of Luke that's of primary importance, but that, as stated in the gospel's prologue: 'Luke received the "narratives" of the "eyewitnesses" *while they were still alive* and their memory of the historical Christ was current.'[110]

The Gospel according to John
As for John and our final missionary grouping, Michael Green explains:

> It now seems certain that it was written either by the apostle himself, or by a close associate at John's direction. Some people think it was written before the fall of Jerusalem in 70 AD, but most scholars agree with Christians of the second century in seeing it as the last of the Gospels to be written, in the 80s or early 90s, when the apostle was an old man, shepherding the church in the Roman province of Asia.[111]

We have noted that some of John plausibly pre-dates the time of its composition.

Dating the gospels from Acts
Scholars advocating composition dates for the gospels after AD 70 often rely upon the question-begging assumption that miracles of prophecy are impossible: 'all the Gospels record Jesus prophesying the destruction of Jerusalem. Now, scholars who don't believe anything supernatural can occur, argue that this shows that the Gospels must be written after the fall of Jerusalem [in AD 70] (a main reason they date the Gospels late).'[112] However, 'Josephus actually records the prophecy of another Jesus, a rude peasant and son of Ananias, who, at the feast of the Tabernacle, prophesized the destruction of Jerusalem and its Temple in AD 60 when Albinus was governor of Judea. If Jesus, son of Ananias, could make such a prediction prior to AD 70, why could not Jesus of Nazareth?'[113]

   The objection based upon Jesus' fulfilled prophecy is in head-on collision with the historical evidence. The book of Acts (the sequel to Luke) ends with Paul in prison c. AD 62. That nothing is said about Paul's trial or martyrdom c. AD 64, the martyrdom of James the brother of Jesus (in AD 62), or the destruction of Jerusalem in AD 70, indicates that Acts was written before these events. Luke's gospel shouldn't be dated later than its sequel; and given that Luke was written after Matthew, and Matthew after Mark, we must conclude that the 'synoptic' gospels were all written *within thirty years of Jesus' death*.

Moreover, 'various passages in Matthew refer to details of temple worship, which would be unnecessary anachronisms after AD 70, and one passage (17:24–27) would be positively misleading since it approves the payment of the temple tax, which after AD 70 was diverted to the upkeep of the temple of Jupiter in Rome!'[114] Likewise, Luke's explanation of Jesus' ritualistic presentation at the temple thirty-two days after circumcision (Luke 2:22–24) is anachronistic unless the temple was still standing when he wrote.

Dating the gospels from the earliest manuscripts and quotations
Michael Green notes the disputed claim that 'we now have a small fragment of Mark's Gospel chapter 6, found among the Dead Sea Scrolls, which were hidden in the caves by the Dead Sea when the Romans came to "settle the Jewish problem" in 66 AD.'[115] Again, Green states: 'We have fragments of Matthew chapter 26 in Oxford which look on palaeographical grounds to have been written before 70 AD, though this is disputed.'[116]

What can be said with some certainty is that Clement, writing to Corinth c. AD 96, quotes from all three synoptic gospels. Likewise, Ignatius refers to all four gospels (as well as Acts) c. AD 108; as does Polycarp c. AD 110. Moreover, as Blomberg reports: 'Older views that placed John well into the second century have been discarded ... with the discovery of the John Ryland's fragment – already at least one stage of copying removed from John's original and yet dating from c. 125–140.'[117]

In sum, then, the synoptic gospels were probably published *within c. 30 years of the crucifixion*, in the order of Mark (c. AD 49), Matthew (mid-50s AD–c. AD 62) and Luke (c. AD 62). Finally, John's gospel arrived on the scene *within c. 60 years* of the crucifixion (c. AD 80–90).

A favourable time-lapse
As the following charts show, even when we ignore hypotheses about earlier written sources and/or first drafts, and even using the earlier of the two dates usually given for Jesus' crucifixion, the gospels compare favourably with other ancient works in terms of the interval between the events they report and their date of composition:[118]

Author/ Work	Reported Events	Report Written	Lapse Between Events and Report	Average Lapse
Mark	c. AD 27–30	c. AD 49	c. 19–22 yrs	c. 20.5 yrs
Matthew	c. 6 BC–AD 30	c. AD 60	c. 30–66 yrs	c. 48 yrs
Luke	c. 6 BC–AD 30	c. AD 60	c. 30–66 yrs	c. 48 yrs
John	c. AD 27–30	c. AD 90	c. 60–63 yrs	c. 62 yrs
Pliny, *Letters*	AD 97–112	AD 100–112	0–3 yrs	1.5 yrs
Thucydides, *History*	431–411 BC	410–400 BC	0–30 yrs	15 yrs
Xenophon, *Anabasis*	401–399 BC	385–375 BC	15–25 yrs	20 yrs
Polybius, *History*	200–146 BC	c. 167–118 BC	53–102 yrs	77.5 yrs
Tacitus, *Annals*	AD 14–68	c. AD 100–110	c. 32–100 yrs	c. 66 yrs
Heroditus, *History*	546–478 BC	430–425 BC	50–125 yrs	87.5 yrs
Suetonius, *Lives*	50 BC–AD 95	c. 120	c. 25–170 yrs	c. 97.5 yrs
Josephus, *War*	200 BC–AD 70	c. AD 80	c. 10–280 yrs	c. 145 yrs
Josephus, *Antiquities*	200 BC–AD 65	c. AD 95	c. 30–295 yrs	c. 162.5 yrs
Plutarch, *Lives*	500 BC–AD 70	c. AD 100	c. 30–600 yrs	c. 315 yrs

Figure 11

The average gap between event and written report for the ten non-biblical sources listed above is c. 98 years. Even if we exclude Plutarch's *Lives*, the average time-gap for the nine remaining texts is c. 75 years. The average gap between the completed four gospels and the events they report is c. 45 years. This drops to an average of c. 39 years for just the synoptic gospels. Indeed, if we ignore Matthew and Luke's stories about Jesus' infancy and focus upon the synoptic gospels' testimony concerning Jesus' ministry, the average time-gap drops to c. 28 years. Even if we relied upon later, 'liberal' dates for the gospels, it's clear that they would still

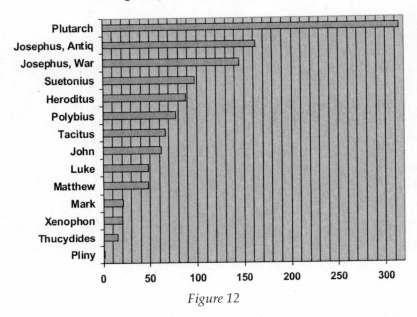

Figure 12

compare favourably to a range of other ancient literature in terms of the average time-lapse between event and written report.

What's canonical?

Michael Green reports that 'by 100, if not a little earlier – that is to say within the lifetime of some who had known Jesus – the New Testament was not only written but was on the way to being collected.'[119] Philip W. Comfort and Jason Driesbach concur that 'the Gospels and the major epistles of Paul were "canonized" in the minds of many Christians as early as A.D. 90–100 ...'[120] As Charlotte Allen explains:

> Within a century of Jesus' death, all four Gospels were in wide circulation, often as a unit ... Today's Christian 'canon' of the New Testament ... was not the product of church councils, although the rulings of bishops and the opinions of theologians undoubtedly played a role in its formation. By and large, it was created by consensus ... While the New Testament canon was not officially codified until sometime during the fourth century, as early as

[AD] 200 it was more or less in place, and at least one definitive list of canonical books was already in circulation.[121]

Richard Dawkins' assertion that 'the four gospels that made it into the official canon were chosen, more or less arbitrarily, out of a larger sample of at least a dozen ... additional gospels'[122] is highly misleading, for as Barnett comments, 'our earliest and in fact our only first century gospels are those by Matthew, Mark, Luke, and John.'[123] As for the later, 'apocryphal gospels' mentioned by Dawkins (e.g. the gospels of Thomas, Peter, etc.), the reason they 'were omitted by those ecclesiastics'[124] was because 'early Christians knew that these documents came too late to represent eyewitness testimony about Jesus.'[125] John Dickson comments:

> The four New Testament Gospels were a fixed, authoritative collection by at least the middle of the second century, before most of the Gnostics had even begun to put pen to papyrus ... When the great church councils got together in the third and fourth centuries to discuss which books were part of the canon (which means 'rule, standard'), there was no argument about the Gospels. Their inclusion, along with the letters of the apostle Paul, had long been established.[126]

According to Comfort and Driesbach:

> it is almost universally recognized that the four Gospels were penned in the first century and that all others came in the second century or thereafter ... The four Gospels (1) were written on the basis of eyewitness authority; (2) were written in the first century; (3) have substantial second-century manuscript support; (4) were written as memoirs of the apostles in the form of narratives; and (5) ring true and accord with what the apostles taught about Jesus [in their first-century letters]. On the other hand, the noncanonical Gospels were not eyewitnesses' accounts ... These Gospels were written in the second century or thereafter; they usually have no manuscript support earlier than the third century or no Greek manuscript support at all. They were written in the form of dialogues or sayings, thereby revealing the authors' lack of credibility

as eyewitnesses; and they lacked that ring of truth, failing to accord with what the apostles taught about Jesus.[127]

As Craig A. Evans concludes: 'these extracanonical Gospels do not offer early, reliable tradition, independent of what we possess in the New Testament Gospels. The extracanonical Gospels are late and almost always reflect a context far removed in time and place from first-century Palestine.'[128]

The Transmission of the Gospel Testimonies

> The New Testament manuscripts stand closer to the original and are more plentiful than probably any other literature of that era. The New Testament is far and away the best-attested work of Greek or Latin literature from the ancient world.
>
> Darrell L. Bock and Daniel B. Wallace[129]

Having covered the link between the original events of Jesus' life and the written reports of those events in the canonical gospels, we now turn to the transmission of those reports over time to the present day.

Link 3

According to Winfried Corduan, 'No other ancient document equals the New Testament when it comes to the preservation of manuscripts, both in terms of number and closeness in time to the original autographs.'[130] Consider the link between the writing of the 'autographs' and the earliest surviving manuscripts in each of the following cases:

- Between Aristotle and our earliest copy lie 1,450 years
- Between both Plato and Herodotus and our copies lie 1,300 years
- Between Pliny the Younger and our copies lie 750 years
- Between Homer and our earliest copy lie 500 years

Between the gospel autographs and our *complete copies* lie c. 275–300 years *at most*.

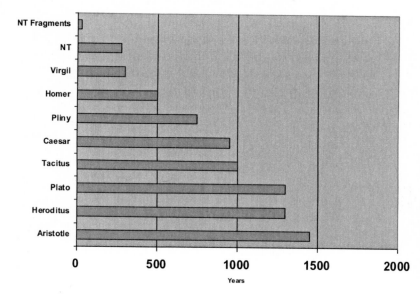

Figure 13

Indeed, 'The average time span between the original and earliest copy of the other ancient texts is over 1,000 years. However, the New Testament has a fragment within one generation of its original composition. Whole books appear within 100 years of the original, most of the New Testament within 200 years, and the entire New Testament within [275–300] years from the date of its completion.'[131]

- We have *complete copies of all the gospels* from AD 325–50 (e.g. Codex Vaticanus,[132] Codex Sinaiticus,[133] and Codex Ephraemi Rescriptus[134]).
- We have *major portions of all four gospels* (and Acts) from c. AD 250 (Chester Beatty Papyri[135]).
- We have several *pages of Luke and John* from c. AD 200 (Bodmer Papyri[136]).
- We also have *fragments of gospel* – including the Rylands Papyrus[137] containing John 18:31–33, 37–38, which dates from c. AD 117–38.

As an atheist, Antony Flew acknowledged that 'the textual authority, the earliness and the number of manuscripts for most of the
Christian documents, is unusually great … that's … very good
authority for the accuracy of the text that is provided in translation in the New Testament.'[138]

Verses from all four gospels are quoted in extra-biblical texts by
the likes of Ignatius and Clement (in his letter to the Corinthians of
AD 95). All but eleven verses of the NT are preserved in quotations
used by the early church fathers of the first to fourth centuries.
Between them, they quoted over 20,000 times from the gospels
and Acts, over 14,000 times from the NT letters, and over 600
times from Revelation. That's over 36,000 quotations from the NT
as a whole![139] Hence it's been said that 'if all the copies of the New
Testament were destroyed, it could be reconstructed solely from
external references by others.'[140] As Wright confirms: 'There is
better evidence for the New Testament than for any other ancient
book … The New Testament we have printed in our Bibles does
indeed go back to what the very early Christians wrote.'[141]

Link 4

Consider the *number* of New Testament manuscripts compared to
other ancient works:

- The writings of Plato survive in 7 manuscripts
- The work of the Roman historian Livy comes to us through 10
  manuscripts
- Homer's *Iliad* is the closest comparison, with c. 650 surviving
  manuscripts
- The New Testament comes to us through over 24,000 manuscripts (including c. 5,700 Greek manuscripts)

As Norman L. Geisler and Frank Turek note: 'there is nothing from
the ancient world that even comes close in terms of manuscript
support [to the New Testament] … Most other ancient works
survive on fewer than a dozen manuscripts, yet few historians
question the historicity of the events those works describe.'[142]

The following chart compares just the *Greek* manuscript evidence
for the New Testament text with the *total* manuscript evidence for

other ancient texts (including the next closest, which is the *Iliad* by Homer):

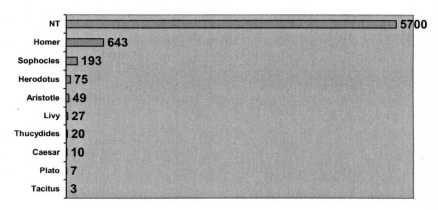

Manuscript Evidence

Figure 14

Atheist Ed Turner grasps the wrong end of the stick in reviewing this data: 'This is little more than an argument based on strength of sales. Is anyone going to argue that Dan Brown's work is more truthful and more intelligent than Aristotle's simply because he has sold more copies?'[143] But of course, the point here isn't that the greater number of NT copies compared to other ancient works shows that the NT is more likely to be truthful or intelligent! The point here is simply that the greater number of manuscript copies means that we can be more certain that our NT text reflects the original NT text than we can be that our text of other ancient works reflects the original text of those works. As Timothy Paul Jones explains:

> the 5,700 or so [Greek] New Testament manuscripts that are available to us may differ from one another in as many as 400,000 places – and there are only 138,000 or so words in the Greek New Testament in the first place ... Most of these 400,000 variations stem from differences in spelling, word order, or the relationships between nouns and definite articles – variants that are easily recognizable and, in most cases, virtually unnoticeable in translations ... In the end, more than 99 percent of the 400,000 differences fall into

this category of virtually unnoticeable variants! Of the remaining 1 percent or so of variants, only a few have any significance for interpreting the biblical text. Most important, *none* of the differences affects any central element of the Christian faith.[144]

Mark D. Roberts' summary is carefully considered:

the abundance of manuscripts and the antiquity of manuscripts, when run through the mill of text-critical methodology, allows us to know with a very high level of probability what the evangelists and other New Testament authors wrote ... We can have confidence that the critical Greek texts of Matthew, Mark, Luke, and John represent, with a very high degree of probability, what the autographs of the Gospels actually contained.[145]

In light of all the above we can see why Craig L. Blomberg concludes that 'on sheer historical grounds alone there is substantial reason to believe in the *general* trustworthiness of the Gospel tradition.'[146]

Other Relevant Sources

Of course, the canonical gospels are not the only relevant first-century sources ...

Paul's letters

J.P. Moreland notes that 'we possess from seven to thirteen letters from the hand of Paul. Most of these letters are dated from 49 to 65.'[147] Alister McGrath confirms that Paul's letters 'date mainly from the period AD 49–69, and provide confirmation of the importance and interpretations of Jesus in this formative period.'[148] Luke Timothy Johnson observes that 'Paul's letters (and probably other epistolary literature such as James and Hebrews) provide firsthand evidence for the Christian movement in its first three decades.'[149] As Barnett comments:

there are early copies (of copies?) of Paul's original letters that have survived and are safely housed in museums around the world. Furthermore, as well as their earliness, the number and wide geographic distribution of editions of the whole NT mean that textual critics are able to reconstitute versions of Paul's original texts that are for practical purposes what Paul actually wrote. Disputed readings of Paul's texts are minimal and are usually limited to isolated words. As well, the next wave of Christian writers (in the early second century) quotes extensively from Paul and provides a further check alongside his manuscripts.[150]

This evidence demonstrates that, 'a concept of a divine Jesus was already present, at the latest, within sixteen to twenty years after the crucifixion.'[151] Not only are some of these letters contemporaneous with Mark's gospel, but:

> Paul's letters contain a number of creeds and hymns (Rom. 1:3–4; 1 Cor. 11:23 ff.; 15:3–8; Phil. 2:6–11; Col. 1:15–18; 1 Tim. 2:8 …) … they use language which is not characteristically Pauline, they often translate easily back into Aramaic, and they show features of Hebrew poetry and thought-forms. This means that they came into existence while the church was heavily Jewish and that they became standard, recognized creeds and hymns well before their incorporation into Paul's letters.[152]

These early creeds and hymns testify to 'the death, resurrection, and deity of Christ. They consistently present a portrait of a miraculous and divine Jesus who rose from the dead … In sum, the idea of a fully divine, miracle-working Jesus who rose from the dead was present during the first decade of Christianity.'[153]

External confirmation

Atheist Michel Onfray asserts that there are only 'two or three vague references' to Jesus 'in ancient texts.'[154] However, Habermas explains that:

> a number of ancient secular sources mention various aspects of Jesus' life, corroborating the picture presented by the Gospels. The

writers of these sources include ancient historians such as Tacitus, Suetonius, and Thallus. Jewish sources such as Josephus and the Talmud add to our knowledge. Government officials such as Pliny the Younger and even Roman Caesars Trajan and Hadrian describe early Christian beliefs and practices. Greek historian and satirist Lucian and Syrian Mara Bar-Serapion provide other details … at least seventeen non-Christian writings record more than fifty details concerning the life, teachings, death, and resurrection of Jesus, plus details concerning the earliest church. Most frequently reported is Jesus' death, mentioned by twelve sources. Dated approximately 20 to 150 years after Jesus' death, these secular sources are quite early by the standards of ancient historiography.[155]

These sources state:

- Jesus lived during the time of Tiberius Caesar
- He was virtuous
- He worked wonders
- He had a brother named James
- He was acclaimed as the Messiah
- He was crucified under Pontius Pilate
- He was crucified on the eve of the Jewish Passover
- Darkness and an earthquake occurred when he died
- His disciples believed he rose from the dead
- His disciples were willing to die for their belief
- Christianity spread rapidly as far as Rome
- His disciples denied the Roman gods and worshiped Jesus as God.[156]

By combining the evidence from first- to third-century Graeco-Roman writers:

> one can clearly accumulate enough evidence to refute the fanciful notion that Jesus never existed, without even appealing to the testimony of Jewish or Christian sources. [This evidence includes] references to his crucifixion, being worshipped as a god, working miracles, having an unusual birth, and being viewed as a sage, king and an instigator of a controversy …[157]

Moreover, archaeology supports the reliability of the NT writers in various matters, and when a reporter proves accurate in matters we can check, our confidence concerning their accuracy in matters we cannot check is increased. As Blomberg observes: 'A particularly significant subcategory of corroborating external evidence outside of the Gospels and Acts, or any other explicitly Christian sources, is that which archaeology unearths ... there are books filled with items that confirm the kinds of details in the New Testament that lend themselves to archaeological proof or disproof. In no instance has any detail been disproved; countless items have been corroborated.'[158] For an introduction to this evidence, I refer interested readers to my paper 'Archaeology and the Historical Reliability of the New Testament'.[159]

Conclusion

> There is much to be said for Jesus at a historical level as one studies the Gospels as ancient literary texts. The thrust of that unique story can be told with confidence that the Gospels are a solid source of information.
>
> Darrell L. Bock[160]

I have presented a cumulative argument for the general historical reliability of the NT gospels that combines: 1) non-inferential (and at least *pro tanto*) justification on the basis of testimony, with 2) justification from testimony conjoined with subconscious premises and 3) justification from testimony conjoined with conscious premises. This cumulative case establishes that, as C. Stephen Evans concludes, 'it is reasonable to take the picture of Jesus provided in the New Testament as basically reliable as history in its main outlines.'[161]

In considering the testimony of the NT, one must distinguish between a) doubts based upon philosophical assumptions (e.g. that miracles can't happen) and b) doubts about the chain of testimony from the historical events to the reports available today. The critique of the NT given by Dawkins and his fellow 'new atheists' is clearly grounded in a philosophical pre-commitment to naturalism, not an unbiased reading of the texts or an objective analysis of the chain of testimony. With R.T. France, we should recognize that: 'At the level of their literary and historical character we have good reason to treat the gospels seriously ... Beyond that point, the decision as to how far a scholar is willing to accept the record they offer is likely to be influenced more by his openness to a "supernaturalist" world-view than by strictly historical considerations.'[162]

Recommended Resources

Websites

Bethinking – Jesus and the Bible http://www.bethinking.org/bible-jesus/.
Biblical Archaeology Review http://www.bib-arch.org/.
Craig, William Lane, 'Reasonable Faith: Jesus of Nazareth' http://www.
    reasonablefaith.org/site/PageServer?pagename=popular_articles_
    Jesus_Of_Nazareth.
4Gospels http://www.4gospels.com/index.html.
Last Seminary – NT Biblical Studies Articles http://www.lastseminary.
    com/nt-biblical-studies-articles/.
Roberts, Mark D. 'Are the New Testament Gospels Reliable?' http://
    www.markdroberts.com/htmfiles/resources/gospelsreliable.htm.

Video

Bauckham, Richard. 'The Gospels as Eyewitness Testimony' http://
    www.youtube.com/watch?v=292NTf1cCNw&feature=related.
*Bible and Church Conference: Providing reliable scholarly evidence in support
    of the historical basis of the Christian faith – Westminster Chapel, London,
    Saturday 20 June 2009*, DVD (Tyndale House, 2009).
Blomberg, Craig L. 'New Developments in Historical Jesus Research'
    http://www.veritas.org/Media.aspx#/v/190.
Bock, Darrell L. http://www.publicchristianity.com/bock.html.
Capernaum: City of Skeptics http://www.dod.org/Products/Capernaum-
    -City-of-Skeptics__DOD2135.aspx.Forbes, Chris. 'Josephus and Jesus'
    http://www.publicchristianity.com/Videos/josephus.html.
First-century Nazareth House http://www.msnbc.msn.com/id/
    34511072/ns/technology_and_science-science/#34523421.

Forbes, Chris. 'Zeitgeist: Time to Discard the Christian Story?' http://www.publicchristianity.com/Videos/zeitgeist.html.

Habermas, Gary R. 'The Veracity of the New Testament' http://www.veritas.org/Media.aspx#/v/332.

Hagner, Don. 'How was the New Testament put together?' http://www.publicchristianity.com/Videos/hagner5.html.

Jesus and the Gospels: Answers to Tough Questions Part 1 http://www.dod.org/Products/Jesus-and-The-Gospels--Answers-to-Tough-Questions--Part-I__DOD2116.aspx and Part 2 http://www.dod.org/Products/DOD2117.aspx.

Licona, Michael. 'Bart Ehrman Answered' http://www.4truth.net/fourtruthpbbible.aspx?pageid=8589952763&terms=licona+bart+answered.

Reformed Seminary Videos of Israel Trip 2000 http://www.youtube.com/user/ReformedSeminary.

Audio

Bock, Darrell L. 'Apocryphal Gospels' http://www.imagesaes.316networks.com/namb/Darrell_Bock_Interview_on_Apocryphal_Gospels.mp3.

Boyd, Gregory and Paul Eddy. 'The Historical Jesus' http://www.reclaimingthemind.org/content/files/CWS/boydeddyhistoricaljesus.mp3.

Craig, William Lane. 'The Work of Bart Ehrman' http://www.rfmedia.org/av/audio/gracepoint-the-work-of-bart-ehrman/.

Habermas, Gary R., et al. 'The Talpiot Tomb' http://www.reclaimingthemind.org/content/files/CWS/cwstalpiot.mp3.

Keener, Craig. 'Gospel Evidence for the Historical Jesus' http://www.imagesaes.316networks.com/namb/Apologetics_Craig_Keener_Interview.mp3.

Roberts, Mark D. 'Can We Trust the Gospels?' http://www.reclaimingthemind.org/content/files/CWS/markrobertsgospels.mp3.

Wallace, Daniel. 'New Testament Textual Criticism' http://imagesaes.316networks.com/namb/Apologetics_Wallace_Interview.mp3.

Williams, Peter S. 'The Historical Reliability of the Canonical Gospels' http://www.damaris.org/cm/podcasts/340.

— 'New Testament Archaeology' http://www.damaris.org/cm/podcasts/215.

Online papers

Barnett, Paul. 'Did Jesus Exist? Early Non-Christian References' http://www.ivpress.com/title/exc/2768-3.pdf.

Blomberg, Craig L. 'The Historical Reliability of the Gospels' http://www.4truth.net/fourtruthpbbible.aspx?pageid=8589952775&terms=blomberg+reliability+gospels.

— 'The Historical Reliability of John' http://www.4truth.net/fourtruthpbbible.aspx?pageid=8589952783&terms=blomberg+reliability+gospels.

Butt, Kyle. 'Archaeology and the New Testament' http://www.apologeticspress.org/articles/2591.

Evans, Craig A. 'Archaeology and the Historical Jesus: Recent Developments' http://216.12.134.73/publications/article.aspx?articleId=335.

Geisler, Norman L. 'The Dating of the New Testament' http://www.bethinking.org/bible-jesus/advanced/the-dating-of-the-new-testament.htm.

Habermas, Gary R. 'The Lost Tomb of Jesus: A Response' http://www.garyhabermas.com/articles/The_Lost_Tomb_of_Jesus/losttombofjesus_response.htm.

— 'Recent Perspectives on the Historical Reliability of the Gospels' http://www.bethinking.org/bible-jesus/intermediate/recent-perspectives-on-the-reliability-of-the-gospels.htm.

— 'Why I Believe the New Testament is Historically Reliable' http://www.theapologiaproject.org/WHYIBE~1.pdf.

Maier, Paul L. 'The James Ossuary' http://www.mtio.com/articles/bissar95.htm.

McRay, John. 'Archaeology and the Bible' http://www.4truth.net/fourtruthpbbible.aspx?pageid=8589952738&terms=mcray+archaeology.

— 'Archaeology and the Book of Acts' http://faculty.gordon.edu/hu/bi/Ted_Hildebrandt/NTeSources/NTArticles/CTR-NT/McRay-ArchaeologyActs-CTR.pdf.

Moreland, J.P. 'The Historicity of the New Testament' http://www.bethinking.org/bible-jesus/advanced/the-historicity-of-the-new-testament.htm.

Nigro, H.L. 'Misunderstanding Christianity: Do Scribal Changes Really Matter and Why? (A Response to Bart Ehrman)' http://www.answeringinfidels.com/answering-skeptics/others/misunderstanding-christianity-do-scribal-changes-really-matter-and-why.html.

Shanks, Hershel. 'Supporters of James Ossuary Inscription's Authenticity Vindicated' http://www.bib-arch.org/news/forgery-trial-news.asp.

Williams, Peter S. 'Archaeology and the Historical Reliability of the New Testament' http://www.bethinking.org/bible-jesus/advanced/archaeology-and-the-historical-reliability-of-the-new-testament.htm.

Witherington III, Ben. 'Top Ten New Testament Archaeological Finds of the Past 150 Years' http://www.christianitytoday.com/ct/2003/septemberweb-only/9-22-21.0.html.

Books

Arnold, Clinton E., ed. *Zondervan Illustrated Bible Backgrounds Commentary* (Grand Rapids, MI: Zondervan, 2002).

Bauckham, Richard. *Jesus and the Eyewitnesses: The Gospels as Eyewitness Testimony* (Grand Rapids, MI: Eerdmans, 2006).

Barnett, Paul. *Finding the Historical Christ* (Grand Rapids, MI: Eerdmans, 2009).

— *Is The New Testament Reliable?* (Downers Grove, IL: IVP, rev. edn, 2003).

Blomberg, Craig L. *The Historical Reliability of the Gospels* (Leicester: Apollos, 2008).

— *The Historical Reliability of John's Gospel* (Leicester: Apollos, 2001).

Bock, Darrell L. *The Missing Gospels: Unearthing the Truth about Alternative Christianities* (Nashville, TN: Thomas Nelson, 2006).

— *Breaking the Da Vinci Code* (Nashville, TN: Thomas Nelson, 2004).

— *Studying the Historical Jesus: A Guide to Sources and Methods* (Leicester: Apollos, 2002).

Bockmuehl, Markus, ed. *The Cambridge Companion to Jesus* (Cambridge University Press, 2001).

Boyd, Gregory A. and Paul R. Eddy. *Lord or Legend? Wrestling with the Jesus Dilemma* (Grand Rapids, MI: Baker, 2007).

Bruce, F.F. *The New Testament Documents: Are They Reliable?* (Leicester: IVP, 2006). Older edition available online http://www.bible.ca/b-new-testament-documents-f-f-bruce.htm.

— *The Books and the Parchments* (London: Marshall Pickering, 1991).

Dickson, John. *Investigating Jesus: An Historian's Quest* (Oxford: Lion, 5th edn, 2010).

Eddy, Paul Rhodes and Gregory A. Boyd. *The Jesus Legend: A Case for the Historical Reliability of the Synoptic Jesus Tradition* (Grand Rapids, MI: Baker Academic, 2007).

Evans, Craig A. *Fabricating Jesus: How Modern Scholars Distort the Gospels* (Downers Grove, IL: IVP, 2007).

Finegan, Jack. *The Archeology of the New Testament: The Life of Jesus and the Beginning of the Early Church* (Princeton University Press, rev. edn, 1992).

Green, Michael. *The Books the Church Suppressed: What* The Da Vinci Code *Doesn't Tell You* (Crowborough: Monarch, 2006).

Greenleaf, Simon. *The Testimony of the Evangelists: The Gospels Examined by the Rules of Evidence* (Grand Rapids, MI: Kregel, 1995).

Habermas, Gary R. *The Secret of the Talpiot Tomb: Unravelling the Mystery of the Jesus Family Tomb* (Nashville, TN: Holman Reference, 2007).

— *The Historical Jesus: Ancient Evidence for the Life of Christ* (Joplin, MO: College Press, 1996).

Jones, Timothy Paul. *Misquoting Jesus: A Guide to the Fallacies of Bart Ehrman's* Misquoting Jesus (Downers Grove, IL: IVP, 2007).

Keener, Craig A., *The Historical Jesus of the Gospels* (Grand Rapids, MI: Eerdmans, 2009).

Komoszewski, J. Ed, M. James Sawyer and Daniel B. Wallace. *Reinventing Jesus: How Contemporary Skeptics Miss the Real Jesus and Mislead Popular Culture* (Grand Rapids, MI: Kregel, 2006).

Lackey, Jennifer and Ernest Sosa, eds. *The Epistemology of Testimony* (Oxford: Clarendon Press, 2006).

Lightfoot, Neil R. *How We Got the Bible* (Grand Rapids, MI: Baker, 3rd edn, 2003).

McRay, John. *Archaeology and the New Testament* (Grand Rapids, MI: Baker Academic, 1991).

Metzger, Bruce M. *The Canon of the New Testament: Its Origin, Development, and Significance* (Oxford: Clarendon Press, 1987).

— and Bart D. Ehrman. *The Text of the New Testament: Its Transmission, Corruption, and Restoration* (Oxford University Press, 4th edn, 2005).

Neufeld, Thomas R. Yoder. *Recovering Jesus: The Witness of the New Testament* (London: SPCK, 2007).

New International Version Archaeological Study Bible: An Illustrated Walk through Biblical History and Culture (Grand Rapids, MI: Zondervan, 2005).

Orr-Ewing, Amy. *Why Trust the Bible? Answers to 10 Tough Questions* (Nottingham: IVP, 2005).

Overman, Dean L. *A Case for the Divinity of Jesus: Examining the Ancient Evidence* (Plymouth: Rowman and Littlefield, 2009).

Price, Randall. *The Stones Cry Out: What Archaeology Reveals about the Truth of the Bible* (Eugene, OR: Harvest House, 1997).

Quarles, Charles L. *Buried Hope or Risen Savior? The Search for the Jesus Tomb* (Nashville, TN: B&H Academic, 2008).

Roberts, Mark D. *Can We Trust the Gospels? Investigating the Reliability of Matthew, Mark, Luke and John* (Wheaton, IL: Crossway, 2007).

Shanks, Hershel and Ben Witherington III. *The Brother of Jesus: The Dramatic Story and Meaning of the First Archaeological Link to Jesus and His Family* (London: Continuum, 2003).

Sheler, Jeffrey L. *Is The Bible True? How Modern Debates and Discoveries Affirm the Essence of the Scriptures* (London: HarperCollins, 2000).

Stanton, Graham. *The Gospels and Jesus* (Oxford University Press, 2nd edn, 2002).

Stewart, Robert B. and Gary R. Habermas, ed. *Memories of Jesus: A Critical Appraisal of James D.G. Dunn's* Jesus Remembered (Nashville, TN: B&H Academic, 2010).

Strobel, Lee. *The Case for the Real Jesus* (Grand Rapids, MI: Zondervan, 2007).

Strauss, Mark L. *Four Portraits, One Jesus: An Introduction to Jesus and the Gospels* (Grand Rapids, MI: Zondervan, 2007).

Thiede, Carsten Peter. *Jesus: Life or Legend?* (Oxford: Lion, 1997).

Voorst, Robert E. Van. *Jesus outside the New Testament: An Introduction to the Ancient Evidence* (Grand Rapids, MI: Eerdmans, 2000).

Walker, Peter. *In the Footsteps of Jesus: An Illustrated Guide to the Places of the Holy Land* (Oxford: Lion, 2009).

Wenham, David, *Did St Paul Get Jesus Right?* (Oxford: Lion, 2010).

— and Steve Walton. *Exploring the New Testament, vol. 1: A Guide to the Gospels and Acts* (Leicester: IVP, 2001).

Wilkins, Michael J. and J.P. Moreland, eds. *Jesus under Fire: Modern Scholarship Reinvents the Historical Jesus* (Grand Rapids, MI: Zondervan, 1995).

Witherington III, Ben. *The Gospel Code: Novel Claims about Jesus, Mary Magdalene and Da Vinci* (Downers Grove, IL: IVP, 2004).

— *The Jesus Quest: The Third Search for the Jew from Nazareth* (Downers Grove, IL: IVP, 1997).

3

The First Way – Jesus' Self-Centred Teaching

Who do people say I am?

Jesus (Mark 8:27)

We've seen good reason to think that the New Testament (NT) offers generally reliable testimony about Jesus. An accumulation of factors 'suggests a presumption in favor of the quality of the tradition as it appears in the New Testament.'[1] However, it will be useful in what follows to bear in mind the standard historical 'criteria of authenticity' that the field of 'Tradition Criticism'[2] utilizes to establish historical facts *without reference to our background knowledge about the historical reliability of the NT*. These criteria 'contribute to a cumulative argument about particular texts',[3] such that even if one thought the NT was a *generally unreliable* witness to the historical Jesus, those elements of the NT that meet one or more of these criteria should nevertheless be regarded as generally reliable. Given the evidence for the historical reliability of the NT reviewed in Chapter 2, use of these 'criteria of authenticity' provides a belt-and-braces approach to the evidence for Jesus.

Words of Caution

William Lane Craig observes that:

> it is somewhat misleading to call these 'criteria,' for they aim at stating sufficient, not necessary, conditions of historicity ... what

the criteria really amount to are statements about the effect of certain types of evidence upon the probability of various sayings or events ... the criteria would state that, all else being equal ... the probability of some event or saying is greater given, for example, its multiple attestation than it would have been without it ... these 'critera' ... focus on a particular saying or event and give evidence for thinking that specific element of Jesus' life to be historical, regardless of the general reliability of the document in which the particular saying or event is reported.[4]

As Darrell L. Bock notes: 'One should remember that failure to meet the criteria does not establish a text's inauthenticity, because the criteria cover only a limited amount of assessment factors ...'[5], a fact which means that 'these criteria serve better as a supplemental argument for authenticity ...'[6] Finally, Bock cautions that, generally speaking 'it is important to recognize that some of these criteria can only test the conceptual level of Jesus' teaching – i.e., did Jesus teach this theme with this emphasis? These criteria cannot prove that he used a specific wording to make his point. Such tests are almost impossible to create for any ancient document.'[7]

Ten criteria of authenticity

1) Criterion of date
All things being equal, we should privilege earlier sources over later sources: 'The less time there is between an event and its written description, the less the margin for error – for forgetting or adding.'[8]

2) Multiple attestation
David Wenham and Steve Walton explain:

> The simple logic is that, if it is attested by several NT writings, then this is in its favour... There is, however, a problem with this criterion: if, for example, we argue that the feeding of the 5,000 has a high claim to being historical, being attested in the four canonical Gospels, the immediate objection could be that the other evangelists were using Mark as a source, so what appears to be four

witnesses is really only one. This objection is not a total knockout blow to the proposed criterion: even if it is correct that the other evangelists used Mark, it is also clear that they had their own non-Markan sources, and very likely that they knew a story such as the feeding of the 5,000 independently of Mark.[9]

That a later writer recounts the same event as an earlier writer (whether in similar language, or via direct quotation) doesn't mean that the later writer didn't check the veracity of this information with independent sources. Literary dependence doesn't negate multiple attestation. Even though Luke is sometimes dependent upon Mark, he states in his prologue that he has carefully checked the truth of his account with many different sources.

That said, we can distinguish other forms of multiple attestation. For example, 'if a story or saying is found in more than one of the Gospel sources which scholars postulate (e.g. Mark, Q, M, L), then this is possibly more significant.'[10] Then again, 'another form of multiple attestation that has been proposed looks for ideas or themes that are found in different types of Gospel teaching: thus the "kingdom of God" is a theme that permeates all sorts of Jesus' teaching (parables, miracle stories, etc.) and is seen therefore as having huge historical probability.'[11] These more stringent forms of multiple attestation occur 'when a saying appears either in multiple sources (M, L, Q, Mark) or in multiple forms (i.e. in a miracle account, a parable, and/or apocalyptic sayings).'[12] Thus Blomberg argues: 'That which appears in more than one Gospel, more than one Gospel source, or more than one form stands a better chance of being authentic than that which is singly attested.'[13] Hence we can distinguish between three different forms of multiple attestation: 'multiple attestation', 'multiple source attestation' and 'multiple form attestation'. As Thomas R. Yoder Neufeld states: 'if one can find the same saying or deed attributed to Jesus in several different sources, especially different kinds of sources and different layers of tradition, confidence in its authenticity is greatly strengthened.'[14]

3) Criterion of embarrassment

'The criterion of embarrassment refers to sayings or deeds that are not easily explained as inauthentic creations of the early church, simply because there are aspects about them that would have been potentially embarrassing.'[15]

4) Criterion of divergent traditions/enemy attestation

'The *criterion of divergent traditions* says that when an author preserves traditions which do not serve his purposes, they are more than likely to be authentic.'[16] As Wenham and Walton note: 'if a Gospel contains a saying or story of Jesus which is contrary to the evangelist's own particular interests or tendencies, then this is likely to be a tradition that is being passed on, not something coming from the evangelist himself.'[17] Information from sources opposed to the gospel writers' viewpoint but which nevertheless agrees with some element of that viewpoint is often called 'enemy attestation'.

5) Criterion of dissimilarity

A saying or deed of Jesus that doesn't fit the mindset of either Judaism or the early church probably goes back to Jesus: 'Such a criterion shows those places where Jesus' teaching is entirely unique.'[18]

6) Criterion of Palestinian colouring

This criteria looks for 'linguistic and cultural features that fit what we know of first-century Palestine.'[19] For example, 'There are particular words in the Gospels, such as *"Abba"*, *"talitha cum"*, *"eloi, eloi, lama sabachthani"*, which are Aramaic, the common language of Palestine in Jesus' day (Mark 5:41; 14:36; 15:34). Their appearance in the Greek Gospels is most simply explained in terms of Jesus' own usage.'[20] Moreover, 'Sometimes translating the text from Greek back into Aramaic will reveal Semitic meter, word plays, or other evidence that points to a Semitic context.'[21]

7) Criterion of unintentional signs of history

This criterion 'argues that particularly vivid details of an eyewitness can demonstrate accurate knowledge of the environment and the event. This contributes to the credibility of a text.'[22]

8) Criterion of memorability

'The criterion of memorability suggests that teachings of Jesus which are inherently memorable are more likely to have been remembered accurately in oral tradition and therefore recorded correctly in the later Gospels.'[23] Much of Jesus' teaching seems to have been designed for memorization using mnemonic devices 'such as rhyme, rhythm, alliteration and parallelism which aid the disciple to recall and pass on the teaching.'[24]

9) Criterion of rejection and execution

This criterion asks 'What sayings and deeds are attributed to Jesus that cohere with the kind of end he met?'[25] Since Jesus' death by crucifixion is one of the best attested historical facts about Jesus, any plausible reconstruction of his life must include some explanation of this fact.

10) Criterion of coherence

Wenham and Walton explain that this criterion is really 'ancillary to the other criteria. If any of the other criteria enable us to identify some sayings or stories of Jesus that are probably historical, then we may build on that, and include other sayings and stories, which may not "pass the test" in their own right, but which fit in with the emerging picture.'[26] As Bock observes: 'This criterion is dependent upon the previous ... It argues that whatever coheres or "jives" with the application of the other criteria should be accepted as authentic.'[27]

Belt and braces

Given that the criteria of authenticity are sufficient but not necessary conditions of historicity, and given that we already have some warrant for trusting the NT, the applicability of the above criteria of authenticity in specific instances should be seen as further contributing to our cumulative grounds for a more general trust in the NT. In other words (and in line with the principle of testimony) it seems reasonable to assume the coherence of the NT witness in any specific instance, even in cases that aren't supported by the criteria of authenticity, just so long as there is an absence of any reason for mistrust. After all, as Wenham and Walton comment:

Historians working with the writings of people like Julius Caesar and Josephus are much more open to their historical sources than skeptical Gospel critics – they do not insist on weighing individual sayings and stories with a criterion such as that as dissimilarity (which would indeed be the death knell of much ancient history [were it made a necessary condition of authenticity]). The Gospels are prima facie evidence for what the historical Jesus said and did … they describe the same real Palestinian world as does Josephus, and they deserve to be taken at least as seriously.[28]

Exploring the Evidence of Jesus' Self-Centred Teaching

Jesus was aware of a call, a vocation, to do and be what, according to the scriptures, only Israel's God gets to do and be.

N.T. Wright[29]

We will first examine *indirect* evidence of Jesus' self-understanding, before examining *direct* evidence for Jesus' self-understanding. The indirect evidence comes from the understanding of Jesus adopted by the earliest Christians. The direct evidence comes from Jesus' self-understanding as expressed in his explicit teaching about himself, as well as from his implicit claims.

Exploring the indirect evidence

The earliest faith of the first Christians is not a hindrance or barrier to our perceiving the reality of what Jesus did and said and the effect he had. On the contrary, the impact thus made by Jesus is itself the evidence needed by those who want to appreciate the character and effectiveness of Jesus' mission.

James D.G. Dunn[30]

Jesus Seminar co-founder Robert W. Funk thought he could uncover a four-stage development within Christology (i.e. the Christian understanding of Jesus) during which Jesus went from being seen as a human being who became 'a son of God by virtue of his resurrection' to being 'pre-existent from the beginning' by the time of the Gospel of John.[31] Atheist John W. Loftus appeals

to Funk's thesis to support his claim that Christians gradually
'developed a higher, more glorified view of Jesus'[32] in a process
of deification 'that took at least seventy years …'[33] This theory is
flatly contradicted by our earliest example of a Christian hymn,
which Paul incorporates into his letter to the Philippians c. AD
60 (i.e. within thirty years after Jesus' death). This ode speaks of
Christ Jesus 'being in the form of God [*en morphe theou*]' prior to
his incarnation, wherein 'he emptied himself, taking the form of
a slave, and becoming in human likeness' (cf. Philippians 2:5–11).
As Michael Green comments: 'In the face of this, to argue that the
full deity of Christ was only gradually asserted after decades had
rolled by is not only inaccurate, it is very bad scholarship. Jesus
was accorded this status by his followers from the earliest days of
the Christian church.'[34]

Having made an in-depth study of the earliest Christians' devotion to Jesus (including Philippians 2:5–11), Larry W. Hurtado
concludes that:

> well within the first couple of decades of the Christian movement
> … Jesus was treated as a recipient of religious devotion and was
> associated with God in striking ways … devotion to Jesus was not
> a late development … it was an immediate feature of the circles
> of those who identified themselves with reference to him … this
> intense devotion to Jesus, *which includes reverencing him as divine*,
> was offered and articulated characteristically within a firm stance
> of exclusivist monotheism.[35]

Such a radical worldview shift demands explanation; and the most
plausible explanation is surely that Jesus personally encouraged
his disciples to adopt such an attitude towards him, and that he
did so in a manner sufficiently compelling to convince them that
this attitude was rationally warranted and thus morally obligatory:
'Orthodox Jews considered worshipping a mere human blasphemous and detestable (Acts 10:25–26; 14:11–15), so the church's
without-controversy acceptance of Christ-worship is stunning. As
we read in the New Testament, Jesus shares in God's identity – in
the *honours* due to God, the *attributes* of God, the *names* of God,
the *deeds* of God, and the *seat* of God's throne (which spells the
acronym H-A-N-D-S).'[36]

That the earliest Christians believed in Jesus' deity is a fact attested in many ways by multiple independent sources. Little surprise, then, to find theologians J. Ed Komoszewski, M. James Sawyer and Daniel B. Wallace affirming that 'this much is certain: Jesus' earliest followers viewed him as divine. Even scholars who do not personally embrace the divinity of Jesus readily recognize that the New Testament authors did.'[37] Paul Barnett confirms: 'We are on firm ground historically in asserting that the early Christians worshipped Jesus as Lord.'[38] Dan Brown's novel *The Da Vinci Code* may promulgate the outlandish idea that Jesus had divinity conceptually foisted upon him by the Council of Nicea in AD 325, but: 'This is simply untrue historically! In the immediate years after Jesus, the New Testament authors refer to him as God [Romans 9:5; Hebrews 1:8; John 1:1]. Paul's letters contain evidence 270 years *before* Nicea that Christians worshipped Jesus as God. Pliny's letter to his emperor, written 215 years *before* Nicea, reports that Christians expressed worship to Jesus, "as if to a god".'[39]

Let's review some key evidence.

Paul's Maran atha *prayer and the Lord's Supper*
Paul closes 1 Corinthians, a letter written to a Gentile congregation in c. AD 54, with the Aramaic phrase *Maran atha* (from *mar*, meaning 'God' or 'Deity'). This phrase implores Jesus *as deity* to 'come':

> Why would Paul use an Aramaic word of closing to a Greek-speaking congregation which did not understand Aramaic? The answer would seem to be that this had become a standard form of address by the time Paul had visited Corinth in [AD] 50 … Where did this form of address arise? It would surely be in the early Jewish church. Thus, once again we have historical evidence that belief in a divine Jesus … originated in [an early] Jewish context.[40]

Wright calls the *Maran atha* prayer an 'extremely early and pre-Pauline tradition.'[41] Indeed, as Barnett comments: 'the Semitic language identifies the words as a prayer written in Palestine from earlier times, arguably much earlier times, going back almost to the time of Jesus … The overwhelming likelihood is that the prayer was formulated for church use in Jerusalem, soon after the historic lifespan of Jesus.'[42] Thus 'it is evident … that the early Christians worshipped Jesus as Lord and prayed *to* him …'[43] Dean L. Overman observes: 'it is in the meaning of *mar* as divine ruler that we have very early evidence that the earliest Christian church, the church in Palestine, worshipped Jesus as God.'[44]

Barnett highlights 'another key reference to "the Lord" [in 1 Corinthians] … Paul's mention of the Lord's Supper. This reference also goes back to formulated prayers of the earliest Jerusalem church, which would also originally have been in Aramaic.'[45] In light of the Jewish creed or *Shema* – 'Hear, O Israel: The LORD our God, the LORD is one' (Deuteronomy 6:4), Barnett argues:

> In calling Jesus *Lord*, Paul was identifying the risen and ascended Jesus with the Lord of the Old Testament. This is clear from Paul's word's, which echo but radically adapt the Jewish creed … "There is *one* God, the Father … and one Lord, Jesus Christ" (1 Corinthians 8:6). The *one* Lord of his Jewish faith Paul now redefined as the *one* Father and the *one* Lord.[46]

Nor was this worldview shift original to Paul:

> Paul the early convert [has an understanding of Jesus that is] as advanced and developed as any within the pages of the NT … his Christology in all essential points was not of his making but was formulated by those who were believers before him. This would mean that the Christology he articulates was formulated within the brief span between the crucifixion of Jesus and the conversion of Paul.[47]

The crucifixion is generally agreed to have happened in either AD 30 or 33 (with the majority of scholars favouring AD 33), while Paul's conversion to Christianity happened 'within a very few years at most after Jesus' execution'.[48] Moreover, as Barnett notes elsewhere: 'every contributor to our New Testament calls Jesus "Christ" and "Lord". And they are all Jews except Luke … What I write here is historical fact no serious scholar doubts … *all* the letter writers in the New Testament teach that the post-resurrection Jesus is Lord, to be worshipped, served and obeyed.'[49]

Jesus as Kyrios

The phrase 'Jesus is Lord [*kyrios*]' was 'a confession of the earliest Christians.'[50] Overman explains:

> By the time of Jesus' birth, devout Jews avoided speaking the Hebrew name for God because the word was considered too sacred to be pronounced out loud. God's name was composed of four Hebrew letters: YHWH (*Yahweh*), known as the Hebrew tetragrammaton. When Jewish believers referred to God, they used the Hebrew word *adonai* in speaking about or to God. Among Greek-speaking Jews, the Greek word *kyrios* was read out loud for the tetragrammaton (*Yahweh*).[51]

The Greek word *kyrios*, or 'Lord', had a range of reference that included but wasn't limited to meaning the same thing as *adonai* or *Yahweh*. However, Josephus reports that first-century Jews refused to address the Roman emperor as *kyrios* because they believed this term should only be applied to *Yahweh*.[52] Moreover, the NT writers repeatedly use *kyrios* to translate the Hebrew term *Yahweh*:

> When the early church proclaimed that 'Jesus is Lord,' it was using *kyrios* in its most exalted sense. For example, the author of the first letter of Peter, writing in the early 60's, ascribes to Jesus an Old Testament passage in which the term 'Lord' refers to the Hebrew *Yahweh*. In First Peter 3:15, the author writes: '… but in your hearts sanctify Christ as Lord (*kyrios*).' (Careful study shows that 'Christ' in the New Testament always refers to Jesus.) This passage refers to Isaiah 8:13: '*Yahweh Saboath*, him you shall sanctify.'[53]

Other NT writers do the same: 'Time and time again, Paul ascribes *kyrios* the same meaning as *Yahweh* in reference to Jesus in Old Testament passages.'[54] A passage from Isaiah 40:3, which describes a voice crying out in the wilderness 'prepare the way for the Lord; make straight in the desert a highway for our God' is quoted in the NT in relation to John the Baptist paving the way *for Jesus* (cf. Mark 1:3; Matthew 3:3; Luke 3:4; John 1:23).

Early devotion to Jesus – explaining the indirect evidence

> Jesus-devotion did not commence at some secondary stage but
> goes back to the earliest known circles of believers.
>
> Larry W. Hurtado[55]

As shown by the *multiple* and *embarrassing* reports in the gospels
about how slow the disciples were to embrace Jesus' self-understanding, it's clear that 'the disciples did not readily or uncritically
embrace the divinity of Jesus. The reason for this is plain to see:
they were Jewish monotheists devoted to one true God. To see a
man as both on a par with God and, indeed, as God himself was
a radical paradigm shift that took some time to sink in.'[56] Michael
Green puts the disciples' belief into historical context:

> The Jews had really learnt one lesson by the first century AD. That
> there is only one God, and no runners up. They believed this so
> strongly that they would allow no images of the divine to deco-
> rate their synagogue ... Tacitus in his Histories preserves the utter
> amazement of the Romans when Pompey burst his way into the
> Holy of Holies in the Temple at Jerusalem – and found no statue
> there! So jealously did they stick to the Second Commandment that
> the Jews fought to the death rather than allow the Roman military
> standards, with their imperial medallions, to enter the Holy City.
> So seriously did Jews take their monotheism that they would not
> take the sacred name of God (Yahweh) upon their lips. At Qumran
> hand basins have been found in the scriptorium where the scrolls
> were written which were manifestly used for a ceremonial washing
> of the hands when the divine name was penned. In other words, if
> you had looked the whole world over for more stony and improb-
> able soil in which to plan the idea of an incarnation you could not
> have done better than light upon Israel![57]

And yet 'it was in this background, no other, that the conviction arose that God had incarnated himself in human flesh.'[58]
Astonishingly, then, 'some time' was not, by all reports, very
much time. As Overman notes:

the earliest literary sources in our possession that we know for certain were written within decades of Jesus' death ... contain devotional creeds, hymns, and liturgical formulae that preexisted these literary sources and were then incorporated into them. They present compelling evidence of a pattern of worship of Jesus of Nazareth as a resurrected, divine being, dating from a time almost contemporaneous with the events they describe ... This means that we have solid, historical evidence that persons who were alive and presumably eyewitnesses to Jesus' life worshipped him as divine within an astonishingly short time frame of the crucifixion.[59]

Indeed:

The devotional practices of the primitive church, for which there is substantial evidence, clearly demonstrate that Jesus was worshipped as divine right from the beginning of the Christian movement. This is nothing short of astounding, considering that this worship practice erupted in the context of an exclusivist monotheistic Judaism and that the early disciples did not see this worship as inconsistent with Judaism, but as the fulfillment of Jewish prophecy.[60]

All of this goes to show, as Michael Bird writes, that 'there is no question of an evolution from Jewish prophet to gentile God.'[61] Hurtado agrees: 'our earliest Christian writings ... already presuppose cultic devotion to Jesus as a familiar and defining feature of Christian circles wherever they are found ... So, instead of an evolutionary/incremental model, we have to think in terms of something more adequate ... a religious development that was more like a volcanic eruption.'[62] But as agnostic philosopher Anthony O'Hear admits: 'We should remember that his first followers were pious Jews, to whom the claims being made would have seemed blasphemous had they not been given strong reason to believe them – and where better than from Jesus himself?'[63]

It's hard to see how the earliest, Jewish disciples of Jesus could have been any clearer in affirming their belief in the divinity of Jesus the Christ: 'In Colossians Paul forthrightly declares Christ to be the one in whom "the whole fullness of deity dwells bodily" (2:9). In Titus Jesus is called "our great God and Savior" (2:13) and the writer of Hebrews addresses Christ thus: "Thy throne, O God, is for ever and ever" (1:8).[64] As Richard Bauckham observes, the first Christians:

> include Jesus in the unique divine identity as Jewish monotheism understood it. The writers do this deliberately and comprehensively by using precisely those characteristics of the divine identity on which Jewish monotheism focused in characterizing God as unique. They included Jesus in the unique divine sovereignty over all things, they included him in the unique divine creation of all things, they identified him by the divine name which names the unique divine identity, and they portray him as accorded the worship which, for Jewish monotheists, is recognition of the divine identity.[65]

On the basis of the evidence, philosopher James E. Taylor argues:

> critics need to avoid committing themselves to the extremely implausible view that the followers of Jesus did not believe he was the Messiah and the Son of God and deliberately fabricated the grounds for attributing divine status to him. It is unlikely that they would have subjected themselves (as they did) to ridicule, persecution, ostracism, imprisonment, and, in some cases, death for the sake of a claim they did not really believe to be true. But if we assume, as we must, that the early Christians *believed* Jesus was Lord and God, we must look for the best explanation of this fact. In particular, could so many have come to believe this – including many eyewitnesses to the life of Jesus – within so few years of Jesus' death if Jesus himself had never explicitly claimed or implied that he was divine? There must have been some objective facts about Jesus that led to widespread conviction concerning his divinity. It is implausible to hold that merely subjective factors, such as self-deception and wishful thinking – especially among hardcore monotheistic Jews – could account for the worship of Jesus as God.[66]

The best explanation of this historical data is that 'the New Testament deification of Jesus Christ ... has its roots in the words and activities of the historical Jesus.'[67]

In the midst of a Jewish–Christian dialogue on the question *Who Was Jesus?* (WJK, 2001), Jewish professor of religious studies Peter Zaas said: 'Did Jesus claim to be divine? I don't think that's quite as closed a question as you think it is. But perhaps he did. Did his followers claim that he was not only divine, but the only way that people could achieve some kind of notion of salvation? They certainly did.'[68] However, the conundrum produced by admitting that Jesus' disciples claimed that he was divine, whilst denying that Jesus claimed that he was divine, is both obvious and very great. As Craig A. Evans comments:

> To assert that Jesus did not regard himself as in some sense God's son makes the historian wonder why others did. From the earliest time Jesus was regarded by Christians as the son of God. Why not regard him as the great Prophet, if that is all that he had claimed or accepted? Why not regard him as the great Teacher, if that had been all that he had ever pretended to be? Earliest Christianity regarded Jesus as Messiah and as son of God, I think, because that is how his disciples understood him and how Jesus permitted them to understand him.[69]

If Jesus didn't claim to be divine, then, when his disciples claimed that he was, were they promulgating a deliberate lie about their teacher? That seems highly unlikely. As Kreeft writes:

> if the story in the Gospels is a myth, if the historical Jesus never claimed divinity ... then this myth was invented by Jesus' apostles themselves, not by later generations or the early Christian community. But why would the apostles lie? What would motivate such a massive conspiracy of deceit? Liars always lie for selfish reasons. If they lied, what was their motive, what did they get out of it? What they got out of it was misunderstanding, rejection, persecution, torture, and martyrdom. Hardly a list of perks! And if they lied, why did not one of the liars ever confess this, even under torture? Martyrdom does not prove truth, but it certainly proves sincerity.[70]

Atheist Michel Onfray concedes that 'Mark, Matthew, Luke, and John did not knowingly deceive. Neither did Paul ... they said that what they believed was true and believed that what they said was true ... Clearly they believed what they wrote.'[71] But if not a lie, then the disciples' claim must, if false, have been a sincere delusion; a case of mistaken identity to be sure, but one qualifying as the most radical and blasphemous of misunderstandings regarding the identity of a fellow human being available to any Jew. Hence Onfray accuses the disciples of suffering from 'intellectual self-intoxication, ontological blindness.'[72] However, the hypothesis of such a radically blasphemous misunderstanding, *by such people and despite the lack of sufficient prompting in this direction from Jesus himself*, seems highly unlikely. By the elimination of alternatives, then, it appears most plausible to think that the disciples' declaration of Jesus' divinity, *whether or not this belief was a true insight or a false delusion on their part*, was at least a *sincere belief rooted in Jesus' own teaching*; that is, in the communication of his own self-image to his disciples in the context of everything else that he said and did.

Exploring the Direct Evidence

> The historical evidence that Jesus claimed any sort of divine status is minimal.
>
> Richard Dawkins[73]

Turning to Jesus' own claims, Taylor writes:

> Jesus' central message was that the kingdom of God had arrived and that his hearers should repent of their sins in order to share in the blessings of God's reign, which would be brought about fully by a future act of God (even the severest critics agree with this). The character of Jesus' earthly ministry was such as to embody, enact, and anticipate this kingdom – as if Jesus himself were the one to usher in God's kingdom.[74]

According to Mark L. Strauss: 'All scholars accept that the kingdom of God was at the center of Jesus' message.'[75] Blomberg reports: 'It is widely agreed that the heart of Jesus' authentic message centres on the kingdom of God.'[76] As philosopher Dallas Willard explains,

'Our "kingdom" is simply the *range of our effective will*.'[77] Neufeld helpfully describes 'the kingdom of God' as:

> a comprehensive symbol that encompasses the relationship of humanity with God but also the relationships within humanity; indeed, it encompasses creation as a whole. It has a *future* dimension, necessarily so because this world is presently still deeply in need of mending. It also implies a strong *present* expression of God's reign and rule whenever the power of God comes to expression. All these dimensions mark Jesus' ministry, in which the kingdom of God as liberator, savior, creator, law-giver, and judge comes to expression. Jesus makes sense in light of the story in which the symbol of the kingdom of God makes sense.[78]

Michael F. Bird explains:

> When Jesus begins his ministry in Galilee proclaiming the gospel [good news] of the kingdom of God … he was proclaiming that Israel's God was now acting in a dramatic way to make good his promises that had been announced in the prophets … the 'kingdom' … is a way of speaking of the dynamic rule or reign of God that is now invading the present … This kingdom is simultaneously present in Jesus' exorcisms, miracles, preaching, and in the experience of the Spirit, and yet it also awaits a future consummation. Jesus calls for faith in God given the appearance of the kingdom and also calls for repentance of sins.[79]

These *already present* and *to-be-consummated* elements of what Matthew (with typical Jewish reverence for the name of God) calls the 'kingdom of heaven' are key to understanding Jesus' messianic self-image. Old Testament prophecy is a genre in which 'The distant and transcendent and the immediate and mundane were typically connected, as if there were no expanse of time separating them. The prophet did not distinguish between the immediate and distant future.'[80] A Jew would have read the prophets 'with one eye on their immediate political situation but the other on their God-given insight into the long-term future.'[81] Roman occupation had brought to the fore a focus upon those elements of the prophecies that spoke of a mighty warrior-king in the line of David who would triumph over God's enemies:

> The hoped for Messiah in ... the general era of Jesus is based on only one or two of the many aspects of the Messiah from [the OT] prophets ... times of great disappointment about the Maccabean and Herodian rulers evoked nationalistic hopes of a king like the bloodied warrior David, who defeated his enemies. But these interpretations ignore, for example, those prophecies about the Messiah's deity ('Immanuel', 'mighty God'), humility, peacemaking and his violent death that are so prominent in the prophetic writings.[82]

As Blomberg writes: 'Jesus developed the idea of the kingdom as the *in-breaking of God into history to realize his redemptive purposes* but dissociated his current ministry from the establishment of a politically free Israel ...'[83] Jesus' kingdom-centred gospel, and his self-image, both turn on his atypical interpretation of the prophetic hope for a Messiah:

> the answer is in Jesus' attitude to himself as the fulfilment of the prophets *within* history and his attitude to the ultimate fulfilment of the prophets *at the end of* history. *Within history* Jesus saw himself fulfilling the hopes of the prophets, which he interpreted in terms of the messiah's humility in service of others and humiliation in death as a ransom for many [cf. Isaiah 52 – 53] ... He was the Servant-Messiah, who was at the same time humble *and* majestic. At the end of history Jesus foresaw the final and absolute judgment of the nations, which would depend on their welcome or rejection of those who came to them in Jesus' name. For to welcome these messengers was to welcome Jesus, and to reject them was to reject him. Christ will sit on his throne as judge and separate the people of the nations as a shepherd separates sheep from goats [Matthew 25:31–46]. He will consign his enemies to the eternal fire, thus fulfilling the warrior-Messiah prophecies of Psalm 2:8 and Isaiah 11:4.[84]

Jesus turned contemporary Jewish expectations about the Messiah on their head. As Wright observes: 'Jesus was articulating *a new way of understanding the fulfillment of Israel's hope.'*[85] While his fellow Jews' immediate desire for a warrior-Messiah overshadowed scriptural prophecies about the Messiah as a humble yet divine servant, Jesus saw himself (except in relationship to the spiritual kingdom of Satan) as a humble yet divine servant in the immediate and mundane here-and-now, whose death and subsequent vindication would lead to his role as a warrior-king bringing cosmic justice in the last judgement: 'Jesus saw the great messianic prophecies converging on himself, yet differently and in such a way that by his life, death and resurrection he inaugurated in the final, universal and absolute fulfillment of those ancient prophecies.'[86]

God's self-disposing love incarnate

James D.G. Dunn argues that *'the characteristic emphases and motifs of the Jesus tradition give us a broad, clear and compelling picture of the characteristic Jesus.'*[87] Dunn summarizes this picture: 'A Galilean Jesus who called Israel to repentance and disciples to faith, one through whose ministry the blessings of God's final reign were experienced, one who was heard as speaking for God and with the authority of God, and one who antagonized the priestly authorities and was crucified by the Romans.'[88]

In a similar overview, Luke Timothy Johnson affirms: 'The most obvious element defining Jesus' human character is his obedient faith in God, whom he calls Father. Jesus is defined above all by his relationship with God ... The second major element in Jesus' character as depicted in all the Gospel narratives is his self-disposing love toward other people.'[89] Jesus not only embodied this spirituality, but invited everyone to answer the call to 'Love the Lord your God with all your heart ... and with all your mind, and with all your strength' (Mark 12:30,33; cf. Deuteronomy 6:5); a duty that organically results in loving 'your neighbor as yourself' (Mark 12:31; cf. Leviticus 19:18). As Norman L. Geisler and Peter Bocchino put it:

> These two commandments are concomitant principles. In order for us to love our neighbor, there must be a correct understanding of who we are and what it means to love ourselves; an appropriate

view of self-love (valuing oneself) can only be understood in the context of a true and loving relationship with God. It is the Creator who endows us with intrinsic value and who seeks us out in order to love us. It is this intimate love relationship that must engulf our entire being, both inside and out – heart, soul, mind, and strength. According to Jesus, once we embrace God in a love relationship, love will manifest itself in the way we value and treat others.[90]

Bock elaborates upon Johnson's observations:

> Jesus was obedient to God, engaged in self-disposing love and called for a discipleship defined by the example of Jesus' character. I want to add that this call to discipleship went beyond a mere call to imitation. It was ultimately rooted in what Jesus presented about himself as the figure at the hub of the presence of the kingdom of God ... There is more here than Jesus' being obedient to God's will; he is the bearer of promise and the presence of divine rule ... Whether as Son of Man or Messiah in the Synoptics, or as the Way and Word in John, Jesus pointed to God beyond his example by revealing God and God's way in ways that pointed to himself as possessing a unique, indispensible role in the program.[91]

Jesus saw himself as more than a prophet called to *teach*, or even to *embody*, a spirituality of love for God, self and neighbour. Jesus understood the blessings of the kingdom of God as coming *in and through his own ministry and person*. As Craig notes:

> One of the undisputed facts about Jesus of Nazareth is the centrality of the advent of the kingdom of God to his proclamation. Moreover, it is clear that Jesus thought of himself as central to the coming of God's kingdom ... most New Testament critics acknowledge that the historical Jesus acted and spoke with a self-consciousness of divine authority and that, furthermore, he saw in his own person the coming of the long-awaited kingdom of God and invited people into its fellowship.[92]

Indeed, it would appear that Jesus saw himself as *the personal instantiation of God's redemptive purpose*, a purpose grounded in the fact that any objective evaluation of humanity in comparison to God's essentially holy character reveals our need for divine forgiveness as a prerequisite to personal relationship between humanity and divinity. Jesus' call to 'love God' wasn't a call to an impersonal relationship, a one-way act of adoration that impacts our relationship with neighbour but not with God. Rather, it was a plea for humans to *enter into a dynamic relationship with God by accepting his offer of forgiveness made through Jesus.* This is why Jesus interpreted his crucifixion in light of Jewish beliefs about the role of sacrifices in facilitating forgiveness, and it explains why he abrogated to himself the divine authority to forgive sins (cf. Luke 7:36–50):

> Some men came, bringing to him a paralyzed man, carried by four of them. Since they could not get him to Jesus because of the crowd, they made an opening in the roof above Jesus by digging through it and then lowered the mat the man was lying on. When Jesus saw their faith, he said to the paralyzed man, 'Son, your sins are forgiven.'
>
> Now some teachers of the law were sitting there, thinking to themselves, 'Why does this fellow talk like that? He's blaspheming! Who can forgive sins but God alone?'
>
> Immediately Jesus knew in his spirit that this was what they were thinking in their hearts, and he said to them, 'Why are you thinking these things? Which is easier: to say to this paralyzed man, "Your sins are forgiven," or to say, "Get up, take your mat and walk"? But I want you to know that the Son of Man has authority on earth to forgive sins.' So he said to the man, 'I tell you, get up, take your mat and go home.' He got up, took his mat and walked out in full view of them all. This amazed everyone and they praised God, saying, 'We have never seen anything like this!' (Mark 2:3–12)

As Kreeft comments: 'Whoever forgives assumes he has the *right* to forgive … and who has the right to forgive an offender? The one offended … Jesus' claim to forgive all sins assumed that he was the one offended in all sins. And who is that? … God.'[93] Donald Guthrie says of this incident: 'Jesus as Son of man was exercising authority which he himself knew was legitimate only for God.'[94] Oscar Cullman recognizes that 'this meant a conscious identification with God.'[95]

Jesus' gospel was the arrival of a new (but long planned) phase in God's relationship with creation, and most especially with humanity; hence Michael Green defines the kingdom of God as 'what life would be like if God was really enthroned as king in human lives.'[96] However, this gospel centred upon Jesus himself as the divine 'Son of Man' who paradoxically combined the role of messianic king (cf. Zechariah 9:9; Mark 11:1–11; John 12:12–19; Mark 15:26; John 19:9) with that of suffering servant, a prophe-sied-yet-unexpected figure who wasn't merely inaugurating the kingdom through his own 'self-disposing love', but *who was himself the divinely appointed divine entry-point into the spirituality of the divine kingdom* (e.g. Matthew 11:27; 16:24–27; 19:29; 25:1–46; Luke 12:8–9; John 3:13–15; 5:25; 11:25). As Jesus put it in a passage from John's gospel that passes the criterion of Palestinian colouring:

> I tell you the truth, I am the gate for the sheep. All who ever came before me were thieves and robbers, but the sheep did not listen to them. I am the gate; whoever enters through me will be saved. He will come in and go out, and find pasture. The thief comes only to steal and kill and destroy; I have come that they may have life, and have it to the full.
>
> I am the good shepherd. The good shepherd lays down his life for the sheep …
>
> I am the way and the truth and the life. No-one comes to the Father except through me (John 10:7–11; 14:6 [NIV]).

Jesus' kingdom-centred gospel was, in this sense, *a self-centred gospel*.

The Son of Man on trial

> Famous terms for Jesus such as 'son of man' and 'son of God' really were being used by or of Jesus when he was alive.
>
> James G. Crossley[97]

As Scott McKnight observes, 'there is a consistent strain in the records about Jesus that he, in some way, claimed to be uniquely the Son of God.'[98] As Bird points out, there are multi-ply attested examples of Jesus referring to himself as God's 'Son', thereby laying claim to a 'unique filial relation to God and his special role in ushering in the kingdom.'[99] For example, Craig explains:

> Jesus' parable of the wicked tenants of the vineyard (Mk 12.1–9) tells us that Jesus thought of himself as God's only son, distinct from all the prophets, God's final messenger, and even the heir of Israel itself. Notice that one cannot delete the figure of the son from the parable as an inauthentic, later addition, for then the parable lacks any climax and point. Moreover, the uniqueness of the son is not only explicitly stated but inherently implied by the tenants' stratagem of murdering the heir in order to claim possession of the vineyard. So this parable discloses to us that the historical Jesus believed and taught that he was the *only* Son of God.[100]

Nevertheless, 'Jesus' preferred self-designation was "Son of Man" (the title features in Mark, Q and L) and this title in the Gospels is central for spelling out Jesus' relation to the coming kingdom.'[101] David Wenham and Steve Walton caution that 'a common mistake that is made is to think that "son of man" refers to Jesus' humanity and "son of God" to his divinity, whereas … both phrases seem to have both elements at least to some degree.'[102] Indeed, if anything, it is actually the 'Son of Man' title that carries the more explicit claim to divinity, as we saw above in connection to Jesus' claim to forgive sins. Cullmann concludes that 'by means of this very term Jesus spoke of his divine heavenly character …'[103]

Robert H. Stein affirms the authenticity of Jesus' self-designation as *the* (not merely 'a') 'Son of Man', stating that 'the only clear instance of this title in contemporary Judaism in the sense in which Jesus used it is found in [Daniel] 7:13.'[104] Daniel wrote:

> In my vision at night I looked, and there before me was one like a son of man, coming with the clouds of heaven. He approached the Ancient of Days and was led into his presence. He was given authority, glory and sovereign power; all nations and peoples of every language worshiped him. His dominion is an everlasting dominion that will not pass away, and his kingdom is one that will never be destroyed (Daniel 7:13–14).

Here, God the Father ('the Ancient of Days') receives *into his divine presence* 'one like a son of man' who 'was given [*the divine qualities of*] authority, glory and sovereign power', and who is then described as the appropriate recipient of worship (something appropriately given only to divinity), an 'everlasting dominion' (a dominion *only an everlasting being* can have) and a 'kingdom' (i.e. *the kingdom of God*) that will never be destroyed! In the light of this background, consider Mark's report of Jesus' trial (which report passes the criterion of rejection and execution, and since it is interwoven with Peter's denial of Christ, the criterion of embarrassment as well):

> They took Jesus to the high priest, and all the chief priests, the elders and the teachers of the law came together. Peter followed him at a distance, right into the courtyard of the high priest. There he sat with the guards and warmed himself at the fire.
>
> The chief priests and the whole Sanhedrin were looking for evidence against Jesus so that they could put him to death, but they did not find any. Many testified falsely against him, but their statements did not agree.
>
> Then some stood up and gave this false testimony against him: 'We heard him say, "I will destroy this temple made with human hands and in three days will build another, not made with hands."' Yet even then their testimony did not agree.
>
> Then the high priest stood up before them and asked Jesus, 'Are you not going to answer? What is this testimony that these men are bringing against you?' But Jesus remained silent and gave no answer … (Mark 14:53–61)

Craig explains that 'in Jewish thinking God is the one who built the temple … and who threatens the destruction of the temple … The charges brought against Jesus, that he threatened the destruction of the temple and promised to rebuild it, show that he was being charged with arrogating to himself divine roles.'[105] With the witnesses' testimony failing to cohere, the trial seems to be going well for Jesus; so the high priest gambles upon a more direct approach: 'Again the high priest asked him, "Are you the Messiah, the Son of the Blessed One?" "I am," said Jesus. "And you will see the Son of Man sitting at the right hand of the Mighty One and coming on the clouds of heaven"' (Mark 14:61–62).

Jesus' response is made in terms of highly charged symbolic images:

1) Jesus identifies himself as the 'Son of Man' from Daniel 7.
2) Moreover, 'it was one thing to enter God's presence and yet another to sit in it. But to sit *at God's right side* was another matter altogether. In the religious and cultural milieu of Jesus' day, to claim to sit at God's right hand was tantamount to claiming equality with God ...'[106]
3) Then again, 'In other Old Testament writings, the image of riding on clouds was used exclusively of divinity [Exodus 14:19–20; 34:5; Numbers 10:34; Psalm 104:3; Isaiah 19:1]. Daniel employed this image, and Jesus embraced it as his own.'[107]
4) Finally, Jesus 'had claimed to exercise the authority of God, implying that he would sit in judgment over the Jewish council – not the other way around.'[108]

Jesus' self-designation here coheres with 'Documents like 4 *Ezra* and Parts of 1 *Enoch*, probably written in the same century in which Jesus lived, [which] clearly make the Son of Man a messianic figure.'[109] Moreover, as Geisler observes: 'The Old Testament not only predicted the Messiah but also proclaimed him to be God [e.g. Isaiah 9:6; Psalm 45:6]. And when Jesus claimed to be a fulfillment of the Old Testament messianic passages, he laid claim to possessing the deity these passages ascribed to the Messiah. Jesus removed all doubts of his intentions by his answer before the high priest at his trial.'[110]

Jesus *deliberately incriminated himself in the council's eyes*: 'The high priest tore his clothes. "Why do we need any more witnesses?" he asked. "You have heard the blasphemy. What do you think?" They all condemned him as worthy of death' (Mark 14:63–64).

Overman explains that 'in Jewish tradition the high priest was to tear his garments if he ever heard blasphemy.'[111] In his reply to the high priest:

> Jesus affirms that he is the Messiah, the Son of God, and the coming Son of Man. He compounds his crime by adding that he is to be seated at God's right hand, a claim that is truly blasphemous in Jewish ears. The trial scene beautifully illustrates how in Jesus'

self-understanding all the diverse claims blend together, thereby taking on connotations that outstrip any single term taken out of context.[112]

People sometimes wonder what the source could have been for this conversation between Jesus and the high priest. In response, Craig A. Evans asks: 'Are we really to imagine that the disciples, who later became zealous proclaimers of their master and his teaching, never learned what happened, and that they had no idea on what grounds the Jewish authorities condemned him? This defies common sense.'[113] After all, 'Some court records were public, and therefore available to those willing to do some research (such as Luke: cf. Luke 1:1–4).'[114] Several relevant sources were certainly available to the gospel writers. Since the trial was 'probably carried out at Herod's palace, the Praetorium',[115] Luke's mention that one of the women who supported Jesus financially was Joanna, the wife of Herod's steward (cf. Luke 8:3; 24:10), has an obvious relevance. Moreover, 'The texts say that the "whole" council was gathered. This would have included Joseph of Arimathea and Nicodemus. They could easily have given eyewitness testimony to what happened.'[116] Finally, it should be remembered that Peter was present at the trial, having been taken along by John, who was known personally to the high priest (cf. John 18:15).

In sum, we have excellent grounds for thinking with J.P. Moreland that 'a high Christology goes back to Jesus himself.'[117] As Carsten Peter Thiede concludes: 'There is no room for doubt. Jesus claimed to be the Messiah, the Son of God and God himself.'[118]

Explaining Jesus' Self-Understanding: The Trilemma

> Divinity is great enough to be divine; it is great enough to call itself divine. But as humanity grows greater, it grows less and less likely to do so ... a great man knows he is not God, and the greater he is the better he knows it. That is the paradox.
>
> G.K. Chesterton[119]

Having investigated Jesus' claims for himself, John Rist (professor of classics and philosophy at the University of Toronto) concluded:

the full range of Christian claims must go back to the very earliest followers of Jesus, and in all probability to Jesus himself. The solution that either Jesus was a lunatic or his earliest followers were all blatant liars again seemed the only alternative possibility if their claims were false. I could no longer delude myself that 'real' scholarship told us that we have no evidence that Jesus himself, as well as the earliest generation of his followers, made claims for his divinity. The attempt of the biblical critics to show that such claims grew up (or were fabricated) within the Church seemed to be a tissue of bad argument, unhistorical treatment of the sources and wishful thinking: the wish being to make Christianity acceptable to the conventional 'liberal' orthodoxy ... of the nineteenth and twentieth centuries. The resulting 'scholarship' was defective to a degree that would not be acceptable in other philological disciplines. When I saw this clearly, [liberal] biblical scholarship no longer stood in the way of my return to Christianity. I had to decide only whether the totality of Jesus' recorded behavior looked like that of a madman; it was not difficult to see that it did not.[120]

Rist's musings bring us to the task of explaining the data we have accumulated concerning Jesus' message and self-understanding. For, having concluded that 'the full range of Christian claims must go back to the very earliest followers of Jesus, and in all probability to Jesus himself', we face an iteration of the conundrum that applied to the disciples' claim that Jesus was divine, only this time *with respect to Jesus himself*. Was Jesus' claim the blasphemy of a lying imposter, a deluded man's lunacy, or a verity of divine revelation?

Given that Jesus claimed to be divine, our explanatory options are severely limited. For this claim was either sincere or insincere on the one hand and either true or false on the other. If Jesus' claim to divinity was insincere, he was a liar and a blasphemer. If his claim to divinity was sincere but false, then he was suffering from a divinity complex – i.e. he was 'mad' or 'a lunatic'. Hence John Duncan (1796–1870) observed that: 'Christ either deceived mankind by conscious fraud, or He was Himself deluded and self-deceived, or He was Divine. There is no getting out of this trilemma. It is inexorable.'[121] C.S. Lewis famously phrased this observation as an argument against the conception of Jesus as a merely human moral teacher:

> I am trying here to prevent anyone saying the really foolish thing that people often say about Him: I'm ready to accept Jesus as a great moral teacher, but I don't accept his claim to be God. That is the one thing we must not say. A man who was merely a man and said the sort of things Jesus said would not be a great moral teacher. He would either be a lunatic – on the level with the man who says he is a poached egg – or else he would be the Devil of Hell. You must make your choice. Either this man was, and is, the Son of God, or else a madman or something worse. You can shut him up for a fool, you can spit at him and kill him as a demon or you can fall at his feet and call him Lord and God, but let us not come with any patronising nonsense about his being a great human teacher. He has not left that open to us. He did not intend to ... Now it seems to me obvious that He was neither a lunatic nor a fiend: and consequently, however strange or terrifying or unlikely it may seem, I have to accept the view that He was and is God.[122]

As Josh McDowell notes: 'The issue with these three alternatives is not which is possible, for it is obvious that all three are possible. Rather, the question is, "Which is more probable?"'[123]

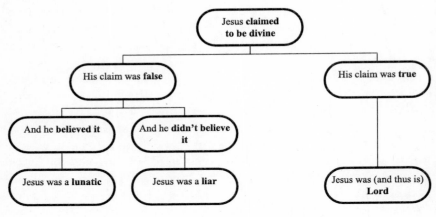

Figure 15

To the extent to which one thinks that the evidence militates against describing Jesus as either a lunatic or a liar, so to that extent one should think it more likely that his claim to divinity was true. Craig comments: 'certainly the majority of scholars today would agree that Jesus was neither a liar nor a lunatic; but that does not mean that they acknowledge him as Lord. Rather, many would say that the Jesus who claimed to be divine is a legend, a theological product of the Christian church.'[124] Yet, as we've seen: 'We have good evidence that Jesus thought of himself as the unique Son of God ... most New Testament critics acknowledge that the historical Jesus acted and spoke with a self-consciousness of divine authority and that, furthermore, he saw in his own person the coming of the long-awaited kingdom of God and invited people into its fellowship.'[125]

Horst Georg Pohlmann states that 'there is virtually a consensus ... that Jesus came on the scene with an *unheard of authority*, namely with the authority of God, with the *claim of the authority to stand in God's place and speak to us and bring us to salvation ...*'[126] How does the hypothesis that Jesus' claim to be the Messiah (and more besides) was wrong square with the rest of our data? Badly. As William Paley argued:

> The Jews ... had understood their prophecies to foretell the advent of a person who by some supernatural assistance should advance their nation to independence, and to a supreme degree of splendour and prosperity. This was the reigning opinion and expectation of the times. Now, had Jesus been an enthusiast, it is probable that his enthusiasm would have fallen in with the popular delusion, and that, while he gave himself out to be the person intended by these predictions, he would have assumed the character to which they were universally supposed to relate. Had he been an impostor, it was his business to have flattered the prevailing hopes, because these hopes were to be the instruments of his attraction and success. But what is better than conjectures is the fact, that all the pretended Messiahs actually did so. We learn from Josephus that there were many of these. Some of them, it is probable, might be impostors, who thought that an advantage was to be taken of the state of public opinion. Others, perhaps, were enthusiasts, whose imagination had been drawn to this particular object by

the language and sentiments which prevailed around them. But whether impostors or enthusiasts, they concurred in producing themselves in the character which their countrymen looked for ... Why therefore Jesus, if he was, like them, either an enthusiast or impostor, did not pursue the same conduct as they did, in framing his character and pretensions, it will be found difficult to explain. A mission, the operation and benefit of which was to take place in another life, was a thing unthought of as the subject of these prophecies. That Jesus, coming to them as their Messiah, should come under a character totally different from that in which they expected him; should deviate from the general persuasion, and deviate into pretensions absolutely singular and original – appears to be inconsistent with the imputation of enthusiasm or imposture ... If it be said that Jesus, having tried the other plan, turned at length to this; I answer, that the thing is said without evidence; against evidence; that it was competent to the rest to have done the same, yet that nothing of this sort was thought of by any.[127]

Lunatic?

There is no indication in the Gospels that Jesus fit the profile of a genuinely deranged person.

James E. Taylor[128]

If Jesus sincerely but mistakenly believed himself to be divine, then he was a lunatic, for as Kreeft argues:

A measure of your insanity is the size of the gap between what you think you are and what you really are. If I think I am the greatest philosopher in America, I am only an arrogant fool; if I think I am Napoleon, I am probably over the edge; if I think I am a butterfly, I am fully embarked from the sunny shores of sanity. But if I think I am God, I am even more insane because the gap between anything finite and the infinite God is even greater than the gap between any two finite things, even a man and a butterfly.[129]

However, the hypothesis that Jesus was a lunatic is both *ad hoc* and contrary to the known facts: 'There are lunatics in asylums who sincerely believe they are God. The "divinity complex" is a recognized form of psychopathology. Its character traits are well known: egotism, narcissism, inflexibility, dullness, predictability, inability to understand and love others as they really are and creatively relate to others. In other words, this is the polar opposite of the personality of Jesus!'[130]

As Chesterton mused:

> Buddha never said he was Bramah. Zoroaster no more claimed to be Ormuz than to be Ahriman ... Normally speaking, the greater a man is, the less likely he is to make the very greatest claim. Outside the unique case we are considering, the only kind of man who ever does make that kind of claim is a very small man; a secretive or self-centred monomaniac ... It is by rather an unlucky metaphor that we talk of a madman as cracked; for in a sense he is not cracked enough. He is cramped rather than cracked; there are not enough holes in his head to ventilate it. This impossibility of letting in daylight on a delusion does sometimes cover and conceal a delusion of divinity. It can be found, not among prophets and sages and founders of religions, but only among a low set of lunatics. But ... nobody supposes that Jesus of Nazareth was *that* sort of person. No modern critic in his five wits thinks that the preacher of the Sermon on the Mount was a horrible half-witted imbecile that might be scrawling stars on the walls of a cell ... Upon any possible historical criticism he must be put higher in the scale of human beings than that. Yet by all analogy we have really to put him there or else in the highest place of all ... If Christ was simply a human character he really was a highly complex and contradictory human character. For he combined exactly the two things that lie at the two extremes of human variation. He was exactly what a man with a delusion never is; he was wise; he was a good judge. What he said was always unexpected ... I really do not see how these two characters could be convincingly combined, except in the astonishing way in which the creed combines them.[131]

Liar?

If Jesus was a mere human being who was sane when he proclaimed his divinity, he must have been lying; and as David Horner explains:

for Jesus to be a liar in this context is for him to be monstrously wicked. This is because of the nature of the lie. For not only did Jesus deliberately misrepresent himself concerning his own identity and fundamental purpose (thus deceiving people about what was the very core and primary focus of his teaching); he also was in fact engaged in calling upon people to give up their livelihoods and follow him, even to trust their very eternal destinies into his hand – all under false pretences. He was deliberately and callously misleading vulnerable people concerning what is of supreme importance.[132]

The point at issue isn't whether Jesus is likely to have been a liar, but whether he is likely to have been a 'monstrously wicked' liar. However, as James E. Taylor writes: 'from what the Gospels tell us about Jesus, he is not the kind of person who would be likely to lie, especially about something as important as whether he is divine. Even people who do not believe that Jesus is God think of him as a good man whose ethical teachings demand unselfish love and moral integrity.'[133] Indeed, Richard Dawkins acknowledges 'the moral superiority of Jesus',[134] judging that:

> Jesus, if he existed … was surely one of the great ethical innovators of history. The Sermon on the Mount is way ahead of its time. His 'turn the other cheek' anticipated Gandhi and Martin Luther King by two thousand years. It was not for nothing that I wrote an article called 'Atheists for Jesus' (and was later delighted to be presented with a T-shirt bearing the legend).[135]

Dawkins takes issue with Jesus' theistic worldview; but he also describes Jesus as 'a charismatic young preacher who advocated generous forgiveness …'[136] Dawkins praises Jesus for 'his genuinely original and radical ethics', saying that 'he publicly advocated niceness and was one of the first to do so'.[137] Moreover, as Taylor notes, 'Jesus had no conceivable motive to lie in this way …'[138] After all, it was his claim to deity (which Jesus appears to have gone out of his way to press with particular rhetorical flourish at his trial) that secured his death sentence.

Lord

The characteristic picture of Jesus available to us through the gospels is at odds with the hypothesis that Jesus was either a lunatic or a liar:

> The savviness, the canniness, the human wisdom, the attractive-ness of Jesus emerge from the Gospels with unavoidable force to any but the most hardened and prejudiced reader ... Jesus has in abundance precisely those three qualities that liars and lunatics most conspicuously lack: (1) his practical wisdom, his ability to read human hearts, to understand people and the real, unspoken question behind their words, his ability to heal people's spirits as well as their bodies; (2) his deep and winning love, his passion-ate compassion, his ability to attract people and make them feel at home and forgiven, his authority, 'not as the scribes'; and above all (3) his ability to astonish, his unpredictability, his creativity. Liars and lunatics are all so dull and predictable! No one who knows both the Gospels and human beings can seriously entertain the possibility that Jesus was a liar or a lunatic ...[139]

Kreeft boils this argument down to the following dilemma:

> the unbeliever almost always believes that Jesus was a good man, a prophet, a sage. Well then, if he was a sage, you can trust him and believe the essential things he says. And the essential thing he says is that he is the divine Savior of the world and that you must come to him for salvation. If he is a sage, you must accept his essential teaching as true. If his teaching is false, then he is not a sage.[140]

Dawkins' objection

In an interview on Canadian TV Richard Dawkins objected that the 'Lunatic, Liar or Lord' argument unfairly constrains the explana-tory options:

> **Fanny Kiefer:** When you read some of C.S. Lewis' work ... a Christian communicator with a fertile mind and a great intellect, why do you think someone who is a scholar ... is grabbed by faith?

Richard Dawkins: Well, you could pick a much better target than C.S. Lewis … He, after all, was a professor of English, and no doubt a very good one. But when you read some of his arguments, they are just pathetic. Things like: Well, Jesus claimed to be the Son of God, so either Jesus was mad, or bad, or He really was the Son of God. It did not seem to occur to him that Jesus could simply be mistaken, sincerely and honestly mistaken. I mean, what a pathetic argument.[141]

As Dawkins wrote in *The God Delusion*: 'A fourth possibility, almost too obvious to need mentioning, is that Jesus was honestly mistaken. Plenty of people are.'[142] Plenty of people are of course honestly mistaken about plenty of things, but *not about their sharing in the divinity of Yahweh*! Thinking that one is divine in this sense is clearly not on a par with holding the mistaken belief that, say, one has a good objection to the trilemma argument! Besides, Dawkins' purported alternative interpretation can easily be incorporated into our argument:

1) If Jesus claimed to be divine and his claim wasn't a lie, the result of lunacy, *or an honest mistake*, then he was divine
2) If Jesus claimed to be divine, it is unlikely that his claim was a lie, the result of lunacy, *or an honest mistake*
3) Therefore, if Jesus claimed to be divine, this claim was probably true
4) Jesus claimed to be divine
5) Therefore, Jesus' claim to be divine was probably true

However, as Chesterton mused concerning Jesus' claims:

> Stark staring incredulity is a far more loyal tribute to that truth than a modernist metaphysic that would make it merely a matter of degree. It were better to rend our robes with a great cry against blasphemy, like Caiaphas in the judgment, or to lay hold of the man as a maniac possessed of devils like the kinsmen and the crowd, rather than to stand stupidly debating … in the presence of so catastrophic a claim. There is more of the wisdom that is one with surprise in any simple person, full of the sensitiveness of simplicity, who should expect the grass to wither and the birds to drop

dead out of the air, when a strolling carpenter's apprentice said calmly and almost carelessly, like one looking over his shoulder: 'Before Abraham was, I am.'[143]

Jesus' appropriation of God's metaphysical self-description, given to Moses upon the incident of the burning bush in Exodus 3:14, as referenced by Chesterton, enjoys independent source attestation from John 8:58 (see also John 18:5–6) and Mark 14:62. As Nicky Gumbel wittily comments: 'The irony of *The God Delusion* is that Dawkins ... says that all Christians are deluded because they believe there is a God, but Jesus was not deluded even though he thought he was God.'[144] With philosopher Stephen T. Davis, I think 'it is not easy to see how any sane religious first-century Jew could sincerely but mistakenly hold the belief, *I am divine*.'[145] Mike King's response to Dawkins really hits the nail on the head: 'anyone "honestly mistaken" in such a way would inevitably be considered insane. But why should Dawkins *et al.* not be content to simply dismiss Jesus as mad or bad? Quite clearly, it is because even a rudimentary flick through Jesus' life demonstrates both of these possibilities to be untenable.'[146] As Richard Purtill affirms: 'the old dilemma still holds: if Christ claimed to be God, he was speaking the truth, or was lying, or was insane. If common sense and available evidence rule out the last two hypotheses, the first must be true.'[147]

Conclusion

I agree with Michael Green when he says that 'no man ought to accept the [incarnation] without having agonized over [it], without having started by believing [it] incredible.'[148] However, if one is convinced that the only alternative explanations are that Jesus was either a blaspheming liar or else a lunatic, then, to the degree one thinks these alternatives are implausible on our background knowledge, so to that degree will one be more seriously disposed towards the hypothesis that Jesus was Lord.

Of course, given a sufficient degree of initial scepticism, one may accept the force of the trilemma whilst yet saying to oneself:

'It is indeed rather implausible to think of Jesus as either a liar or a lunatic, but yet I think it still more implausible to think of him as Lord.' In which case, one must simply bite the bullet and endorse the interim conclusion that Jesus was either a liar or a lunatic (even if one cannot work out which of these implausible alternatives seems the least implausible). Nevertheless, given that consideration of the trilemma leads one to be that little bit less comfortable with denying the hypothesis that 'Jesus is Lord', because one is less sanguine than before about the explanatory merits of the consequential hypothesis that 'Jesus was a liar/lunatic', then the trilemma will nevertheless play a role within the cumulative case for the deity of Jesus laid out herein. Someone in this position will acknowledge that there is something in Craig's comment that 'contemporary New Testament criticism has actually served to support rather than undermine a high view of Christ. The refusal of radical critics to draw the obvious Christological implications of unquestionably authentic sayings of Jesus is due not to lack of historical evidence but to their personal anti-metaphysical ... prejudices.'[149] If the trilemma thus makes the hypothesis 'Jesus is Lord' *less implausible* to the reader, it will at least soak up a portion of their prior scepticism about the Christian understanding of Jesus, whether or not readers think it sufficient in and of itself to warrant the conclusion that Jesus is Lord. The lower the degree of one's prior scepticism, the closer to the Christian hypothesis one will be moved by the trilemma. At the very least, I think it is an argument that should leave every sceptic in the position described by Chesterton:

> imagine what would happen to a man who did really read the story of Christ as the story of a man; and even of a man of whom he had never heard before ... I wish to point out that a really impartial reading of that kind would lead, if not immediately to belief, at least to a bewilderment of which there is really no solution except in belief.[150]

Recommended Resources

Video website

Jesus: Man, Messiah, or More? http://www.dod.org/Products/DOD2121.
aspx.

Audio

Craig, William Lane. 'Who Does Jesus Think He Was?' http://www.
rfmedia.org/RF_audio_video/Other_clips/National_Faculty_
Leadership_Conf_2008/Who_Jesus_Think_He_Was.mp3.
— 'The Work of Bart Ehrman' http://www.rfmedia.org/av/audio/
gracepoint-the-work-of-bart-ehrman.
Groothuis, Douglas. 'Claims of Jesus and Resurrection' http://www.
relyonchrist.com/Lecture/Audio/31.mp3.
Williams, Peter S. 'Defending the Trilemma' http://www.damaris.org/
cm/podcasts/314.

Online papers

Craig, William Lane. 'Jesus the Son of God' http://www.reasonablefaith.
org/site/News2?page=NewsArticle&id=6247.
Kreeft, Peter. 'The Divinity of Christ' http://www.peterkreeft.com/
topics/christ-divinity.htm.
Last Seminary – Trilemma http://www.lastseminary.com/trilemma/.

Books

Barnett, Paul. *Messiah: Jesus – the Evidence of History* (Nottingham: IVP,
2009).
Bock, Darrell L. *Studying the Historical Jesus: A Guide to Sources and Methods*
(Leicester: Apollos, 2002).
Bowman, Robert and J. Ed Komoszewski. *Putting Jesus in His Place: The
Case for the Deity of Christ* (Grand Rapids, MI: Kregel, 2007).
Boyd, Gregory A. and Paul R. Eddy. *Lord or Legend? Wrestling with the
Jesus Dilemma* (Grand Rapids, MI: Baker, 2007).
Craig, William Lane. *On Guard: Defending Your Faith with Reason and Pre-
cision* (Colorado Springs: David C. Cook, 2010).

— *Reasonable Faith: Christian Truth and Apologetics* (Wheaton, IL: Crossway, 3rd edn, 2008).

Davis, Stephen T. *Christian Philosophical Theology* (Oxford University Press, 2006).

Dickson, John. *Investigating Jesus: An Historian's Quest* (Oxford: Lion, 2010).

Hurtado, Larry W. *How on Earth Did Jesus Become a God? Historical Questions about Earliest Devotion to Jesus* (Grand Rapids, MI: Eerdmans, 2005).

— *Lord Jesus Christ: Devotion to Jesus in Earliest Christianity* (Grand Rapids, MI: Eerdmans, 2003).

Horner, David A. '*Aut Deus aut Malus Homo*: A Defense of C.S. Lewis' "Shocking Alternative".' Pages 68–84 in *C.S. Lewis as Philosopher: Truth, Goodness and Beauty* (ed. David Baggett, Gary R. Habermas and Jerry L. Walls; Downers Grove, IL: IVP Academic, 2008).

Kreeft, Peter. 'Why I Believe Jesus Is the Messiah and Son of God.' Pages 239–52 in *Why I Am a Christian* (ed. Norman L. Geisler and Paul K. Hoffman; Grand Rapids, MI: Baker, rev. edn, 2006).

— *Between Heaven and Hell* (Leicester: IVP, 1982).

Neufeld, Thomas R. Yoder. *Recovering Jesus: The Witness of the New Testament* (London: SPCK, 2007).

Overman, Dean L. *A Case for the Divinity of Jesus: Examining the Earliest Evidence* (London: Rowman & Littlefield, 2009).

Owen, Paul. 'Monotheism, Mormonism, and the New Testament Witness.' Pages 271–314 in *The New Mormon Challenge* (ed. Francis J. Beckwith, Carl Mosser and Paul Owen; Grand Rapids, MI: Zondervan, 2002).

Taylor, James E. *Introducing Apologetics: Cultivating Christian Commitment* (Grand Rapids, MI: Baker Academic, 2006).

Wilkins, Michael J. and J.P. Moreland, eds. *Jesus under Fire: Modern Scholarship Reinvents the Historical Jesus* (Grand Rapids, MI: Zondervan, 1995).

4

The Second Way – Jesus' Dynamic Deeds

The miracles I do in my Father's name speak for me.

Jesus (John 10:25 [NIV])

As G.E.M. Anscombe observes, a good way of discovering something about a person's beliefs is to take note of what they *do*:

> if you want to say at least some true things about a man's intentions, you will have a strong chance of success if you mention what he actually did or is doing. For whatever else he may intend, or whatever else may be his intentions in doing what he does, the greater number of the things which you would say straight off a man did or was doing, will be things he intends.[1]

Jesus' deeds are part of the context against which we have to wrestle with the paradox posed by his claims to divinity. For example:

> One of the most radical features of the historical Jesus was His practice of inviting prostitutes, tax collectors, and other outcasts into fellowship with Him around the dinner table. This was a living illustration of God's forgiveness of them and His invitation to them to fellowship in the kingdom of God. In table fellowship with the immoral and unclean, Jesus is acting in the place of God to welcome them into God's kingdom.[2]

This chapter will explore a particularly illuminating and 'exceedingly well attested'[3] category of Jesus' deeds that simultaneously expresses his self-understanding *and provides independent valida-tion thereof*; namely, his miracles. As T.C. Hammond comments: 'Miracles may be evidences of a supernatural agent, and may also afford evidence of moral intent.'[4]

We must distinguish the *a priori* (before experience) questions of a) what 'miracle' means, b) whether miracles can happen, and c) whether miracles can in principle be known to have happened, from the *a posteriori* (after experience) question of d) whether Jesus performed any miracles. Since a miracle is by definition some-thing contrasted with merely natural events, the wisest preamble to defining what we mean by 'miracle' is surely to define what we mean by 'nature'.

The Nature of Nature

> Miracles do not, in fact, break the laws of nature.
>
> C.S. Lewis[5]

C.S. Lewis traces the developing meaning of 'nature': 'By far the commonest native meaning of *natura* is something like sort, kind, quality, or character. When you ask, in our modern idiom, what something "is like", you are asking for its *natura* … In nineteenth century English the word "description" itself ("I do not associate with persons of that description") is often an exact synonym for *natura*.'[6]

In this native sense of the term, to give a 'natural' or 'naturalis-tic' explanation is to give an explanation in terms of 'some idea of a thing's *natura* as its original or "innate" character'.[7] One could thus give a 'natural' or 'naturalistic' explanation of a supernatu-ral reality (e.g. 'God knows what I am praying for because he is by nature omniscient'), no less than the behaviour of an atom. In a related explanatory sense: 'The nature of anything, its original, innate character, its spontaneous behaviour, can be contrasted with what it is made to be or do by some external agency. A yew tree is *natural* before the topiarist has carved it; water in a fountain is forced upwards against its *nature* …'[8] It's not 'natural' for a yew tree to form itself into the shape of an elephant; to do so outstrips the innate behavioural capacities of a yew tree, and our observation of such a tree therefore excites an experience-based sense of wonder best resolved by explaining this form as the product of intelligent design.

This design inference immediately raises questions about the nature of the designer. We might consider attributing this design to any number of potential designer candidates. In this case the simplest adequate explanation of an elephant-shaped yew tree is the actions of a human being. However, there could, in principle, be occasions where divine agency is the best explanation of an event that outstrips the innate behavioural capacities of the natural world.[9]

Lewis explains that the distinction between natural and non-natural (i.e. supernatural) explanations arose during the development of Greek thought:

> The pre-Socratic Greek philosophers had had the idea of taking all the things they knew or believed in – gods, men, animals, plants, minerals, what you will – and impounding them under a single name; in fact, of regarding Everything as a thing, turning this amorphous and heterogeneous collection of things into an object or pseudo-object. And for some reason the name they chose for it was *phusis* ... From *phusis* this meaning ['everything'] passed to *natura* ... Parmenides and Empedocles [materialists] had thought that they were giving, in principle, an account of everything. Later thinkers denied this; but in the sense that they believed in realities of a quite different order from any that their predecessors took account of. They expressed this not in the form '*phusis* contains more than our ancestors supposed', but in the form (explicitly or implicitly), 'there is something else besides *phusis*.' The moment you say this, *phusis* is being used in what I call its demoted sense. For it had meant 'everything' and you are now saying there is something in addition to it.[10]

Hence, Lewis notes, 'Aristotle criticised thinkers like Parmenides because "they never conceived of anything other than the substance of things perceivable by the senses."'[11] In the same vein, Lewis observes that 'Christianity involves a God as transcendent as Aristotle's, but adds (this was what it inherited from Judaism and could also have inherited from Plato's *Timaeus*) the conception that this God is the Creator of *phusis. Nature* (d.s.) *demoted* is now both distinct from God [i.e. monotheism isn't pantheism] and also related to him as artefact to artist, or as servant to master [i.e. monotheism isn't deism].'[12]

The Judaeo-Christian theistic tradition believes in a transcendent, supernatural God who is the creator of a nature (in the demoted sense – 'd.s.') able to achieve certain ends simply in virtue of its divinely given and sustained character or *natura*. For example, Jesus (using phenomenological language) says: 'All by itself the soil produces grain ...' (Mark 4:28).

Nature (d.s.) can attain ends beyond its *natura* with the help of an agent. That agent may be a finite agent, as when a human shapes a yew tree into topiary. However, if we admit that a transcendent-yet-immanent divine agent (i.e. God) *might* exist, it follows that nature *might* attain ends beyond its *natura* with the help of this divine agent. Indeed, given that this 'infinite' agent is omnipotent, the only ends that nature couldn't attain with divine assistance would be ends that are logically impossible for God to bring about. That is, the only relevant limiting factor where miracles are concerned is not the *natura* of created reality (which is by definition surpassed in any miracle), but the character of God: 'it seems plain that divine interventions could not be capricious exercises of power, nor convenient responses to the would-be manipulations of [humans]. Rather, they would necessarily be expressions of God's characteristics: they would be not arbitrary, but rational and intelligible; they would be ... manifestations of deep love and goodness.'[13]

We may surely call any instance of nature achieving an end beyond its *natura* due to the assistance of divine agency 'a miracle'. Therefore we conclude that 'if there is a God, miracles are possible',[14] and hence that 'an atheist must have reasons for thinking that theism is untenable or evidentially suspect in the extreme in order for his or her resistance to the miraculous to be principled ...'[15]

The Nature of Miracles

> If there is a God who can act, there can be acts of God (miracles).
>   Norman L. Geisler and Frank Turek[16]

According to Christopher Hitchens, the Scottish philosopher David Hume (1711–76) 'wrote the last word on the subject'[17] of miracles. Hume notoriously defined a miracle as 'a violation of the laws of nature'[18] and '[a] transgression of a law of nature by a particular volition of the Deity'.[19] Richard Dawkins follows Hume in defining a miracle as 'a violation of the normal running of the natural world'[20] that is 'flatly contradictory not just to the facts of science but to the spirit of science.'[21] However, Hume's definition is rather obviously prejudicial, as J.A. Cover complains:

> Miracles are not 'violations' of the laws of nature at all. The laws of nature ... describe what objects in nature are capable of producing in light of the powers that they have. And miracles ... are occurrences that are beyond the natural power of any created thing to cause or bring about. Thus, miraculous events – those events not caused by the operation of natural powers in created objects – do nothing to threaten the truth of natural laws about natural causes ... believing in events having supernatural causes needn't saddle one with believing that there are *false laws of nature*, laws having exceptions. Miracles are ... occurrences having causes about which laws of nature are simply silent. The laws are true, but simply don't speak to events caused by divine intervention. (Laws of nature are, after all, laws of nature, not supernature. As our Church Fathers might have expressed it, miracles can be *supra natura* without being *contra natura*.) In short, then, miracles are anomalous ... not because they violate laws of nature, but because the laws of nature don't speak to their causes at all.[22]

Hume inadvertently 'gives away the store' by posing the rhetorical question: 'Why is it more than probable, that all men must die; that lead cannot, *of itself*, remain suspended in the air ... unless it be, that these events are found agreeable to the laws of nature, and there is required a violation of these laws, or in other words, a miracle to prevent them?'[23] If God were to keep some lead suspended in the air, then the lead would clearly not remain suspended in the air 'of itself' (i.e. as part of 'the normal running of the natural world'), but *by the action of divine power*. Hence, *according to the definition given by Hume and Dawkins, no 'miracle'* – that is, no 'violation' of the law that 'lead cannot, *of itself*, remain

suspended in the air' via 'the normal running of the natural world'
– *would have taken place*! As Michael L. Peterson *et al*. note:

> *if* we assume that the water has been turned into wine as the
> result of direct divine activity, then those scientific laws leading
> us to believe that water does not turn into wine under any set of
> natural conditions have not been rendered inadequate. What has
> been rendered inadequate, rather, is the belief that all events can
> be explained adequately in terms of natural laws. And if this is so,
> then *unless* it can be demonstrated that supernatural causal activity
> is an impossibility, we can ... claim to have both the exception and
> the rule ... However, few philosophers today believe that God's
> existence or ability to intervene directly can be shown to be impos-
> sible. And, accordingly, few philosophers today claim that miracles
> are impossible.[24]

C. Stephen Evans muses:

> there are regular processes which bring about results in the natural
> order. These processes are certainly divine in origin, but they rep-
> resent God's 'constant' [secondary] activity. When God steps in in
> a special [primary] way, his activity is by definition exceptional in
> nature ... Since God has acted specially, the effects will be some-
> what special. No laws are violated in the sense that something
> irrational has occurred. Still, the events in question will be *different*
> from the normal course of nature.[25]

In other words:

• A miracle is an event brought about by God acting as a primary
  cause, the addition of whose agency makes a created reality
  achieve an end that lies beyond its *natura*.

Note that the *natura* acted upon by God in a miracle may be natural
(d.s.) or supernatural. Note too that:

> Given a God who created the universe, who conserves the world
> in being, and who is capable of acting freely, miracles are evidently
> possible ... Only to the extent that one has good grounds for
> believing atheism to be true could one be rationally justified in

denying the possibility of miracles. In this light, arguments for the impossibility of miracles based on defining them as violations of the laws of nature are vacuous.[26]

Kinds of miracle

Winfried Corduan states: 'A Miracle is an event so unusual that, given all the circumstances, the best explanation is that God intervened directly ... this unusualness can show up in one of two ways. Either the event appears to defy known physical laws (the superceding miracle), or a set of events seems too improbable to come together on the basis of coincidence alone (the configuration miracle).'[27] This seems like a useful distinction, even if one might argue that a) it is a matter of degree rather than of kind and b) that it should incorporate God's primary action upon supernatural as well as natural realities. Clear examples of a first order, superseding miracles would be Jesus rising from the dead or exorcising demons against their will. A clear example of a second order, configuration miracle would be the occasion when, as the Israelites approached the Jordan on their journey out of slavery in Egypt, a mudslide upstream temporarily blocked the water's flow, enabling them to cross into Israel as God had promised (cf. Joshua 3:14–17).[28] There's nothing about a mudslide *per se* that goes beyond the *natura* of mud. However, the *naturally unlikely timing* of this particular mudslide *in the context of God's specific promise* to Israel makes it reasonable to think that the 'specified complexity' of this event was a configuration miracle wherein the mud achieved an end that it would not have achieved apart from the intervention of divine agency.

God's wonderful signs

The New Testament writers use various Greek words to describe 'miracles', including:

- *Dunamis* – an act of power ('*dunamis*' is the root of English words such as 'dynamic' and 'dynamo')
- *Teras* – a wonder
- *Semeion* – a 'sign'

Michael Poole explains that '*Dunamis* focuses attention on the cause of a miracle in the power of God. *Teras* refers to its effect, and *Semeion* to its purpose.'[29] Hence we may more precisely define a miracle as:

- A wondrous event (i.e. an event wherein a created reality achieves an end that lies beyond its *natura*) best explained as caused (directly or indirectly) by a special application of God's willpower and which therefore signifies something of God's character and/or purposes.

Contextual Considerations

One might be tempted to think that, rather than attributing wondrous events to the input of God's primary causal agency, a better response would be to simply revise our understanding of the *natura* of the physical world. However, as Moreland and Craig observe, to justify revising our understanding of natural causes: 'the anomaly must occur repeatedly whenever the [natural] conditions for it are present. If an anomalous event occurs and we have reason to believe that this event would not occur again under similar circumstances [where we limit those circumstances to natural causes alone], then the law in question will not be abandoned.'[30]

Furthermore, the proposal that we always give preference to revising our understanding of nature over the hypothesis that a miracle has happened ignores the *context-dependent significance* of the event in question: 'A miracle without a context is inherently ambiguous. But if a purported miracle occurs in a significant religio-historical context, then the chances of its being a genuine miracle are increased.'[31] As Kreeft and Tacelli comment:

> context is crucially important. When we consider ... the extraordinary deeds attributed to Jesus, and the special relationship he claimed to have with 'the Father' (i.e., God), it is difficult to avoid one of three conclusions. Either Jesus was a sincere lunatic, or a demonic fraud, or he really was the Son of God – and his extraordinary deeds were in the fullest sense miracles. This triple possibility arises not merely from the deeds considered by themselves; it

arises primarily from the life, character and message of the one who performed them.[32]

Indeed, the more reason we think there is *a priori* to expect God to work miraculously to achieve certain goals, the lighter the evidential load will fall upon *a posteriori* experience in convincing us that a miracle has happened; but as James Taylor writes:

> there are good reasons to think that God would sometimes choose to diverge from his normal mode of managing the universe, so long as sufficient regularity and predictability could be maintained. Among these reasons is the likelihood that a supremely good, wise, and powerful God would choose nonnatural (miraculous) means to get the attention of his intelligent but lost and alienated creatures for the immediate purpose of communicating with them and for the ultimate purpose of making it possible to commune with them (by providing them with indicators of his existence, nature, and will as a way to encourage an appropriate response from them).[33]

The plausibility of these motives increases the *a priori* plausibility of purported miracles that appear to cohere with these motives, as the miracles of Jesus do. The same point applies to any case where we have sufficient reason to believe that God has revealed his intention to work a specific miracle.

Methodological Naturalism and History

> There is no valid reason supernatural explanations should be excluded from an academic endeavour interested in finding and teaching the truth about our world.
>
> Norman L. Geisler[34]

According to R.T. France: 'the historical evidence [concerning Jesus] points to conclusions which lie outside the area which some modern scholars will allow to be "historical".'[35] However, as William P. Alston observes: 'There are Gospel critics who reject, on principle, any reports of divine intervention in the affairs of the world, anything that God is reported to have brought about other than what would have happened had only natural, this-worldly influences been involved.'[36] Such critics do not reject miracles as events that cannot happen, or even as events that cannot be known to have happened, but merely as events that *by definition* cannot feature within the account of reality provided by their academic discipline. As William Lane Craig notes: 'It is frequently asserted that the professional scientist or historian is methodologically committed to seeking only natural causes as explanations of their respective data, which procedure rules out inference to God as the best explanation.'[37] For example, according to Albert Schweitzer: 'the exclusion of miracle from our view of history has been universally recognized as a principle of criticism, so that miracle no longer concerns the historian either positively or negatively.'[38] Likewise, the Jesus Seminar contends that 'the historical Jesus' must *by definition* be a non-supernatural figure.[39] The Seminar endorses nineteenth-century German Bible critic D.F. Strauss's distinction between the historical Jesus and the Christ of faith as 'the first pillar of scholarly wisdom.'[40] However, by adopting methodological naturalism (MN) as a necessary condition of historical theory making, the Seminar *guarantees by definition* that miraculous explanations are non-historical, *irrespective of the evidence.*

As Craig complains: 'If you *begin* by presupposing naturalism, then of course what you wind up with is a purely natural Jesus! This reconstructed, naturalistic Jesus is not based on evidence, but on definition. What is amazing is that the Jesus Seminar makes no attempt to defend this naturalism; it is just presupposed. But this presupposition is wholly unjustified.'[41]

MN is a discredited philosophical rule. As Garry DeWeese and J.P. Moreland report: 'The inadequacy of methodological naturalism [is] widely acknowledged by philosophers ... even among those who are atheists ...'[42] For example, Michael Ruse states that 'it would indeed be very odd were I and others to simply characterize "science" as something which, by definition, is based on (methodological) naturalistic philosophy and hence excludes God.'[43] What goes for MN within science goes within history. In both cases, as Stephen C. Meyer points out, 'Theoretically there are at least two possible types of causes: mechanistic and intelligent'[44] – and ruling out either type of cause *a priori* when arguing that the other type of cause is the best explanation of a given dataset is question begging.

Philosopher of science Del Ratzsch takes a dim view of begging the question against supernatural causation:

> The scientific attitude has usually been characterized as a commitment to following the evidence wherever it leads. That does not look like promising ammunition for someone pushing an official policy of refusing to allow science to follow evidence to supernatural design no matter what the evidence turns out to be ... [Such an approach] commits science to either having to deliberately ignore major (possibly even *observable*) features of the material realm or having to refrain from even considering the obvious and only workable explanation, should it turn out that those features clearly resulted from supernatural activity ... any imposed policy of naturalism in science has the potential not only of eroding any self-correcting capacity of science but of preventing science from reaching certain truths. Any imposed policy of methodological naturalism will have precisely the same potential consequences.[45]

As atheist philosopher of science Bradley Monton argues: 'it's a dangerous practice to try to impose rigid boundaries on what counts as science. For example ... a consequence of [methodological naturalism] is that the aim of science is not truth.'[46] Likewise, MN contradicts the fundamental aim of history, which is to seek the truth about the past.

We can preserve the truth-seeking spirit of history by rejecting MN and adopting instead the eminently sensible rule that 'historians should seek a natural [i.e. non-miraculous] cause for historical events unless there are sufficient reasons to think that these events do not have a natural cause.'[47] That is, a miraculous explanation should never be our first port of call (after all, even people who believe in miracles think they are the exception rather than the rule); but neither should our epistemology exclude miracles regardless of the evidence. As Wright affirms: 'Sometimes, to make sense of the actual evidence before us, we have to pull our worldviews, our sense of what is after all possible, into a new shape.'[48]

Hume's Arguments against Miracles

> I flatter myself that I have discovered an argument ... which, if just, will, with the wise and learned, be an everlasting check to all kinds of superstitious delusion, and consequently will be useful as long as the world endures.
>
> David Hume[49]

One's openness to miracles is deeply affected by one's beliefs about God: 'For nearly all people who deny that miracles have actually happened have done so because of some philosophical argument which is supposed to prove that miracles cannot happen.'[50] It is of course impossible for a human being to know *by investigation of the evidence* that no miracles have happened: 'Did they examine every alleged miracle story, sift through *all* the evidence on a case-by-case basis? Of course not [and what about the possibility of miracles in pre-history, or on unknown alien worlds?]'[51] People who reject belief in miracles outright therefore do so by arguing *a priori* that miracles can't happen and/or that we can't rationally believe in them even if they do happen. This amounts to arguing that God doesn't exist to work any miracles, or that (despite being omnipotent) God can't work miracles even if he exists, or that even if God exists and can work miracles, he can't work them in such a way that we could ever be warranted in believing that a miracle has occurred (again, despite being omnipotent). The outright rejection of miracles clearly shoulders a heavy burden of proof.

Despite the fact that 'it is generally recognised among philosophers that Hume overstates his case',[52] Hume's outright rejection of miracles is highly influential among many contemporary atheists. In Hume's own words:

1) 'A miracle is a violation of the laws of nature'
2) 'Firm and unalterable experience has established these laws'
3) 'A wise man proportions his belief to the evidence'
4) Therefore: 'the proof against miracles ... is as entire as any argument from experience can possibly be imagined.'[53]

Hume's rejection of miracles has received 'hard' and 'soft' interpretations.

Hume's 'hard' argument

According to the 'hard' interpretation, Hume is arguing as follows:

1) Miracles, by definition, are a violation of natural law
2) Natural laws are unalterably uniform
3) Therefore, miracles cannot occur

Hume uses a form of the 'hard' argument when he says: 'it is a miracle that a dead man should come to life, because that has never been observed in any age or century.'[54] This argument begs the question by *defining* miracles as events that have never been observed. As Lewis observed:

> we must agree with Hume that if there is absolutely 'uniform experience' against miracles, if in other words they have never happened, why then they never have. Unfortunately we know the experience against them to be uniform only if we know that all reports of them are false. And we can know all the reports to be false only if we know already that miracles have never occurred. In fact, we are arguing in a circle.[55]

Lewis pointed out that belief in God, which renders belief in the uniformity of nature more than a mere 'determination of the mind', also renders miracles possible:

> Theology says to you in effect, 'Admit God and with Him the risk of a few miracles, and I in return will ratify your faith in uniformity as regards the overwhelming majority of events.' The philosophy which forbids you to make uniformity absolute is also the philosophy which offers you solid grounds for believing it to be general … The alternative is really much worse. Try to make Nature absolute and you find that her uniformity is not even probable. You get the deadlock, as in Hume.[56]

The God who created and sustains nature is able to intervene within nature to achieve his good purposes (just as I can intervene to stop a piece of rock falling, simply by holding it). Hence the theistic worldview rationally grounds trust in the *general* course of nature whilst leaving the door open to exceptions.

Hume's 'soft' argument

Hume can more charitably be interpreted as arguing 'not for the impossibility of miracles but for the *incredibility* of accepting miracles.'[57] That is:

1) A miracle is by definition a rare occurrence
2) A natural law is by definition a description of a regular occurrence
3) The evidence for the regular is always greater than the evidence for the rare
4) A wise man always bases his belief on the greater evidence
5) Therefore, a wise man should never believe a miracle has happened

Geisler explains that on this 'soft' interpretation of the argument 'the rationality of belief in miracles is eliminated, since by the very nature of the case no thoughtful person should ever hold that a miracle has indeed occurred.'[58] However, Winfried Corduan objects that 'this is really no argument at all. It is nothing more than an expression of a predisposition against miracles at all costs …'[59] As atheist John Earman argues: 'An epistemology [theory of knowledge] that does not allow for the possibility that evidence, whether from eyewitness testimony or from some other source, can establish the credibility of a UFO landing, a walking on water, or a resurrection is inadequate.'[60] Hume implicitly depends upon his prejudicial definition of miracles in order to create a false opposition between evidence for the laws of nature and evidence for miracles. Correctly defining a miracle as an event wherein God causes something to achieve an end that lies beyond its *natura* shows that there's no either/or choice between evidence for laws of nature and evidence for miracles.

Geisler points out that 'Hume's policy of "adding" evidence would eliminate belief in any unusual or unique event from the past [e.g. the Big Bang].'[61] Indeed, Charles Taliaferro and Anders Hendrickson note that 'there is a significant parallel between

Hume's stand on white supremacy and on miracles'[62] in that, on the basis of one and the same principle about proportioning belief to evidence: 'Hume winds up assuming that to expect black intelligence is as unreasonable as to expect a miracle.'[63] Hume's argument 'proves' too much.

One might expect Hume to argue that it is irrational to believe in miracles without *sufficient* evidence; but Hume argues that the evidence for a miracle can *never* be sufficient for rational belief *even if a miracle has happened*. Even if Jesus *did* rise from the dead, and you were one of those who *saw him die and met him alive on the third day*, Hume says that you oughtn't to believe your experience, *even if it is veridical*, because regular experience establishes that people do not *naturally* rise from the dead! This is surely a 'reduction to absurdity' (*reductio absurdum*) of Hume's argument, which begs the question even in its 'soft' form. As J. Huston argues:

> Hume reaches his conclusion that evidence for a supposed miracle will always be overridden [by] the large body of (as Hume sees it) undeniably relevant evidence in favour of natural law, only by *assuming* that no god has acted miraculously ... It is only by presupposing a conclusively justified *atheism*, or presupposing belief in a non-miracle-working god ... that you are entitled to adduce with any cogency, say, evidence for Archimedes' Principle ... as evidence against Christ's having walked on water. *Agnosticism*, by contrast, leaves it open whether there is a god who works miracles, and so does not rule out the possibility that, for example, Archimedes' Principle may be an unsound guide to what occurred on some particular occasion. Agnosticism may be shifted by some well-attested miracle report ... Only what one might call a fideistic atheism which refuses to consider its rational credentials will refuse to countenance the possibility that a theistic explanation may account *better* for the range of phenomena, including some putatively miraculous phenomena, than atheism.[64]

Hume says we should always believe what is most probable on the basis of prior experience, but 'On these grounds ... we should never believe we have been dealt a perfect bridge hand (though this has happened) since the odds against it are 1,635,013,559,600 to 1!'[65] Sometimes the probability of an event based on past experience is low, but the evidence for the event is good based on current evidence. Moreland and Craig comment that 'the cumulative power of independent witnesses is such that individually they could be *un*reliable more than 50% of the time and yet their testimony combine to make an event of apparently enormous improbability quite probable in light of their testimony.'[66] Hence, 'if a number of independent probabilities converge upon an alleged miraculous event, and alternative naturalistic explanations are inadequate to explain the data ... it becomes entirely reasonable to believe that this miraculous event has occurred.'[67] As David Baggett explains:

> Hume failed to distinguish ... between the intrinsic probability of something like the resurrection, which may well be very low, and the probability of the resurrection in the light of the evidence we have for it, the improbability of having that evidence if the resurrection didn't happen and the low probability of naturalistic alternatives, which collectively could render the probability of the resurrection considerably higher than judgements of its intrinsic probability that fail to take such considerations into account.[68]

As Geisler concludes:

> Hume's argument confuses *quantity* of evidence with the *quality* of evidence ... in the 'hard' form it begs the question by assuming that miracles are by definition impossible ... in the 'soft' form the argument engages in special pleading, begs the question, proves too much ... is inconsistent with Hume's own epistemology and makes scientific progress impossible ... The wise do not *legislate* in advance that miracles cannot be believed to have happened; rather, they *look* at the evidence to see if God has indeed acted in history.[69]

Despite his continuing influence upon the public at large, 'the fallaciousness of Hume's reasoning has been recognized by the majority of philosophers writing on the subject today.'[70] Earman muses: 'I find it astonishing how well posterity has treated "Of Miracles," given how completely the confection collapses under a little probing ... I suspect that in more than a few cases it ... involves the all too familiar phenomenon of endorsing an argument because the conclusion is liked.'[71] 'Prejudice has rarely been quite so clearly expressed in the history of philosophy,'[72] writes Keith Ward: 'any dispassionate thinker would have to conclude that David Hume's arguments against miracles are not at all convincing ...'[73] Stephen T. Davis affirms: 'Humean arguments against rational belief in miracles fail ... miracles (so far as we know) *can* occur; the real question is whether any *have* occurred.'[74] In sum, we may agree with Evans:

> Miracles seem possible, and it also seems possible for there to be compelling evidence for their occurrence ... One's judgement here will be heavily shaped by his view of the likelihood of God's existence and his view of God's nature and purposes. It seems at least possible, however, that a reasonable person could be convinced that miracles have occurred even if he does not have a previously high estimate of the likelihood of God's existence, as long as he is not firmly convinced that God's existence is impossible. Indeed, it seems reasonable that God might reveal much about his character and purposes through miracles.[75]

Openness to Evidence

Of course, 'not everyone who believes in God believes in miracles. If there is a God, miracles are *possible*. But perhaps God did not choose to actualize this possibility.'[76] Those who believe some miracle claims don't necessarily believe all miracle claims. We need not and should not be gullible when it comes to assessing miracle claims. Rather, we should ask in each case whether there is sufficient evidence to convince us that a miracle has occurred:

> secondary causality is God's usual mode and primary causality is infrequent, comparatively speaking. This is why Christianity, far from hindering the development of science, actually provided the womb for its birth and development. Armed with the primary/secondary causal distinction, Christian scientists did not abandon a search for natural (secondary) causes simply because they believed in primary causes as well. The postulation of a primary cause must be justified – it cannot be claimed willy-nilly.[77]

With this in mind, we turn to an exploration of the evidence for Jesus' miracles.

Exploring the Evidence for Jesus' Miracles

> The only *historical* evidence that we possess is that of a Jesus whose deeds as well as His words led His disciples to perceive that He was the Christ, the Son of God.
>
> Alan Richardson[78]

According to Anthony Harvey: 'There are ... certain facts about Jesus which, by any normal criterion of historical evidence, it would be altogether unreasonable to doubt. Such facts are that Jesus ... *carried out cures of various illnesses, particularly demon-possession, and that these were widely regarded as miraculous ...*'[79] Jesus Seminar member Marcus Borg states that 'despite the difficulty which miracles pose for the modern mind, on historical grounds it is virtually indisputable that Jesus was a healer and exorcist.'[80] Joachim Jeremias confirms that 'even when strict critical standards have been applied to the miracle stories, a demonstrably historical nucleus remains.'[81] John Dominic Crossan notes that while some might assume:

> that miracles come into the tradition later ... as creative confirmation rather than as original data [such an assumption] would be completely wrong. The better explanation is just the opposite. Miracles were, at a very early stage, being washed out of the tradition and, when retained, were being very carefully interpreted ... [e.g. Matthew excludes or shortens Mark's miracle stories and John doesn't mention any exorcisms] I hold, in summary, that Jesus, as ... miracle worker, was a very problematic and controversial phenomenon not only for his enemies but even for his friends.[82]

As Daniel Morias and Michael Gleghorn argue: 'it's especially unlikely that Jesus would be made into a miracle worker since many Jews didn't expect that the Messiah would perform miracles.'[83] Nevertheless, we have multiple source attestation for the fact that Jesus had no compunction about appealing to his miracles as evidence supporting his teaching about the kingdom of God and his central role therein: 'Believe me when I say that I am in the Father and the Father is in me; or at least believe on the evidence of the [miracles] themselves' (John 14:11; cf. John 10:25; Luke 13:32).

The early Q tradition reports that when John the Baptist languished in Herod's jail suffering *embarrassing* doubts about Jesus, he sent messengers asking 'Are you the one who was to come, or should we expect someone else?' (Matthew 11:2) Jesus replied: 'Go back and report to John what you hear and see: The blind receive sight, the lame walk, those who have leprosy are cleansed, the deaf hear, the dead are raised, and the good news is proclaimed to the poor' (Matthew 11:4–5; cf. Luke 7:22). This response (which 'Joachim Jeremias, an authority on Aramaic, argues ... originally occurred in a speech rhythm characteristic of the way Jesus spoke'[84]) echoed the prophecies of Isaiah:

> Then will the eyes of the blind be opened
>   and the ears of the deaf unstopped.
> Then will the lame leap like a deer,
>   and the mute tongue shout for joy (Isaiah 35:5–6; cf. Isaiah 61:1).

Jesus was arguing:

1) If someone does X-kinds of actions then they are the Messiah
2) I do X-kinds of actions
3) Therefore, I am the Messiah[85]

Before his arrest, John publically proclaimed Jesus as Messiah (cf. Matthew 3:1–15; John 1:19–34) and in Matthew 11:10 and Luke 7:27 Jesus identified John as the messenger prophesied by Malachi 3:1: '"I will send my messenger, who will prepare the way before me. Then suddenly the Lord you are seeking will come to his temple; the messenger of the covenant, whom you desire, will come," says the Lord Almighty.' Matthew 3:3 and Luke 3:4–6 both apply the prophecy of Isaiah 40:3 to John:

> A voice of one calling:
> 'In the wilderness prepare

the way for the LORD;
make straight in the desert
a highway for our God.'

Hence we see the entailment of Jesus' reply to John:

1) Jesus is the Messiah
2) The Messiah is God
3) Therefore, Jesus is God

Miracles and Historical Criteria

Contemporary consideration of the argument from miracles doesn't simply rest upon the cumulative case for the general reliability of the gospel testimonies adduced in Chapter 2, for as Robert H. Stein affirms, 'by various criteria ... the authenticity of the miracles stories is strongly attested.'[86]

Multiple source attestation

According to John P. Meier, 'the single most important criterion in the investigation of Jesus' miracles is the criterion of multiple attestation of sources and forms.'[87] The gospels present us with a plethora of significant evidence in just such terms:

the *sheer number and variety* of Jesus' miracles are extraordinary. Mark reports no fewer than *eighteen* miracles, the majority of which are reproduced in Matthew and Luke. Found only in the source common to Matthew and Luke (Q) are *two* miracles, Matthew's special source (M) has *three*, Luke's special source (L) has *seven* and John has *six*. In other words, five independent sources report about forty miracles of Jesus.[88]

Barry Blackburn thus observes: 'the miracle-working activity of Jesus ... easily passes the criterion of multiple attestation. Such miracles are attested in Q, Mark, material unique to Matthew and to Luke, and the Gospel of John (healings only), including the "signs source".'[89] Thus Meier states that if the tradition that Jesus worked miracles is rejected, 'so should every other gospel tradition about him.'[90]

In terms of *categories* of miracle, 'there are many examples of multiple attestations to exorcisms, nature miracles, healings and the raising of the dead spread across the primary Gospel sources Mark, John [SQ], Q, L and M ...'[91] This testimony includes:

- *17 healing miracles*, with representatives in all four gospels – including one healing (the centurion's servant) reported by Q, Luke and John and one (Peter's mother-in-law) reported by Mark, Matthew and John (multiple source attestation)
- *3 revivification miracles*, with representatives in all four gospels (multiple source attestation)
- *9 nature miracles* with representatives in all four gospels (multiple source attestation) including:
- Two incidents of food multiplication (one with multiple attestation and one with multiple source attestation)
- Walking on water, with multiple source attestation
- Calming a storm, with multiple attestation
- Withering of fig tree, with multiple attestation
- *7 incidents of exorcism* (an activity not predicated of the Messiah by the OT), with representatives in all three synoptic gospels, including reports from Q and L (i.e. multiple source attestation)[92]

Figure 16 lists the miracles of Jesus that appear in more than one gospel.

Hence, not only is each and every *category* of miracle reportedly performed by Jesus attested by multiple, early, independent sources; but even *specific* miracles are attested in this way. As Paula Fredriksen observes: 'Jesus as exorcist, healer (even to the point of raising the dead), and miracle worker is one of the strongest, most ubiquitous, and most variously attested depictions in the Gospels. All strata of this material – Mark, John, M-traditions, L-traditions, and Q – make this claim.'[93] Moreover, this testimony – which includes eyewitnesses' reports (i.e. John, Matthew/Q) as well as reports based upon eyewitness evidence (i.e. Mark and Luke) – follows close upon the events reported by comparison with many other works of ancient history (especially in the cases of Mark and

Miracle	Type	Mark	Matthew	Luke	John
In all four gospels					
1. Feeding 5,000 people	Nature	6:35f.	14:15f.	9:12f.	6:5f.
In three gospels including John					
2. Walking on water	Nature	6:48f.	14:25f.		6:19f.
3. Peter's mother-in-law	Healing	1:30f.	8:14f.		4:38f.
4. Roman centurion's servant	Healing (at a distance)		8:5f.	7:1f.	4:47f.
In all three synoptic gospels					
5. Man with leprosy	Healing	1:40f.	8:24f.	5:12f.	
6. Paralyzed man	Healing	2:3f.	9:2f.	5:18f.	
7. Man with shrivelled hand	Healing	3:1f.	12:10f.	6:6f.	
8. Calming the storm	Nature	4:37f.	8:23f.	8:22f.	
9. Gadarene demoniac(s)	Exorcism	5:1f.	8:28f.	8:27f.	
10. Raising Jairus' daughter	Revivification	5:22f.	9:18f.	8:41f.	
11. Haemorrhaging woman	Healing	5:25f.	9:20f.	8:43f.	
12. Demon-possessed boy	Exorcism	9:17f.	17:14f.	9:38f.	
13. Two blind men	Healing	10:46f.	20:29f.	18:35f.	
In two gospels (Mark and Matthew)					
14. Canaanite woman's daughter	Exorcism (at a distance)	7:24f.	15:21f.		
15. Feeding of 4,000	Nature	8:1f.	15:32f.		
16. Fig tree withered	Nature	11:12f.	21:18f.		
In two gospels (Mark and Luke)					
17. Possessed man in synagogue	Exorcism	1:23f.		4:33f.	
In two gospels (Matthew and Luke)					
18. Blind, mute, and possessed man	Exorcism		12:22	11:14	

Figure 16

Q). Nor is this testimony restricted to the NT. Quadratus, writing c. AD 125, provides independent evidence of Jesus' miraculous power: 'But the works of our Saviour were always present, for they were true, those who were cured, those who rose from the dead, who not merely appeared as cured and risen, but were constantly present, not only while the Saviour was living, but even for some time after he had gone, so that some of them survived even to our own time.'[94]

'Such multiple attestation in textual evidence,' writes Gary R. Habermas, 'is overwhelming in terms of ancient documents.'[95]

Agreement among divergent traditions

> We must be clear that Jesus' contemporaries, both those who became his followers and those who were determined not to become his followers, certainly regarded him as possessed of remarkable powers.
>
> N.T. Wright[96]

'It cannot be disputed upon historical grounds that all the people who came into contact with Jesus during his ministry in Galilee believed that He worked miracles,' writes Alan Richardson, for 'even his enemies believed it.'[97] Both 'Mark and Q include the accusation of Jesus' opponents that he was able to exorcise demons *because he was in league with the devil* (Mark 3:20–30; Matthew 12:22–32). Not only is this doubly attested, but it is an unlikely fabrication.'[98] As Wright argues: 'the Church did not invent the charge that Jesus was in league with Beelzebub, but charges like that are not advanced unless they are needed as an explanation for some quite remarkable phenomenon.'[99] *Jesus' enemies didn't attempt to refute the fact of his exorcisms.* Instead, they sought to reinterpret those facts to suit their own worldview. Jesus' critics thereby testify to the fact that Jesus engaged in apparently successful exorcisms. Moreover, the first Christian preachers were able to appeal to Jesus' miracles *as a matter of public knowledge* (cf. Acts 2:22; 10:38).

That non-Christians believed Jesus did miracles is born out by Josephus' comment that 'at this time there appeared Jesus, a wise man. For he was *a doer of startling deeds* …'[100] Again, the following charge appears in the Babylonian Talmud:

> It has been taught: On the eve of Passover they hanged Yeshu. And an announcer went out, in front of him, for forty days (saying): 'He is going to be stoned, because *he practiced sorcery* and enticed and led Israel astray. Anyone who knows anything in his favor, let him

come and plead in his behalf.' But, not having found anything in his favor, they hanged him on the eve of Passover.[101]

Geza Vermes notes that 'even rabbinic literature records that an early Jewish-Christian, Jacob of Kfar Sama, offered to heal the sick "in the name of Jesus".'[102]

Writing c. AD 180 the pagan philosopher Celsus recorded his opinion that 'Christians get the power which they seem to possess by pronouncing the names of certain demons and incantations ... It was by magic that [Jesus] was able to do *the miracles which he appears to have done*.'[103] Moreover:

> [In] a well-known exorcism formula from the Greek Magical Papyrus ... we see Jesus' name invoked, right along with magical names and names of deities. We also see reference to the 'seal' associated with Solomon. But what is astonishing is that Jesus is referred to as 'the God of the Hebrews.' A pagan exorcist, familiar with various Jewish traditions, was aware of the power of Jesus' name (through firsthand observation?) and probably knew that Jesus was Jewish and that early Christians confessed him as God's Son. Accordingly, from this pagan's point of view Jesus could be described as the God of the Hebrews.[104]

Indeed, the NT records that strangers used the name of Jesus to perform exorcism: '"Teacher," said John, "we saw someone driving out demons in your name and we told him to stop, because he was not one of us." "Do not stop him," Jesus said. "No one who does a miracle in my name can in the next moment say anything bad about me"' (Mark 9:38–39; cf. Luke 9:49). This report triggers the criterion of embarrassment, since it calls into question any claim of the church to be the sole purveyor of Jesus' power and teaching, 'especially as Jesus does not condemn the practice.'[105] This story also embarrasses the disciple John. But why would strangers use Jesus' name in exorcism unless Jesus was well known as an exorcist? Again, we find Jews experimenting with Jesus' name as an authority in exorcism, although without success, in Acts 19:13–17:

Some Jews who went around driving out evil spirits tried to invoke the name of the Lord Jesus over those who were demon-possessed. They would say, 'In the name of the Jesus whom Paul preaches, I command you to come out.' Seven sons of Sceva, a Jewish chief priest, were doing this. One day the evil spirit answered them, 'Jesus I know, and I know about Paul, but who are you?' Then the man who had the evil spirit jumped on them and overpowered them all. He gave them such a beating that they ran out of the house naked and bleeding.

It's unlikely that anyone would have invented this story, involving as it does the sons of a supposedly prominent member of society in such a publicly embarrassing situation. Jewish sources would hardly want to lampoon themselves with such a tale, and Luke would hardly have made up a story that important contemporaries would have been in a position to deny. It's also interesting to note that the possessed man was able to overpower, beat and strip naked seven men!

Coherence and dissimilarity

John Drane observes that Jesus' miracles taken as a whole *cohere* with his teaching: 'It is not difficult to see how the various types of miracle that Jesus performed were meant to emphasize in a striking way the different things he said in the parables about the kingdom of God.'[106] Craig A. Evans agrees that Jesus' 'healings and exorcisms were an intrinsic part of his proclamation of the kingdom …'[107] Moreover, as Raymond Brown says: 'Jesus is remembered as combining teaching with miracles intimately related to his teaching, and that combination was unique.'[108] So unique, indeed, that it passes the criteria of *dissimilarity*.

Twelftree notes several marks of authenticity in Jesus' exorcisms, unusual facts about his mode of operation that cannot have been borrowed from the common practice of the day: Jesus used no material devices (in contrast to other ancient cases), neither did he require departing demons to give proof of their exit, nor did he use common formulas such as 'I bind you'. Finally, Jesus didn't pray to remove the evil spirits or invoke any authority beyond his own: '"Be quiet!" said Jesus sternly. "Come out of him!" The evil spirit shook the man and came out of him with a shriek. The people were all so amazed, they asked each other, "What is this? A new teaching – and with authority! He even gives orders to evil spirits and they obey him"' (Mark 1:25–27; cf. Luke 4:31–37). Mark's account stresses Jesus' spiritual power, in that Jesus commands the demon to depart *by his own authority, without the use of material or magical devices.* As Warrington writes: 'The amazement of the people may have been due to the fact that Jesus dealt with the demon by a word, without resorting to magic.'[109] It also highlights the fact that the inauguration of God's kingdom through Jesus would entail, and be evinced by, the waning of demonic power. This authoritative exorcism serves to validate the authority of Jesus' teaching: 'new teaching – and with authority!' (Mark 1:27)

Additional evidence for specific miracles

Even specific miracles in each of the categories receive support from additional criteria of authenticity. For example, the passage in Matthew 16:5–12 which recounts the disciples' failure to understand Jesus' analogy between the Pharisees and yeast, which testifies to both incidents of miraculous feeding, is *embarrassing*. So is their fear and lack of faith before Jesus calms the storm. Likewise, all three synoptic gospels recount Jesus' healing of a boy suffering demonically caused epilepsy (Matthew 17:14–21; Mark 9:14–29; Luke 9:37–43) after his disciples fail to do so, although they've recently been given authority by Jesus to do just that (Matthew 10:1, Luke 9:1). Matthew and Mark record the disciples asking Jesus to explain their failure and Matthew records that it was due to their lack of faith (Matthew 21:21f. cf. Luke 17:5f). This episode is both multiply attested and highly *embarrassing*.

Then again: 'at least two of Mark's miracle stories contain *Aramaisms*: the raising of Jairus' daughter from death (5:41) and the healing of the deaf man (7:34).'[110] Hugh Montefiore points out that in the story of Jesus healing the son/servant (the Greek *pais* can have either meaning) of a Roman centurion (Matthew 8:5–13; Luke 7:1–10; John 4:47–54) 'there is multiple attestation; there are Semitisms in the Q accounts; there is discontinuity and embarrassment at the faith of a Gentile.'[111]

Explaining the Evidence

> We can no longer neatly separate historical-critical debates about the interpretation of pieces of historical evidence from philosophical debates about the nature of reality.
>
> Paul Rhodes Eddy and Gregory A. Boyd[112]

As Paul Rhodes Eddy and James K. Beilby comment:

> Contrary to previous times, virtually everyone in the field today acknowledges that Jesus was considered by his contemporaries to be an exorcist and a worker of miracles. However, when it comes to historical assessment of the miracles tradition itself, the consensus quickly shatters. Some, following in the footsteps of Bultmann, embrace an explicit methodological naturalism such that the very idea of a miracle is ruled out *a priori*.[113]

Thus Habermas observes that among many NT scholars today Jesus' healings and exorcisms 'are recognized as historical and explained cognitively. Both sick individuals as well as those who thought they were possessed by demons got better when they *believed* they were well.'[114] Notice, first of all, that we need not resolve this debate for Jesus' miraculous deeds to play *a purely phenomenological role* (i.e. a role as events recognized to be historical on the one hand however they are to be explained on the other) in expressing and sharpening the dilemma posed by his self-image. For example, however one understands Jesus' ministry of exorcism *metaphysically speaking*,[115] *historically speaking* the evidence at least shows that Jesus engaged in what friend and foe alike believed was a unique ministry of exorcism (one conducted on his own authority), a ministry that restored 'possessed' people to their right minds and which Jesus himself interpreted as a sign of his own authority: 'if it is by the finger of God [cf. Exodus 8:18–19] that I cast out demons, then the kingdom of God has come upon you' (Luke 11:20 [ESV]; cf. Mark 3:23–27). Craig comments:

> This saying, which is recognized by New Testament scholarship as authentic, is remarkable for two reasons. First, it shows that Jesus claimed divine authority over the spiritual forces of evil. Second,

it shows that Jesus believed that in himself the kingdom of God had come ... In claiming that in himself the kingdom of God had already arrived, as visibly demonstrated by his exorcisms, Jesus was, in effect, saying that in himself God had drawn near, thus putting himself in God's place.[116]

As Michael Symmons Roberts observes, many of Jesus' miracles 'were acts that first-century Jews expected only God to perform.'[117] Whatever one's worldview, then, Jesus' exorcisms (and other miracles) sharpen the dilemma of his person explored in Chapter 3.

In addition to such phenomenological considerations:

It may be granted that some of the people Jesus cured were suffering from psychosomatic rather than 'physical' illness. But what of that? Psychosomatic illnesses usually take a long time to heal, even with the use of modern-day drugs and therapies. They certainly cannot be treated 'on the spot'. The same is true of lameness, deafness, dumbness and blindness – and miraculous cures of these conditions were virtually unheard of in first-century Palestine. The possibility that Jesus was just another faith healer must, on the evidence, be ruled out.[118]

Moreover, it's hard to give miracles of healing and exorcism that are worked at a distance a psychosomatic explanation (cf. Matthew 8:5–13; Luke 7:1–10; John 4:47–54; Mark 7:24–30; Matthew 15:21–28)! Points like these open up an entirely new avenue of argument. As Richard Purtill writes:

Christ might have cured a paralytic because the paralysis was hysterical and subject to psychological healing. But what about the cure of leprosy? What about the cure of the man blind from birth? And it is no use saying that psychomatic illnesses cured by the impact of a charismatic personality account for *some* of Christ's cures and that the rest are fictional, for this would be to pick and choose among the evidence in a blatant way. If I am allowed to pick which of the evidence I will explain and reject the rest, I can make almost any theory look plausible.[119]

Graham Stanton notes that 'in antiquity miracles were not accepted without question … it is a mistake to write off the miracles of Jesus as a result of the naivety and gullibility of people in the ancient world.'[120] Stanton observes that while there are some 'reports of Jewish miracle workers who lived at about the time of Jesus … they are not common [and] rather surprisingly, they do not include cures of the deaf, the dumb and the lame.'[121] 'The people of Jesus' day could be as skeptical as people today,' writes Mark L. Strauss. 'The Gospels treat Jesus' miracles not as commonplace or as the expected norm for charismatic leaders but as surprising and astonishing to those who witnessed them.'[122] Twelftree reports that people 'were not uncritical in their acceptance of a report of a miracle … Not everyone believed in demons and exorcism …'[123] Moreover, even amongst those who did believe in such things, 'People in the New Testament world [were able] to discriminate between those sicknesses which were and those which were not thought to be caused by demons.'[124] For example, 'All three synoptic Gospels record that, during the evening of the day on which Peter's mother-in-law was healed, many who were sick and demonised were brought to Jesus for ministry, each category of affliction kept separate in the accounts.'[125] Again, compare the cures of deaf, dumb, and blind persons in Mark 7 and 8, where there is no exorcism (despite Mark's interest in such events) with the similar cases in Matthew 9 and 12, where dumb and blind people *are* exorcised: 'There must have been some diagnosis or discernment by Jesus at the time, whereby he was able to tell which cases required the casting-out of evil spirits and which did not.'[126] There were:

> well-established maladies like fever, leprosy and paralysis it was not thought necessary to attribute either to Satan or to demons (Mark 1:29–31, 40–4, 2:1–12; cf. Mark 4:19). [Rather] the idea of demon-possession was reserved for conditions where the individual seemed to be totally in the grip of an evil power (using his vocal chords, Mark 1:24, 5:7, 9; Acts 16:16; convulsing him, Mark 1:26, 9:20–2, 26; superhuman strength, Mark 5:3–4; Acts 19:16).[127]

Some of these symptoms can be given psychiatric explanations. However, 'The presence of a diagnosable psychiatric disorder does not ... invalidate a possible spiritual basis or trigger for the disturbance itself ...'[128] As psychiatrist and exorcist M. Scott Peck concluded: 'there has to be a significant emotional problem for the possession to occur in the first place. Then the possession itself will both enhance that problem and create new ones. The proper question is: "Is the patient just mentally ill or is he or she mentally ill and possessed?"'[129] Nor is all the evidence amenable to psychiatric explanation. David Instone-Brewer, whose approach is informed both by modern psychiatric thinking and personal experience of exorcism, testifies that while a psychiatrist might suggest reinterpreting biblical accounts of exorcism in terms of various psychiatric disorders, such an approach has 'only limited value as explanations of what is described in the Gospels.'[130] For example, psychiatry cannot explain the insight than many of the demonized have into Jesus' self-image:

> The man in the synagogue shouted out that Jesus was the Holy One of God (Mk. 1:24/Lk. 4:34). The mad man of Gadera called him Son of the Most High God (Mk. 5:7/Mt. 8:29/Lk. 8:28). Many other demonised people are also recorded as shouting that he was the Son of God, and having to be silenced (Mk. 1:34; 3:11; Lk. 4:41). This insight into Jesus' character cannot be explained in psychiatric terms.[131]

Keith Warrington suggests that demons attempted to complicate life for Jesus by proclaiming his status at an inopportune time, but that 'Jesus refused to allow any slowing down of his ministry and saw through the unsubtle (at least to him) strategy of the demons.'[132]

The fact that Jesus healed an epileptic boy through exorcism indicates that he wasn't *merely* epileptic:

> liberal New Testament scholars have attempted to explain cases of demonization and exorcism such as the one in Mark 9 as merely primitive ways of describing and dealing with epilepsy or similar disorders ... But if one grants that this account in the Gospels is at least minimally rooted in actual history – and few today deny it – this explanation must be judged inadequate, for it does not fully explain what transpired. This exclusively naturalistic explanation

fails to account for why the boy fell into convulsions when he saw Jesus or for why the seizures involved suicidal behaviour. Nor does it account for why Jesus' exorcism worked, why the demon 'shrieked' when it left (though the boy had been mute), or how Jesus ... could have misdiagnosed the boy's condition (while still getting the cure right).[133]

In the multiply attested incident of the Gadarene demonic (Matthew 8:28–34; Mark 5:1–20; Luke 8:26–39), signs of possession include great strength (Mark 5:3) and a stampede of pigs into which the demons flee: 'the evil spirits came out and went into the pigs. The herd, about two thousand in number, rushed down the steep bank into the lake and were drowned' (Mark 5:13). This event caused public uproar:

> Those tending the pigs ran off and reported this in the town and countryside, and the people went out to see what had happened. When they came to Jesus, they saw the man who had been possessed by the legion of demons, sitting there, dressed and in his right mind; and they were afraid. Those who had seen it told the people what had happened to the demon-possessed man – and told about the pigs as well. Then the people began to plead with Jesus to leave their region (Mark 5:14–16).

Such disquiet may reflect the false assumption that Jesus' power over the demonic came from the prince of demons himself, or the simple realization that someone stronger than the demons was in their midst. As for the previously possessed man, he 'went away and began to tell in the Decapolis [ten cities] how much Jesus had done for him. And all the people were amazed' (Mark 5:20). To lay claim to widespread public knowledge of a particular exorcism and its highly memorable results, and to do so within twenty years of its advent, is no way to make up a story! One can only conclude that the story wasn't made up.[134]

In the light of the OT background (cf. Psalm 107:28–29; Exodus 16:4; 2 Kings 4:42–44; Job 9:8; Psalm 77:19) Jesus' miracles of calming the storm (evidenced by early, multiple – including eye-witnesses – and embarrassing testimony), feeding 5,000 people from very little (evidenced by early, multiple sources – including eyewitnesses – and the criteria of eyewitness detail) and walking on water (evidenced by early, multiple sources – including eyewitnesses) are best understood as *enacted claims to divinity*. Thus Jesus' miracles add to the evidence that he claimed to be divine, and they do so in a way that both adds to our knowledge of his character and puts a divine stamp of approval upon his teaching.

Conclusion

> Jesus of Nazareth, a man attested to you by God with mighty works and wonders and signs which God did through him in your midst, as you yourselves know.
>
> Peter (Acts 2:22)

On the one hand, as James Taylor observes:

> Many of the things the Gospels report that Jesus did are not only supernatural in character ... but also alleged acts of God ... They are, therefore (if they really happened), miracles. Moreover, if Jesus really performed them ... then Jesus' claim to be the Messiah and the Son of God receives substantial further confirmation. This confirmation is the result not only of the fact that it is highly likely that God is working in Jesus to perform miracles but also of what the miracles communicate about the nature and character of Jesus as a person ... In sum, if Jesus really performed the miracles the Gospels say he did, then both the existence and the character of these miracles add substantial confirmation to Jesus' claim to be the Messiah and one with the Creator and Redeemer God.[135]

On the other hand, as Bruce Chilton and Craig A. Evans affirm:

> Any fair reading of the Gospels and other ancient sources (including Josephus) inexorably leads to the conclusion that Jesus was well known in his time as a healer and exorcist. The miracle stories are now treated seriously and are widely accepted by Jesus scholars as deriving from Jesus' ministry. Several specialized studies have appeared in recent years, which conclude that Jesus did things that were viewed as 'miracles'.[136]

Whether we are prepared to infer that Jesus performed miracles, and thus to draw a conclusion in support of Jesus' claims, will depend in part upon our philosophical openness to miracles and in part upon our assessment of the relevant historical evidence. There are good philosophical reasons for adopting a cautious openness to the occurrence of miracles. Moreover, the general claim that Jesus performed miracles is supported by multiple, early sources of testimony (including the testimony of eyewitnesses) that pass numerous other standard criteria of historical reliability; and the same can be said of several specific and highly significant miracles. Hence, as philosopher Steven B. Cowan concludes, 'the evidence for the veracity of at least some of the biblical miracles is quite strong.'[137]

In the context of Jesus' teaching about the kingdom of God and his role therein, the conclusion that Jesus was a worker of miracles clearly confirms the truth of his teaching. In addition to this, those specific miracles for which we have the strongest historical evidence both *express and validate* Jesus' divine self-image. As Paul Barnett concludes:

> The miracles of Jesus were not 'contrary' to natural patterns: freakish or bizarre like the 'signs' and 'portents' the Jews sought. His miracles were restrained, done for the good of those in need and not as spectacles in the manner of magicians. They served to point to Jesus as at one with the Creator in revealing in advance his generous, end-time purposes on earth. In the miracles of Jesus, the kingdom of God was present among people as the Son of Man went about doing good.[138]

Recommended Resources

Websites

Bethinking – 'Resurrection and Miracles' http://www.bethinking.org/categories.php?CategoryID=5.

Video

The Miracles of Jesus: What Do They Reveal? http://www.dod.org/ Products/The-Miracles-of-Jesus--What-Do-They-Reveal-Part-II__ DOD2023.aspx.

Online papers

Corduan, Winfried. 'Miracles: Liability and Asset' http://www.uk apologetics.net/07/miraclesla.htm.

Craig, William Lane. 'The Problem of Miracles: A Historical and Philosophical Perspective' http://www.reasonablefaith.org/site/News2? page=NewsArticle&id=5212.

— vs. Bart Ehrman. 'Is There Historical Evidence for the Resurrection of Jesus?' http://www.bringyou.to/apologetics/p96.htm.

Geisler, Norman L. 'Miracles and Modern Scientific Thought' http:// www.leaderu.com/truth/1truth19.html.

Hartwig, Mark. 'In Defense of the Supernatural' http://www.boundless. org/2005/articles/a0000039.cfm.

Instone-Brewer, David. 'Jesus and the Psychiatrists' http://www. tyndale.cam.ac.uk/Tyndale/staff/Instone-Brewer/JESUS%20- %20Psychaitrists%20UC.pdf.

Kreeft, Peter. 'The Argument from History' http://www.peterkreeft. com/topics/history.htm.

Lennox, John. 'The Question of Miracles: The Contemporary Influence of David Hume' http://www.bethinking.org/resource.php?ID=59.

Lindsley, Art. 'C.S. Lewis on Miracles' http://www.cslewisinstitute. org/pages/resources/publications/knowingDoing/2004/Miracles. pdf.

McGrew, Linda. 'Historical Inquiry: Epistemology, Miracles, and the God Who Speaks' http://www.lydiamcgrew.com/Wholepaper draft.pdf.

Morais, Daniel and Michael Gleghorn. 'Did Jesus Really Perform Miracles?' http://www.probe.org/site/c.fdKEIMNsEoG/b.4227257/ k.3E6C/Did_Jesus_Really_Perform_Miracles.htm.

Reppert, Victor. 'Hume on Miracles, Frequencies and Prior Probabilities' http://www.infidels.org/library/modern/victor_reppert/miracles. html.

Roberts, Michael Symmons. 'The Miracles of Jesus' http://www.bbc. co.uk/religion/religions/christianity/history/miraclesofjesus_ 1.shtml.

Saunders, Peter and Mark Pickering. 'Miracles' http://www.bethinking. org/resource.php?ID=172.

Wade, Rick. 'Miracles' http://www.leaderu.com/orgs/probe/docs/ miracles.html.

Williams, Peter S. 'The Impossible Planet and The Satin Pit' http://www. damaris.org/content/content.php?type=5&id=492.

— 'New Testament Criticism and Jesus the Exorcist' http://www. quodlibet.net/articles/williams-criticism.shtml.

Books

Adler, Mortimer J. *The Angels and Us* (London: Collier, 1982).

Barnett, Paul. *Messiah: Jesus – the Evidence of History* (Nottingham: IVP, 2009).

Beckwith, Francis J., ed. *To Everyone an Answer: A Case for the Christian Worldview* (Downers Grove, IL: IVP, 2004).

— 'Theism, Miracles, and the Modern Mind.' Pages 221–36 in *The Rationality of Theism* (ed. Paul Copan and Paul K. Moser; London: Routledge, 2003).

Boa, Kenneth D. and Robert M. Bowman Jr. *Sense and Nonsense about Angels and Demons* (Grand Rapids, MI: Zondervan, 2007).

Copan, Paul. *Loving Wisdom: Christian Philosophy of Religion* (St Louis, MO: Chalice Press, 2007).

Corduan, Winfried. *No Doubt about It: The Case for Christianity* (Nashville, TN: Broadman, Holman & Hunt, 1997).

Cover, J.A. 'Miracles and Christian Theism.' Pages 345–74 in *Reason for the Hope Within* (ed. Michael J. Murray; Grand Rapids, MI: Eerdmans, 1999).

Craig, William Lane. *Reasonable Faith: Christian Truth and Apologetics* (Wheaton, IL: Crossway, 3rd edn, 2008).

Davies, Brian. *An Introduction to the Philosophy of Religion* (Oxford University Press, 3rd edn, 2004).

Earman, John. *Hume's Abject Failure: The Argument against Miracles* (Oxford University Press, 2000).

Evans, Craig A. *Fabricating Jesus: How Modern Scholars Distort the Gospels* (Downers Grove, IL: IVP, 2006).

Foster, Charles. *The Christmas Mystery* (Milton Keynes: Authentic, 2007).

Geisler, Norman L. and Paul K. Hoffman, eds. *Why I Am a Christian* (Grand Rapids, MI: Baker, 2nd edn, 2006).

— and Frank Turek. *I Don't Have Enough Faith to Be an Atheist* (Wheaton, IL: Crossway, 2004).

Geivett, R. Douglas and Gary R. Habermas, eds. *In Defence of Miracles: A Comprehensive Case for God's Action in History* (Leicester: Apollos, 1997).

Humphreys, Colin J. *The Miracles of Exodus* (London: Continuum, 2003).

Huston, J. *Reported Miracles* (Cambridge University Press, 2007).

Kreeft, Peter. *Angels and Demons: What Do We Really Know about Them?* (San Francisco: Ignatius, 1995).

Lane, Anthony N.S., ed. *The Unseen World* (Carlisle: Paternoster, 1996).

Lennox, John C. *God's Undertaker: Has Science Buried God?* (Oxford: Lion, 2nd edn, 2009).

Lewis, C.S. *Miracles* (London: Fount, 1998).

Molnar, Michael R. *The Star of Bethlehem: The Legacy of the Magi* (Rutgers University Press, 2000).

Peck, M. Scott. *Glimpses of the Devil: A Psychiatrist's Personal Accounts of Possession, Exorcism, and Redemption* (New York: Free Press, 2005).

Redford, John. *Born of a Virgin: Proving the Miracle from the Gospels* (London: St Paul's, 2007).

Stanton, Graham. 'Message and Miracles.' Pages 56–71 in *The Cambridge Companion to Jesus* (ed. Markus Bockmuehl; Cambridge University Press, 2001).

Taylor, James E. *Introducing Christian Apologetics: Cultivating Christian Commitment* (Grand Rapids, MI: Baker Academic, 2006).

Twelftree, Graham. *Jesus the Miracle Worker: A Historical and Theological Study* (Leicester: IVP, 1999).

— *In the Name of Jesus: Exorcism among Early Christians* (Grand Rapids, MI: Baker, 2007).

Wiebe, Phillip H. *God and Other Spirits: Intimations of Transcendence in Christian Experience* (Oxford University Press, 2004).

Willard, Dallas. *Knowing Christ Today: Why We Can Trust Spiritual Knowledge* (New York: HarperOne, 2009).

Williams, Peter S. *The Case for Angels* (Carlisle: Paternoster, 2002).

Woolmer, John. *Healing and Deliverance* (Crowborough: Monarch, 1999).

5

The Third Way – Jesus' Resurrection

> And last of all he appeared to me also, as to one abnormally born. For I am the least of the apostles and do not even deserve to be called an apostle, because I persecuted the church of God.
>
> Paul (1 Corinthians 15:8–9)

David Winter observes that the Graeco-Roman world of the first century:

> was not an age of gullibility, but of cynicism and scepticism. The dominant school of Greek thought, Stoicism, rejected any idea of life beyond death. So did one of the two major Jewish schools of thought, the Sadducees. There was no shortage of eloquent and learned voices ready to do battle with any religion or philosophy that proposed as its central belief that a person came back from the dead.[1]

Even Jews who accepted the concept of resurrection (the Greek term is *anastasis*, literally meaning 'to stand up') thought in terms of a 'general resurrection' at the 'final judgement'. Yet it was against this background (and in the very city in which he had been publically executed and buried) that Jesus' disciples proclaimed *one man's resurrection within history* as the fulcrum at the heart of God's relationship with humanity.

The first Christians placed Jesus' resurrection 'at the centre of their characteristic praxis, narrative, symbol and belief; it was the basis of their recognition of Jesus as Messiah and Lord, their insistence that the creator god had inaugurated the long-awaited new age, and above all their hope for their own future bodily resurrection.'[2] It was in this hope that many of the disciples (and their disciples in turn) were martyred. As Lucian of Samosata wrote c. AD 165:

> The poor wretches have convinced themselves, first and foremost, that they are going to be immortal and live for all time, in consequence of which they despise death and even willingly give themselves into custody ... Furthermore, their first lawgiver persuaded them that they are all brothers of one another after they have transgressed once by denying the Greek gods and by worshipping the crucified sophist himself and living under his laws.[3]

Paul discourses upon *the resurrection body* in his first letter to the Corinthians (c. AD 54): 'The body that is sown is perishable, it is raised imperishable; it is sown in dishonor, it is raised in glory; it is sown in weakness, it is raised in power; it is sown a natural body, it is raised a spiritual body' (1 Corinthians 15:42–44; cf. Philippians 3:21). As Bart Ehrman observes: 'The resurrection claims are claims that not only [did] Jesus' body [come] back alive; it came back alive never to die again.'[4] Atheist John W. Loftus notes: 'What little Jesus himself said about the resurrection leads us to think both he and Paul shared the same view [of the resurrection body].'[5] On this view, the dead body laid in the earth is raised from the earth in *a metaphysically renovated but recognizably physical form*: 'from the start within early Christianity it was built in as part of the belief in resurrection that the new body, though it would certainly be a body in the sense of a physical object occupying space and time, will be a *transformed* body, a body whose material, created from the old material, will have new properties.'[6]

Paul's use of the terms 'natural' (*psychikon*, which literally means 'soulish') and 'spiritual' (*pneumatikon*) does *not* contrast physicality with non-physicality.[7] After all, both terms apply to the same 'body'. As William Lane Craig notes: 'Virtually every modern commentator agrees on this point: Paul is not talking about a rarefied body made out of spirit or ether; he means a body under the lordship and direction of God's Spirit ... The contrast is not between physical body/non-physical body, but between naturally oriented body/spiritually oriented body.'[8] Hence Paul writes that 'the natural person does not [welcome] the things of the Spirit of God, for they are folly to him, and he is not able to understand them because they are spiritually discerned. The spiritual person judges all things, but is himself to be judged by no one' (1 Corinthians 2:14–15 [ESV]).

While Paul believes that the non-physical souls of the Christian dead go to be 'with Christ' (Philippians 1:22–24),[9] he nevertheless looks forward to the end of earthly history wherein:

> We will not all sleep [i.e. die physically], but we will all be changed – in a flash, in the twinkling of an eye … the dead will be raised imperishable, and we [i.e. humans living then] will be changed. For the perishable [human body] must clothe itself with the imperishable, and the mortal [human body] with immortality. When the perishable has been clothed with the imperishable, and the mortal with immortality, then the saying that is written will come true: 'Death has been swallowed up in victory.' [Isaiah 25:8]
>
>   Where, O death, is your victory?
>   Where, O death, is your sting?' [Hosea 13:14]
>
> The sting of death is sin, and the power of sin is the law. But thanks be to God! He gives us the victory through our Lord Jesus Christ (1 Corinthians 15:51–53).

The 'spiritual body' is thus physical human nature *transformed by God so that it is no longer conditioned by sin, but fitted to life in a re-created 'spiritual' cosmos* (the 'new heavens and earth' – cf. 2 Peter 3:13; Revelation 21:1) of which Jesus' resurrection is our advanced sample: 'Christ has indeed been raised from the dead, the first-fruits of those who have fallen asleep' (1 Corinthians 15:20).[10] Hence, if Jesus was not resurrected, Christian spirituality is false. *Theism* could be true without *Christianity* being true; but there's no objective point in anyone being a *Christian* unless the belief that Jesus rose from the dead is true: 'if Christ has not been raised, our preaching is useless [fallacious] and so is your faith. More than that, we are then found to be false witnesses about God, for we have testified about God that he raised Christ from the dead …' (1 Corinthians 15:14–15). On the other hand, if Jesus has been resurrected, that clearly confirms his teaching (including his teaching about himself).

The Puzzle of Belief in Jesus' Resurrection

> Whatever transpired in Jerusalem on that 'first day', it was evidently so inexplicable and yet undeniable that it stretched inherited explanatory categories to breaking point – and ended up reconstituting the very centre of faith in the God of Israel.
>
> Markus Bockmuehl[11]

As Bart Erhman observes: 'Historians ... have no difficulty whatsoever speaking about the belief in Jesus' resurrection, since this is a matter of public record. For it is a historical fact that some of Jesus' followers came to believe that he had been raised from the dead soon after his execution.'[12] Francis Watson concurs that 'historical research can confirm that belief in Jesus' resurrection goes back to the earliest days of the Christian community.'[13] It is worth noting that 'the great majority of scholars believe that the passion narratives assumed a fairly fixed form early on rather than coming together at the tail end of the process ...'[14] German NT scholar Rudolph Pesch thinks that Mark's passion source goes back to at least AD 37. Wright argues that the lack of OT allusion, the lack of explicit connection to Christian eschatology and the inclusion of culturally embarrassing *female* witnesses who were sidelined by the early creedal material quoted by Paul in 1 Corinthians 15 all point to the gospel resurrection narratives being 'essentially very early, pre-Pauline ... The stories, though lightly edited and written down later, are basically very, very early.'[15]

The common structure and content of the disciples' testimony about Jesus' death and resurrection can be firmly established from the *multiple, independent* and *early* testimonies contained within: the pre-Pauline creed of 1 Corinthians 15:3–5, the pre-Marcan passion narrative of Mark 15:37 – 16:7; Peter's Pentecost sermon in Acts 2:22–32 and Paul's sermon in Acts 13:28–31. Concerning speeches in Acts, James D.G. Dunn comments that there are 'sufficient indications that Luke has sought out much earlier material and has incorporated it into the brief formalized expositions which he attributes to Peter, Stephen, Paul, etc.':

1 Corinthians 15:3–5 (Early creed, c. AD 35)	Mark 15:37 – 16:7 (Pre-Marcan passion narrative)	Acts 2:22–32 (Peter's Pentecost sermon)	Acts 13:28–31 (Paul's sermon in Pisidian Antioch)
Christ died...	Jesus breathed his last.	you ... put him to death by nailing him to the cross.	they asked Pilate to have him executed.
he was buried...	Joseph bought some linen cloth, took down the body, wrapped it in the linen, and placed it in a tomb...	David died and was buried, and his tomb is here to this day [Peter implies Jesus' empty tomb].	they took him down from the cross and laid him in a tomb.
he was raised...	He has risen!	God has raised this Jesus to life...	But God raised him from the dead...
he appeared...	He is going ahead of you into Galilee. There you will see him...	we are all witnesses of the fact...	for many days he was seen by those who had travelled with him from Galilee to Jerusalem.

Figure 17

The question is: *is this story true?* If it isn't true, it is either a deliberate deception or a profound delusion. Of course, some people think that first-century folk were easily duped or deluded into thinking that Jesus had risen from the dead. For example, atheist Walter Sinnott-Armstrong condescendingly states: 'Most people at the time were gullible ...'[16] However, both Jesus' Jewish disciples – including doubters and enemies who became followers after purported encounters with a post-mortem Jesus (e.g. James and Saul/Paul) – and first-century Greek converts (e.g. Apollos, Damaris, Dionysius) had *every expectation* that once Jesus was dead and buried he would stay put: 'contrary to the claims of some twentieth-century theologians (who make it sound as if first-century folk were almost pantingly eager to believe in resurrection and other miracles, and would do so at the drop of a hat), they were as convinced as we are that dead people stay dead. They were definitely not expecting to encounter Jesus.'[17]

However, 'It can hardly be doubted that proclamation of the resurrection of Jesus Christ was central to the earliest preaching of the Christian community ...'[18] For example:

Don't you know that all of us who were baptized into Christ Jesus were baptized into his death? We were therefore buried with him through baptism into death in order that, just as Christ was raised from the dead through the glory of the Father, we too may live a new life.

If we have been united with him in a death like his, we will certainly also be united with him in a resurrection like his (Romans 6:3–5, c. AD 55).

Praise be to the God and Father of our Lord Jesus Christ! In his great mercy he has given us new birth into a living hope through the resurrection of Jesus Christ from the dead, and into an inheritance that can never perish, spoil or fade. This inheritance is kept in heaven for you, who through faith are shielded by God's power until the coming of the salvation that is ready to be revealed in the last time (1 Peter 1:3–5, c. AD 63).

Belief in Jesus' resurrection was *the* catalytic, central component of the earliest Christian *kerygma* ('a Greek word meaning "the declaration" '[19]), something typified by the very first apostolic sermon, given by Peter just fifty days after Jesus' crucifixion:

People of Israel, listen to this: Jesus of Nazareth was a man accredited by God to you by miracles, wonders and signs, which God did among you through him, as you yourselves know. This man was handed over to you by God's deliberate plan and foreknowledge; and you, with the help of wicked men ['of those not having the law'], put him to death by nailing him to the cross. But God raised him from the dead, freeing him from the agony of death, because it was impossible for death to keep its hold on him. David said about him:

'I saw the Lord always before me.
   Because he is at my right hand,
   I will not be shaken.
Therefore my heart is glad and my tongue rejoices;
   my body also will rest in hope,
because you will not abandon me to the realm of the dead,
   you will not let your holy one see decay.

You have made known to me the paths of life;
    you will fill me with joy in your presence.' [Psalm 16:8–11]

Brothers and sisters, we all know that the patriarch David died and was buried, and his tomb is here to this day. But he was a prophet and knew that God had promised him on oath that he would place one of his descendants on his throne. Seeing what was to come, he spoke of the resurrection of the Messiah, that he was not abandoned to the realm of the dead, nor did his body see decay. God has raised this Jesus to life, and we are all witnesses of the fact (Acts 2:29–32).

Geza Vermes affirms that 'the ideas attributed to the beginnings of the Jesus movement in Jerusalem and Judea, chronicled in the Acts of the Apostles, have every probability of mirroring in substance the earliest thoughts of the first Jewish-Christian communities of Palestine',[20] and he encapsulates the historical conundrum posed by the sudden emergence, in this context, of the belief that Jesus had been resurrected from the dead:

> the idea of the resurrection of the dead was a latecomer in Jewish thought [and] it occupied only a small area of the broad religious canvas of late Second Temple Judaism. The New Testament completely altered the vista and changed the perspective. In it the individual resurrection of one Jew, Jesus of Nazareth, predominates. It is set in time and space and integrated into history … The situation is profoundly perplexing and the historian must come to grips with this puzzle.[21]

Just the Facts

N.T. Wright argues:

> The very strong historical probability is that, when Matthew, Luke, and John describe the risen Jesus, they are writing down very early oral tradition, representing three different ways in which the original astonished participants told the stories. These traditions have received only minimal development, and most of that

probably at the final editorial stage, for the very good reason that stories as earth-shattering as this, stories as community-forming as this, once told, are not easily modified. Too much depends upon them.[22]

Some will point to perceived discrepancies in the NT resurrection accounts with the aim of casting doubt upon their general historical reliability. On the one hand, in most cases it's possible to argue that these accounts are complementary rather than contradictory.[23] On the other hand, 'the presence of discrepancies in circumstantial detail is no proof that the central fact is unhistorical.'[24] The level of genuine discrepancy is well within the character of historically reliable oral tradition. As atheist John W. Loftus concedes: 'all the New Testament writers agree … that God raised Jesus from the dead. Should this unanimous agreement alone be enough of a reason to believe Jesus was resurrected from the dead? It is a reason, no doubt.'[25]

Besides, arguments for miracles such as the resurrection *needn't* assume that the NT accounts are even *generally* reliable. Instead, arguments can be grounded in data that passes one or more of the criteria of authenticity reviewed in Chapter 3, and which are therefore 'generally admitted by critical scholars who research this particular area.'[26] As Gary R. Habermas and Terry L. Miethe comment: 'Our arguments [for the resurrection are] based on a *limited number* of knowable historical facts and *verified by critical procedures*. Therefore, contemporary scholars should not spurn such evidence by referring to "discrepancies" in the New Testament texts or to its general "unreliability" … Jesus' resurrection appearances can be historically demonstrated *based only on a limited amount of critically recognized historical facts*.'[27]

Likewise, Craig reports: 'Wolfhart Pannenberg has opined that the Gospel accounts of Jesus' resurrection are so legendary that they have scarcely a historical kernel in them; yet he stunned German theology by arguing for the historicity of Jesus' post-mortem appearances and empty tomb and, hence, for his resurrection sheerly on historical grounds.'[28] Thus: 'Any historical argument for Jesus' resurrection will have two steps, even if these are not clearly delineated: (1) to establish the facts which will serve as historical evidence and (2) to argue that the hypothesis of Jesus' resurrection is the best or most probable explanation of those facts.'[29]

Whatever their personal viewpoint, 'Scholars agree that there is an irreducible historical core to the resurrection story that can't be explained away as pious legend or wholesale deceit.'[30] Habermas lists some of the *minimal facts* acknowledged by the relevant community of scholars:

> The vast majority of critical scholars allow for a surprisingly strong basis of known historical data surrounding the end of Jesus' life and the birth of the Christian church ... virtually all scholars, whatever their personal beliefs, espouse or at least concede that Jesus died by Roman crucifixion and that his disciples experienced grief and disillusionment at his death, usually allowing that Jesus' burial tomb was later found empty. Then, due to experiences that they believed were appearances of the risen Jesus, the disciples were transformed, even to the point of being willing to die for their faith. At a very early date they began to proclaim the death and resurrection of Jesus Christ, and the church was born shortly afterward, founded on this gospel message. Even a few former sceptics, such as James, the brother of Jesus, and Paul, became believers after they, too, believed that they had seen the risen Jesus.[31]

In addition to Jesus' death, the most crucially relevant data consists in the following:

> the tomb of Jesus was found empty by a group of his women followers on the first day of the week following his crucifixion, various individuals and groups thereafter experienced on different occasions and under varying circumstances appearances of Jesus alive, and the first disciples came sincerely to believe in Jesus' resurrection in the absence of sufficient antecedent historical influences from either Judaism or pagan religions.[32]

To solve the puzzle of the resurrection we must seek the best explanation for this data.

Fact 1: Jesus' death by crucifixion

As Charles Foster reports: 'The overwhelming conclusion of the mainstream literature, even that written by virulent opponents of Christianity, is that Jesus did indeed die on the cross.'[33] According to Habermas, 'Almost no scholar today questions Jesus' death by crucifixion.'[34] After all, multiple, independent Christian (e.g. all four gospels and various NT letters) and non-Christian sources confirm that Jesus was put to death under Pilate (e.g. Tacitus and Josephus), by crucifixion (e.g. Josephus and the Talmud).

Graham Stanton notes that 'traditions which would have been an embarrassment to followers of Jesus in the post-Easter period are unlikely to have been invented.'[35] The crucifixion would surely have been so embarrassing to Jesus' followers (who expected him to destroy the Romans in battle) that they wouldn't have made it up. As David Wenham notes,[36] as early as the first century there were cartoons in Pompeii mocking the idea of Jesus being crucified. Why would the disciples make up something that turned their leader into a laughing stock? As Professors Gerd Theissen and Annette Merz argue: 'The execution was offensive for any worship of Jesus. As a "scandal" it cannot have been invented.'[37] Furthermore, the abandonment of Jesus at the crucifixion by most of his disciples, as reported by his disciples, is embarrassing.

The NT accounts of Jesus' crucifixion mention people that the audience (especially of Mark's gospel) would have known and been able to check facts with. For example, the synoptic gospels all mention Simon of Cyrene, who is compelled to carry Jesus' crossbeam for a time (cf. Mark 15.21; Matthew 27:32; Luke 23:26). Simon's sons Alexander and Rufus were known within the early church and are mentioned by the pre-Marcan passion account as if to say: 'if you don't believe this, go and check with them' (cf. Mark 15:21; Romans 16:13). In 1941, Israeli archaeologist Eleazar Sukenik discovered a tomb in the Kidron valley in eastern Jerusalem. Pottery dated it to the first century AD. The tomb contained eleven ossuaries bearing twelve names in fifteen inscriptions. Some of the names were particularly common in Cyrenaica. An inscription on one of these ossuaries says: 'Alexandros (son of) Simon'. The lid of this ossuary bears an inscription with the name Alexandros in Greek, followed by the Hebrew QRNYT. The meaning of this isn't clear, but one possibility is that the person making the inscription meant to write *QRNYH* – the Hebrew for 'Cyrenian'. Writing in *Biblical Archaeology Review*, Tom Powers comments: 'When we consider how uncommon the name Alexander was, and note that the ossuary inscription lists him in the same relationship to Simon as the New Testament does and recall that the burial cave contains the remains of people from Cyrenaica, the chance that the Simon on the ossuary refers to the Simon of Cyrene mentioned in the Gospels seems very likely.'[38] Archaeology thus confirms the existence of sources woven into the pre-Marcan passion account.

After his flogging (which left victims with severe injuries), Jesus was hung on a cross:

> Once a person is hanging in the vertical position ... crucifixion is essentially an agonizingly slow death by asphyxiation. The reason is that the stresses on the muscles and diaphragm put the chest into the inhaled position; basically, in order to exhale, the individual must push up on his feet so the tension on the muscles would be eased for a moment. In doing so, the nail would tear through the foot, eventually locking up against the tarsal bones. After managing to exhale, the person would then be able to relax down and take another breath in. Again he'd have to push himself up to exhale, scraping his bloodied back against the coarse wood of the cross. This would go on and on until complete exhaustion would take over, and the person wouldn't be able to push up and breathe anymore. As the person slows down his breathing, he goes into what is called respiratory acidosis – the carbon dioxide in the blood is dissolved as carbonic acid, causing the acidity of the blood to increase. This eventually leads to an irregular heartbeat ... then ... cardiac arrest.[39]

In Jesus' case, death is confirmed by two facts. First, by the fact that the soldiers didn't bother to break his legs (victims' legs were broken to stop them being able to breathe), showing they were sure he was already dead. As Ronald H. Nash observes: 'the necessarily laboured breathing of anyone still alive could not be missed. Moreover, the collapsed state in which any crucified victim would hang while either unconscious or pretending to be dead would make breathing impossible.'[40] Roman law placed a death penalty 'on any soldier who let a capital prisoner escape in any way, including bungling a crucifixion. It was never done.'[41] Moreover, not just the highly motivated Roman soldiers, but 'the priests and His friends who buried Him would all look carefully to make certain that He was dead.'[42]

Second, Jesus' death is confirmed by the fact that a soldier stabbed Jesus through his lung and into his heart with a spear. John provides an eyewitness report of the fluid coming out of Jesus from this wound as 'blood and water' (John 19:34). Truman Davies MD argues that, although no first-century writer would have known the specific medical significance of this observation, it is 'conclusive post-mortem evidence that [Jesus] died ... of heart failure due to shock and constriction of the heart by fluid in the pericardium.'[43] John wouldn't have known this, and so can't have added this detail in a deceptive attempt to prove that Jesus was dead. Rather, this detail is best explained as a genuine eyewitness report that proves Jesus was dead before the soldier stabbed him. As an article in the *Journal of the American Medical Association* (21 March 1986) concluded:

> Clearly, the weight of historical and medical evidence indicates that Jesus was dead before the wound to his side was inflicted and supports the traditional view that the spear, thrust between his right rib, probably perforated not only the right lung but also the pericardium and heart and thereby ensured his death. Accordingly, interpretations based on the assumption that Jesus did not die on the cross appear to be at odds with modern medical knowledge.[44]

Fact 2: Jesus' burial

Like most NT scholars, Vermes acknowledges the burial of Jesus: 'The Bible orders that a person condemned to death by a court should be buried on the day of his execution before sunset [Deuteronomy 21:22–23], as happened to Jesus, too.'[45] Of course, Jesus' burial is indirect evidence for his death. John A.T. Robinson attests that the burial of Jesus is 'one of the earliest and best attested facts about Jesus.'[46] Gerd Ludemann argues that 'Jesus was obviously buried ... There is the tradition of the burial in Paul; it's a very old tradition, and it's likely to be historical.'[47] Klaus Berger observes that 'the reports about the empty tomb are related by all four Gospels (and other writings of early Christianity) in a form independent of one another …'[48] Craig notes that 'even the most skeptical scholars acknowledge that Joseph was probably the genuine, historical individual who buried Jesus, since it is unlikely that early Christian believers would invent an individual, give him a name and nearby town of origin, and place that fictional character on the historical council of the Sanhedrin, whose members were well known.'[49]

Raymond Brown acknowledges: 'a Christian fictional creation from nothing of a Jewish Sanhedrist who does what is right is almost inexplicable.'[50] Hence, as Wolfgang Trilling states: 'It appears unfounded to doubt the fact of Jesus' honorable burial.'[51]

Fact 3: Jesus' empty tomb

John Dickson reports that 'most experts accept that Jesus' tomb was empty within days of his burial.'[52] Of course, the only notable thing about the empty tomb is *that it was previously occupied*. Hence evidence for the empty tomb is also evidence that the tomb was previously occupied (and hence evidence that Jesus was dead).

According to Alister McGrath: 'the empty tomb … is such a major element in each of the four gospels … that it must be considered to have a basis in historical fact.'[53] The gospels provide independent attestation for the empty tomb. J.P. Moreland notes that 'the absence of explicit mention of the empty tomb in the speeches in Acts [the empty tomb is indirectly mentioned by Peter in his Pentecost sermon] is best explained by noting that the fact of the empty tomb was not in dispute and thus it was not at issue. The main debate was over why it was empty, not whether it was empty.'[54]

Wright observes that 'Jewish tombs, especially those of martyrs, were venerated and often became shrines. There is no sign whatever of that having happened with Jesus' grave.'[55] The lack of veneration at Jesus' tomb is understandable if there was no body there to venerate (it is the body and not the tomb which is the subject of veneration).

Moreover, if the tomb were not empty, the authorities (who would have had an interest in disproving this story) could and probably would have produced Jesus' body to quash the disciples' story:

> the resurrection was preached in Jerusalem just a few weeks after the crucifixion. If the tomb had not been empty, such preaching could not have occurred. The body of Jesus could have been produced, and since it is likely that the location of Joseph of Arimathea's tomb was well known (he was a respected member of the Sanhedrin), it would not have been difficult to find where Jesus was buried.[56]

The gospels report that women first discovered the empty tomb. A standard objection to the women being witnesses is that the gospels name different women on the scene. However, this is a secondary detail; all four gospels agree on the primary point that it was *some women* who discovered the empty tomb. Indeed, all four gospels mention Mary Magdalene by name and either indicate or at least allow for the presence of other women. The relevant reports are thus wholly compatible with one another.[57] The significant thing about the women's role in the story of the empty tomb is that women were considered so unreliable in first-century Jewish culture that their testimony was automatically suspect. For example, the *Mishnah* states that women are 'unsuitable to bear witness.'[58] As Vermes argues: 'The evidence furnished by female witnesses had no standing in a male-dominated Jewish society … If the empty tomb story had been manufactured by the primitive Church to demonstrate the reality of the resurrection of Jesus, one would have expected a uniform and foolproof account attributed to patently reliable witnesses.'[59]

If the gospel writers were to invent the story of an empty tomb, they would have placed men as witnesses instead of women, in order to add credibility to their story. As it stands, the discovery of the empty tomb by a group of women is a report that passes the criterion of embarrassment: 'the fact that it is women, rather than men, who are the chief witnesses to the empty tomb is best explained by the historical facticity of the narrative in this regard.'[60]

As Craig A. Evans reports:

the consensus of scholarship affirms the historicity of the empty tomb of Jesus. According to Jacob Kremer, 'By far most exegetes hold firmly to the reliability of the biblical statements concerning the empty tomb.' Thus it is today widely recognized that the empty tomb of Jesus is a simple historical fact. As New Testament critic D.H. Van Dallen points out, 'It is extremely difficult to object to the empty tomb on historical grounds; those who deny it do so on the basis of theological or philosophical assumptions.'[61]

Fact 4: Jesus' post-mortem appearances

Antony Flew admitted that 'there is apparently immensely strong evidence' for 'the resurrection appearances' of Jesus.[62] Many of the appearance reports pass the criteria of embarrassment, since they show founding members of the church as slow to believe (cf. Matthew 28:17; Luke 24:11; John 20:24–29). Embarrassingly (in its patriarchal context), the first resurrection appearance recorded by John's gospel is to Mary Magdalene (John 20:11–18; see also Mark 16:9–11). The resurrected Jesus likewise appears to women in Matthew 28:8–10. Moreover, the NT provides *multiple, independent* and *early* sources for Jesus' resurrection appearances:

> The appearance to Peter is independently attested by Paul and Luke [1 Corinthians 15:5; Luke 24:34], the appearance to the Twelve by Paul, Luke and John [1 Corinthians 15:5; Luke 24:36–43; John 20:19–20], the appearance to the women disciples by Matthew and John [Matthew 28:8–10; John 20:11–18], and appearances to the disciples in Galilee by Mark … and John [Mark 16:7; John 21].[63]

Indeed, multiple independent sources attest that after his death Jesus was not only *seen* alive (e.g. 1 Corinthians 15:3–8; Matthew 28:17; Luke 24:34; John 20:14, 18), but also *heard* (e.g. Matthew 28:9, 18–20; Luke 24:17–30, 36–49; John 20:15–17) and *touched* (Matthew 28:9; Luke 24:39; John 20:17, 27).

Craig notes that: 'Given its early date, as well as Paul's personal acquaintance with the people involved, the list of eyewitnesses to Jesus' resurrection appearances, quoted by Paul [in 1 Corinthians 15:3–8], guarantees that such appearances occurred.'[64] Jake O'Connell concurs that 'the pre-Pauline material of 1 Corinthians

15:3–8, which surely dates to within years of the resurrection, and is nearly universally regarded as summarising extremely early material, ensures that the appearances enumerated there cannot be legendary.'[65] Written c. AD 54, Paul's first letter to the Corinthian church refers to the testimony that he had 'received' (*paralambano*) as oral tradition before he had personally 'handed over' or 'delivered' (*paradidomi*) said tradition to the Corinthians in AD 51:

> For I delivered to you as of first importance what I also received, that
>
> *Christ died for our sins in accordance with the scriptures,*
> *that he was buried,*
> *that he was raised on the third day in accordance with the scriptures,*
> *and that he appeared to Cephas,*
> *then to the twelve.*
> *Then he appeared to more than five hundred brethren at one time*
> [most of whom are still alive, though some have fallen asleep].
> *Then he appeared to James,*
> *then to all the apostles.*
> Last of all, as to one untimely born, he appeared also to me (1 Corinthians 15:3–8 [RSV], my italics, layout and square brackets).

The italicized section of this passage, excepting Paul's editorial comment (which I have placed in square brackets), is the earliest known Christian creed. Theologian Robert L. Reymond explains:

> This assertion is based upon (1) Paul's references to his 'delivering' to the Corinthians what he had first 'received,' terms suggesting that we are dealing with a piece of 'tradition,' (2) the stylized parallelism of the 'delivered' material itself (see the four *hoti* clauses and the repeated *kata tas graphas* phrases in the first and third of them), (3) the Aramaic 'Cephas' for Peter, suggesting an earlier Palestinian mileu, not a later Greco-Roman mileu, for this tradition, (4) the traditional description of the disciples as 'the Twelve,' and (5) the omission of the appearances to the women from the list.[66]

James G. Crossley notes that '1 Corinthians 15:4 ("that he was buried, and that he was raised") refers to bodily resurrection in the strongest sense: Jesus was literally and bodily *raised* up from the dead.'[67] Habermas summarizes the generally accepted scholarly reconstruction of how Paul received this creed:

> Critical scholars take very seriously Paul's statement in Galatians 1:18–19 that he went up to Jerusalem just three years after his conversion, to meet with Peter and James the brother of Jesus. The immediate context concerns the gospel, which the New Testament defines repeatedly and clearly as including the resurrection. Just a few verses later, Paul tells us that he went back to Jerusalem fourteen years later, specifically to discuss the nature of the gospel [2:2]. The other apostles, Peter, James and John, agreed with his message and added nothing to it [2:6,9]. As Paul said several years later, he and the other apostles were preaching the same message with regards to Jesus' resurrection [1 Corinthians 15:11]. So the consensus among scholars is that Paul probably received the creedal material when he visited Jerusalem the first time [in AD 35]. At the very least, from an exceptionally early date, these four major disciples discussed the nature of the gospel message and agreed on the details. This is rarely questioned by critical scholars. But note carefully, this is when Paul received and confirmed the message. The other apostles who passed it on to him had it before he did, and the events themselves are earlier still. So we are essentially back to the exact time when it all happened, as critical scholars have noted.[68]

Whilst the gospel resurrection accounts reflect oral history that may pre-date even the original formulation of the 1 Corinthian creed, that oral history reaches us through later publications that involved an editorial process, however minimal. What Paul preserves for us in 1 Corinthians 15 is *an example of early oral history itself*. As Reymond concludes, the 1 Corinthians 15 creed 'reflects what those who were the earliest eye-witnesses to the events that had taken place in Jerusalem were teaching on Palestinian soil within days after the crucifixion … the material in 1 Corinthians 15:3b–5 is based on *early, Palestinian* eyewitness testimony …'[69] According to James D.G. Dunn, 'This tradition, we can be entirely confident, was formulated as tradition within months of Jesus' death.'[70] Jewish scholar Pinchas Lapide confirms that 1 Corinthians 15:3ff. 'may be considered as a statement of eyewitnesses ...'[71]

That many of the eyewitnesses listed in the 1 Corinthians creed (and Paul himself) died for belief in the resurrection confirms their certainty that it happened. If they were unsure, they would have admitted their doubts and been spared execution. None did. This shows the disciples were convinced:

> Consider James the brother of Jesus. Josephus ... tells us that he died a martyr's death for his faith in his brother. Yet the Gospels tell us that during Jesus' life, he was an unbeliever and opposed to Jesus. Why did he change? What could cause a Jew to believe that his own brother was the very Son of God and to be willing to die for such a belief? ... Only the appearance of Jesus to James (1 Cor. 15:7) can explain his transformation. As with James, so it is with the other disciples. One who denies the resurrection owes us an explanation of this transformation which does justice to the historical facts.[72]

Moreover, Paul claims that he is an eyewitness to the resurrected Jesus (cf. 1 Corinthians 9:1; 15:8; Galatians 1:13–17; Acts 9:1–30) – a claim given the stamp of sincerity by his martyrdom. As Flew observes:

> the evidence of Paul is certainly important and strong precisely because he was a convert. He was not a prior believer, and the evidence that he hadn't been previously a believer is about as clear as it could have been because he had been an active opponent. I think this has to be accepted as one of the most powerful bits of evidence that there is.[73]

Little wonder, then, that 'most New Testament critics are prepared to admit that the disciples did see appearances of Jesus ...'[74] Flew concedes: 'I believe they had some sort of experience.'[75] Reginald Fuller confirms that the disciples' experience of seeing Jesus after his death 'is a fact upon which both believer and unbeliever may agree.'[76] Vermes comments: 'No doubt the New Testament characters believed in the reality of their visions of Jesus.'[77] James G. Crossley affirms that 'certain people believed they saw Jesus ...'[78]

E.P. Sanders states: 'That Jesus' followers (and later Paul) had resurrection experiences is, in my judgment a fact. What the reality was that gave rise to the experiences I do not know.'[79]

Beyond Consensus

Summarizing the consensus of scholarship, based upon multiple lines of evidence (only some of which we have had the space to review), N.T. Wright affirms: 'Historical investigation ... brings us to the point where we must say that the tomb previously housing a thoroughly dead Jesus was empty and that His followers saw and met someone they were convinced was this same Jesus, bodily alive though in a new, transformed fashion ...'[80] The evidence establishes that Jesus died and that he was buried in a tomb (by Joseph of Arimathea), that his tomb was later found empty (a discovery first made by a group of women), and that both individuals and groups of people, including sceptics, subsequently had several experiences in which they sincerely believed they interacted with a very much alive (albeit transformed) Jesus. This series of events convinced numerous people (including sceptics), against the intellectual and social expectations of their culture, that Jesus was resurrected. So convinced were the first Christians of Jesus' resurrection that they were willing to make the ultimate sacrifice in defence of its proclamation.

From this point on, we leave behind any hope of a scholarly consensus, for the question of how best to explain the historical data inevitably intersects with philosophical issues about miracles. In the course of a debate on the resurrection of Jesus, Bart Ehrman commented: 'The reason [the resurrection is] rational and makes sense to Bill [Craig] is because he's a believer in God, and so, of course, God can act in the world. Why not? ... Well, that presupposes a belief in God.'[81] On the one hand, it's important to note Ehrman's admission that *belief in Jesus' resurrection makes sense if you already believe in God*. However, Ehrman's admission doesn't go far enough, because agnostics and non-dogmatic atheists must also admit the possibility of God acting miraculously in the world. As Habermas argues:

it is undeniable that everyone generally operates within his or her own concept of reality ... Having said this, however, the factual data are still equally crucial ... We do need to be informed by the data we receive. And sometimes this is precisely what happens – the evidence on a subject convinces us against our indecisiveness or even contrary to our former position.[82]

Argument by Elimination

The following explanations are put forward concerning Jesus' purported resurrection:

1) The primary explanation (given by those closest to the events) is that Jesus was resurrected.
2) The second explanation (the 'myth theory') is that the NT reports of the resurrection were written as myth and weren't meant literally.
3) The third explanation (the 'conspiracy theory') is that the disciples lied about Jesus being resurrected.
4) The fourth explanation (the 'swoon theory') is that the disciples were themselves deceived by Jesus, who had not died on the cross, but who only faked his death and later appeared to his followers pretending to be resurrected.
5) The fifth explanation (the 'delusion theory') is that the witnesses to Jesus' resurrection were sincerely deluded (e.g. by experiencing hallucinations).

(Note that the second, third and fourth theories get off to a bad start by denying one or more of the minimal facts established above.) As Kreeft and Tacelli write: 'All five possibilities are logically possible, and therefore must be fairly investigated – even [the resurrection] ... They are also the *only* possibilities, unless we include really far-out ideas that responsible historians have never taken seriously, such as that Jesus was really a Martian who came in a flying saucer.'[83]

They note: 'If we can refute all [the] other theories ... we will have proved the truth of the resurrection ...'[84] Let's consider the alternatives.

Alternative 1: myth

A once common objection to the resurrection was that the disciples were inspired by pagan myths of dying and rising gods: the resurrection was a story intended to be read as myth, a story of metaphorical but not historical import. The most obvious problem with this theory is that the NT claims concerning Jesus' resurrection simply don't read like myths. As C.S. Lewis argued (cf. Chapter 2), they read as historical claims about a specific event experienced by real people in space-time. Michael Green comments:

> The really special thing [about Jesus] was this: nobody had ever attributed divinity and a virgin birth, resurrection and ascension to a *historical person* whom lots of people knew. And certainly nobody claimed that the one and only God, the creator and judge of the whole earth, had embodied himself in Apollo, Hercules, Augustus, and the rest. Folk like Apollo were mythical figures ... As for the ruler cult, it was a convenient tool with which to bind together a religiously, culturally and politically disparate empire ... Augustus had temples erected to him as *divus Augustus* in the East (whilst being more circumspect in the Roman West), but of course neither he nor anybody else imagined that by so doing he laid claim to embody the Godhead ... Vespasian, dying in the seventies, quipped 'Alas, I fear I am becoming a god!' It is very difficult to see the Christian conviction about Jesus springing from such roots. But no better ones have been put forward. Analogies from the Hermetic literature, the Gnostic Redeemer myth to the Mandean literature are all post-Christian and therefore quite unable to account for the rise of the Christian belief; they may all also be influenced (two of them certainly are) by Christian beliefs.[85]

Craig argues:

> there is no causal connection between pagan myths and the disciples' belief in Jesus' resurrection. Jews were familiar with the seasonal deities (Ezek. 37:1–14) and found them abhorrent ... Grass does not exaggerate when he says that it would be 'completely unthinkable' that the original disciples would have sincerely come to believe that Jesus of Nazareth was risen from the dead because

they had heard of pagan myths about dying and rising seasonal gods.[86]

As Gerald O'Collins observes, the myth thesis 'runs against the present tide of main-line scholarship, which – now drawing on extensive data from the Dead Sea Scrolls, recent archaeological discoveries, and other sources – insists that Jesus and the first Christians must be interpreted primarily against a Jewish and not a Hellenistic background.'[87] Besides, Green notes that 'similarity would not prove borrowing (and the early Christians showed no sign of syncretism with the mystery religions) ...'[88] Moreover, Habermas reports: 'There is no clear and early evidence for a resurrection occurring in a mystery religion before the late second century AD.'[89] Craig L. Blomberg concludes: 'the evidence suggests that the Gnostic redeemer myth does not predate the writing of the gospels and that other alleged parallels are not that close or numerous.'[90]

The death and resurrection of Jesus is presented by multiple, independent and early sources as *an observed historical reality*. This historical claim is either true, or it is the product of deceiving or deceived minds. The one thing the resurrection cannot be is a myth. Little wonder, then, to find J.N.D. Anderson reporting that 'no critic today suggests that these stories are either lies or mere legends.'[91] Carl Braaten confirms that 'even the more sceptical historians agree that for primitive Christianity ... the resurrection of Jesus from the dead was a real event in history, the very foundation of faith, and not a mythical idea arising out of the creative imagination of believers.'[92] As atheist Kai Nielsen acknowledges: 'it wasn't a myth that the Christian community tried to purvey, rather they were recording what they actually believed happened.'[93]

Alternative 2: conspiracy

The conspiracy theory latches upon the *ad hoc* possibility that someone stole away the body of Jesus and that the disciples consequently *invented* the story of Jesus' resurrection.

Having considered the hypothesis that the disciples stole Jesus' body away from the tomb (admitted to be empty by all the interested parties), Vermes concludes that 'its value for the interpretation of the resurrection is next to nil.'[94] Alternatively, if it isn't the disciples, but rather Joseph and/or Nicodemus, and/ or the person in charge of the burial place (i.e. 'the gardener' of John 20:15), who are supposed to have emptied the tomb, then, as Vermes argues, 'the fact that the organizer(s) of the burial was/ were well known and could have easily been asked for and supplied an explanation, strongly mitigates against this theory.'[95] Richard Purtill eliminates the more obvious candidates:

> Early Christians claimed that the tomb of Christ was empty and that Christ had risen from the dead. The Roman and Jewish authorities did not refute this claim by producing the body, as they certainly would have done had *they* removed it from the tomb. The Apostles suffered persecution, hardship, and martyrdom to proclaim the message of Christ risen from the dead, which they surely would not have done if *they* had removed and hidden Christ's body.[96]

Perhaps even harder for the conspiracy theory to accommodate than the empty tomb is the disciples' proclamation of Jesus' resurrection. As William Paley asked:

> Would men in such circumstances pretend to have seen what they never saw; assert facts which they had not knowledge of, go about lying to teach virtue; and, though not only convinced of Christ's being an imposter, but having seen the success of his imposture in his crucifixion, yet persist in carrying on; and so persist, as to bring upon themselves, for nothing, and with full knowledge of the consequences, enmity and hatred, danger and death?[97]

After the crucifixion (indeed, mainly *before* the crucifixion) the disciples very sensibly, albeit embarrassingly in light of the story they would subsequently tell, *ran away*:

> In the everyday religious politics of the time, if the Messiah you followed died it was proof positive that you had backed the wrong man. The movement surrounding a failed Messiah was either wiped out or broke up as quickly as possible. Nobody wanted to voice support for Judas the Galilean when he and his rebel army ended up on crosses, and we have no reason to think that Peter,

James and John had any other hope after the death of Jesus than to distance themselves from him and disappear unnoticed. A hint of this attempt is preserved in the story of Peter's [embarrassing] denial, which all four Gospels relate.[98]

These are not the moves made by a group of men with a cunning plan.

The intellectual climate in which the disciples supposedly invented their story was against anyone even thinking of such an idea. In fact, in the absence of an actual resurrection, the disciples' religious views would have discredited the possibility of Jesus' resurrection (rather than, say, his assumption into heaven). Craig gives three reasons for this conclusion:

> 1) Their leader was dead, and Jewish Messianic expectations included no idea of a Messiah who, instead of triumphing over Israel's enemies, would be shamefully executed by them as a criminal. 2) According to Old Testament law, Jesus' execution exposed him as a heretic, a man literally accursed by God. 3) Jewish beliefs about the afterlife precluded anyone's rising from the dead to glory and immortality before the general resurrection of the dead at the end of the world.[99]

The story of Jesus' resurrection departs radically from contemporary Jewish and pagan thinking. Indeed, outside the occurrence of the event itself, it's hard to imagine why *any* first-century Jew would have proclaimed, whether sincerely or insincerely, Jesus' resurrection.

Calculated deception would likely produce unanimity among the conspiratorial sources. Instead we get independent reports from different viewpoints that contain a host of variation in matters of secondary detail. This pattern of data is generally seen as indicating historical reliability.

One must take into account the fact that 'the testimony on behalf of Christ's Resurrection held firm under the most extraordinary affliction.'[100] If nothing else, *martyrdom assures sincerity*:

> no one, weak or strong … Christian or heretic, ever confessed, freely or under pressure, bribe or even torture, that the whole story

of the resurrection was a fake, a lie, a deliberate deception. Even when people broke under torture, denied Christ and worshiped Caesar, they never let that cat out of the bag, never revealed that the resurrection was their conspiracy. For that cat was never in that bag. No Christians believed the resurrection was a conspiracy; if they had, they wouldn't have become Christians.[101]

Any conspiracy theory for the origin of Christian belief is morally and psychologically implausible given what we know about the disciples, and especially given what we know about Jesus' antago-nistic brother James and the Christian-persecuting Saul, who were converted by their experiences of Jesus after his death. As Flew admits: 'virtually all the major people are people who are above suspicion of deliberate distortion ... I believe they had some sort of experience.'[102] In short, the principle witnesses to the resur-rection are, to borrow a phrase from Hume 'of such undoubted integrity, as to place them beyond all suspicion of any design to deceive others ...'[103]

Craig observes: 'this explanation has been completely given up by modern scholarship ... No scholar would defend the Conspiracy Hypothesis today. The only place you read about such things is in the popular, sensationalist press or in former propaganda from behind the iron curtain.'[104]

Alternative 3: 'swoon'

The 'swoon' theory holds, contrary to our first minimal fact, that Jesus didn't die on the cross, but either fell unconscious or somehow faked his death. Then (despite having been flogged, crucified and speared in the side), he *revived* in the tomb, removed his shroud,[105] rolled away the tombstone, evaded the guard,[106] appeared to his disciples, deceiving them into thinking (against their expectations) that he'd been *resurrected*, leaving them to spread this delusion in his name without him, before finally dying elsewhere.

Lee Strobel notes: 'The idea that Jesus never really died on the cross can be found in the Koran, which was written in the seventh century – in fact, Ahmadiya Muslims contend that Jesus actually fled to India. To this day there's a shrine that supposedly marks his real burial place in Srinagar, Kashmir.'[107] But as Foster reports,

such claims 'have been laughed out of court by serious scholars.'[108] If Jesus avoided death on the cross 'he abandoned all those
who loved and trusted him, leaving them to their own fate, and
crept away out of Palestine with his tail between his legs …'[109]
The 'swoon' theory is contradicted by our evidence about Jesus'
character.

Even if Jesus survived crucifixion and being entombed – and he
managed to get out of the tomb (despite the guard) – how did he
convince his disciples that he was the resurrected Lord? As liberal
theologian David Strauss wrote:

> It is impossible that a being who had stolen half-dead out of the
> sepulchre, who crept about weak and ill, wanting medical treat-
> ment, who required bandaging, strengthening and indulgence, and
> who was still at last yielding to his sufferings, could have given the
> disciples the impression that he was a Conqueror over death and
> the grave, the Prince of life, an impression which lay at the bottom
> of their future ministry.[110]

In the end, the swoon theory requires either a conspiracy theory
or a delusion theory: 'for the disciples testified that Jesus did not
swoon, but really died and really rose.'[111]

Alternative 4: delusion

The most plausible and popular delusion hypothesis is the suggestion that the disciples suffered from a series of individual and
collective hallucinations that convinced them Jesus had been
raised from the dead.

Hallucinations are unusual occurrences, collective hallucinations even more so. Yet those who witnessed the resurrected
Jesus included *several* individuals as well as several large *groups* of
people (such as the eleven disciples gathered in the upper room).
Indeed, Paul reports that Jesus appeared to more than 500 people
at once (1 Corinthians 15:6), noting that while some had died,
some still lived. In effect Paul said: 'If you don't believe me, go
and ask them yourselves.' However, 'Given the rarity of hallucinations, the odds that everyone in a large group of people would
be in the proper frame of mind for a hallucination is certainly

low.'[112] (About 15 per cent of people *on average* experience one or more hallucinations in their lives, but with men less likely to experience them than women and young people less likely than old people.[113]) A coherently co-ordinated series of individual and collective hallucinations, such as would be necessary to cover the data concerning Jesus' apparent resurrection appearances, is extremely unlikely. As Craig notes: 'it is unlikely that hallucinations could be experienced by so many various people under so many varied circumstances. The suggestion that there was a chain reaction of hallucinations among believers in Jesus does not alleviate the difficulty because neither James nor Paul stood in the chain.'[114]

The resurrection appearances of Jesus contradict the known nature of subjective psychological experiences: 'The problem with this theory is that, in the case of the Resurrection appearances, everything we know about hallucinations is violated.'[115] Hallucinations usually last seconds or minutes. Jesus was present for long stretches of time. Hallucinations usually happen only once, except to the insane. Jesus returned to the disciples many times, but they weren't insane (John 20:19; Acts 1:3). Hallucinations don't consume food. Jesus ate on at least two separate and independently reported occasions (Luke 24:42–43; John 21:1–14). Hallucinations don't hold extended, profound conversations with people. Jesus did (e.g. Acts 1:3). Hallucinations come from within and draw upon what we already know, so are unlikely to do surprising or unexpected things, but the resurrected Jesus did: 'hallucinations cannot exceed the content of a person's mind. But … the resurrection of Jesus involved ideas utterly foreign to the disciples' minds.'[116]

C.S. Lewis makes a very telling point when he argues that 'any theory of hallucination breaks down on the fact … that on three separate occasions this hallucination was not immediately recognized as Jesus [Luke 24:13–31; John 20:15; 21:4].'[117] Why would the disciples hallucinate a Jesus they didn't recognize? This data is explicable if we attribute it to the resurrected nature of Jesus' body. Another point about expectations is made by Jake O'Connell:

> Hallucinations must accord with the hallucinator's (or hallucinators') expectations and … many of those at the resurrection appearances would have expected Jesus to make a glorious

appearance [cf. Daniel 12:2; Mark 12:25; 2 Baruch; 1 Enoch; Testament of Job 40:3] ... but the Gospels present us with purely non-glorious appearances ... the evidence indicates that if stories of glorious appearances ever existed they would have been preserved by the tradition, and the absence of glorious appearances from the Gospel narratives is therefore indicative of the absence of any stories of glorious appearances at any point between AD 30 and 70. Since stories of glorious appearances should have been preserved if the resurrection appearances were hallucinatory, their absence from the Gospel narratives serves as a strong argument against the hallucinatory nature of the appearances.[118]

Indeed, the need for multiple collective hallucinatory episodes puts an intolerable strain on the delusion hypothesis. In documented cases of collective hallucination 'expectation is a necessary prerequisite for these occurrences',[119] but the evidence indicates that the disciples weren't expecting the resurrection. In documented cases of collective hallucination 'not all present see the vision',[120] but the evidence suggests that everyone present saw the resurrected Jesus. In documented cases of collective hallucination 'those who do see the vision see it differently',[121] but in the case of the resurrection appearances, everyone apparently saw the same thing (e.g. neither disciple on the road to Emmaus recognized Jesus; all the disciples saw Jesus cooking fish for breakfast, and ascending to heaven). Perhaps most damningly:

> a group conversation would be impossible if the vision was a hallucination ... while expectation seems theoretically capable of accounting for collective visual hallucinations, it would not be able to give rise to a collective hallucinatory conversation. This is because, while a group of people could go expecting to see Mary, or even go expecting to hear a short statement from Mary ... they could not possibly go with an entire conversation planned out in their mind.[122]

The resurrection narratives present us with multiple conversations between Jesus and the disciples (e.g. Luke 24:13–35; John 20:10–18, 24–29; John 21:15–24; Acts 1:3–9; Acts 9:1–9). Hence, O'Connell argues:

if the hallucination hypothesis is correct [the] group appearances ... 1) would have been expected; 2) would probably have involved some external signs of extreme stress (e.g. fainting); would have involved Jesus being seen only by some members of the group; 4) would have involved Jesus being seen differently by those who did see him; 5) would not have involved Jesus conducting group conversations.[123]

O'Connell concludes that 'the [resurrection] narratives are inconsistent with collective hallucinations ...'[124]

Moreover, the hallucination theory fails to provide an adequate explanation for the disciples' belief in Jesus' *resurrection*: 'Normally, visions of deceased people have not been thought to imply physical resurrections resulting in empty tombs; rather, they have been thought to consist of ghostly apparitions. So it is hard to accept [the] thesis that reports concerning the emptiness of Jesus' tomb were made up because subjective visions of the post-mortem Jesus were thought to imply his physical resurrection.'[125]

As Wright argues, any hypothesis proposed to explain the relevant historical data must grapple with the fact that:

> the disciples really did encounter [Jesus after his death] in ways which convinced them that he was not simply a ghost or hallucination ... If the disciples had simply seen, or thought they had seen, someone they took to be Jesus, that would not by itself have generated the stories we have. Everyone in the ancient world took it for granted that people sometimes had strange experiences involving encounters with the dead, particularly the recently dead. They knew at least as much as we do about such visions, about ghosts and dreams – and the fact that such things often occurred within the context of bereavement or grief. They had language for this, and it wasn't 'resurrection'. However many such visions they had had, they wouldn't have said Jesus was raised from the dead; they weren't expecting such a resurrection.[126]

James D.G. Dunn likewise stresses the need to convincingly account for:

the first disciples' interpretation of their experience. For them to have understood that they were seeing the crucified Jesus *as risen from the dead* rather than as (simply!) translated or glorified was quite extraordinary. That it led them to the conclusion that God had raised Jesus from the dead, that Jesus had been raised as the beginning of the end-time general resurrection of the dead, was exceptional and unprecedented. That is why I am [confident] that this first Christian interpretation deserves a very high respect, and that Christians, on its basis, need have no qualms about affirming their faith in Jesus as risen.[127]

Far from being in a state of mind that expected Jesus' death and resurrection, and which might therefore be susceptible to hallucinations, Vermes points out that 'the cross and the resurrection were unexpected, perplexing, indeed incomprehensible for the apostles ... As for the resurrection, no one was awaiting it, nor were the apostles willing to believe the good news brought to them by the women who had visited the tomb of Jesus.'[128] It is *doubly embarrassing* that the disciples a) failed to believe the good news brought to them b) by the initial female witnesses.

Finally, as Kreeft and Tacelli note: 'The apostles could not have believed in the "hallucination" if Jesus' corpse had still been in the tomb ... for if it was a hallucination, where was the corpse? They would have checked for it [cf. Luke 24:12; John 20:3–9]; if it was there, they could not have believed.'[129] Hence agnostic Antony O'Hear acknowledges that 'the standard rationalistic explanations in terms of auto-suggestion seem altogether too glib ...'[130]

In sum, if the resurrection appearances were hallucinations of some kind, they were hallucinations *of a miraculous kind* that were then misinterpreted by Jesus' own disciples in a manner radically at odds with their prior religious beliefs; a hypothesis that fails to account for the empty tomb. Indeed, the fact of the empty tomb means that the 'delusion' theory ultimately depends upon the 'swoon' or 'conspiracy' theories, and is therefore worse off than either: 'A hallucination would explain [at most] only the post-resurrection appearances; it would not explain the empty tomb, the rolled-away stone, or the inability [of the antagonistic authorities] to produce the corpse.'[131]

Last Hypothesis Standing

> That he arose is the only plausible explanation for what happened after his death and what still exists today as a consequence.
>
> Dallas Willard[132]

The only remaining hypothesis is that Jesus was resurrected: 'Modern scholarship recognizes no plausible explanatory alternative to the resurrection of Jesus. Those who refuse to accept the resurrection as a fact of history are simply self-confessedly left without an explanation.'[133] As Stephen T. Davis writes: 'no one who denies that Jesus was raised from the dead or who offers reductive theories of the resurrection has yet been able to account adequately for these widely accepted facts.'[134] For example, Flew admits: 'I don't think it's possible to offer any satisfactory naturalistic account of what happened.'[135] Having decided to reject all miracle claims, philosopher Charles Hartshorne comments: 'it is remarkable that a crucified man should have been the source of so vast a company of believers. I cannot explain this convincingly.'[136] The failure of arguments against the occurrence and rational acceptability of miracles means that resurrection is *the only adequate explanation*.

Argument to the Best Explanation

> The one interpretation which best accounts for all the data ... is that Jesus' bodily resurrection from the dead was a real objective event.
>
> F.F. Bruce[137]

The argument for Jesus' resurrection needn't be framed in terms of an argument by the elimination of alternatives. It can also be viewed in terms of an argument to the best explanation. William Lane Craig asks us to:

> [consider] six tests which historians use in determining what is the best explanation for given historical facts. The hypothesis 'God raised Jesus from the dead' passes all these tests:

1. It has great *explanatory scope*: it explains why the tomb was found empty, why the disciples saw post-mortem appearances of Jesus, and why the Christian faith came into being.

2. It has great *explanatory power*: it explains why the body of Jesus was gone, why people repeatedly saw Jesus alive despite his earlier public execution, and so forth.

3. It is *plausible*: given the historical context of Jesus' own unparalleled life and claims, the resurrection serves as divine confirmation of those radical claims.

4. It is *not ad hoc* or *contrived*: it requires only one additional hypothesis: that God exists. And even that needn't be an additional hypothesis if one already believes that God exists.

5. It is *in accord with accepted beliefs*. The hypothesis: 'God raised Jesus from the dead' doesn't in any way conflict with the accepted belief that people don't rise *naturally* from the dead …

6. It *far outstrips any of its rival hypotheses in meeting conditions (1)–(5)*.[138]

As Wright argues:

Historical investigation … brings us to the point where we must say that the tomb previously housing a thoroughly dead Jesus was empty and that His followers saw and met someone they were convinced was this same Jesus, bodily alive though in a new, transformed fashion … the historian may and must say that all other explanations for why Christianity arose and took the shape it did are far less convincing as historical explanations than the one the early Christians themselves offer: that Jesus really did rise from the dead … the sort of reasoning historians characteristically employ – inference to the best explanations, tested rigorously in terms of the explanatory power of the hypothesis thus generated – points strongly toward the bodily resurrection of Jesus.[139]

Revivification or Resurrection?

The evidence for the proposition that 'after his death on the cross Jesus was physically alive again' is stronger than it is for the proposition that his renewed physical form had the nature of what Paul called the 'spiritual body'. Of course, the first proposition still constitutes a miracle. Moreover, the second proposition *is* evidentially supported. For one thing, it explains why Jesus' disciples came to believe in his *resurrection* and not merely in his *revivification*, and why they made Jesus' *resurrection* the foundation of their eschatology (their theology of the future). For another, it provides a unifying explanation for the facts (attested by independent sources) that a) several people who knew Jesus failed to recognize him for a while when they met him after his death (Luke 24:13–35; John 20:14; 21:12), and b) Jesus suddenly appeared to multiple witnesses inside a locked room (Luke 24:36–43; John 20:19, 26). The best explanation of the evidence is that Jesus not only came back to life after his death, but that he was *resurrected*.

Ascension

The 'ascension' of Jesus designates the event, narrated in Luke-Acts (Luke 24:50–53; Acts 1:1–11) and referred to or implied frequently elsewhere in the NT, wherein Jesus miraculously indicated to the disciples that they would no longer meet him in the resurrected flesh. As an atheist friend of mine once asked: 'Am I expected to believe that Jesus' disciples saw him floating like a red balloon, up, up, up and finally disappearing?' Well, why not? Wright observes:

> If Jesus really was alive again in (what we would call) a physical body of some sort ... and if after a short while this physical body ceased to be present (without the body being in a tomb anywhere), then some kind of explanation for the new state of affairs is called for. The real problem ... is not so much the ascension itself, but the idea of a body which is both physical (in the sense that the tomb was empty after it had gone) and 'transphysical' (in the sense that it can appear and disappear, is not always immediately recognized, and so on).[140]

The resurrection makes sense of the ascension. As Stephen T. Davis comments:

Philosophers and scientists alike, quite apart from theology, have discussed models that involve passing from one space-time manifold to another, and such a concept seems to be coherent ... Although I accept Luke's account of the ascension of Jesus as trustworthy, I see the event primarily as a symbolic act performed for the sake of the disciples. By means of it, God showed them that Jesus was henceforth to be apart from them in space and time ... The ascension of Jesus was primarily a change of state rather than a change of location, but it was visibly symbolized for the disciples by a change of location.[141]

Conclusion

The historical evidence is quite strong enough, given the background evidence, to make it considerably more probable than not that Jesus Christ rose from the dead on the first Easter Day.

Richard Swinburne[142]

With theologian Clark H. Pinnock I affirm that 'the historical evidence for the resurrection of Jesus, so long as it is not ruled out from the start as inherently impossible, is impressive and solid.'[143] Of course, as philosopher R. Douglas Geivett explains, 'events are made more or less likely not only by circumstantial evidence susceptible of historical analysis but also by metaphysical possibilities that fall outside of the special province of historical investigation.'[144] Despite the evidence for the resurrection, some atheists may hold, on *a priori* grounds, that *whatever happened that first Easter day* (and they might be agnostic about the answer to the question 'What happened?') *it wasn't a miracle*. However, to seek refuge in *a priori* dogma like this is to concede that, *in the absence of a principled, counterbalancing philosophical anchor*, the evidence points to Jesus' miraculous resurrection from the dead in vindication of his radical teaching and personal claims. As David Baggett concludes: 'Both the failure of the naturalistic explanations and the positive reasons to believe in the resurrection render belief in the historicity of the resurrection altogether rational ...'[145] – at least, that is, for anyone whose *a priori* resistance is insufficient to the task of principled disagreement. But of course, we have already seen (cf. Chapter 4) that, granted even the mere possibility of God's existence, the philosophical case against the possibility and believability of miracles is insubstantial.

Against the background of the philosophical cases against naturalism and for theism, and in the context of the cumulative case presented thus far, readers will have to make their own minds up about the standing of their own *a priori* resistance to miracles in the face of the evidence for the resurrection. However, it seems to me that, if one grants that miracles are both possible and knowable, the simplest and most – indeed the only – adequate explanation of the minimal facts established by standard historical criteria is the one given by the eyewitnesses: God raised Jesus from the dead. As Michael R. Licona writes: 'no plausible alternative theories exist that can explain the known historical facts of Jesus' death by crucifixion, the empty tomb, and the beliefs of a number of Jesus' friends and foes that He had been resurrected and had appeared to them. These three facts are pieces of a puzzle that, no matter how you arrange them, only look like the resurrection of Jesus.'[146]

Moreover, as Craig comments: 'The resurrection of Jesus is significant not just because anyone or someone rose from the dead, but because Jesus of Nazareth, who claimed to be the absolute revelation from God, rose from the dead.'[147]

Recommended Resources

Video

Collins, Robin. 'A New Heaven and A New Earth' http://www.closer totruth.com/video-profile/A-New-Heaven-A-New-Earth-Robin-Collins-/720.

Craig, William Lane vs. Richard Carrier, 'Did Jesus Rise from the Dead? Part One' http://www.rfmedia.org/av/video/craig-vs-carrier-did-jesus-rise-from-the-dead-1/and Part Two http://www.rfmedia.org/av/video/craig-vs-carrier-did-jesus-rise-from-the-dead-2/.

Dickson, John. 'The New Atheists Challenge the Crucifixion' http://www.publicchristianity.com/crucifixionvid.html.

Habermas, Gary R. – Debates and Lectures http://www.garyhabermas.com/video/video.htm.

— 'The Resurrection Argument That Changed a Generation of Scholars' http://www.veritas.org/Media.aspx#/v/305.

— *Tools for Talks* Video Clips http://www.youtube.com/user/tools fortalks#p/u/0/v7PMHdQtJlc.

Jesus: Man, Messiah, or More? 'The Resurrection of Jesus' http://www. dod.org/Products/DOD2128.aspx.

Licona, Mike vs. Bart Ehrman, 'Can Historians Prove that Jesus Rose from the Dead?' http://www.4truth.net/debate/.

Moreland, J.P. 'The Search for the Historical Jesus', Parts 1–7 http:// www.youtube.com/watch?v=HA2d5jOpsH0&feature=PlayList&p= 5C3ED050A38A301B&index=0.

Williams, Peter S. 'Did Jesus Rise from the Dead?' http://www.damaris. org/cm/podcasts/135 and http://www.idpluspeterswilliams. blogspot.com/2008/10/blog-post.html.

Wright, N.T. *Resurrection: Did It Happen? What Could It Mean?* (Blakeway-IVP-Channel 4, 2004).

Audio

Craig, William Lane. 'Contemporary Scholarship and the Resurrection of Jesus' http://www.bethinking.org/bible-jesus/contemporary-scholarship-and-the-resurrection-of.htm.

— 'The Evidence for Christianity' http://www.bethinking.org/bible-jesus/the-evidence-for-christianity-reasonable-faith.htm.

— 'The Historicity of the Resurrection of Jesus' http://www.rfmedia. org/RF_audio_video/Other_clips/William_Lane_Craig-Evidence_ for_resurrection-2004-06-08-Liszt-1030.mp3.

— vs. Hector Avalos. 'The Resurrection: Fact or Fiction?' http://www. bringyou.to/CraigAvalosResurrectionDebate.mp3.

— vs. John Dominic Crossan. 'Will the Real Jesus Please Stand Up?' http://www.bringyou.to/CraigCrossanDebate.mp3.

— vs. Gerd Ludemann. 'Jesus' Resurrection: Fact or Figment?' http:// www.bringyou.to/CraigLudemannResurrectionDebate.mp3.

Habermas, Gary R. 'Interview: The Case for the Resurrection of Jesus' http://imagesaes.316networks.com/namb/Habermas_interview_ on_the_Resurrection.mp3.

— 'Interview on the Resurrection' http://www.thethingsthatmatter most.org/Sound/05-28-06.mp3.

— 'The Minimal Facts Approach' http://www.garyhabermas.com/audio/habermas_minimal_facts_approach.mp3.

Komoszewski, Ed, James Sawyer and Daniel B. Wallace. 'Reinventing Jesus' http://www.reclaimingthemind.org/content/files/CWS/reinventingJesus.mp3.

Moreland, J.P. 'How Do We Know Christianity Is Right out of All the Religions?' http://www.bethinking.org/bible-jesus/how-do-we-know-christianity-is-right-out-of-all.htm.

Swinburne, Richard. 'Historical Evidence for the Resurrection' http://www.blackhawkmedia.org/MP3/Swinburne3.mp3.

Williams, Peter S. 'The Resurrection Puzzle: Putting the Pieces Together' http://www.damaris.org/cm/podcasts/317.

Websites

Bethinking – 'Resurrection and Miracles' http://www.bethinking.org/categories.php?CategoryID=5.

Christian CADRE – The Resurrection http://www.christiancadre.org/topics/resurrection.html.

William Lane Craig http://www.reasonablefaith.org.

Gary R. Habermas http://www.garyhabermas.com.

Shroud Story http://www.shroudstory.com.

The Shroud of Turin Education Project http://www.shroud2000.com.

Shroud of Turin Website http://www.shroud.com/menu.htm.

Lee Strobel http://www.leestrobel.com.

Online papers

Brown, John L. 'Microscopial Investigation of Selected Raes Threads from the Shroud of Turin' http://www.shroud.com/pdfs/brown1.pdf.

Craig, William Lane. 'Contemporary Scholarship and the Historical Evidence for the Resurrection of Jesus' http://www.reasonablefaith.org/site/News2?page=NewsArticle&id=5214.

— 'Dale Allison on Jesus' Empty Tomb, His Post-Mortem Appearances, and the Origin of the Disciples' Belief in His Resurrection' http://www.reasonablefaith.org/site/News2?page=NewsArticle&id=6887.

— '*Noli Me Tangere*: Why John Meier Won't Touch the Risen Lord' http://www.reasonablefaith.org/site/News2?page=NewsArticle&id=7367.

— vs. Bart Ehrman. 'Is There Historical Evidence for the Resurrection of Jesus?' http://www.holycross.edu/departments/crec/website/resurrection-debate-transcript.pdf.

Edwards, William D. et al. 'On the Physical Death of Jesus Christ' http://www.godandscience.org/apologetics/deathjesus.pdf.

Habermas, Gary R. 'Historical Epistemology, Jesus' Resurrection and the Shroud of Turin' http://www.shroud.com/pdfs/habermas.pdf.

— 'Jesus' Resurrection and Contemporary Criticism: An Apologetic (Part I)' http://www.faculty.gordon.edu/hu/bi/Ted_Hildebrandt/NTe Sources/NTArticles/CTR-NT/Habermas-Resurrection1-CTR.pdf.

— 'Jesus' Resurrection and Contemporary Criticism: An Apologetic (Part II)' http://www.faculty.gordon.edu/hu/bi/Ted_Hildebrandt/NTe Sources/NTArticles/CTR-NT/Habermas-Resurrection2-CTR.pdf.

— 'The Shroud of Turin and its Significance for Biblical Studies', *Journal of the Evangelical Theological Society* 24:1 (1981) http://www.gary habermas.com/articles/J_Evangelical_Theological_Soc/habermas_ shroud_turin_significance_1981.htm.

— 'The Shroud of Turin: A Rejoinder to Basinger and Basinger', *Journal of the Evangelical Theological Society* 25:2 (1982) http://www.garyhabermas. com/articles/J_Evangelical_Theological_Soc/habermas_JETS_ Shroud_Rejoinder_Basinger.htm.

Kreeft, Peter and Ronald Tacelli. 'Evidence for the Resurrection of Christ' http://www.hometown.aol.com/philvaz/articles/num9.htm.

McGrew, Timothy and Linda McGrew. 'The Argument from Miracles: A Cumulative Case for the Resurrection of Jesus of Nazareth' http://www.lydiamcgrew.com/Resurrectionarticlesinglefile.pdf.

Rogers, Raymond N. 'Studies on the Radiocarbon Sample from the Shroud of Turin', *Thermochimica Acta* 425, pp. 189–94 http://www.shroud.it/ROGERS-3.PDF.

Williams, Peter S. 'The Shroud of Turin: A Cumulative Case for Authenticity' http://www.case.edu.au/uploads/media/The_20Shroud_20of _20Turin.pdf.

Wright, N.T. 'Jesus' Resurrection and Christian Origins' http://www. ntwrightpage.com/Wright_Jesus_Resurrection.htm.

Books

Ankerberg, John F., ed. *Resurrected? An Atheist and Theist Dialogue* (Oxford: Rowman & Littlefield, 2005).

Baggett, David, ed. *Did the Resurrection Happen? A Conversation with Gary Habermas and Antony Flew* (Downers Grove, IL: IVP, 2009).

Beckwith, Francis J., ed. *To Everyone an Answer: A Case for the Christian Worldview* (Downers Grove, IL: IVP, 2004).

Blomberg, Craig L. *The Historical Reliability of the Gospels* (Leicester: Apollos, 2nd edn, 2007).

Bock, Darrell L. and Daniel B. Wallace. *Dethroning Jesus: Exposing Popular Culture's Quest to Unseat the Biblical Christ* (Nashville, TN: Thomas Nelson, 2007).

Clifford, Ross. *The Case for the Empty Tomb: Leading Lawyers Look at the Resurrection* (Oxford: Albatross Books, 1991).

Cooper, John W. *Body, Soul and Life Everlasting: Biblical Anthropology and the Monism–Dualism Debate* (Leicester; Apollos, 1989).

Copan, Paul, ed. *Will the Real Jesus Please Stand Up? A Debate between William Lane Craig and John Dominic Crossan* (Grand Rapids, MI: Baker, 1998).

— and William Lane Craig, eds. *Passionate Conviction: Contemporary Discourses on Christian Apologetics* (Nashville, TN: B&H Academic, 2007).

— and Ronald K. Tacelli, eds. *Jesus' Resurrection: Fact or Figment? A Debate between William Lane Craig and Gerd Ludemann* (Downers Grove, IL: IVP, 2000).

Craig, William Lane. *On Guard: Defending Your Faith with Reason and Precision* (Colorado Springs: David C. Cook, 2010).

— *Reasonable Faith: Christian Truth and Apologetics* (Wheaton, IL: Crossway, 3rd edn, 2008).

— *The Son Rises* (Eugene, OR: Wipf & Stock, 2000).

Davis, Stephen T. 'Have the Infidels Refuted the Resurrection?' Pages 49–75 in *Disputed Issues: Contending for Christian Faith in Today's Academic Setting* (Baylor University Press, 2009).

—, Daniel Kendall SJ and Gerald O'Collins SJ, eds. *The Resurrection* (Oxford University Press, 1997).

— *Risen Indeed: Making Sense of the Resurrection* (London: SPCK, 1993).

Foster, Charles. *The Jesus Inquest: The Case for and against the Resurrection of the Christ* (Oxford: Monarch, 2006).

Geisler, Norman L. and Frank Turek. *I Don't Have Enough Faith to Be an Atheist* (Wheaton, IL: Crossway, 2004).

Geivett, R. Douglas and Gary R. Habermas, eds. *In Defence of Miracles: A Comprehensive Case for God's Action in History* (Leicester: Apollos, 1997).

Habermas, Gary R. 'The Resurrection of Jesus and Recent Agnosticism.' Pages 281–94 in *Reasons for Faith: Making a Case for the Christian Faith* (ed. Norman L. Geisler and Chad V. Meister; Wheaton, IL: Crossway, 2007).

— 'The Resurrection of Jesus: A Rational Inquiry' (PhD dissertation – MI State University, 1976) http://www.garyhabermas.com/books/dissertation/Pensgard-v1c_Resurrection_Dissertation_1976_Habermas_FRAMES.htm.

— *The Secret of the Talpiot Tomb: Unravelling the Mystery of the Jesus Family Tomb* (Nashville, TN: Holman Reference, 2007).

— and Michael R. Licona, *The Case for the Resurrection of Jesus* (Grand Rapids, MI: Kregel, 2004).

— and J.P. Moreland, *Beyond Death: Exploring the Evidence for Immortality* (Wheaton, IL: Crossway, 1998).

Iannone, John C. *The Mystery of the Shroud of Turin* (New York: St Paul's, 1998).

Licona, Michael R. *Paul Meets Muhammad: A Christian–Muslim Debate on the Resurrection* (Grand Rapids, MI: Baker, 2006).

— *The Resurrection of Jesus: A New Historiographical Approach* (Downers Grove, IL: IVP, 2010).

McGrew, Timothy and Linda McGrew. 'The Argument from Miracles.' Pages 593–662 in *The Blackwell Companion to Natural Theology* (ed. William Lane Craig and J.P. Moreland; Oxford: Wiley-Blackwell, 2009). Available online at http://www.lydiamcgrew.com/Resurrection articlesinglefile.pdf.

Miethe, Terry L. ed. Gary R. Habermas and Anthony Flew, *Did Jesus Rise from the Dead? The Resurrection Debate* (Eugene, OR: Wipf & Stock, 2003).

Miller, Troy A. ed. Craig A. Evans and Tom Wright, *Jesus: The Final Days* (London: SPCK, 2008).

Polkinghorne, John. *The God of Hope and the End of the World* (London: SPCK, 2002).

Quarles, Charles L. ed. *Buried Hope or Risen Savior? The Search for the Jesus Tomb* (Nashville, TN: B&H Academic, 2008).

Stevenson, Kenneth E. *Image of The Risen Christ: Remarkable New Evidence about the Shroud* (Ontario: Frontier Research, 1999).

— and Gary R. Habermas, *Verdict on the Shroud* (London: Robert Hale, 1982).

Stewart, Robert B., ed. *The Resurrection of Jesus: The Crossan–Wright Dialogue* (London: SPCK, 2006).

Strobel, Lee. *The Case for the Real Jesus: A Journalist Investigates Current Attacks on the Identity of Christ* (Grand Rapids, MI: Zondervan, 2007).

— *The Case for Christ: A Journalist's Personal Investigation of the Evidence for Jesus* (Grand Rapids, MI: Zondervan, 1998).

Swinburne, Richard. *The Resurrection of God Incarnate* (Oxford: Clarendon Press, 2003).

Taliaferro, Charles and Chad Meister, eds. *Christian Philosophical Theology* (Cambridge University Press, 2010).

Walker, Peter. *The Weekend That Changed the World: The Mystery of Jerusalem's Empty Tomb* (London: Marshall Pickering, 1999).

Walls, Jerry L. *Heaven: The Logic of Eternal Joy* (Oxford University Press, 2002).

Wenham, John. *Easter Enigma: Are the Resurrection Accounts in Conflict?* (London: Paternoster, 2nd edn, 1992).

Wilkins, Michael J. and J.P. Moreland, eds. *Jesus under Fire: Modern Scholarship Reinvents the Historical Jesus* (Grand Rapids, MI: Zondervan, 1996).

Wright, N.T. 'Appendix B: The Self-Revelation of God in Human History.' Pages 185–213 in Antony Flew with Roy Abraham Varghese, *There Is a God* (New York: HarperOne, 2007).

— *The Resurrection of the Son of God* (London: SPCK, 2003).

— *Surprised by Hope* (London: SPCK, 2007).

6

The Fourth Way – Jesus and Fulfilled Prophecy

Beginning with Moses and all the Prophets, he explained to them what was said in all the Scriptures concerning himself.

(Luke 24:27)

Luke recounts how two dispirited disciples, on their way to Emmaus,[1] on the Sunday evening following Jesus' crucifixion:

were talking with each other about everything that had happened. As they talked and discussed these things with each other, Jesus himself came up and walked along with them; but they were kept from recognizing him.

He asked them, 'What are you discussing together as you walk along?'

They stood still, their faces downcast. One of them, named Cleopas, asked him, 'Are you only a visitor to Jerusalem and do not know the things that have happened there in these days?'

'What things?' he asked.

'About Jesus of Nazareth,' they replied. 'He was a prophet, powerful in word and deed before God and all the people. The chief priests and our rulers handed him over to be sentenced to death, and they crucified him; but we had hoped that he was the one who was going to redeem Israel. And what is more, it is the third day since all this took place. In addition, some of our women amazed us. They went to the tomb early this morning but didn't find his body. They came and told us that they had seen a vision of angels, who said he was alive. Then some of our companions went to the tomb and found it just as the women had said, but him they did not see' (Luke 24:14–24).

Despite Jesus' authoritative teaching and his miraculous deeds, these disciples just couldn't square Jesus' execution with their interpretation of 'Messiah'. They certainly didn't know what to make of the recently discovered empty tomb. In response, the resurrected Jesus called into question their interpretation of 'Messiah'. He argued that, far from falsifying his messianic claims, his death (and even his resurrection – cf. Psalm 16:10; 30:3; 41:9–10; Isaiah 53:9–10) was just what one should expect on the basis of the Jewish scriptures: '"How foolish you are, and how slow to believe all that the prophets have spoken! Did not the Christ have to suffer these things and then enter his glory?" And beginning with Moses and all the Prophets, he explained to them what was said in all the Scriptures concerning himself' (Luke 24:25–27).

Jesus' perspective on the Old Testament scriptures combined with the reality of his resurrection as mutually reinforcing evidence. The disciples' understanding of the OT was illuminated by Jesus' death *in the light of his resurrection* (absent the resurrection they wouldn't have continued to think that he was the Messiah); and, with the benefit of hindsight, the OT shed new light on Jesus' life, death and resurrection. Far from feeling that the Jewish scriptures presented an obstacle to Christian belief, like the disciples on the road to Emmaus, by the time Peter makes his speech at the Pentecost festival (cf. Acts 2) we find him weaving several OT passages into his argument. Indeed, the apostle Peter wrote a letter to Christians in Asia in which he argued: 'Some prophets told how kind God would be to you, and they searched hard to find out more about the way you would be saved. The Spirit of Christ was in them and was telling them how Christ would suffer and would then be given great honour. So they searched to find out exactly who Christ would be and when this would happen' (1 Peter 1:10–11 [CEV]).

Peter makes several distinct claims about the match between OT prophecy and Jesus:

1) OT prophecy sought to discern *when* the Messiah would be active – and Jesus' ministry satisfies this prediction

2) OT prophecy sought to discern *who* the Messiah would be (something we can analyze in terms of both his *origins* and his *actions*) – and Jesus satisfies this OT 'portrait' of the Messiah
3) OT prophecy discerned that the Messiah would suffer in the cause of salvation – like Jesus
4) OT prophecy discerned the manner of the Messiah's suffering – and Jesus' suffering comports with these prophetic insights
5) OT prophecy discerned that having suffered, the Messiah would be given great honour – like Jesus

The OT prophetically specifies the Messiah's historical era, his biological and geographical origins, his messianic actions, his suffering and death for a new covenant of forgiveness, and his resurrection from the dead. However, before we use Peter's claims as a framework for examining Jesus' fulfilment of prophecy, we should make an excursus into the distinction between implicit and explicit prophecy, and we should establish some criteria by which to assess arguments from fulfilled prophecy.

Prophecy: Implicit and Explicit

To authenticate a work of art one can take two approaches. The first relies upon implicit signs that a particular artist was responsible for the work in question. By drawing attention to certain characteristic qualities of an artist's style one proceeds to argue by analogy: since the work in question exhibits these same artistic qualities, it probably has the same artistic cause. The stronger the analogy, the stronger this argument becomes. The second approach relies upon explicit signs that a particular artist is responsible for the work in question. For example, spotting the artist's signature in the corner of a painting. If a work of art can be authenticated by both implicit and explicit approaches, so much the better.

In order to support their claim that God was at work in Jesus, the NT writers (especially Matthew) sometimes make implicit, analogical appeals to OT passages that aren't explicitly predictive either in their original literary context or in the established Jewish interpretation thereof (of course, if the Bible is the Word of God as well as the writing of humans, then the meaning of a passage for the human author is not a definitive guide to the meaning of the passage as God's word). The theological term for this approach to prophecy is *typology*: 'Typology comes from the Greek word for "type" or "pattern" and was a recognized means of analyzing current events in both Jewish and Greco-Roman circles prior to the dawn of Christianity.'[2]

Typological application seeks to exhibit *consonance* between the OT and the life of Jesus:

> It is an argument of which the real strength is known only by means of the careful and scholarly study of the Bible, and it is in proportion as our minds are steeped in the words and thoughts of the Bible that its analogies make their full impression upon us and we come to discern in them real correspondences within the whole pattern of biblical history, which in whole and in part become effective testimony to the truth of Christ.[3]

Thus certain OT passages are applied to Jesus *typologically*. For example, Hosea 11:1 is applied to Christ in Matthew 2:15 because, with the benefit of hindsight, it is seen to speak to his situation analogically. As Alan Richardson wrote:

> If we think of prophecy as primarily the discernment of the underlying purpose of contemporary events, which carries with it an insight into the pattern and goal of history, we shall understand that the fulfillment of prophecy means the corroboration by later historical happenings of the prophetic fore-shadowings of the truth, the typological fulfillment, that is to say, of patterns that have been given in the earlier stages of Israel's history. It is this fulfillment of Israel's history, and therefore of the insights of the prophets, which the New Testament claims to have been accomplished in the coming of Jesus and His church.[4]

However, prophecy isn't merely a matter of analogical hindsight. Prophecy is sometimes concerned with the more or less explicit prediction of future events. Isaiah lays down the following challenge:

> Bring in your idols to tell us
>   what is going to happen …
> declare to us the things to come,
>   tell us what the future holds,
>   so that we may know you are gods (Isaiah 41:22 [NIV]).

Isaiah clearly sets up a distinction between idols who cannot reveal the future, and God, who can and does. As Norman L. Geisler asserts: 'There are certainly … a sufficient number of examples of prophecies that are clearly predictive …'[5] Hence Richardson concludes that: 'Underlying all the prophetic writings, and also in a sense the whole of the Old Testament, there is an atmosphere of expectation, a looking-forward to a climax of history or a fulfillment of God's sovereign purpose …'[6]

Criteria for Explicit Prophecy

In discussing how the validity of a religious experience might be scientifically tested, atheist Victor J. Stenger observes that 'all that has to happen is that the person returning from such an experience report some fact that she could not have known ahead of time. This could be the successful prediction of some future event.'[7] As Thomas V. Morris argues:

> A single successful prediction about a remote or unlikely event can be just a lucky guess, a shot in the dark that just happened to hit its target. But the more successful predictions of that sort a person is able to make, the less likely we are to be fully satisfied with just ascribing it all to luck. At a certain point we have to hypothesize some explanation for the success, some connection, mechanism, ability, or power responsible for the otherwise highly improbable accuracy.[8]

According to mathematician and philosopher William A. Dembski, it is precisely this combination of *a highly improbable hit upon an independently specified target* that rationally grounds design inferences in scientific fields as diverse as cryptography, psychology, fraud detection, the search for extra-terrestrial intelligence (SETI) and forensic science: 'given an event, object, or structure, to convince ourselves that it is designed we need to show that it is improbably (i.e. complex) and suitably patterned (i.e. specified).'[9] Dembski has defended 'specified complexity' – or 'complex specified information' (CSI) – as a reliable design detection criterion in numerous writings,[10] including his peer-reviewed monograph *The Design Inference* (Cambridge University Press, 1998).

In sum: A long string of random letters is complex without being specified (that is, without conforming to an independently given pattern that we haven't simply read off the object or event in question). A short sequence of letters like 'this' or 'that' is specified without being sufficiently complex to outstrip the capacity of chance to explain this conformity (e.g. letters drawn at random from a scrabble bag will occasionally form a short word). Neither complexity without specificity nor specificity without complexity compels us to infer design. However, this book is both specified (conforming to the functional requirements of grammatical English) *and* sufficiently complex (doing so at a level of complexity that makes it unreasonable to attribute this match to luck) to trigger a design inference on the basis of our experience that whenever we know the cause of CSI that cause is an intelligent one.

That CSI is a sound method of design detection is something accepted both implicitly and explicitly by a wide range of scholars from a variety of disciplines and metaphysical positions.[11] For example, in *The Blind Watchmaker* Richard Dawkins argues that: 'Of all the unique and, with hindsight equally improbable [i.e. complexity], positions of the combination lock, only one opens the lock [i.e. specification] … The uniqueness of the arrangement … that opens the safe [has] nothing to do with hindsight. It is *specified* in advance.'[12] The best explanation of an open safe isn't that someone got lucky, but that someone knew the *specific* and *complex* combination required to open it. Likewise, in *Climbing Mount Improbable* Dawkins draws a distinction between objects that are clearly designed and objects that are not clearly designed but superficially look like they are – which he calls '*designoid*'.[13] Dawkins illustrates the concept of being designoid with a hillside that suggests a human profile: 'Once you have been told, you can just see a slight resemblance to either John or Robert Kennedy. But some don't see it and it is certainly easy to believe that the resemblance is accidental.'[14] Dawkins contrasts this Kennedy-esque hillside with the four president's heads carved into Mt Rushmore in America, which 'are obviously not accidental: they have design written all over them.'[15] He argues that while 'a rock can weather into the shape of a nose seen from a certain vantage point ...'[16] such a rock (e.g. the Kennedy-esque hillside) is designoid. Mt Rushmore, on the other hand, is clearly not designoid: 'Its four heads are clearly *designed* ...'[17] The fact that Rushmore is designed is, according to Dawkins, empirically detectable: 'The sheer number of details [i.e. the amount of complexity] in which the Mount Rushmore faces resemble the real things [i.e. the complexity fits four specifications] is too great to have come about by chance.'[18] In terms of mere possibility, says Dawkins: 'The weather *could* have done the same job ... But of all the possible ways of weathering a mountain, only a tiny minority [complexity] would be speaking likenesses of four particular human beings [specification].'[19] Hence: 'Even if we didn't know the history of Mount Rushmore, we'd estimate the odds against its four heads [specification] being carved by accidental weathering as astronomically high ... [complexity]'[20] While Dawkins makes an *implicit* use of CSI in these examples, in a 2004 editorial piece for *Free Inquiry* Dawkins *explicitly* acknowledged that CSI is a valid criterion of design detection:

> 'specified complexity' takes care of the sensible point that any particular rubbish heap is improbable, with hindsight, in the unique disposition of its parts. A pile of detached watch parts tossed in a box is, with hindsight, as improbable as a fully functioning, genuinely complicated watch. What is specified about a watch is that it is improbable in the specific direction of telling the time.[21]

Dembski observes that fulfilled 'predictive prophecies in Scripture are instances of specified complexity.'[22] As theologian Robert C. Newman writes:

> Fulfilled predictions are one type of miracle that can be tested centuries after the event took place. All we need is good evidence (1) that the text clearly envisions the sort of event alleged to be the fulfillment, (2) that the prophecy was made well in advance

of the event predicted, (3) that the prediction actually came true and (4) that the event predicted could not have been staged [or known in advance] by anyone but God. The strength of the evidence is greatly enhanced if (5) the event itself is so unusual that the apparent fulfillment cannot be plausibly explained as a good guess.[23]

Messiah – *When?*

Two independent OT prophecies specify the time of the Messiah. One talks of his arrival, the other of his death.

The Messiah's arrival

According to Genesis 49:10:

> The scepter will not depart from Judah,
> nor the ruler's staff from between his feet,
> until he to whom it belongs shall come
> and the obedience of the nations be his.

The 'sceptre' traditionally referred to the administrative control of the death penalty; a control that the Jewish nation retained even through its exile in Babylon, until the Romans took over in AD 11. At that time, the Jewish leadership 'tore their garments' in mourning because the sceptre had departed from Judah and no Messiah had come. They didn't realize that the Messiah had already come, as a baby born in Bethlehem c. 6 BC.[24]

The Messiah's death

Josephus wrote:

> what more than all else incited [the Jews to revolt against Rome, AD 66–73] was an ambiguous oracle, *likewise found in their sacred scriptures*, to the effect that *at that time* one from their country would become ruler of the world. This they understood to mean someone of their own race, and many of their own wise men went astray

in their interpretation of it. The oracle, however, in reality signified the sovereignty of Vespasian, who was proclaimed [Roman] Emperor on Jewish soil.[25]

The existence of this prophecy is likewise referenced by the Roman historians Tacitus (*Histories* 5.13) and Suetonius (*The Lives of the Caesars*, 'The deified Vespasian,' 4.5). The only candidate for this oracle 'found in [the Jewish] sacred scriptures' occurs in the book of Daniel (9:24–26):

> Seventy 'sevens' are decreed for your people and your holy city to finish transgression, to put an end to sin, to atone for wickedness, to bring in everlasting righteousness, to seal up vision and prophecy and to anoint the most holy.
> Know and understand this: From the issuing of the decree to restore and rebuild Jerusalem until the Anointed One, the ruler, comes, there will be seven 'sevens,' and sixty-two 'sevens.' It will be rebuilt with streets and a trench, but in times of trouble. After the sixty-two 'sevens,' the Anointed One will be cut off and will have nothing. The people of the ruler who will come will destroy the city and the sanctuary. [NIV]

The interpretation of this passage is much discussed,[26] but one plausible reading notes the significance of the decree issued by the Persian king Artaxerxes I in 445 BC, officially approving Nehemiah's return to Jerusalem to rebuild its walls (cf. Nehemiah 2:1–9). The 'sevens' of Daniel 9 may refer to the recurring seven-year sabbatical cycle for land use: 'Using these cycles as units of measurement, the sixty-ninth such cycle (7 + 62), measured from the starting point of 445 BC, spans the years AD 28–35. One cannot help but note with interest that on this analysis the "Anointed One" [i.e. Jesus] is "cut off" precisely when Jesus is crucified.'[27] Jesus was indeed 'cut off' with 'nothing' before 'the people of the ruler' (i.e. the Romans) destroyed 'the city and the sanctuary'; for the Jews rebelled against Rome in AD 66 and Jerusalem fell to the Roman army in AD 70. As seen in the above quotation from Josephus, the Roman propaganda machine decided to use this prophecy for the glorification of Vespasian. Their method involved sacrificing the specificity required of a genuine prophetic fulfilment, for unlike

Jesus, Vespasian wasn't 'cut off' with nothing before the destruction of Jerusalem.

Messiah – *Who?*

Vespasian failed to fulfil any of the necessary conditions of the OT prophecies concerning the Messiah's identity. Jesus, on the other hand, fit them all. For example:

Prophecy re Messiah's Origins	Old Testament Prediction	New Testament Fulfilment	Estimated Odds
The Messiah will come from Abraham	Genesis 17:7–8; 18:17–18; 26:3–4	Matthew 1:1; Acts 3:25–26; Galatians 3:16; Hebrews 2:16	0.1
Messiah will come from the tribe of Judah[28]	Micah 5:2	Matthew 1:1–3; Hebrews 7:14; Revelation 5:5	0.08
Messiah will come from the seed of Isaac	Genesis 17:19; 21:12; 26:2–4	Matthew 1:2, 17; Romans 9:7; Hebrews 11:17–19	0.5
Messiah will come from the seed of Jacob	Genesis 28:13–14; Numbers 24:17–19	Matthew 1:2; Luke 1:33; 3:23–38	0.5
Messiah will be a firstborn son, sanctified	Exodus 13:2; Numbers 3:13; 8:17	Matthew 1:18–25; Luke 2:7, 23	0.125
Messiah will come from the stem of Jesse	Isaiah 11:1–2	Matthew 1:6; Acts 13:22–23	0.5
Messiah will be born in Bethlehem[29]	Micah 5:2–5	Matthew 2:1–6; Luke 2:4–7	0.005
Messiah will be born from the line of King David	Isaiah 9:7; 2 Samuel 7:12–13; Jeremiah 23:5–6; 30:9	Matthew 1:1; Luke 1:32; Acts 13:22–23	0.1
Total Odds:			0.00000006 – that's c. 1 chance in 17 million

Figure 19

Prophecy re Messiah's Actions	Old Testament Prediction	New Testament Fulfilment	Estimated Odds
Messiah will be preceded by a messenger sent to prepare his way	Malachi 3:1	Mark 1:2–4; Matthew 11:10; Luke 7:27–28; John 1:19–35	0.1
Messiah will be a prophet[30]	Deuteronomy 18:15	Matthew 21:11; Luke 7:16; John 6:14; Acts 3:20–22; 7:37	0.01
Messiah will heal various ailments[31]	Isaiah 29:18; 35:5	Mark 7:37; Matthew 11:5; Luke 7:19–22; John 9:39	0.001
Messiah will be rejected by rulers	Psalm 2:2	Matthew 12:14; 26:3–4, 47; Luke 23:11–12; John 18 – 19	0.1
Total Odds:			0.0000001 – that's 1 chance in 10 million

Figure 20

The odds of just these twelve prophecies (the fulfilments of which are all multiply, and often independently, attested) being fulfilled by chance in one individual, calculated conservatively, are about 1 chance in 170, million, million (1 in 1.7×10^{14}).

Messiah – his Passion

Perhaps the greatest examples of fulfilled prophecy in the person of Jesus are the striking parallels with Jesus' 'passion' (the events of his trial, death and resurrection) found in Isaiah 53 and Psalm 22.

Isaiah 53

As Roy Williams notes, among the c. 800 documents of the Dead Sea Scrolls, which were discovered in 1947 near the ruins of the desert city of Qumran and which date from between 200 BC and AD 50, was a copy of Isaiah pre-dating Jesus by c. 150 years: 'Before 1947, the oldest complete copy of Isaiah was the so-called

Masoretic Text of AD 916. Incredibly, despite being over a thousand years older, the words appearing on the Isaiah scroll are virtually identical to those in the Masoretic Text – including the prophecies about the Resurrection in Chapter 53.'[32] Here's the passage in question:

> Who has believed our message and to whom has the arm of the LORD been revealed?
> He grew up before him like a tender shoot, and like a root out of dry ground.
> He had no beauty or majesty to attract us to him,
> nothing in his appearance that we should desire him.
> He was despised and rejected by others, a man of suffering, and familiar with pain.
> Like one from whom people hide their faces he was despised, and we held him in low esteem.
> Surely he took up our pain and bore our suffering,
> yet we considered him punished by God, stricken by him, and afflicted.
> But he was pierced for our transgressions, he was crushed for our iniquities;
> the punishment that brought us peace was on him,
> and by his wounds we are healed.
> We all, like sheep, have gone astray, each of us has turned to our own way;
> and the LORD has laid on him the iniquity of us all.
> He was oppressed and afflicted, yet he did not open his mouth;
> he was led like a lamb to the slaughter, and as a sheep before its shearers is silent,
> so he did not open his mouth.
> By oppression ['arrest'] and judgment he was taken away.
> Yet who of his generation protested?
> For he was cut off from the land of the living; for the transgression of my people he was punished.
> He was assigned a grave with the wicked, and with the rich in his death,
> though he had done no violence, nor was any deceit in his mouth.
> Yet it was the LORD's will to crush him and cause him to suffer,

and though the Lord makes ['though you make'] his life an offering for sin,
he will see his offspring and prolong his days,
and the will of the Lord will prosper in his hand.
After he has suffered, he will see the light of life [or 'the fruit of his
suffering'] and be satisfied;
by his knowledge ['by knowledge of him'] my righteous servant
will justify many, and he will bear their iniquities.
Therefore I will give him a portion among the great ['many'],
and he will divide the spoils with the strong ['numerous'],
because he poured out his life unto death,
and was numbered with the transgressors.
For he bore the sin of many, and made intercession for the transgressors (Isaiah 53:1–13, my layout).

Norman L. Geisler comments:

> In Old Testament times, the Jewish rabbis *did* consider this to be a
> prophecy concerning the Messiah. That's the opinion that's really
> relevant. Only later, after Christians pointed out this was obviously
> referring to Jesus, did they begin saying it was really about the suf-
> fering Jewish nation. But clearly that's wrong. Isaiah customarily
> refers to the Jewish people in the first-person-plural ... [we, us, our]
> but he always refers to the Messiah in the third-person singular ...
> [he, him, his] and that's what he did in Isaiah 53. Plus, anyone who
> reads it for themselves will readily see it's referring to Jesus.[33]

Turning to the NT accounts, we find that Jesus (and later his
disciples and the church) viewed his death as a sacrifice for the
forgiveness of sins (Acts 2:38), a sacrifice he made 'willingly'
for people whom he 'prayed ... might be forgiven' (Luke 23:34),
and that while the Jews thought of his death as a punishment for
blasphemy (Matthew 26:62–66), he was in fact God's 'Son' with
whom God was 'pleased' (Matthew 17:5). Jesus received 'blows'
(Luke 22:63), made no answer before his accusers (Luke 23:9),
was 'arrested and sentenced and led off to die' (John 18:12,39,16),
although he had committed no crime (Luke 23:4); and while he
died ('was assigned a grave') among criminals (Luke 23:32), he
was 'buried with the rich' (Luke 23:50–53), and after 'a life of suffering' he nevertheless lived to see the fruit of his suffering (John

19:30; Acts 1:1–9). That Jesus fulfilled all this by chance seems unlikely.

Psalm 22

In quoting Psalm 22 from the cross (Mark 15:34; Matthew 27:46) Jesus takes King David's song and applies it to his own circumstance. As Angela Tilby writes: 'Jesus died a loyal Jew, reciting scripture. Perhaps the familiar words of the psalms brought him comfort. Perhaps he was consciously offering his death as a sacrifice, and recited the psalms as they might be recited to accompany the sacrifices offered in the temple.'[34]

As an aside, anyone tempted to take Jesus' cry of 'My God, my God, why have you forsaken me?' as indicating that God the Father actually abandoned God the Son in some moment of divine wrath-sating on the cross should note verse 24:

> For he has not despised or scorned
>   the suffering of the afflicted one;
> *he has not hidden his face from him*
>   but has listened to his cry for help (Psalm 22:24, my italics).

At the very most, Jesus may have *felt* abandoned, whilst nevertheless knowing – in the light of Psalm 22 – that the Father was with him even on the cross.

Of course, the original context of David's writing Psalm 22 and the context of Jesus' application of the psalm to his own situation on the cross are not identical. Still, the resonance between these two hermeneutical horizons is such a striking example of specified complexity that it seems inappropriate to categorize the psalm as merely 'typological', or its application to Jesus as merely 'analogical'. Indeed, in light of Jesus' passion, it would seem more appropriate to say that the psalm was actually analogical *in its Davidic context*! Psalm 22 can be seen as a fusion of temporal modes best explained in terms of God's omniscience and inspiration. As Norman L. Geisler and Frank Turek comment concerning Psalm 22: 'This goes beyond coincidence … It may be true that certain messianic prophecies in the Old Testament become clear only in light of Christ's life. But that doesn't mean those prophecies are any less amazing.'[35] Here is the psalm in question:

My God, my God, why have you forsaken me?
  Why are you so far from saving me,
  so far from the words of my groaning?
My God, I cry out by day, but you do not answer,
  by night, but I find no rest.
Yet you are enthroned as the Holy One;
  you are the praise of Israel.
In you our ancestors put their trust;
  they trusted and you delivered them.
They cried to you and were saved;
  in you they trusted and were not disappointed.

But I am a worm, not a human being;
  I am scorned by everyone, despised by the people.
All who see me mock me;
  they hurl insults, shaking their heads.
'He trusts in the LORD,' they say,
  'let the LORD rescue him.
Let him deliver him,
  since he delights in him.'

Yet you brought me out of the womb;
  you made me feel secure on my mother's breast.
From birth I was cast on you;
  from my mother's womb you have been my God.
Do not be far from me,
  for trouble is near
  and there is no one to help.

Many bulls surround me;
  strong bulls of Bashan encircle me.
Roaring lions that tear their prey
  open their mouths wide against me.
I am poured out like water,
  and all my bones are out of joint.
My heart has turned to wax;
  it has melted within me.
My mouth is dried up like a potsherd,
  and my tongue sticks to the roof of my mouth;

you lay me in the dust of death.
Dogs surround me,
   a pack of villains encircles me;
   they pierce my hands and my feet.
All my bones are on display;
   people stare and gloat over me.
They divide my clothes among them
   and cast lots for my garment.

But you, LORD, do not be far from me.
   You are my strength; come quickly to help me.
Deliver me from the sword,
   my precious life from the power of the dogs.
Rescue me from the mouth of the lions;
   save me from the horns of the wild oxen.

I will declare your name to my people;
   in the assembly I will praise you.
You who fear the LORD, praise him!
   All you descendants of Jacob, honor him!
Revere him,
   all you descendants of Israel!
For he has not despised or scorned
   the suffering of the afflicted one;
he has not hidden his face from him
   but has listened to his cry for help.

From you comes the theme of my praise in the great assembly;
   before those who fear you I will fulfil my vows.
The poor will eat and be satisfied;
   those who seek the LORD will praise him –
   may your hearts live forever!
All the ends of the earth
   will remember and turn to the LORD,
and all the families of the nations
   will bow down before him,
for dominion belongs to the LORD
   and he rules over the nations.

All the rich of the earth will feast and worship;
　all who go down to the dust will kneel before him –
　those who cannot keep themselves alive.
Posterity will serve him;
　future generations will be told about the Lord.
They will proclaim his righteousness,
　declaring to a people yet unborn:
　He has done it! [cf. John 19:30]

Crucified by gentiles ('dogs' in Jewish vernacular) after the usual flogging,[36] Christ had his clothing divided among the soldiers by the casting of lots (Mark 15:24; Matthew 27:35; Luke 23:34; John 19:23–24);[37] he was scorned, mocked and insulted (Mark 15:26–30; Matthew 27:41); he was taunted with his lack of divine deliverance (Mark 15:32; Matthew 27:43), he suffered from dehydration (Mark 15:36; John 19:36), and the separation of his red blood cells from the serum, seen when he was pierced by a spear, confirmed his death (John 19:33–37; cf. Mark 15:37). Christ underwent all this to declare the character of God to humanity, a God who does ultimately vindicate his servant, thereby legitimizing Psalm 22's theme of praise for his servant whose suffering somehow feeds the spiritually hungry with righteousness and causes their hearts to live forever when they recognize that they cannot keep themselves alive.

The combined odds of Jesus fulfilling so many specific aspects of both Isaiah 53 and Psalm 22 are pretty steep. If we take just 15 aspects of Jesus' fulfilment of just these passages, and we assign a generous 1 in 2 chance to each aspect's fulfilment, the combined odds of Jesus fulfilling them by chance are 1 in 32,768. At odds of 1 in 4 for each aspect, the combined odds of fulfilment drop to about 1 in 1074 million.[38] In combination with the odds previously calculated concerning Jesus' origins and actions, we can conservatively estimate that Jesus had between 1 chance in 5,610,000, million, million (1 in 5.6×10^{18}) and 1 chance in 182,580, million, million, million (1 in 1.8×10^{23}) of having fulfilled just these 27 prophecies by chance. These odds are roughly comparable to your chances of successfully picking, at random and on your first attempt, a single pre-specified grain of sand *out of all the grains of sand on the planet.*[39]

Understanding Atonement

Jesus viewed his death as an act of sacrifice that would inaugurate a new phase in the relationship between God and humanity. As theologian Mark L. Strauss explains, the so-called 'Last Supper' was a Jewish 'Passover' celebration with a twist:

> this is no ordinary Passover but the establishment of a new Passover for the new age of salvation – the kingdom of God. The original Passover represented God's greatest act of deliverance in the Hebrew scriptures and the creation of Israel as a nation ... Yahweh defeated Pharaoh ... delivered his people through the sacrificial blood of the Passover lamb, and brought them out of slavery in Egypt. Giving them his law at Mount Sinai, he established a covenant relationship with them. When Israel was later oppressed and defeated by her enemies, the prophets would predict the day when Yahweh would return to Zion to accomplish a new and greater exodus [Isaiah 11:11–16; 35:1–10; 40:1–5; Jeremiah 23:5–8; etc.]. Jesus' eucharistic words recall and transform the rich symbols of Passover ... The unleavened bread of the Passover meal represents Jesus' body, given for his disciples. The implication is that he is the new Passover lamb [cf. 1 Corinthians 5:7]. The Passover wine represents the blood of the new covenant. Jesus' words in Mark 14:24, 'This is my blood of the covenant,' echo Exodus 24:8 ... Jesus speaks explicitly of the new covenant, a clear allusion to Jeremiah 31 ... Jesus' words at the Last Supper thus fit well his preaching about the kingdom of God ... They also provide important clues as to how he viewed his approaching death. Drawing symbolism from the Passover meal, the covenant at Sinai, and the new exodus and new covenant imagery in the prophets, Jesus inaugurates a new Passover meal celebrating the new covenant and the arrival of the kingdom of God. While the first covenant was instituted with the blood of sacrificial animals, this new covenant will be established through his own blood. It seems likely, therefore, that Jesus viewed his death as a sacrifice of atonement, leading his people in a new exodus from bondage to sin and death.[40]

In light of the divine vindication provided by his resurrection, Jesus' multiply and independently attested re-purposing of the Passover (cf. 1 Corinthians 10:16; 11:23–26; Mark 14:22–24; Matthew 26:26–29; Luke 22:19–20; John 6:54–56) meant that his crucifixion was a performative act inaugurating the new age covenant predicted by the OT. That is, just as the act of a properly authorized personage breaking a bottle of champagne on the side of a ship whilst uttering the words 'I name this ship …' *brings about the naming of a ship,* so Jesus' death and his interpretation thereof *brings about the existence of a new covenant* in light of the fact that his resurrection (etc.) shows him to be someone with the authority so to do.

Jesus' death and resurrection bring about and advertise the fact of a new covenantal relationship between God and humanity. Exactly *how* God bridges the gulf between sinful human beings and his own perfect nature so as to permit this 'at-one-ment' is the subject matter for theories of 'atonement'. Theologian Alister E. McGrath explains that:

> the New Testament is not … concerned with the detailed and intricate mechanics of redemption. The New Testament actually presents us with a series of images of what Christ achieved for us through his death and resurrection. It is dominated by proclamation of the *fact* that the cross and resurrection have the power to change us, along with a number of superb illustrations of the ways in which we can visualize this potential.[41]

Philosopher C. Stephen Evans concurs that 'it is the *fact* of atonement that Christians are asked to believe, not any particular *theory* as to how this is achieved by Christ's death and resurrection. Indeed, Christians have over the centuries held a variety of theories about how this occurred.'[42]

The study of the 'intricate mechanics of redemption', the philosophical elaboration of various 'theories of atonement', takes place in dialogue with a complex set of scriptural symbols or images. Taking any of these images literally is analogous to taking scientific images of atoms being like billiard-balls literally. Just as thinking of atoms as billiard balls is useful for relating to atoms in certain situations, so thinking of Jesus' death as a 'ransom' (Mark 20:45) that buys us back from the clutches of sin is useful for relating to Jesus' death in certain situations. However, just as thinking of atoms as being literally like billiard balls leads to theoretical problems, so thinking of Jesus' death as a literal ransom leads to theological problems. Likewise, theologians deploy multiple analogies to capture multiple aspects of atonement just as scientists deploy multiple analogies to capture multiple aspects, for example, of light (which is described as both wave-like and particle-like – a description that is incoherent if taken literally but useful when taken as a metaphor).

Some Christians advance a 'strict retributionist' interpretation of the biblical image of 'substitutory atonement':

> The image of 'substitution' is often used in Scripture, along with others, of course. The problem with this theory is, I think, that it often is presented in an overly legalistic manner. God the Father is the stern lawgiver who imposes a punishment on Jesus, the innocent victim, so that he will not have to pour out his wrath on the rest of us. The whole business sounds like a cold, legal transaction ... What is forgotten in this picture is that Christians are monotheists as well as Trinitarians. God the Father and God the Son are one. When Jesus gives his life for us, it is not God punishing an innocent victim, but God giving himself for us.[43]

Even with some Trinitarian adjustment, this model can sound like an angry man who diverts his rage away from its real object (such as a wife or child), if not by hitting an innocent bystander, then by smashing his own fist through a window, self-harming out of the kind of 'love' that co-exists with loathing and turns into self-loathing. Hence, with Christian philosopher Richard Purtill: 'I think that strict retribution is a profoundly unchristian view and that this view of the Atonement leads to the mistaken view that Christ was *punished* for our sins, a view quite different from the view that Christ *suffered* for our sins.'[44] Indeed, Isaiah 53 doesn't say that the servant suffers 'the punishment due to our sin', but that *he suffers our sin* (cf. Isaiah 53:6, 12). That is, as the suffering servant, Jesus *exhibited the fact of divine sin-bearing through the medium of the unjust punishment he received from the authorities upon the cross* (Isaiah 53:5b). As Paul writes: 'This grace was given us in Christ Jesus before the beginning of time, but it has now been revealed through the appearing of our Savior, Christ Jesus, who has destroyed death and has brought life and immortality to light through the gospel' (2 Timothy 1:9–10). That is, the new covenant brought about by Jesus' death is the eternally planned explicit enactment of a previously implicit reality (cf. Romans 3:21; Ephesians 1:9; 3:2–6; Revelation 13:8).

Jesus' death doesn't make or allow God to love us. As theologians Joel B. Green and Mark D. Baker affirm: 'Whatever meaning atonement might have, it would be a grave error to imagine that it focused on assuaging God's anger or winning God's merciful attention.'[45] Rather, Jesus died for us *because* God already loved us: 'This is love: not that we loved God, but that he loved us and sent his Son as an atoning sacrifice for our sins' (1 John 4:10). Paul states that 'God demonstrates his own love for us in this: While we were still sinners, Christ died for us' (Romans 5:8).[46]

Keith Ward elaborates upon the theme of God's sacrificial suffering of sin displayed on the cross:

> Sin, we might well say, causes a change in the divine nature – the realization of anger, even when transformed by compassion, the frustration of divine purpose, and the frustration of joy. These are costs that God [freely] bears whenever sin impairs a possible divine-creaturely relationship. The crucifixion of Jesus, in so far as it is an act of God as well as the self-offering of a human life, is the particular and definitive historical expression of the universal sacrifice of God in bearing the cost of sin [cf. Revelation 13:8]. Sin is a harm done to God, inasmuch as it causes God to know, and to share, the suffering and reality of evil. The 'ransom' God pays is to accept this cost, to bear with evil, in order that it should be redeemed, transfigured, in God ... The patience of God, bearing the cost of sin, takes the life and death and resurrection of Jesus as its own self-manifestation, and makes it the means by which the liberating life of God is made available in its essential form to the world.[47]

This makes a good deal of intuitive sense to me, for what is forgiveness, in our experience, but the willingness of a wronged individual to suffer and absorb the wrong done to them in the hope of relationship with the person who wronged them? To forgive someone is *not* to excuse them as not being guilty, but rather to affirm their guilt whilst willingly suffering their sin and the pain it causes. As Evans comments: 'In the death and resurrection of Jesus, God shows us how complete his love for us is … He takes on human form and suffers the consequences of sin, expressing both the seriousness with which he views our sin and the exuberant love with which he is willing to forgive our sins.'[48] Moreover, with Tim Bayne and Greg Restall we should note that:

> Paul doesn't see Christ's death and resurrection as the salve for a troubled conscience … he regards Christ's death as dealing with sin as part of the human (indeed: cosmic) condition. The participatory strand in Paul's theology takes sin to be a problem of our *identity*. The atonement does not merely adjust our 'moral standing' but instead [if we respond to it positively] inaugurates a change in the kind of beings we are.[49]

Hence Paul describes 'the way' of Christianity as a continuous spiritual participation in Jesus' death and resurrection:

> Don't you know that all of us who were baptized into Christ Jesus were baptized into his death? We were therefore buried with him through baptism into death in order that, just as Christ was raised from the dead through the glory of the Father, we too may live a new life …
>
> The death he died, he died to sin once for all; but the life he lives, he lives to God.
>
> In the same way, count yourselves dead to sin but alive to God in Christ Jesus … Do not offer any part of yourself to sin as an instrument of wickedness, but rather offer yourselves to God as those who have been brought from death to life; and offer every part of yourself to him as an instrument of righteousness …
>
> For the wages of sin is death, but the gift of God is eternal life in Christ Jesus our Lord (Romans 6:3–4, 10–11, 13, 23).

In the final analysis, I agree with Evans that 'the critical question is not whether you fully understand God's action in suffering on your behalf. It is whether you are moved by his suffering to "turn around," to repent. Then the power of God that conquered death in Jesus will be at work in your life as well.'[50] Whether or not you understand *how* a medicine works, the main thing is to trust the doctor who testifies *that* it works by taking your medicine.

Jesus' Prophecies

As Roy Williams observes, the Old Testament prophecies fulfilled in Jesus don't stand alone: 'Also deserving of the most serious study are the predictions recorded in the Gospels as having been made by Jesus Himself – of His betrayal by Judas, of the future work of the Apostles, and (centrally) of His death and resurrection.'[51]

Concerning Jesus' prophecy about Jerusalem and the temple (which one can see as following from the combination of OT prophecy with Jesus' messianic self-image), historian Ian Wilson comments:

> it is a straight fact of history that Herod's seemingly so-permanent Temple, which Jesus had predicted would be destroyed within a generation of his time (Matthew 24:1–3; Mark 13:1–4; Luke 21:5–7), did indeed suffer this very fate. When Jewish nationalists revolted in AD 66, putting up such strong resistance that it took the Romans four hard years to bring them all to heel, the Roman reprisal was to destroy the Temple. This task was carried out so completely that by the end of a second and final revolt in AD 130–5, not a stone of it was left standing above its platform base.[52]

Warned by Jesus' prophecy, Christians left Jerusalem during a temporary Roman retreat in the winter of AD 66–7: 'during the interval when the Roman troops withdrew, the Christians fled down to the east to the Jordan River and then crossed the river and went up its east side to a town named Pella, where they sat out the war ...'[53]

Jesus' prophecy about Jerusalem and the temple is intermixed with his prediction of his own 'second coming':

> Jesus ... foretells how not one stone of the temple will be left standing on another, and the disciples say 'Tell us, (a) when will these things be, and (b) what will be the sign of your coming and of the close of the age?' (Matt. 24:3). Then, at the close of the following

discourse, Jesus answers their twofold question by saying that (a) 'this generation will not pass away till all *these things* take place' (Matt. 24:34) while, (b) with regard to his coming and 'the close of the age', he tells them that 'of *that* day and hour no one knows, not even the angels of heaven, nor the Son, but the Father only' (Matt. 24:36). The distinction between the two predications is clear in Matthew [and] it was already implicit, though not so clear, in Mark.[54]

As David Winter explains: 'here is no blueprint or timetable of future events, such as some have professed to discover. Jesus was not offering any such scheme or schedule, but a set of visionary pictures of the near and more distant future, to which he attached warnings about the dangers of resisting or rejecting God's will for his people.'[55] While some early Christians (e.g. the Thessalonians) do seem to have been naïve about these prophecies, 'Paul was at pains to warn them against any obsession with dates and timings … History has proved that they and others were wrong to expect an imminent fulfilment of the second prophecy, but in the nature of things "history" cannot prove that it will not one day be fulfilled.'[56] Geza Vermes is, therefore, not entirely correct when he asserts that 'Paul and his Thessalonian and Corinthian Christians were fired by the sure faith that the return of the Lord would occur at any moment, and certainly during their lifetime.'[57] Paul's language of 'the end of the ages' (1 Corinthians 10:11 [RSV]) doesn't imply an end to history 'during their lifetime', as Wright explains:

> The significance of Jesus' resurrection, for Saul of Tarsus [Paul] as he lay blinded and perhaps bruised on the road to Damascus, was this. *The one true God had done for Jesus of Nazareth, in the middle of time, what Saul had thought he was going to do for Israel at the end of time* … Saul had imagined that the great reversal, the great apocalyptic event, would take place all at once, inaugurating the kingdom of God … setting all wrongs to right, defeating evil once and for all, and ushering in the age to come. Instead, the great reversal, the great resurrection had happened to one man, all by himself … The death and resurrection of Jesus were themselves the great eschatological event, revealing God's covenant faithfulness, his way of putting the world to rights … Saul was already living in the time

of the end, even though the previous dimension of time was still carrying on around him. The Present Age and the Age to Come overlapped, and he was ... liberated in the middle ... If the Age to Come had arrived, if the resurrection had already begun to take place, then this was the time when the Gentiles were to come in.[58]

Paul is no more specific concerning the second coming than saying: 'the appointed time has grown very short ... the form of this world is passing away' (1 Corinthians 7:29,31 [RSV]). It's worth remembering that Paul would have been aquainted with the psalmist's declaration that:

> A thousand years in [God's] sight
>   are like a day that has just gone by,
> or like a watch in the night (Psalm 90:4; cf. 2 Peter 3:8).

Jesus taught that the timing of the end was unknown to all but God the Father: 'You will hear of wars and rumors of wars, but see to it that you are not alarmed. Such things must happen, but the end is still to come ... about that day or hour no one knows, not even the angels in heaven, nor the Son, but only the Father' (Matthew 24:6, 36).

Moreover, the statement that 'this generation will certainly not pass away until all these things have happened' (Matthew 24:34) is ambiguous. The word translated as 'generation' could be translated as 'race'. Matthew 16:28 (derived from Mark 9:1), which has Jesus saying 'There be some standing here, which shall not taste of death, till they see the Son of man coming in his kingdom' [AV] doesn't necessarily refer to Jesus' second coming. Reading Matthew 16:28 in context (taking into account the teaching of Jesus and Paul on avoiding speculation about the timing of the end, as well as its Marcan original and Luke's redaction thereof), it seems clear that Matthew 16:28 reflects Paul's understanding of the immanence of the 'Age to Come' in the present age, an understanding that we can trace back to Jesus' proclamation that 'the kingdom of God is near' (Mark 1:15 [NIV]). The disciples (except Judas) did live to see 'the great eschatological event' of the resurrection ushering in the end for the old order of things and the beginning of the new order of Jesus' kingdom rule through the Holy Spirit (cf. Acts 2).

Of course, Matthew 16:28 *might* reflect a misunderstanding corrected by the later gospel of John: 'the rumour spread among the brothers that this disciple would not die. But Jesus did not say that he would not die; he only said, "If I want him to remain alive until I return, what is that to you?"' (John 21:23 [NIV]) Either way, Jesus certainly didn't intend his affirmation that 'some who are standing here will not taste death before they see the kingdom of God come with *power*' (Mark 9:1 [NIV], my italics) to refer to his second coming, since he explicitly taught that the timing of his second coming was a mystery. Rather, Jesus was referring to the imminent events of his resurrection and the outpouring of the Holy Spirit in accordance with the prophecy of Joel 2:28–31: 'you will receive *power* when the Holy Spirit comes on you …' (Acts 1:8, my italics). We should allow this context, reflected in the Marcan original, to determine our reading of Matthew's redaction.[59]

Some Objections to the Argument from Fulfilled Prophecy

It might be suggested that the disciples and/or gospel writers simply *invented* the fulfilment of various prophecies. In the nineteenth century Professor A.B. Bruce noted that while it was formerly 'maintained by Strauss and others that the gospel miracles were the product of faith in Jesus as the Christ', being myths born of Old Testament precedents and prophecies 'setting forth the marvellous works Messiah must have wrought after Jesus had been accepted as Messiah', nevertheless 'there is good reason … to believe that these miracles were not the creations of faith, but rather … were in part the ground of the belief that Jesus was the Christ among the first generation of disciples.'[60] For example, if the disciples and/or gospel writers were creating 'historicized prophecy' they seem to have been rather poor at both producing and exploiting it; as Craig L. Blomberg points out concerning the psalmic casting of lots for Jesus' clothing that is described in all four gospels:

> Only John sees a fulfilment of Scripture … suggesting that it was not the Old Testament that inspired the Gospel writers to invent

details of Christ's passion narrative but rather the Gospel writers in different ways looking back on the events of the passion and finding Old Testament parallels in various places ... John introduces two separate garments where the Old Testament speaks only of clothing in general and says nothing about a seamless robe. An inventor of fiction would probably have made the 'prophecy' and its fulfilment correspond more exactly.[61]

Another major problem with the 'historicized prophecy' hypothesis is that, following Jesus' crucifixion (an event reported by non-Christian sources), the frightened and dispirited disciples were clearly in no state of mind to propagate spurious stories about how Jesus fulfilled prophecy. To the disciples' deflated, post-crucifixion way of thinking (and this is something that would prove an embarrassment in light of future events), Jesus had flunked out of the Messiah category when he was executed by Rome. As we saw in the case of the disciples on their way to Emmaus, it was only belief in the resurrection that overturned their negative verdict on Jesus' messianic status, emboldening them to face persecution and death for his sake. The disciples can hardly have invented Jesus' death and resurrection in order to justify a faith that they only adopted as a consequence of sincerely believing that the crucified Jesus had appeared to them having been resurrected from the dead! As Stuart C. Hackett argues:

the resurrection of Jesus ... is virtually the historical condition of the very existence of the Christian community from the first, since without it the band of disciples would doubtless have ceased to exist as a group by reason of the overwhelming discouragement that would have been occasioned by the irreversible loss of the one on whom they had pinned all their hopes ... So sincere and so unexceptionable is the confidence of that first circle of disciples in Jesus' resurrection that any supposition of a joint deception here cannot be taken seriously, since the disciples had everything to lose and nothing to gain if they unitedly proclaimed the resurrection of Jesus when in fact they knew it was a lie.[62]

Moreover, given that the disciples and/or gospel writers were sincerely telling the truth as they saw it about Jesus' resurrection, why think they abandoned testimonial honesty when it came to less significant events? Occam's Razor thus discourages us from accepting the independently implausible hypothesis that the disciples invented non-historical details in their reports of Jesus' death and resurrection in order to 'historicize' prophecies *that they only interpreted as predicting such events after the (perceived) fact of the resurrection.* Besides, as Hackett asks: 'If the early Christian communities created the very content of the Gospels, then what satisfactory account can be given to explain the origin of those communities themselves?'[63]

Finally, the 'historicized prophecy' hypothesis is implausible given the integrity displayed in the gospel writers' use of material that passes the criterion of embarrassment (e.g. Peter's denial of Christ), or seen in the distinction Paul draws between what Jesus did and did not say (cf. 1 Corinthians 7:10, 12, 25, 40). As Stephen T. Davis argues:

> had the early Christians engaged in such a practice, it is highly probable that sayings would have been placed in the mouth of Jesus that were relevant to the central concerns and controversies of the church in the second half of the first century. But notice that there are no sayings of Jesus in the canonical gospels that are directly relevant to such burning issues in the late-first-century church as the proper use of spiritual gifts, whether male Gentile converts were obliged to be circumcised, whether Christians should divorce their non-Christian spouses, the proper practice of the Lord's supper, how churches ought to be governed, etc. Second, notice that the church preserved and passed on 'difficult' sayings of Jesus – sayings that it would have been convenient for the church to forget – for example, sayings about the human failings of some of the church's greatest leaders (e.g. Peter, in Mark 14:66–72).[64]

People who don't feel free to omit things that embarrass their cause, or to put words in Jesus' mouth that would support their opinion, probably wouldn't feel free to invent events either. The personal testimony of Peter (the major source behind Mark's gospel) is clear on this score: 'we did not follow cleverly devised stories when we told you about the coming of our Lord Jesus Christ in power, but we were eyewitnesses of his majesty' (2 Peter

1:16).[65] The letter of 1 John similarly affirms: 'That which was from the beginning, which we have heard, which we have seen with our eyes, which we have looked at and our hands have touched – this we proclaim concerning the Word of life' (1 John 1:1–2). Indeed, the moral commitment and character of the first followers of the one who famously commanded 'Simply let your "Yes" be "Yes", and your "No", "No"' (Matthew 5:37 [NIV], cf. James 5:12) is firmly against the hypothesis that they formed a conspiracy of liars (see also 2 Timothy 4:3–4). Whatever else it evinces, the disciples' willingness to be martyred demonstrates both a sincerity and a concern for truth (cf. the prologue to Luke's gospel or the epilogue to John's gospel) wholly at odds with the hypothesis that they 'made up' Jesus' fulfilment of prophecy.

Alternatively, it might be objected that some events were (or at least may have been) humanly manipulated so as to deliberately fulfil prophecy. When Jesus claimed to make a new covenant (cf. Jeremiah 31:31–34; 1 Corinthians 10:16; 11:23–26; Mark 14:22–24; Matthew 26:26–29; Luke 22:19–20; John 6:54–56), or when he rode a donkey into Jerusalem (cf. Zechariah 9:9; Matthew 21:4–5), he was in all probability deliberately fulfilling prophecy in order to make a messianic claim. However, there are many fulfilled prophecies over which Jesus could, humanly, have had little or no control (including his lineage, the time of his birth, the place of his birth, his healings, his rejection by the authorities, his repudiation by Peter, the time and detailed circumstances of his death, his resurrection from the dead and the destruction of the temple). Jesus' fulfilment of prophecies in circumstances he could humanly control wouldn't have been accepted as genuine signs without the context provided by his fulfilment of prophecies not in this category, as well as by his teaching in the context of his life, his miracles, his resurrection, etc. For example, Jesus' attempt to establish a new covenant in his own blood upon the cross would clearly have been dismissed apart from the validation of the resurrection.

Besides, if one approaches this issue with a belief in God already in hand, one might very well think that God wouldn't allow the 'fulfilment' of any significant portion of OT prophecies concerning the Messiah by anyone but the Messiah:

In a theistic universe where God is in control of the course of events and where God makes predictions hundreds of years in advance about his plan of salvation for the world, an accidental 'fulfilment' will not happen. It is virtually inconceivable that God would allow either a total deception in his name or an accidental 'fulfilment' in the life of the wrong person … An all-powerful, all-knowing, and all-perfect God will not allow anything to thwart his plans. Predictions made hundreds of years in advance in the name of the true and living theistic God cannot fail. This God cannot lie and he cannot break a promise (Heb. 6:18), nor is it in accord with his nature that those desiring truth can be totally deceived (Heb. 11:6, John 7:17).[66]

Even setting to one side the existence of a providential deity, even setting aside any prophecy whose fulfilment we can reasonably attribute to the deliberate human manipulation of events, and even attributing as much 'luck' to Jesus as we sensibly dare, his fulfilment of so many specific prophecies cannot plausibly be explained away as a mere 'fluke of history'. In the first place, as a miracle in its own right, Jesus' resurrection clearly *couldn't* have been the chance fulfilment of prophecy (the same point applies to Jesus' miraculous healings). Second, the relevant odds are simply too large to ignore. The People's Almanac (1976) studied the predictions of twenty-five top psychics and found that of 72 predictions, 66 (92%) were totally inaccurate. The supposed psychics' accuracy rate (of 8%) could easily be chalked up to educated guesswork and chance. Biblical prophecy is in a totally different league, making many specific and accurate predictions hundreds of years in advance of their fulfilment. According to Norman L. Geisler, the odds against one man fulfilling all the OT prophecies about the Messiah by luck are phenomenal: 'It has been computed by mathematicians that the chances for only 16 prophecies about Christ to come true in Jesus' life are 1 in 10^{45}. For 48 prophecies the chances are an even more amazing 1 in 10^{157}. It is almost impossible to conceive how large a figure this really is.'[67] Even when we go out of our way to make every reasonable allowance, Jesus' fulfilment of prophecy continues to exhibit a degree of specified complexity best explained in terms of the omniscience and/or providence of God.

There are, of course, some aspects of messianic prophecy as yet unfulfilled by Jesus (i.e. aspects having to do with his second coming). The Christian understanding of Jesus isn't undermined by such yet-to-be-fulfilled prophecy. If I inserted your debit card into a cash machine and proceeded to enter the first three digits of your Personal Identification Number (PIN), it would be reasonable to infer that I knew the last digit of your PIN as well. You certainly couldn't discount the hypothesis that I knew your entire PIN simply because I hadn't, as yet, entered the final digit. Likewise, since the pattern of Jesus' life has already exhibited a significant portion of the complex information specified by messianic prophecy, we can reasonably infer that he is the Messiah and that his life will, therefore, eventually fulfil all genuinely outstanding elements of messianic prophecy.

Foreknowledge and Freedom

Christian spirituality is predicated upon the assertion that *humans are morally blameworthy for freely choosing to do that which we know to be wrong*. As H.P. Owen explains:

> Christianity presupposes free will in both the religious and the moral spheres. If our wills were not free in the religious sphere there would be no point in preaching the Gospel. Such preaching would do no more than intensify a pre-existing tendency to accept or reject God's Word. There would be no genuine offer of salvation, no genuine invitation to eternal life ... Equally Christianity presupposes free will in the moral sphere. If our wills were not morally free we should not be responsible for our actions and so accountable to God.[68]

God desires loving relationship with all humans (cf. 1 Timothy 2:3–4); and while, as a necessary precondition of such relationships, God has given humans the freedom to reject him (cf. Romans 11:32), he has also provided them the means to be saved from the natural consequence of sin; i.e. by freely receiving his gift of forgiveness displayed in Christ (cf. Acts 4:12). Some welcome relationship with God. Others spurn his advances. Jesus laments:

'O Jerusalem, Jerusalem, you who kill the prophets and stone those sent to you, how often I have longed to gather your children together, as a hen gathers her chicks under her wings, *but you were not willing'* (Matthew 23:37; Luke 13:34, my italics).

Paul Marston and Roger Forster note that 'free will' is a phrase coined by the early church:

> to represent the Bible's teaching that God allows man a choice of whether or not to obey him … Not a single church figure in the first 300 years rejected it and most of them stated it clearly in works still extant … Thus we find striking agreement among early church leaders over the issue of freewill. The same teaching was held by mainstream and fringe groups, by scholars and ordinary ministers, by the Greek, Latin and even Syrian traditions, by everyone, in short, except total heretics … it expressed their universally held belief that God made man free to accept or reject his offer of free pardon and grace.[69]

For example, Irenaeus commented:

> This expression, 'How often would I have gathered thy children together, and thou wouldst not,' set forth the ancient law of human liberty, because God made man a free (agent) from the beginning, possessing his own soul to obey the behests of God voluntarily, and not by compulsion of God. For there is no coercion with God … in man as well as angels, He has placed the power of choice … man is possessed of freewill from the beginning, and God is possessed of freewill in whose likeness man was created.[70]

It is sometimes argued that a belief in free will is incompatible with a belief in divine foreknowledge:

1) Necessarily, if God knows in advance that I will do x, x will come about
2) God knows in advance that I will do x
3) Therefore, x will come about necessarily
4) Anything that will come about necessarily isn't something concerning which I have freedom of choice
5) Therefore, I have no freedom of choice

However, Paul Copan points out that 'God's knowledge of future actions does not by itself hinder human freedom since knowledge does not actually cause anything ... Knowing and bringing about are distinct.'[71] Our knowledge that the average temperature will rise towards mid-summer doesn't *cause* the average temperature to rise towards mid-summer: 'In the same manner, God can have foreknowledge of free human choices without that foreknowledge causing anything. Something else – namely, human choice – must be added to the equation to cause human actions that God foreknows. In this sense, my foreknowledge is no different from God's foreknowledge since by itself foreknowledge does nothing.'[72]

If there is a conflict between foreknowledge and freedom, it isn't a problem introduced with belief in *divine* foreknowledge. Divine foreknowledge is no more incompatible with human freedom than is human foreknowledge. One might as well argue that 'necessarily, if you know in advance that I will do x, then x will come about ...' and so on. Indeed, irrespective of whose knowledge we consider, knowledge of truths about the future isn't the real issue here, but the mere fact that there appear to be truths about the future. Since it is either true that Peter will deny Christ tomorrow or true that he will not deny Christ tomorrow, then, even if no one knows which of these propositions is true, it's still tempting to argue that Peter lacks freedom of choice. However, whatever else might be wrong with the sceptical argument, it makes a mistake in modal logic (the logic of possibility and necessity). Atheist philosopher Peter Cave points out that:

> If God knows that Peter will sin, then, yes, it does necessarily follow that Peter will sin, but it does not necessarily follow that Peter will necessarily sin. To note that something necessarily follows is *not* to note that what follows is itself necessary ... just because someone – anyone – knows something to be true, it does not mean that what is known is a necessary truth and so could not have been otherwise. Foreknowledge alone is no threat to our acting freely.[73]

As Paul Copan explains:

The skeptical argument – that God's foreknowledge nullifies human freedom – results from the confusion between certainty and necessity. Look at the following two statements:

> A. If God knows in advance that I will do x, x will necessarily come about.
> B. Necessarily, if God knows in advance that I will do x, x will come about.

What is the difference between A and B? Statement A implies that the action God foreknows *had to* come about (that it *must* happen); because God foreknows it, it is necessarily so and could not have been otherwise. Statement B implies that my action that God foreknows *may* have been different (e.g. if I had chosen differently), but it *will* happen. Therefore, *if* God knows that [we will x], then we *will* [x], but, logically speaking, this does not mean that we *have to*. While [x] is certain, it is not *necessary*. We must be careful not to confuse these two ideas … While something that is necessary is also certain, what is certain may not be necessary.[74]

The upshot is that *the sceptical argument is invalid because premise 3 doesn't follow from premises 1 and 2*. When we correct the mistaken modal logic, the first syllogism of the sceptical argument reads as follows:

1) Necessarily, if God knows in advance that I will do x, x will come about
2) God knows in advance that I will do x
3) Therefore, necessarily, x will come about

But nothing at all follows from *this* conclusion concerning human freedom. The correctly placed 'necessarily' in the conclusion of this argument adds nothing to the meaning of the phrase 'x will come about'; and so if we ask *how* 'x will come about' we are perfectly within our rights to reply that 'x will come about' *due to my free will*. Likewise, abstracted from the red-herring of knowledge:

1) Necessarily, if it is true that I will do x, x will come about
2) It is true that I will do x
3) Therefore, necessarily, x will come about

Once again, this conclusion is no threat to free will, since it is distinct from the free-will denying conclusion that '*x* will come about *necessarily*'. Free will, divine foreknowledge and fulfilled biblical prophecy are logically compatible.

Conclusion

> I think it wholly reasonable to claim ... that in the plethora of prophecies concerning Jesus, and in their evident fulfilment, predictive prophecy both meets and passes its decisive test.
>
> Stuart C. Hackett[75]

As Robert D. Culver comments:

> Even by using the most extreme tactics it is impossible to date a large number of the Old Testament prophecies so late that they may be considered mere historical accounts rather than predictions. And once we conclude that many of these prophecies are truly prophetic, the whole narrative of human history becomes a vast account of their fulfillment and a vast demonstration of the power and foreknowledge of God and the truth of His Word.[76]

Fulfilled biblical prophecy appears to be a case where the miraculous activity of God can be offered as 'a best causal explanation ... when naturalistic processes seem incapable [or unlikely] of producing the *explanandum* effect, and when intelligence is known to be capable of producing it and thought to be more likely to have produced it.'[77] As Thomas V. Morris argues:

> A confluent series of prophecies made by different people at different times and culminating in a single fulfillment by the life of so remarkable a person as Jesus cries out for an explanation of a quite extraordinary sort ... the most reasonable explanation is that God was involved in the prophecy and fulfillment, thereby giving us an extra ground for accepting Jesus as the culmination of divine revelation.[78]

Recommended Resources

Video

Bock, Darrell L. 'The Historical "Problems" of the New Testament' http://www.publicchristianity.com/Videos/historicalNT.html.
'Jesus the Messiah: Unlocking Old Testament Prophecy' http://www.dod.org/Products/Jesus-the-Messiah--Unlocking-Old-Testament-Prophecy__DOD2170.aspx.

Websites

2005 Evangelical Alliance Symposium on the Atonement http://www.eauk.org/theology/key_papers/Atonement.

Online papers

Bayne, Tim and Greg Restall. 'A Participatory Model of the Atonement' http://www.consequently.org/papers/pa.pdf.
Bloom, John. 'Is Fulfilled Prophecy of Value to Scholarly Apologetics?' http://www.bethinking.org/bible-jesus/is-fulfilled-prophecy-of-value-for-scholarly-apologetics.htm.
Evans, Craig A. 'Did Jesus Predict His Violent Death and Resurrection?' http://www.4truth.net/fourtruthpbjesus.aspx?pageid=8589952879.
Lucas, J.R. 'Reflections on the Atonement' http://www.users.ox.ac.uk/~jrlucas/theology/atone.html.
Rea, Michael. 'Philosophy and Christian Theology' http://www.plato.stanford.edu/entries/christiantheology-philosophy/#BibAto.
Reichenbach, Bruce R. 'Inclusivism and the Atonement' http://www.faithandphilosophy.com/article_atonement.php.

Books

Copan, Paul. *That's Just Your Interpretation: Responding to Skeptics Who Challenge Your Faith* (Grand Rapids, MI: Baker, 2001).
Dembski, William A. *The Design Inference* (Cambridge University Press, 1998).
Dietz, James. 'Christianity for the Technically Minded: Risk Assessment, Probability, and Prophecy.' Pages 414–25 in *Tough-Minded Christianity:*

Honoring the Legacy of John Warwick Montgomery (ed. William Dembski and Thomas Schirrmacher; Nashville, TN: B&H Academic, 2008).

The Doctrine Commission of the Church of England, *The Mystery of Salvation* (Church House, 1995).

Foster, Charles. *The Christmas Mystery: What on Earth Happened at Bethlehem?* (Milton Keynes: Authentic, 2007).

Geivett, R. Douglas and Gary R. Habermas, eds. *In Defence of Miracles: A Comprehensive Case for God's Action in History* (Leicester: Apollos, 1997).

Green, Joel B. and Mark D. Baker, *Recovering the Scandal of the Cross: Atonement in New Testament and Contemporary Contexts* (Carlisle: Paternoster, 2000).

Hackett, Stuart C. *The Reconstruction of the Christian Revelation Claim: A Philosophical and Critical Apologetic* (Eugene, OR: Wipf & Stock, 2008).

Marston, Paul and Roger Forster. *God's Strategy in Human History* (Eugene, OR: Wipf & Stock, 2000).

McDowell, Josh. *The New Evidence That Demands a Verdict* (Nashville, TN: Thomas Nelson, 1999).

McGrath, Alister. *Making Sense of the Cross* (Leicester: IVP, 1992).

Molnar, Michael R. *The Star of Bethlehem: The Legacy of the Magi* (Rutgers University Press, 2000).

Pinnock, Clark H., ed. *The Grace of God and the Will of Man* (Minneapolis, MN: Bethany House, 1989).

Purtill, Richard. *Reason to Believe: Why Faith Makes Sense* (San Francisco: Ignatius, 2009).

Sanders, John. *No Other Name: Can Only Christians Be Saved?* (London: SPCK, 1994).

Strobel, Lee. *The Case for the Real Jesus: A Journalist Investigates Current Attacks on the Identity of Christ* (Grand Rapids, MI: Zondervan, 2007).

— *The Case for Christ: A Journalist's Personal Investigation of the Evidence for Jesus* (Grand Rapids, MI: Zondervan, 1998).

Swinburne, Richard. *Responsibility and Atonement* (Oxford: Clarendon Press, 1998).

Walls, Jerry L. *Heaven: The Logic of Eternal Joy* (Oxford University Press, 2002).

Ward, Keith. *What the Bible Really Teaches: A Challenge for Fundamentalists* (London: SPCK, 2004).

7

The Fifth Way – Jesus and Contemporary Experience

What we need is not experience without Christ, nor Christ without experience, but the experience of Christ; not psychology or theology but religion, lived relationship.

Peter Kreeft[1]

Christian philosopher Dallas Willard explains that:

Those who really do know Christ in the modern world do so by seeking and entering the kingdom of God ... To know Christ in the modern world is to know him in *your* world *now*. To know him in your world now is *to live interactively with him right where you are* in your daily activities. This is the *spiritual life* in Christ. He is, in fact, your contemporary, and he is now about *his* business of moving humanity along toward its destiny ... You don't want to miss out on being a part – *your* part – of that great project. You want to be sure to take your life into his life, and in that way to find your life to be 'eternal,' as God intended it ... 'Entering the kingdom of Heaven' ... is not a matter of 'making it into heaven' after death – though it takes care of that at the appropriate time. It is precisely a matter of *being interactively engaged with the kingdom in your life now*.[2]

One component of life in the kingdom of heaven is a matter of acting on the basis of what one *knows about* God and his business, as revealed by Jesus in the first century and communicated through the testimony of the New Testament. However, another component of life in the kingdom is a matter of *knowing God* and his business in the very act of *knowing Jesus*. Willard notes how philosophers 'distinguish knowledge by *description* from knowledge by *acquaintance*. Only the latter is the interactive relationship … The way of Jesus Christ is the way of firsthand interaction – knowing by acquaintance – direct awareness of him and his kingdom.'[3] As Amy Orr-Ewing observes, claims to this sort of direct religious experience are by no means ubiquitous amongst the world's spiritualities: 'Neither Buddhism nor Islam has any concept equivalent to the idea of relationship with God, which is at the heart of the Christian message … This is why Christian testimony – a personal account of one's relationship with God – underlines the uniqueness of Jesus.'[4] Moreover, Christian spirituality – the spirituality of the kingdom of heaven – involves both personal religious experience and publically available evidence. Christian religious experience straddles the categories of private and public, individual and corporate knowledge.

Credulity and Religious Experience

According to the principle of credulity, unless we have sufficient reason not to take instances of apparent knowledge by acquaintance at face value, we are within our epistemic rights to take them at face value. This applies no less to religious experience centred upon faith in Jesus than to other experiences. As philosopher Basil Mitchell argues, 'here as in other perceptual situations the mere possibility of delusion is not enough to warrant scepticism …'[5]

We shouldn't allow the person-relative nature of experience to obscure the *prima facie* objective intentionality of experience. An experience is of course something had by a subject, but this doesn't necessarily mean that it is a merely subjective awareness. That is, while all experience has a subjective aspect (in that it is something had by a subject) not all experience is wholly subjective (in that at least some experiences have objective referents). *You* experience reading this book; but you experience reading *this book*.

The person who prays for forgiveness in the name of Jesus on the basis of the NT witness and subsequently feels they are relieved of guilt has a spiritual experience that involves not merely *feeling* (e.g. relief), but also *belief* (that they have received the forgiveness they are relieved about receiving). Moreover, the truth of this belief is warranted, *prima facie*, *by that feeling*.

Countering Incredulity

Niles Eldredge expresses a fundamental scepticism about the possibility of warranted religious experience: 'We humans can directly experience [the] material world only through our senses, and *there is no way we can directly experience the supernatural.*'[6] From the fact that humans can only have direct experience of the material world using their material senses (sight, hearing, touch, taste, etc.), it follows that humans cannot directly experience God using those material senses. However, it doesn't follow that humans cannot directly experience the supernatural; because it doesn't follow that humans only have material senses. Such a conclusion would of course follow if naturalism was true, but one can't simply beg the question against the argument from religious experience by assuming that. Besides, the fact that humans cannot have *direct* experience of the supernatural using our material senses doesn't mean that we cannot have *indirect* experience of the supernatural using our material senses, as in the case of witnessing a miracle.

Richard Dawkins observes that 'the brain's simulation software … is well capable of constructing "visions" and "visitations" of the utmost veridical power. To simulate a ghost or an angel or a Virgin Mary would be child's play to software of this sophistication.'[7] This concludes his rebuttal of the theistic argument from religious experience: 'This is really all that needs to be said about personal "experiences" of gods or other religious phenomena. If you've had such an experience, you may well find yourself believing firmly that it was real. But don't expect the rest of us to take your word for it, especially if we have the slightest familiarity with the brain and its powerful workings.'[8]

Dawkins' rebuttal doesn't formally rise to the level of an argument because it fails to contain more than one premise. Merely observing that the brain *can* create illusions provides no reason for the conclusion that all religious experiences *are* illusions. Moreover, without a premise restricting the illusion-giving

power of the brain to religious experiences, Dawkins' objection
counts equally against all experiences, including those which lead
Dawkins to believe that human beings have brains 'capable of
constructing "visions" and "visitations" of the utmost veridical
power.' Dawkins' rebuttal of the argument from religious experience is threatened with self-contradiction.

Public Experience

Christian religious experience isn't restricted to the private side
of the distinction between private and public experience. Before
returning to the more common forms of Christian religious experience, I'd like to consider some more unusual experiences that
fall firmly on the public side of that distinction.

As Luke Timothy Johnson observes, 'the New Testament epistolary literature's focus is on the "signs and wonders" worked
through the power of the Holy Spirit ("in the name of the Lord")
in the present community, rather than on those worked by Jesus
in the past [e.g. Romans 15:19; Galatians 3:5; 2 Corinthians 12:12;
Hebrews 2:4].'[9] Evidence has continued to mount for this argument into the present day. Accepting the principles of credulity
and testimony does *not* mean being gullible, so the following
contemporary examples should be critically assessed on a case-
by-case basis.

Words of knowledge

Clive Calver defines a 'word of knowledge' (or 'prophetic word')
as 'the supernatural revelation by God of information that was not
learned by the efforts of our natural minds.'[10]

For example, I had an acquaintance that everyone called Andy.
He'd been a Christian youth worker, but had become disenchanted
with the church and had drifted away from faith. Nevertheless,
Andy kept up several friendships with Christians and went to
church with them occasionally. The church we both attended had
regular services offering prayer for physical and spiritual healing.
Before these services a small prayer group met to 'listen to God'
for 'words of knowledge' that were then given out in the service

to encourage people to come for prayer (about 70 per cent of the 'words' were reportedly responded to by people who thought that a proffered 'word' was for them). One Sunday, someone in the prayer group believed they had received a 'word' in the form of a symbolic picture depicting someone in a tug of war but feeling they were on the wrong team. The prayer-group leader (known personally to me) felt that this word was too vague, so he asked the group to pray that God would give them a specific name to attach to it. No one in the group knew about Andy's situation, yet someone hesitantly offered 'Andrew', Andy's real name. The picture and the name were duly given out together during the service, and Andy responded. Afterwards he told me that, several times before, he'd heard similar 'words' given out that he *could* have applied to himself, but he didn't respond because he reasoned that if God was really interested in him, God could put his name on an appropriate 'word'. In a congregation of c. 240 people, a non-Christian named Andrew, who felt in a 'tug of war' about accepting God, challenged God to put his name on an appropriate 'word', and God apparently responded. Andy rededicated his life to God, and a straightforward interpretation of the data surely supports the *prima facie* conclusion that Andy was rational in so doing.

In another case, a woman on the church staff I knew was involved in counselling someone, and was surprised to find an image of boots repeatedly coming to mind. Feeling rather foolish, but thinking this image might be a 'word', she asked the person she was counselling if 'boots' meant anything to them. This turned out to be a breakthrough moment, as the boots were a strong childhood memory related to hiding fearfully in a cupboard (for reasons we need not go into here).

Philosopher J.P. Moreland testifies to several verified examples of prophetic words.[11] For instance, in praying for a friend Moreland felt led to say (using an uncharacteristic word choice) that 'God sees you and approves of your ministry'. His friend broke down in tears because he'd been wondering if God even saw him and if his ministry was worthwhile. Again, as the evening speaker at a conference of Korean-Americans, Moreland asked God if there was anything he should say to the students. Moreland testifies that 'by way of a series of thoughts and images that came to me', he came to believe that God wanted him to say: 'There is a young man here named Mike, and he had a confrontation with his pastor before he came here, and he has continued to blame himself for that confrontation, but it wasn't his fault, it was his pastor's, and he needs to share with his pastor how much he was hurt by the confrontation.' Although worried by the fact that he'd never met a Korean-American named 'Mike', Moreland felt '70–30 it was the Lord', and so he 'shared this word with the group' and left for the night. When he returned the next morning to speak again, the conference leader introduced him to Mike (the only 'Mike' at the conference). Mike had indeed been inappropriately blaming himself for a confrontation with his pastor, who'd said some upsetting and untrue things about Mike and his girlfriend. The pastor was actually arriving at the conference later that day, and Mike resolved to speak with him about the incident.

Such 'risky predictions' (to borrow a phrase from philosopher of science Karl Popper), made on the basis of personal religious experience but publically verified after the fact, especially when considered cumulatively, are examples of specified complexity that confirm the reality of the relevant spiritual experiences and, by extension, the spiritual tradition in which these events take place.

Angelic and demonic encounters

As Peter Kreeft argues, there are only two groups of people who would disagree with the conclusion that *some reported experiences of angels are true*: '(1) the materialists, who claim to know that there are no spirits and thus believe *no* angel stories, and (2) people who even believe the *National Enquirer* and thus believe *all* angel stories.'[12] Kenneth D. Boa and Robert M. Bowman note that 'angelic encounters have *always* been rare, even during biblical times' – a fact that highlights the need 'to balance two legitimate concerns' when assessing contemporary reports of such encounters: 'On the one hand, we want to affirm the honest experiences of people who sincerely report encountering angels … On the other hand, we want to reject erroneous reports about angels …'[13] Assessing claims of angelic encounters means considering alternative explanations:

Whenever someone ... thinks he has encountered an angel [there] are actually five possibilities. 1. He saw a human being (and mistook that human for an angel). 2. He was mistaken – he did not see anyone. 3. He lied ... 4. He saw an actual, good angel. 5. He saw an actual angel, but it was a demon ... our study of what the Bible says about angel appearances leads us to expect that most (but not all) such reports today will fall into one of the first three options. We number these three options in the order we think most common ... We should caution that it is not always possible to reach a definite, certain conclusion about each reported angel sighting.[14]

By the negative elimination of alternatives, as well as by positive inference to the best explanation, it is possible to justify the hypothesis that *some* purported angelic and demonic encounters are real. Moreover, as with Jesus' exorcisms, agnosticism about the best *metaphysical* interpretation of the following events is compatible with the fact that they nevertheless provide some *prima facie phenomenological support* to the Christian hypothesis. So let's consider the testimony of three academic witnesses who followed the evidence even though it led them against the grain of their own scepticism.

Philosopher Phillip H. Wiebe

Philosopher Phillip H. Wiebe was a sceptic: 'I was aware that exorcism had been practiced in the church but thought that a worldview allowing for possession, exorcism, and other supernatural beliefs was absurd. I thought that supernatural hypotheses either had been imposed on events capable of being explained in natural terms or that reports of events supposedly favouring a supernaturalistic explanation were exaggerated.'[15]

However, as 'a doctoral student in philosophy at the University of Adelaide [under atheist J.J.C. Smart] ... working on the general problem of defining corroborating evidence for hypotheses',[16] Wiebe met a Christian minister who conducted exorcisms, and he became 'intrigued by the claim that evil spirits exist and startled by the contention, extraordinary to me at the time, that contemporary experiences might corroborate it.'[17] Through the close study of such evidence, Wiebe did a philosophical U-turn, developing 'an abductive approach to defending the existence of transcendent beings ...'[18] In his book *God and Other Spirits: Intimations of Transcendence in Christian Experience* (Oxford University Press, 2004), Wiebe argues that:

> spirits can be meaningfully and plausibly postulated ... to account for several kinds of reputed phenomena ... Physicalism cannot begin to describe what it will replace these explanations with, so it is not rational to abandon explanations provided by a transcendent reality in the absence of a better alternative ... The claim that spirits exist who are capable of acting in our world does not appear to be either self-contradictory or so counterintuitive that it should never be proposed. In fact, phenomena continue to be alleged for which it seems a plausible explanation.[19]

For example, Wiebe reports a particularly intriguing case:

> In one of the exorcisms that Leo [the minister Wiebe knew] conducted, the spirits who were ordered to leave a man responded in a distinctive voice with the threat that if they did so, they would enter a certain young man, who was known to Leo. The young man also lived in Adelaide, which was a city of about 700,000 at the time. Leo said he told the spirits to leave in spite of the threat and ordered them not to enter the young man. Within a half hour or so of this exorcism, he received a telephone call from the mother of the young man who had been named. She begged Leo to come to the house immediately because 'something strange had come over her son.' When Leo arrived at the house [he] went to the young man's room and saw from the doorway that he was lying on his bed. Leo entered the room and shut the door behind him, whereupon the threatening voice that he had heard from the older man a short while ago now spoke to him from the bed, saying, 'we told you we would get him, didn't we?'[20]

Wiebe comments:

> The sequence of the reported events, the close timing of them, the coherence of the utterances involved, and perhaps also the similarity of the distinctive voice coming from the two men suggest that something left the first man and entered the second ... The

suggestion that we are merely looking at two unrelated instances of dissociative identity disorder seems less plausible than the claim that we are confronted with a coherent complex requiring some other kind of explanation.[21]

Psychologist David Instone-Brewer

Consider this account of possession from psychologist David Instone-Brewer:

> I once went to interview a patient but found that he was asleep. He was lying on his bed, facing the wall, and he did not turn around or respond when I walked in. I sat in his room for a while thinking that he might wake up, and after a while I thought I might pray for him. I started to pray silently for him but I was immediately interrupted because he sat bolt upright, looked at me fiercely and said in a voice which was not characteristic of him: 'leave him alone – he belongs to us.' Startled, I wasn't sure how to respond, so we just sat and stared at each other for a while. Then I remembered my fundamentalist past and decided to pray silently against what appeared to be an evil spirit … because I was aware that an hysterical disorder could mimic demon possession. If the person felt that I was treating them as if they were possessed, this would exacerbate the condition and confirm in his mind that he really was possessed. I also prayed silently in case I was making a fool of myself. I can't remember exactly what I prayed but I probably rebuked the spirit in the name of Jesus. Immediately I did so, I got another very hostile outburst along the same lines … I realised then that I was in very deep water and continued to pray, though still silently. An onlooker would have seen a kind of one-sided conversation. I prayed silently and the person retorted very loudly and emphatically. Eventually (I can't remember what was said or what I prayed) the person cried out with a scream and collapsed on his bed. He woke up a little later, unaware of what had happened. I was still trying to act the role of a medic, so I did not tell him anything about what had happened. His behaviour after waking was quite striking in its normality. He no longer heard any of the oppressive voices which had been making him feel cut off and depressed, and his suicidal urges had gone.[22]

Until this event took place, Instone-Brewer was 'fairly satisfied that the Gospel accounts of demonization can be dealt with in terms of modern psychiatry or medicine'.[23] Instone-Brewer's report bears all the marks of a trained observer giving a careful account of something surprising. He is careful to distinguish between what he can and can't remember. He wasn't expecting these events. Nor did he leap to conclusions:

> I have personally been persuaded away from [a sceptical view-point] by a series of events which occurred while I was studying psychiatry, and during my time in pastoral work ... When I was dealing with the strange personalities which spoke out of [a] person I was always careful to speak silently, even if the person appeared to be asleep. If these personalities were part of a multiple personality syndrome or an hysterical reaction, it would have been counter-productive to speak out loud anything which might make him believe that these personalities were distinct from himself. These voices answered specific questions such as What is your name?, When did you come? This gradually convinced me that I was not dealing with a purely psychiatric disorder. After such 'conversations', which often involved much shouting, rage and abuse ... the person usually had no memory of any of these disturbing events.[24]

Instone-Brewer's experience finds corroboration in the experience of other educated people:

> Reading back to myself what I have written above, it seems like the rambling of a rabid fundamentalist or the paranoia of someone who needs urgent psychiatric help. I can only invite you to assess this in the way in which I present it – as a report of experiences which I have been reluctant to air in public in case they provoke ridicule or condemnation. I have heard similar stories ... from other ministers who are also reluctant to mention such things in public.[25]

Psychiatrist M. Scott Peck

Psychiatrist M. Scott Peck relates his involvement with two cases of possession. Having become 'a left-wing liberal'[26] Christian who believed in God and in the reality of human evil, Peck says he 'was left facing an obvious intellectual question: Is there such a thing as evil spirit?'[27] He says: 'I thought not … Still priding myself on being an open-minded scientist, I felt I had to examine the evidence that might challenge my inclination in the matter …'[28] Peck made it known that he was interested in observing cases of purported possession for evaluation:

> The first two cases turned out to be suffering from standard psychiatric disorders, as I had suspected, and I began making marks on my scientific pistol. The third case turned out to be the real thing. Since then I have also been deeply involved with another case of genuine possession … As a hard-headed scientist – which I assume myself to be – I can explain 95 percent of what went on in these two cases by traditional psychiatric dynamics … But I am left with a critical five percent I cannot explain in such ways. I am left with the supernatural – or better yet, subnatural.[29]

Peck argues that while people like to ask whether a patient is possessed or mentally ill, this is an invalid question: 'As far as I can currently understand these matters, there has to be a significant emotional problem for the possession to occur in the first place. Then the possession itself will both enhance that problem and create new ones. The proper question is: "Is the patient just mentally ill or is he or she mentally ill and possessed?"'[30] Peck affirms the importance of free will in possession and exorcism:

> Possession appears to be a gradual process in which the possessed person repeatedly sells out for one reason or another … Free will is basic. It takes precedence over healing. Even God cannot heal a person who does not want to be healed. At the moment of expulsion both these patients voluntarily took the crucifix, held it to their chests and prayed for deliverance. Both chose that moment to cast their lots with God.[31]

Peck concludes: 'Given the severity of their psychopathology before their exorcisms, the rapidity of their progress to health is not explainable in terms of what we know about the ordinary psychotherapeutic process.'[32] I recommend reading Dr Peck's book:

Glimpses of the Devil: A Psychiatrist's Personal Accounts of Possession, Exorcism, and Redemption (Free Press, 2005).

Angelic encounters

Evangelist Billy Graham relates the following incident:

> The Reverend John G. Paton, a missionary in the New Hebrides Islands, tells a thrilling story involving the protective care of angels. Hostile natives surrounded his mission headquarters one night, intent on burning the Patons out and killing them. When daylight came they were amazed to see the attackers unaccountably leave. They thanked God for delivering them. A year later, the chief of the tribe was converted to Jesus Christ, and Mr. Paton, remembering what had happened, asked the chief what had kept him and his men from burning down the house and killing them. The chief replied in surprise, 'Who were all those men you had with you there?' The missionary answered, 'There were no men there; just my wife and I.' The chief argued that they had seen many men standing guard – hundreds of big men in shining garments with drawn swords in their hands. They seemed to circle the mission station so that the natives were afraid to attack. Only then did Mr. Paton realise that God had sent His angels to protect them. The chief agreed that there was no other explanation.[33]

As Weibe argues: 'shared visual experiences of this kind obviously carry the impression that the being that appears is real.'[34]

Having written her PhD thesis on angel experiences, agnostic Emma Heathcote-James reports that 'people from all cultures, backgrounds and faiths relate fundamentally the same types of experience ... agnostics and atheists have the same kinds of experiences as believers in orthodox religions.'[35] Although remaining an agnostic, Heathcote-James concludes that 'angels are a *possibility* ... I simply don't believe [that] all those people who have written to me outlining their experiences have neurological, mental illnesses or undiagnosed temporal lobe epilepsy!'[36] Such naturalistic explanations strain credulity when faced with so many reports of not only individual but group experiences: 'psychological and medical theories have not provided answers that could explain away every experience I have investigated.'[37]

I submit that contemporary experience of angels and demons not only coheres with NT reports, but that many cases evince the ongoing reality of Jesus' ministry through the body of his church.

Healing

Perhaps the most widely claimed contemporary public experience of the supernatural would be the claim to have witnessed miracles of healing in answer to prayers made in the name of Jesus. Richard Dawkins acknowledges that 'the alleged power of intercessory prayer is at least in principle within the reach of science. A double-blind experiment can be done and was done. It could have yielded a positive result.'[38] The failure of a double-blind study on prayer for healing to produce a positive result does not count against the Christian understanding of Jesus, or the hypothesis that Jesus sometimes answers prayer positively. It counts against the hypothesis that God *always* answers prayer positively, but few if any believers accept such a hypothesis.

Dawkins references a study of prayer for healing that failed to yield a positive result:

> Needless to say, the negative results of the experiment [it would be more accurate to state that the study had a 'null' result rather than a 'negative' result] will not shake the faithful. Bob Barth, the spiritual director of the Missouri prayer ministry which supplied some of the experimental prayers, said: 'A person of faith would say that this study is interesting, but we've been praying a long time and we've seen prayer work, we know it works, and the research on prayer and spirituality is just getting started.' Yeah, right: we know from our faith that prayer works, so if evidence fails to show it we'll just soldier on until finally we get the result we want.[39]

Dawkins portrays Barth as claiming to know from *un-evidenced faith* that prayer can lead to real-world changes directly after he quotes Barth claiming to know this *from personal experience*! Dawkins also fails to note that several other scientific studies on prayer have reported positive results.[40] For example:

- 'Dr [Randolf] Byrd divided 393 heart patients into two groups. One was prayed for by Christians; the other did not receive prayers from study participants. Patients didn't know which group they belonged to. The members of the group that was prayed for experienced fewer complications, fewer cases of pneumonia, fewer cardiac arrests, less congestive heart failure and needed fewer antibiotics.'[41]
- Dr Dale Matthews documents how volunteers prayed for selected patients with rheumatoid arthritis: 'To avoid a possible placebo effect from knowing they were being prayed for, the patients were not told which ones were subjects of the test. The recovery rate among those prayed for was measurably higher than among a control group, for which prayers were not offered.'[42]

Such results provide *prima facie* verification of the efficacy of prayer for healing. They certainly show that Dawkins fails to grapple with the full range of available data on this subject. Indeed, a systematic review of the efficacy of distant healing published in 2000 concluded that 'approximately 57% (13 of 23) of the randomised, placebocontrolled trials of distant healing … showed a positive treatment effect'.[43] Moreover: 'David R. Hodge, an assistant professor of social work in the College of Human Services at Arizona State University, conducted a comprehensive analysis of 17 major studies on the effects of intercessory prayer … among people with psychological or medical problems. He found a positive effect.'[44] Hodge's meta-analysis featured in the March 2007 issue of *Research on Social Work Practice*:

> This is the most thorough and all-inclusive study of its kind on this controversial subject that I am aware of … It suggests that more research on the topic may be warranted, and that praying for people with psychological or medical problems may help them recover … Overall, the meta-analysis indicates that prayer is effective.[45]

Case studies in healing

While the Christian views positive answers to prayers for healing as a gift rather than an entitlement, the miraculous exception rather than the normal rule, 'there are numerous documented (and actually quite extraordinary) cases of healings'[46] that occur in apparent response to prayers offered by Christians in the name of Jesus.

Damaged knee/Banished laryngitis
J.P. Moreland testifies:

> I was speaking at a conference in which a young lady who had a damaged knee received healing prayer. She had been on crutches for about a month and walked with a serious limp, and she had not exercised for two full months. After receiving prayer, she was completely healed. She shed her crutches, began walking normally to this very day, and returned the next morning to her daily routine of jogging, all with no pain at all.[47]

Moreland has a personal testimony to offer as well:

> The Sunday evening service on February 20, 2005, had just ended and I wanted to get home ... The previous Thursday a virus landed in my chest and throat, and in a period of less than three hours I went from being normal to having the worst case of laryngitis in the 35 years since college. On Friday I went to our walk-in clinic and received the bad news. The doctor warned that this virus was going around, she had seen several cases of it in the last few weeks, and there was nothing that could be done about it. I just had to wait it out. The laryngitis would last 7–10 days. This couldn't be, I whispered to her. My main day of teaching at the university was Monday, and I was looking at a full day of lecturing. I couldn't afford to cancel classes because I had already missed my limit of canceled classes for that semester. To make matters worse, I was scheduled to deliver a three-hour lecture at a nearby church that Tuesday evening, and I didn't want to let the church down. It made no difference. The doctor said I wasn't going to be able to speak either day, so I had to make other plans. My throat felt as if it had broken glass in it, and I was reduced to whispering. On Sunday evening I whispered a few greetings to various church friends; I tried to speak normally, but it hurt too much. After the service I had to get home, try to contact our department secretary ... and cancel my classes for Monday. I could cancel with the church the

next day. As I was walking out of the sanctuary, two lay elders intercepted me. 'Hey, J.P.,' one yelled, 'you can't leave yet. Hope (my wife) just told us you have laryngitis, and we can't let you get outta here without loving on you a bit and praying for your throat!' So one elder laid hands on my shoulders and the other placed his hand on my lower throat area and started praying. To be honest, I wasn't listening to a word they said. I had already left the church emotionally and wanted to get home to make my phone call. But something happened. As the two men prayed gently for me, I began to feel heat pour into my throat and chest from one elder's hand. After two or three minutes of prayer, I was completely and irreversibly healed! I started talking to the brothers normally with no pain, no effort, no trace that anything had been wrong. I never had to make that call to my secretary.[48]

Multiple sclerosis

Michael Poole, lecturer in science education at King's College London, discusses the case of a female multiple sclerosis sufferer whom he calls Helen Johnson: 'When I first visited her and her husband, she had her left leg in a calliper, used a wheelchair, walked with crutches and was often to be found slumped on a large cushion on the floor ...'[49] On 10 January 1981 Helen attended a talk about the Christian ministry of healing given by the chaplain of the London Healing Mission, who prayed with Helen after the meeting: 'following a private conversation with the speaker [Helen] put down her crutches and, to the horror of her husband ... picked up a tray of bone china and carried it to the kitchen. The expected crash never occurred!'[50] In Helen's own words:

> After the main meeting had concluded Tom wanted to know if I would like him to pray for me. I was hesitant, because of my shyness, but I felt honoured that he should want to pray ... After a brief prayer of confession and asking for forgiveness [the chaplain] asked the Lord to take away the ... multiple sclerosis. Immediately I knew that the Lord had healed me, though I had felt nothing, and the realisation of being well began to dawn on me ... I felt [God] tell me to stand up, unaided, and walk to the opposite side of the room, pick up a tray of bone china mugs and carry them out to the kitchen. This I did, and being faithless, was amazed at how

easy this action was. My healing had started that day and was to go on during the next week until my husband bought me a cycle so that, at last, we could go out together … It was very difficult to persuade the doctors to accept back my mobility allowance but easy to find a buyer for the two wheelchairs. Within two weeks I was riding a new bicycle and swimming lengths of the pool. Some ten years have now passed and I have never felt any MS symptoms return.[51]

Poole reproduces a medical report written on 11 August 1981 by Helen's GP: 'Several months ago this patient attended my Surgery to report that she had been totally cured of her condition, and at that time I could see no residual evidence of disability. With regard to prognosis I am optimistic that the present situation will be maintained …'[52]

Brain tumour
Dr Bill Lees reports the case of 'H.P':

Some while ago she was under the care of neuro-surgeons who removed the main bulk of a benign space-occupying lesion which was becoming life-threatening on account of its size. The surgery was highly successful, although the surgeon reported that some portions of lesion could not be removed without unacceptable risk to H.P.'s normal brain tissue. Her friends, who had prayed for the surgeon in his work, were delighted and proceeded to ask God to complete what the surgeon could not. There was, however, eventually a return of symptoms and H.P. returned to the surgeon. After a full reinvestigation, he was convinced that there was need for further surgery. The friends continued to pray urgently that the tumour might be 'shrunk'. In due course H.P. was allocated a bed and prepared for the reopening of her skull. The surgeon wisely insisted on updating the data that would be available to him in the theatre. After a careful examination of the X-ray scan, he came to her bedside and announced that there was no need for surgery. There was no longer any sign of the tumour.[53]

A miscellany of healings

Consider the following reports from *The Independent on Sunday*:

- After a visit to her local hospital in 2003, [Sharyn] Mackay was diagnosed with cancer of the kidney. The tumour was removed, but soon grew back and spread to her lungs. After being given a year to live, Mackay decided to visit a church that performed healing services. On entering the church, Mackay recalls feeling an 'enormous heat' and the cancer leaving her body. Amazingly, subsequent test results found no traces of the cancer.[54]
- Like many of the 5 million Catholic pilgrims who make the journey to Lourdes each year, wheelchair-bound MS sufferer Jean-Pierre Bely arrived hoping for some respite from his chronic condition. After ignoring voices telling him to 'get up and walk', he went home a few hours later and, to the astonishment of his wife and two children, started walking around the house. In 1999, after a 12-year medical investigation by the Catholic Church, it became the first formally recognised miracle for over 22 years.[55]

Professors J.P. Moreland and Klaus Issler jointly testify:

> We have both seen and heard eyewitness testimony to miraculous healings … During the last two years, in our church alone, there have been at least six cases of cancer miraculously healed, some of them terminal and beyond medical intervention; one person who instantly had her complete eyesight restored from significant, partial blindness after receiving prayer; a Vietnam veteran blinded in one eye for twenty-five years by a grenade explosion who received full sight after being prayed for by a team of several people; and a young deaf boy who miraculously received full hearing after a friend of ours laid hands on him and prayed. These stories are real – in most cases we know the people involved in praying – and they could be multiplied many times over by other examples of miraculous healing.[56]

Andrew Wilson reports 'a number of healings this author has personally witnessed in the last month (September 2006)':[57]

A physiotherapist friend of mine who had been wearing a wrist splint, unable to move her wrist without significant pain, was healed instantly in front of me and ten others three weeks ago, and has since been able to move it completely normally without any discomfort, much to the surprise of many of her (atheist physiotherapist) colleagues. A chef in our church, who had been unable to move his arm above shoulder level for two years, prayed for it two weeks ago during a church meeting, and was instantly able to do so (last time I looked, he had not stopped waving it for several days). A short-sighted student I know, who had never been able to walk around with no glasses without suffering migraines, was instantly healed on being prayed for, and has not worn glasses since (except when, ironically, she cautiously wore them at college, and ended up getting migraines because her eyesight had been corrected). I do not mention these examples because they are the most dramatic I know, nor are they third hand reports ... I mention them because I have personally witnessed them in the last few weeks ... they are neither internalised hallucinations nor empirically untrue, but public, physical events in the space-time world, verifiable by doctors and friends.[58]

These reports are *prima facie* evidence that Jesus continues his ministry of miraculous healing in the world today in response to prayer.

Time we turned to the more common forms of Christian religious experience.

Religious Experience and the Principle of Testimony

Religious experience, like any other type of experience, is obviously more convincing in the first person than in the third person. Nevertheless, even considered in the third person, religious experience can clearly provide some warrant for the Christian understanding of Jesus.

Richard Swinburne argues that even though you may lack religious experience yourself, the principle of testimony means that it is reasonable to trust the reports of those with such experience:

Since (probably) others have the experiences which they report, and since (probably) things are as a subject's experience suggests that they are, then (with some degree of probability) things are as others report ... One who has not himself had an experience apparently of God is not in as strong a position as those who have. He will have less evidence for the existence of God; but not very much less, for he will have testimony of many who have had such experiences.[59]

As H.H. Price affirmed, one should 'accept what you are told, unless you see reason to doubt it.'[60] Other people's testimony regarding their religious experience carries, by the principle of credulity, *prima facie* validity. To deny any evidential value to religious experience considered in the third person involves a double standard:

Much of what a particular individual knows (justifiably believes) about the world is acquired from testimony. If I had to rely on my own experience and reasoning alone, I would know little of history, geography, science, and the arts, to say nothing of what is going on in the world currently. We generally suppose that justification is transferred via testimony from someone who has learned something from perception, memory, reasoning, or some combination thereof, to society at large. Why should it be different in the religious sphere?[61]

Hence, even if one lacks religious experience, one must deal with the fact that: 'a host of individuals have claimed to have known and had a personal relationship with God. This claim has been made across cultural and geographic boundaries as well as over time.'[62] At the very least, such common consent adds to the burden of proof on the sceptic. As Joshua Hoffman and Gary S. Rosenkrantz affirm, 'if entities of a certain kind belong to folk ontology [the ontological presumptions of our common-sense worldview], then there is *prima facie* presumption in favour of their reality ... Those who deny their existence assume the burden of proof.'[63] Throughout history people from different cultures all over the world have not merely believed in Jesus as the divine Son of God, but have claimed to know him as such *by acquaintance*.

It's *possible* that *all* Christians have misinterpreted their religious experience, but it doesn't seem at all *plausible*: 'It seems much more likely that such self-analyzing and self-critical men as Augustine, Blaise Pascal, and Kierkegaard were not totally deceived than that total skepticism is right.'[64]

The 'Direct Perception' Argument

The 'direct perception' argument seeks to demonstrate a close analogy between some forms of religious experience and everyday sensory experience (e.g. seeing or hearing something), in order to argue that: 'since we know the latter to be cognitive and (usually) veridical [i.e. true to reality], there is justification for taking the former to be cognitive and (usually) veridical.'[65] As Moreland argues: 'there are several reasons for holding that there is a close analogy between sensory perception and numinous [religious] perception. And since we know that the former is (usually) veridical, there is good reason to take the latter as (usually) veridical.'[66]

Of course, there are disanalogies between sensory and religious experience; but merely pointing this out doesn't defeat the direct perception argument, because disanalogy is an essential feature of *all* analogy. The question is whether the analogy between sensory and religious experience is *strong enough* for an argument by analogy to work. To be 'strong enough', an analogy merely needs to have more points of relevant coincidence than divergence. At least nine points of coincidence can be noted between religious experiences and such sensory experiences as sight:

1) *Our belief-forming practices can't be justified without epistemic circularity but are innocent until proven guilty.*
Alston points out that none of our belief-forming practices can be justified without begging the question: 'it is a familiar story that our best attempts to establish the reliability of memory, introspection, deductive reasoning or inductive reasoning will make use of premises derived from the practice under consideration, and so fall into epistemic circularity.'[67] While a belief-forming practice must *be* reliable if the beliefs it produces are to *be* reliable, we needn't justify the belief that our belief-forming practices are

reliable in order to be justified in relying upon the beliefs they produce. After all, the demand that we do so is impossible to satisfy since it leads to an infinite regress. Hence the only rational thing to do is to take our stand *within* familiar belief-forming practices 'that have become established, psychologically and socially, in our lives'[68] and to 'follow the lead of Thomas Reid in taking all our established doxastic [belief-forming] practices to be acceptable as such, as innocent until proven guilty.'[69] These considerations apply no less to religious experience than to memory, deductive reasoning, etc: *'for any established doxastic practice it is rational to suppose that it is reliable, and hence rational to suppose that its doxastic outputs are prime facie justified ... [Christian religious experience] is a functioning, socially established, perceptual doxastic practice ... As such it possesses a prima facie title to being rationally engaged in, and its outputs are therefore prima facie justified ...'[70]*

2) *If one seems to see something then this is* prima facie *evidence for the existence of that object, such that in the absence of relevant evidence that undermines this claim, the experience counts as evidence for the object's existence.*
If one seems to experience Jesus, this is *prima facie* evidence for the reality of Jesus. Alston points out that while Swinburne applied the principle of credulity to individual belief-forming *events*, he applies it to belief-forming *practices*: 'Swinburne's principle applies to experience-belief pairs individually, in isolation, while in my approach a principle of justification that applies to individual beliefs is grounded in a defence of the rationality of socially established doxastic practices.'[71]

3) *Certain conditions must be met, both in and out of the perceiving subject, if the perception is to be possible.*
In the sensory case, the perceiving subject must not be blind, must have their eyes open and so on. In the spiritual case, the subject must usually be 'looking' for Jesus, he must develop through practice and discipline the ability to 'recognize Jesus' voice', and so on: 'Among the particular conditions for reliable religious experience, honesty and attentiveness are often singled out as necessities.'[72]
Alston comments:

A priori it seems just as likely that some aspects of reality are accessible only to persons who satisfy certain conditions not satisfied by all human beings, as that some aspects are equally accessible to all. I cannot see any a priori reason for denigrating a practice either for being universal or for being partial ... quite apart from the religious case, we can see many belief-forming practices, universally regarded as rational, that are practiced by only a small minority. Higher mathematics and theoretical physics certainly satisfy this description ... Relatively few persons can follow inner voices in complex orchestral performances. But such belief-forming practices are not denied epistemic credentials on the grounds of narrow distribution ... the most basic point is that God has set certain requirements that must be met before He reveals Himself to our experience, at least consistently and with relative fullness. 'Blessed are the pure in heart for they will see God.'[73]

4) *Such experiences are about or of objects, and these objects usually exist independently of the experience itself.*
Visual experiences are usually experiences of objects that are taken to exist outside the subject. Religious experience is also experience of an object taken to exist outside of the subject: 'the mode of consciousness involved is distinctively perceptual; it seems to the subject that something ... is directly presenting itself to his/her awareness as so-and-so.'[74]

5) *Such experience is 'analogue' (a matter of degree) and not 'digital' (not all-or-nothing).*
'Just as one can sensorily perceive the same physical object with different degrees of attention, and just as a sensorily perceived object can be more or less within the focus of attention, so it would seem to be with the perception of God.'[75]

6) *Successive experiences of the object lead one from a vague experience to a clear experience of that object.*
Seeing a table from a distance is a vague perception; moving closer allows a clear perception. Religious experience occurs in a similar manner:

The initial stage of awareness of God frequently involves an awakening of the self to a vague sense of God's presence accompanied by intense feelings of joy and exultation. This is often followed by a clearer apprehension of God's beauty and holiness with a concomitant awareness of one's own sin and guilt. Eventually, perception becomes clearer to the point that spiritual work is done on the self in that it becomes more unified, whole, and at peace. Further, God has several attributes. Just as a table could appear circular from one angle and elliptical from another, so numinous perception can fasten onto different aspects of God as he is experienced in different ways in different conditions.[76]

Hence: 'one's apprehension of the divine can be self-correcting, just as one can continually correct one's vision as one sees objects from different angles and in different lights.'[77]

7) *The experience is both individual and communal.*
My friend's dog and my friend's God can both feature in the experience of many people at once, although none of these people is sharing the self-same experience in either case: 'people in the Christian community do tend to make the same or similar attributions to God on the basis of similar experiences.'[78]

8) *There are public checks for perception.*
You can ask other people if there is a dog in the room. You can ask someone else to describe what colour it is, etc. Likewise (although it *is* harder to do), religious experiences can be cross-referenced with multiple subjects, and several tests can be offered to distinguish true from false perceptions. For example: reliable experiences must be internally coherent and externally consistent with those of 'mystics' considered exemplars of religious experience. Such experiences are likely to be repeated, shared by others, and morally beneficial both for the self and for others. Such experience might be expected to conform to an objective body of revelation. Moreover, such experiences can be falsified if they contradict ordinary sense experience. As C. Stephen Layman writes: 'While I resist a dismissive attitude toward religious experience, I think we have to regard sense experience as a paradigm of reliable experience. In my view, any religious

experience that conflicts with sensory experience should be considered unreliable.'[79]

9) *Perceptual doxastic practices allow for a degree of inconsistency in their output.*
Alston observes:

> Witnesses to crimes and automobile accidents often disagree as to what happened, and there are undoubtedly many other cases of disagreement that go unnoticed because they are of no practical importance. It is notorious that people's memories often conflict ... Nevertheless, I doubt that any of our most basic doxastic practices yield enough mutually contradictory pairs to be disqualified as a rational way of forming beliefs. It is only on a fanatically rigoristic epistemology that one would be deemed irrational in holding perceptual beliefs just on the grounds that those beliefs were formed by a sort of mechanism that sometimes yields mutually contradictory beliefs.[80]

The fact that religious experience sometimes yields mutually contradictory beliefs cannot be used to invalidate the belief-forming practice of religious experience, unless one is prepared to jettison memory or sight on the same grounds. However, jettisoning belief in the general reliability of one's memory is self-contradictory. After all, one would have to assume that one had correctly remembered the reason for denying the general reliability of memory in the very process of withdrawing trust from one's memory. Hence, denying the general reliability of religious experience on the same grounds is also self-contradictory, unless one is prepared to endorse a double standard: 'sources of belief can be rationally tapped and can be sources of epistemic justification even if they sometimes yield mutually contradictory pairs of beliefs, provided this is a small proportion of their output.'[81]

Lest we become distracted by the analogy with sight, Alston reminds us that 'touch, unlike seeing, involves direct contact with the object; seeing reveals much more detail concerning the object and provides a much more convincing view of its nature and identity. And some mystical perceptions involve a more intimate contact with God, while others reveal him more fully.'[82] Religious experience doesn't necessarily exhibit 'the kind of clear, unmistakable, chock-full-of-information sort of awareness of God that we have of physical objects when we see them with our eyes.'[83] However: 'this has no tendency to show that we don't have any kind of perception of God. After all, feeling and smell don't give us such a clear, sharp, and loaded-with-information cognition of an object as vision does, but nonetheless they are modes of perception.'[84] Indeed, *this is a ninth analogy between religious experience and sense experience*: both can be divided into different types of experience bearing different types and amounts of information.

Disanalogy

The most obvious disanalogy between sensory and religious perception is that direct religious perception isn't empirical. Rather, experience of the divine is analogous to belief in other minds. No human has ever had empirical sensory perception of another person's experience (although we all know what it is to know what someone else is feeling or thinking). Someone else's experience just isn't the sort of thing that is open to *direct physical perception*; and neither is God the Son. If the fact that 'other minds' aren't directly perceivable by the empirical senses doesn't make belief in 'other minds' irrational (and clearly it doesn't) then neither does the fact that 'God the Son' is not directly perceivable by the empirical senses make belief in 'God the Son' irrational. As Keith Yandell argues: 'perceptual experiences provide evidence that there are physical objects; it is arbitrary not to add that perceptual experience provides evidence that God exists, unless there is some *epistemically relevant* difference between sensory and numinous experience.'[85] The non-empirical nature of religious perception is not obviously an epistemically relevant difference.

Besides, setting up the empirical nature of sensory perception as a necessary condition of reliable experience looks like begging the question: 'Unless the critic can give a convincing reason for supposing that the criteria available for sense perception constitute a necessary condition for any experiential access to objective reality,' observes Yandell, 'he is guilty of *epistemic chauvinism* ...'[86] Moreover, 'it is a category fallacy to fault ... God for not being an empirical entity ... It is not part of the nature of a spirit to be visible empirically as a material object would be. It is a category fallacy to ascribe sensory qualities to God or fault him for not being visible.'[87]

Hence, it would appear that an analogy can be drawn between sensory and religious perception in which there are more points of relevant coincidence than of relevant divergence. As R. Douglas Geivett concludes: 'The strong analogy between sense perception and perception of God ensures strong epistemological parity between the evidence of sense perception in grounding beliefs about the physical world and the perception of God in grounding beliefs about God.'[88] Therefore, Christian mystical experience provides *prima facie* evidence for the Christian understanding of Jesus.

The Causal Argument from Christian Religious Experience

> The final test of the Christian scheme comes from trying it out in one's life.
>
> William P. Alston[89]

In the causal argument from Christian religious experience 'a person cites certain experiences of spiritual power and transformation, his changed life, his new ability to handle problems in a way not available to him before his conversion (or before some special numinous experience after conversion), and postulates God as the best explanation for his change.'[90] As Alston suggests: 'one's experience of the changes in one's life that follow a conversion, or one's experience of the gradual improvement of one's character in the course of sincere attempts to open oneself up to the influence of the Holy Spirit, can be of cognitive significance, in addition to other forms of significance, as presenting explananda that are naturally explained theologically.'[91]

The causal argument can of course be framed in the third person, as Basil Mitchell argues:

> if [religious believers] did in fact exemplify a quality of life of unusual power and grace of a kind and to a degree that their

former personality gave no warrant for expecting, some weight attaches to their testimony that it was 'not I, but the grace of God that was in me', and the value to be given to it is necessarily related to whatever other reasons there may be for believing in the God whose character and purposes they purport to reflect. The situation is analogous to that in which one man claims to have been influenced by another. In assessing his claim we pay attention to such matters as his general truthfulness, the contrast between his performance before and after the alleged influence, the extent to which his words and actions altered in conformity with the other's known views and whether the other was in a position to influence him. To the extent that we are satisfied by such tests as these we are the more inclined to trust his testimony; but his testimony makes its own independent contribution to our final judgement.[92]

The classic biblical example here is the apostle 'Paul', formerly implicated in the murder of Christians under his original name of 'Saul'. Saul believed that he was doing the will of God:

> I too was convinced that I ought to do all that was possible to oppose the name of Jesus of Nazareth. And that is just what I did in Jerusalem. On the authority of the chief priests I put many of the saints in prison, and when they were put to death, I cast my vote against them. Many a time I went from one synagogue to another to have them punished, and I tried to force them to blaspheme. In my obsession against them, I even went to foreign cities to persecute them (Acts 26:9–11 [NIV]).

Then he had an experience of God as revealed in the risen Jesus, and he realized that he hadn't been doing God's will, but opposing it:

> As he neared Damascus on his journey, suddenly a light from heaven flashed around him. He fell to the ground and heard a voice say to him, 'Saul, Saul, why do you persecute me?'
> 'Who are you, Lord?' Saul asked.
> 'I am Jesus, whom you are persecuting,' he replied. 'Now get up and go into the city, and you will be told what you must do' (Acts 9:3–6).

Saul's life turned inside out: 'At once he began to preach in the synagogues that Jesus is the Son of God' (Acts 9:20). Whatever you believe about Jesus, this is certainly the subjective experience that Paul had (cf. 1 Corinthians 9:1), and it transformed him. Millions of people have had similar (if not always so dramatic) life-changing experiences of God/Jesus. Relevant Christian testimony isn't hard to come by:

- William Lane Craig claims: 'God has transformed my life, my attitudes, my relationships, my motivations, my marriage, and my priorities through his very real ongoing presence in my life …'[93]
- John Dickson describes 'experiencing God personally through my reading of the Bible, answered prayer and the slow but real transformation of my life under the influence of his presence.'[94]
- Lee Strobel states: 'It was in 1981 when I originally responded to the evidence by deciding to abandon atheism and cling to Christ … I've never been the same. Opening my life wider and wider to God and his ways, I've found my values, my character, my priorities, my attitudes, my relationships, my desires have been changed over time – for the better.'[95]
- J.P. Moreland remarks: 'As a university student … I met Jesus Christ personally and He changed my life. I have had close to two decades of walking with Him and fellowshipping with Him and falling more and more in love with Him daily. He has given me power for life that I did not know before, and I have had personal experiences of Him … When one tries Christianity based upon these rational considerations, he can put Jesus Christ to the test and see if Christianity works out in his own personal life. I have done this, and I have found that Jesus Christ has changed my life. This is an argument from religious experience that has meant a lot to me intellectually and personally, and I recommend it to you.'[96]

Attempts to explain away religious transformation by the power of psychological and/or sociological factors must, in order to be plausible, assume the existence of a common causal factor (or a small number of factors) responsible for the transformation.

However: 'such a strategy becomes less plausible as the diversity increases in the nature and scope of religious transformation ... since the [apparent] working of God seems to be the major, perhaps the only, constant factor at work in such experiences.'[97] After all:

> Religious transformation has occurred for thousands of years, in primitive cultures and advanced ones, in young and old people, in those well educated and those without education, in cool, calm people and emotional, hysterical people, in those in a religious culture and those in an atheistic culture. Such differences in time, place, upbringing, temperament, and age are good evidence that the common causal factor in such cases is God.[98]

Indeed, the common causal factor is a decision to take Jesus at his word, to trust him and to follow him.

Conclusion

As N.T. Wright comments: 'Christians have claimed from the very beginning that, though Jesus is no longer walking around Palestine and available for us to meet him and get to know him in that sense, he is indeed "with us" in a different sense, and that we can indeed get to know him in a manner not wholly unlike the way we get to know other people.'[99] The veracity of this claim is supported by a multi-stranded argument from 1) Christian religious experience combined with the principles of credulity and testimony, 2) the close analogy between religious and perceptual experience, and 3) the 'best explanation' argument from the spiritual transformation of those who live as Jesus' disciples. The public evidence of changed lives is joined by publically available evidence concerning 4) miraculous 'words of knowledge', 5) angelic/demonic encounters, and 6) physical healings closely associated with prayers offered in Jesus' name.

Of course, Christians remain ignorant about things it would be useful to know, many people are not healed physically (Jesus does not fulfil an obligation when he heals, but rather bestows a supererogatory gift), and so on. These observations clearly raise further theological questions, but these questions don't count against, or permit us to ignore, the evidence that raises them.

Recommended Resources

Video

DeWeese, Garrett. 'Problems of Evil: Does the Fact of Evil in Some Way Disprove God's Existence?' http://www.veritas.org/Media.aspx#/v/285.

Geivett, Douglas. 'Problems of Evil' http://www.hisdefense.org/LinkClick.aspx?link=http%3a%2f%2fhisdefense.org%2fvideo%2fGeivett+-+Problems+of+Evil.WMV&tabid=136&mid=954.

Habermas, Gary R. 'The Death and Resurrection of Debbie' http://www.youtube.com/watch?v=489i38n1gjU

Morse, Neal. *Testimony: Live*, music DVD (SPV, 2004).

Audio

Craig, William Lane. 'The Problem of Evil and Suffering' http://www.rfmedia.org/av/audio/gracepoint-the-problem-of-evil-and-suffering.

— 'Vision in Life' http://www.rfmedia.org/RF_audio_video/Other_clips/BIOLAChapelVisionInLife.mp3.

Habermas, Gary R. 'God's Activity in the World Today' http://www.namb.edgeboss.net/download/namb/4truth/audio/habermas_god_in_world_today.mp3.

Moreland, J.P. 'Kingdom Triangle Talk' http://www.kingdomtriangle. com/audio/kingdom_triangle_5-6-07.mp3.

— 'On the Gift of Prophecy' http://www.jpmoreland.com/media/on-the-gift-of-prophecy.

— 'On the Promises and Problems of Petitionary Prayer' http://www.jpmoreland.com/media/on-the-promises-and-problems-of-petitionary-prayer/.

Williams, Peter S. 'Angels at Advent' http://www.damaris.org/cm/podcasts/269.

Online papers

Clark, Kelly James. 'I Believe in God the Father, Almighty' http://www.calvin.edu/academic/philosophy/writings/ibig.htm.

Copan, Paul. 'God Can't Possibly Exist Given the Evil and Pain I See in the World!' http://www.bethinking.org/resource.php?ID=30&TopicID=3&CategoryID=3.

Cowan, Steven B. 'Peering Through a Glass Darkly: Responding to the Philosophical Problem of Evil'. http://www.arcapologetics.org/articles/article09.htm.

Craig, William Lane. 'The Problem of Evil' http://www.bethinking.org/resource.php?ID=60&TopicID=3&CategoryID=3.

Dembski, William A. 'Faith and Healing: Where's the Evidence?' http://www.bpnews.net/BPnews.asp?ID=28460.

Gibson, Keith. 'Faith Healers or Fake Healers?' http://www.arcapologetics.org/articles/article10.htm.

Habermas, Gary R. 'Atheism and Evil: A Fatal Dilemma' http://www.garyhabermas.com/books/why_believe/whybelieve.htm.

— 'Job and Me and God Will Supply', from *Forever Loved: A Personal Account of Grief and Resurrection* (College Press, 1997) http://www.garyhabermas.com/books/forever_loved/foreverloved.htm.

— 'The Truth and Comfort of the Resurrection' http://www.garyhabermas.com/articles/decision_mag/dec_truth_comfort_res_2000-04.htm.

Snyder, Daniel Howard. 'God, Evil and Suffering' http://www.faculty.wwu.edu/howardd/god,evil,andsuffering.pdf.

Books

Adler, Mortimer J. *The Angels and Us* (New York: Collier, 1982).

Alston, William P. *Perceiving God: The Epistemology of Religious Experience* (Cornell University Press, 1993).

— 'Why Should There *Not* Be Experience of God?' Pages 382–6 in *Philosophy of Religion: A Guide and Anthology* (ed. Brian Davies; Oxford University Press, 2000).

Boa, Kenneth D. and Robert M. Bowman Jr. *Sense and Nonsense about Angels and Demons* (Grand Rapids, MI: Zondervan, 2007).

Burke, Brad. *Does God Still Do Miracles? An MD Examines* (Eastbourne: Victor, 2006).

Calver, Clive. *The Holy Spirit* (Bletchley: Scripture Union, 2001).

Dubay, Thomas. *The Evidential Power of Beauty: Science and Theology Meet* (San Francisco: Ignatius, 1999).

Geivett, R. Douglas. 'The Evidential Value of Religious Experience.' Pages 175–203 in *The Rationality of Theism* (ed. Paul Copan and Paul K. Moser; London: Routledge, 2003).

— 'God and the Evidence of Evil.' Pages 249–68 in *Reasons for Faith: Making a Case for the Christian Faith* (ed. Norman L. Geisler and Chad V. Meister; Wheaton, IL: Crossway, 2007).

Heathcote-James, Emma. *Seeing Angels* (London: John Blake, 2001).

Kwan, Kai-Man. 'The Argument from Religious Experience.' Pages 498–552 in *The Blackwell Companion to Natural Theology* (ed. Craig, William Lane and J.P. Moreland; Oxford: Wiley-Blackwell, 2009).

Lane, Anthony N.S., ed. *The Unseen World: Christian Reflections on Angels, Demons and the Heavenly Realm* (Carlisle: Paternoster, 1996).

Lewis, C.S. *The Problem of Pain* (London: Fount, 1977).

Lucas, Ernest, ed. *Christian Healing: What Can We Believe?* (London: Lynx, 1997).

Moreland, J.P. *Kingdom Triangle* (Grand Rapids, MI: Zondervan, 2007).

— *Scaling the Secular City* (Grand Rapids, MI: Baker, 1987).

— and Klaus Issler. *In Search of a Confident Faith: Overcoming Barriers to Trusting in God* (Nottingham: IVP, 2008).

Nash, Ronald H. 'The Problem of Evil.' Pages 203–23 in *To Everyone an Answer: A Case for the Christian Worldview* (ed. Francis J. Beckwith, William Lane Craig and J.P. Moreland; Downers Grove, IL: IVP, 2004).

Orr-Ewing, Amy. *But Is It Real? Answering 10 Common Objections to the Christian Faith* (Nottingham: IVP, 2008).

Peck, M. Scott. *Glimpses of the Devil* (New York: Free Press, 2005).

Poole, Michael. *Miracles: Science, the Bible and Experience* (London: Scripture Union, 1992).

Rhodes, W.S. *The Christian God* (Delhi: I.S.P.C.K, 1998).

Strobel, Lee. *The Case for Faith: A Journalist Investigates the Toughest Objections to Christianity*, (Grand Rapids, MI: Zondervan, 2000).

Wiebe, Phillip H. *God and Other Spirits: Intimations of Transcendence in Christian Experience* (Oxford University Press, 2004).

Willard, Dallas. *Knowing Christ Today* (New York: HarperOne, 2009).

Williams, Peter S. *The Case for Angels* (Carlisle: Paternoster, 2002).

Woolmer, John. *Healing and Deliverance* (Mill Hill, London: Monarch, 1999).

8

Understanding the Spirituality of Jesus

Christianity makes claims on the entire personality; accepting it as true is not a matter of mere intellectual assent, but of embarking on a new venture in life.

Douglas Groothuis[1]

The Christian understanding of Jesus is that *the self-understanding of the historical Jesus is true.* Jesus' self-understanding was inextricably bound up in his spirituality, a spirituality simultaneously expressed and vouchsafed in word and deed. Jesus' implicit and explicit claims placed him in the category of the divine as understood within the Jewish religious tradition. This forces us to grapple with the incongruities that result from affirming any of the limited range of consequent explanatory options, besides acknowledging Jesus as divine, in the light of everything else we know about his moral and intellectual character. Jesus' symbolic miraculous (and non-miraculous) deeds, amongst which his resurrection is the most significant, cohere with his teaching about himself and the kingdom of God. Across the board, numerous aspects of Jesus' personal history correspond with both the general tenor and specific, unlikely predictions of Old Testament prophecy. The specified complexity of this correspondence provides warrant for a design inference that supports Jesus' self-understanding. Finally, various aspects of contemporary Christian religious experience round out the cumulative case for believing that Jesus really is who he claimed to be. On the basis of a global consideration of these five 'ways' to understanding Jesus, I am personally convinced that

David Hume's 'desire' and 'expectation' that 'Heaven' would be pleased to afford us 'some more particular revelation to mankind'[2] has been met in Jesus, the true source of spiritual enlightenment.

Spiritual Enlightenment

> The life and words that Jesus brought into the world came in the form of information and reality. He and his early associates overwhelmed the ancient world because they brought into it a stream of life at its deepest, along with the best information possible on the most important matters.
>
> Dallas Willard[3]

Although Jesus' central teaching was about the kingdom of God (that is, 'what life would be like if God was really enthroned as king in human lives'[4]) it's also true to say that his teaching was self-centred; for Jesus' proclamation of the kingdom centred upon himself as the divine 'Son of Man', a figure who wasn't merely inaugurating the kingdom through his own teaching and deeds, but *who was himself the divine entry-point into the spiritual life of the divine kingdom*. It is primarily the *quality*, rather than the unlimited *extent* of life in the kingdom that Jesus calls 'eternal life' in John's gospel: 'Now this is eternal life: that they may know you, the only true God, and Jesus Christ, whom you have sent' (John 17:3 [NIV]). Jesus saw himself as more than someone called upon to *teach* and to *embody* the spirituality of love for God, self and neighbour. Jesus saw the lived reality of kingdom spirituality coming *in and through his own ministry and person, such that people's ultimate response to him was their ultimate response to that kingdom and to its king*:

> I tell you the truth, I am the gate for the sheep. All who ever came before me were thieves and robbers, but the sheep did not listen to them. I am the gate; whoever enters through me will be saved. He will come in and go out, and find pasture. The thief comes only to steal and kill and destroy; I have come that they may have life, and have it to the full.
>
> I am the good shepherd. The good shepherd lays down his life for the sheep ...

I am the way and the truth and the life. No-one comes to the Father except through me' (John 10:7–11; 14:6 [NIV]).

As Darrell L. Bock comments:

> Jesus was obedient to God, engaged in self-disposing love and called for a discipleship defined by the example of Jesus' character ... this call to discipleship went beyond a mere call to imitation. It was ultimately rooted in what Jesus presented about himself as the figure at the hub of the presence of the kingdom of God ... There is more here than Jesus' being obedient to God's will; he is the bearer of promise and the presence of divine rule ... Whether as Son of Man or Messiah in the Synoptics, or as the Way and Word in John, Jesus pointed to God beyond his example by revealing God and God's way in ways that pointed to himself as possessing a unique, indispensible role in the program.[5]

Closing his massive study on *Jesus According to Scripture: Restoring the Portrait from the Gospels* (Baker Academic, 2002), Bock summarizes Jesus' ministry:

> Jesus defines his mission as that of the Servant who calls out to the captives to experience release (Luke 4:16–19). Everything about the character of Jesus' ministry wedded together words and deeds of compassion and showed the love of God standing behind his preaching of divine forgiveness and mercy. But the presence of the offer of forgiveness and mercy does not mean that salvation is for everyone. Jesus formed a new community of those who wished to walk in what soon became know as 'the way' (Acts 9:2; 18:25; 19:9). It was to be made up of Jews and eventually Gentiles who came to Jesus in a faith that had turned them to God out of a sense of spiritual need for deliverance and forgiveness. In embracing God and his love, they took on a commitment to love God and their neighbor, taking the message of this fresh walk into eternal life to a needy but rejecting world.[6]

Jesus' interpretation of the messianic redemptive goal wasn't the militarily enforced political transformation for Israel expected by the disciples (cf. Acts 1:6), but the invitation to *a spiritual transformation open to everyone.* And while the faithful response Jesus calls for 'has an intellectual (*notitia*) or cognitive aspect'[7] it is equally 'a faith that is relational and alive towards God, not a dispassionate intellectualism … Faith means a commitment to the truth of God and a heart that delights in the truth … engaging not only heart and mind, but also the will.'[8] As Marcus Borg writes: 'to follow Jesus means in some sense to be "like him," to take seriously what he took seriously,' and doing so leads us to 'an alternative vision of life'[9]; that is, a new spirituality.

Peter Kreeft explains Jesus' perspective on our need for forgiveness and for spiritual transformation that reflects God's character:

> The essence of sin is selfishness, 'me first', self-love or pride. Pride is essentially competitive. 'Me first' necessarily means 'you second' … Self-love, or pride, is not the same as self-respect. Self-respect means treating yourself, like all selves, as valuable. This is true, because self is … made in God's image … is loved by God, offered adoption into his family and destined for spiritual marriage to him in eternal righteousness, truth and joy. Self-love, on the other hand, means making yourself your own God: that is, your own end, good and goal; seeking your happiness and purpose and destiny and meaning in yourself rather than in God. It means Hamlet thinking he's Shakespeare. Christianity teaches that we ought to have more self-respect and less self-love.[10]

As Bock explains,

> Jesus understood that the renunciation of self-focus bound up in his call to turn to God meant that many in the world would not accept the invitation to be a part of God's people. To accept God's gift of grace meant to acknowledge one's own need and limitations … the kingdom comes only to those who embrace their need for life in the way God has established it.[11]

Thus Jesus taught that we should put God at the very heart of our lives:

Do not store up for yourselves treasures on earth, where moth and rust destroy, and where thieves break in and steal. But store up for yourselves treasures in heaven, where moth and rust do not destroy, and where thieves do not break in and steal. For where your treasure is, there your heart will be also.

The eye is the lamp of the body. If your eyes are [generous], your whole body will be full of light. But if your eyes are [stingy], your whole body will be full of darkness. If then the light within you is darkness, how great is that darkness!

No one can serve two masters. Either you will hate the one and love the other, or you will be devoted to the one and despise the other. You cannot serve both God and Money.

Therefore I tell you, do not worry about your life, what you will eat or drink; or about your body, what you will wear. Is not life more important than food, and the body more important than clothes? Look at the birds of the air; they do not sow or reap or store away in barns, and yet your heavenly Father feeds them. Are you not much more valuable than they? Can any one of you by worrying add a single hour to your life?

And why do you worry about clothes? See how the flowers of the field grow. They do not labor or spin. Yet I tell you that not even Solomon in all his splendor was dressed like one of these. If that is how God clothes the grass of the field, which is here today and tomorrow is thrown into the fire, will he not much more clothe you – you of little faith? So do not worry, saying, 'What shall we eat?' or 'What shall we drink?' or 'What shall we wear?' For the pagans run after all these things, and your heavenly Father knows that you need them. But seek first his kingdom and his righteousness, and all these things will be given to you as well (Matthew 6:19–33; cf. Luke 12:22–34).

Jesus' injunction to 'seek first his kingdom' (cf. Mark 8:34–36; Luke 9:24) breaks the 'hedonist's paradox' that the pursuit of pleasure, when elevated to the status of one's primary motive, is ultimately a deeply unpleasurable experience. Jesus does *not* proclaim a 'health and wealth' gospel that links spirituality with earthly prosperity (cf. Mark 10:21–25; Matthew 8:20). What he proclaims is that when the primary motive of one's life is a loving relationship with God, one is freed from the hedonist's paradox to *enjoy earthly pleasures as the by-products they were designed to be.* Charles Colson explains that the 'eternal life' of kingdom spirituality:

> begins with what the Greeks called *metanoia*, which means a 'change of mind' and is translated in the New Testament as 'repentance' ... the repentance God desires of us is not just contrition over particular sins; it is also a daily attitude, a perspective. Repentance is the process by which we see ourselves, day by day, as we really are: sinful, needy, dependent people. It is the process by which we see God as he is: awesome, majestic, and holy. It is the essential manifestation of regeneration that sets us straight in our relationship to God and so radically alters our perspective that we begin to see the world through God's eyes, not our own. Repentance is the ultimate surrender of self.[12]

Jesus takes up the call of John the Baptizer: 'Repent (*metanoieite*), for the kingdom of heaven has come near' (Matthew 3:2; 4:17; cf. Mark 1:4,15). Jesus' concept of 'entering into the kingdom of the heavens' (Matthew 5:20) is, as Dallas Willard observes:

> clearly not a matter of 'making it into heaven' after death – though it takes care of that at the appropriate time. It is precisely a matter of *being interactively engaged with the kingdom in your life now.* That interaction is God's gift of himself to human beings elsewhere referred to as 'the birth from above' (John 3:3, 5). You cannot earn this, but you do have to actively receive it. You do that by welcoming God into every dimension of your character and life ... to know Christ in the kingdom of God we must abandon ourselves to a total transformation of *who we are on the inside*, to taking on the character of Christ through living with him day by day.[13]

N.T. Wright explains:

> following Jesus means just that, *following Jesus*, not ticking a box which says 'Jesus' and then sitting back as though it's all done. To speak, rather, of Jesus' lordship, and of the new creation which results from his victory on [the cross] and at Easter, implies at once that to confess him as Lord and to believe that God raised him from the dead is to allow one's entire life to be reshaped by him,

knowing that, though this will be painful from time to time, it will be the way, not to a diminished or cramped human existence, but to genuine human life in the present, and complete, glorious, resurrected human life in the future.[14]

Thus Paul urges his readers:

> in view of God's mercy, to offer your [life] as a living sacrifice, holy and pleasing to God – this is true worship. Do not conform to the pattern of this world, but be transformed by the renewing of your mind [*nous* – cognitive faculties]. Then you will be able to test [with your mind] and approve [in your heart] what God's will is – his good, pleasing and perfect will (Romans 12:1–2).

The change of perspective demanded by Jesus requires us to repent of the prideful, me-first kind of self-love by embracing a God-first orientation in light of his loving mercy towards us. The result of this *metanoia* is to find oneself loving both self and neighbour in response to God's love: 'Be imitators of God, therefore, as dearly loved children and live a life of love, just as Christ loved us and gave himself up for us … ' (Ephesians 5:1 [NIV]). This is the spiritual context for Jesus' teaching on the 'golden rule':

> One of the teachers of the law … asked [Jesus], 'Of all the commandments, which is the most important?'
> 'The most important one,' answered Jesus, 'is this: "Hear, O Israel: The Lord our God, the Lord is one. Love the Lord your God with all your heart and with all your soul and with all your mind and with all your strength." [cf. Deuteronomy 6:4–5] The second is this: "Love your neighbor as yourself." [cf. Leviticus 19:18.] There is no commandment greater than these.'
> 'Well said, teacher,' the man replied. 'You are right in saying that God is one and there is no other but him. To love him with all your heart, with all your understanding and with all your strength, and to love your neighbor as yourself is more important than all burnt offerings and sacrifices.'
> When Jesus saw that he had answered wisely, he said to him, 'You are not far from the kingdom of God' (Mark 12:28–34; cf. Matthew 22:34–40; Luke 10:25–37).

Jesus' response to the question of the greatest commandment defines the structure of kingdom spirituality: 'At the core of God's commandments is not a set of principles or a list of expectations; at the heart of God's commandments is a relationship. We are to love God with our whole being.'[15] The teacher of the law was 'not far from the kingdom of God' because he believed *that* this was true. However, to enter into the kingdom one must actually enter into loving relationship with God despite one's inherent selfishness; and faith (trust) *in Jesus* in response to his loving forgiveness is the divine doorway into the eternal life of the kingdom (cf. Mark 10:17–31): 'To receive Christ means more than receiving the benefits of the atonement; it means receiving *him*. It means believing that he died for the sins of humanity, loving him, and determining to strive to obey his commands.'[16] As John put it:

> This is how God showed his love among us: He sent his one and only Son into the world that we might live through him. This is love: not that we loved God, but that he loved us and sent his Son as an atoning sacrifice for our sins. Dear friends, since God so loved us, we also ought to love one another … We love [God, self and neighbour] because he [i.e. God] first loved us' (1 John 4:9–11, 19).

Kreeft analyzes Jesus' kingdom spirituality in terms of worldview:

> Think of humanity as a tube with two openings. The openings can be either open or closed, as we choose [our spiritual attitudes]. Think of God, or superhuman reality, as above the tube, and nature, or subhuman reality, as below it. Traditional religious wisdom tells us to be open at both ends so God can flow in one end and out the other: in the receptive end first by faith and then out the active end by works. But if the top opening is closed, our business becomes exclusively human action in the world, without plugging into divine power … There is a third possibility: the tube could be closed at the bottom and open at the top. This would characterize Hinduism and Buddhism, for which the world is illusion (*maya*) … mysticism minimizes worldly action; modern Western secularism denies receptivity to God; and the classical Western tradition synthesizes the two, giving priority to the God-relationship, for

we must first be directed by God before we can wisely direct our world.[17]

Jesus presents kingdom spirituality as a way of life founded upon opening ourselves, through an ongoing act of trust, to God's forgiveness (the divine desire to fellowship with humans despite our selfishness) as it is displayed in, offered through, and vouchsafed by Jesus' own life, death, resurrection and continuing activity in the life of the faithful. The consequent, tripartite content of kingdom spirituality is implicit within Paul's letter to the Colossians:

> Put on then, as God's chosen ones, holy and beloved, compassionate hearts, kindness, humility, meekness, and patience, bearing with one another and, if one has a complaint against another, forgiving each other; as the Lord has forgiven you, so you also must forgive. And *above all these put on love, which binds everything together in perfect harmony*. And *let the peace of Christ rule in your hearts* ['all your heart'], to which indeed you were called in one body. And be thankful. *Let the word of Christ dwell in you richly, teaching and admonishing one another in all wisdom* ['all your mind'], singing psalms and hymns and spiritual songs, with thankfulness in your hearts to God. And *whatever you do* ['all your strength'], in word or deed, do everything in the name [i.e. character] of the Lord Jesus, giving thanks to God the Father through him (Colossians 3:12–17 [ESV], my italics).

Paul's discussion emphasizes the heart-attitude of the Colossians; but it's clear that this attitude is formed in response to understanding the *word* (i.e. *logos*) of Jesus Christ, and that the appropriate attitude to this word (not only to the 'teaching' of Christ but to his life in the round) results in actions reflecting the nature ('the name') of Christ.

Understanding Jesus in the Christian manner is thus inseparable from the Christian understanding of true spirituality, for as Kreeft comments: 'Christianity is not a *hypothesis*, it is a proposal of marriage.'[18]

Jesus' Kingdom Spirituality = Love God (and therefore self and neighbour) with all your:

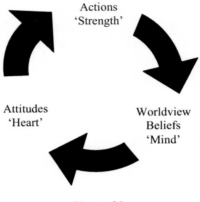

Actions
'Strength'

Attitudes
'Heart'

Worldview
Beliefs
'Mind'

Figure 20

Contemplating Community

Sociologist David Burnett reminds us that 'worldviews are incarnated in the actual ways of life of a person and his society.'[19] Philosopher W. Jay Wood explains:

> we are not alone in our efforts to become morally and intellectually virtuous persons; our careers as moral and intellectual agents are developed in a community context … What goals are worth pursuing, what goals should be subordinated to others, what practices ought to be avoided and which pursued, and what resources are available to assist us in moral and intellectual growth are matters shaped in large measure within families, churches, schools and other social frameworks.[20]

For example, C. Stephen Evans observes:

> In becoming a scientist, an individual becomes part of a scientific community, which is defined by the shared values, attitudes and basic assumptions of its members. These shared commitments are embodied not only in theories but in the life and practice of the community, and they are acquired not only through overt

instruction but by the individual's coming to share in that communal form of life.[21]

Like the scientific community, Christian community acts as a 'plausibility structure', one that makes the faith and works of Jesus' spirituality a more plausible or 'live' option (to borrow a term from William James) than it would otherwise be.

A community isn't the same thing as a family, a friendship group or a neighbourhood. Philip Yancey notes that 'we often surround ourselves with the people we most want to live with, thus forming a club or clique, not a community. Anyone can form a club; it takes grace, shared vision, and hard work to form a community.'[22] Rather, as Charles Colson explains: 'A community is a gathering around shared values; it is a commitment to one another and to common ideas and aspirations.'[23] A spiritual community is *the social embodiment of a common spirituality*, and is therefore constituted by shared beliefs, attitudes, and activities. As Tim Chester and Steve Timmis observe:

> The New Testament word for community is *koinonia*, often translated by the now anaemic word 'fellowship'. *Koinonia* is linked to the words 'common', 'sharing', 'participation'. We are the community of the Holy Spirit (2 Corinthians 13:14) in community with the Son (1 Corinthians 1:9); sharing our lives (1 Thessalonians 2:8), sharing our property (Acts 4:32), sharing in the gospel (Philippians 1:5; Philemon 6) and sharing in Christ's suffering and glory (2 Corinthians 1:6–7; 1 Peter 4:13).[24]

A positive personal response to Jesus results in Christian fellowship:

- *Christian community* (as distinct from other fellowships of common interests and liabilities) *happens* (community is an active thing) *when any group of people love each other and their non-Christian neighbours because they love God, as revealed in and through Jesus, with all their mind, heart and strength.*

Thus Jesus told his followers: 'A new command I give you: Love one another. As I have loved you, so you must love one another. By this everyone will know that you are my disciples, if you love one another' (John 13:34–35). After all, 'Inextricably connected to the doctrine of the Trinity [God's nature as three divine persons in one divine personal being] is love … Because God is a relational community of love, God is the source and model of all that is love.'[25] It was with this love in mind that Paul observed:

> If I have the gift of prophecy and can fathom all mysteries and all knowledge, and if I have a faith that can move mountains, but do not have love, I am nothing. If I give all I possess to the poor and give over my body [to hardship] that I may boast, but do not have love, I gain nothing.
>
> Love is patient, love is kind. It does not envy, it does not boast, it is not proud. It does not dishonor others, it is not self-seeking, it is not easily angered, it keeps no record of wrongs. Love does not delight in evil but rejoices with the truth. It always protects, always trusts, always hopes, always perseveres (1 Corinthians 13:2–7).

Out of the depths of God's love Jesus formed a loving spiritual community around himself, calling and empowering that community to an ongoing purpose; namely, to flourish in true spirituality, growing in the love of God and thus the sharing of God's love with others (Matthew 16:18; 28:16–20; Luke 24:45–49; Acts 1:1–8). As Keith Ward explains:

> Human persons are to find their fulfilment, not in isolation, but in co-operating with one another in many creative enterprises, in helping one another in trouble, and in sharing in the understanding and appreciation of the good things of creation. So if religion is about human fulfilment in relation to God … it is necessarily about the building up of healthy, creative communities. The fact is, however, that human beings have largely turned away from this divine purpose, and now find themselves trapped by selfish egoism, hatred of others, and the pursuit of pleasure at the expense of goodness. Christians believe that God's response to this situation is to create a 'counter-cultural community', a society which will try to counter the forces of egoism and hatred, and encourage the pursuit of creative excellence, universal compassion and worthwhile happiness … To be a Christian is to accept membership of this community of the Spirit.[26]

Although Jesus' spiritual proposal is made to each and every individual, it's emphatically *not* the proposal of an *individualistic* spirituality. Rather, Jesus proposes an innately *corporate* spirituality in which being his disciple means *communing in Jesus* and thereby participating in a community that Paul calls 'the body of Christ' (cf. Romans 12:5; 1 Corinthians 10:16; 11:29; 12:12, 27; Ephesians 3:6; 4:12). In this communion humans find forgiveness for sin (Galatians 6:14; Colossians 2:14) and live in the warranted hope that the Christ-centred community born on earth will one day be raised from the dead just as Jesus was (1 Corinthians 15:20), being transposed by God into the eternal life of 'the new heavens and the new earth' (Isaiah 66:22; cf. 2 Peter 3:13) described in John's visionary experience:

> Then I saw 'a new heaven and a new earth,' [Isaiah 65:17] for the first heaven and the first earth had passed away, and there was no longer any sea [i.e. chaos]. I saw the Holy City, the new Jerusalem [i.e. the church], coming down out of heaven from God, prepared as a bride beautifully dressed for her husband. And I heard a loud voice from the throne saying, 'Look! God's dwelling place is now among the people, and he will dwell with them. They will be his people, and God himself will be with them and be their God. "He will wipe every tear from their eyes. There will be no more death" [Isaiah 25:8] or mourning or crying or pain, for the old order of things has passed away.'
>
> He who was seated on the throne said, 'I am making everything new!' Then he said, 'Write this down, for these words are trustworthy and true.'
>
> He said to me: 'It is done [cf. Psalm 22:31; John 19:30]. I am the Alpha and the Omega, the Beginning and the End. To the thirsty I will give water without cost from the spring of the water of life [cf. John 4:14]' (Revelation 21:1–6).

Whilst this is the ultimate flourishing of the flower of eternal life, growth towards this transcendent sun informs the here-and-now of kingdom life (Colossians 3:1).

Luke describes how the earliest Christian community functioned as a body of believers:

They devoted themselves to the apostles' teaching and to fellowship, to the breaking of bread and to prayer. Everyone was filled with awe at the many wonders and signs performed by the apostles. All the believers were together and had everything in common. They sold property and possessions to give to anyone who had need. Every day they continued to meet together in the temple courts. They broke bread in their homes and ate together with glad and sincere hearts, praising God and enjoying the favor of all the people. And the Lord added to their number daily those who were being saved (Acts 2:42–47).

Atheist philosopher Andre Comte-Sponville observes that:

In monotheistic cultures, people are bound together (horizontally, so to speak) by the fact that all of them feel bound to God (vertically). It is like the warp and woof of the religious material. The community of believers … is as powerful as this double bond is solid … for it is communion that creates the community, far more than the other way around … it is a communion that turns a human group into a community, instead of a series of juxtaposed and competing individualities.[27]

He insightfully explains that:

to commune is to share without dividing. This may sound paradoxical. Where material goods are concerned, it is indeed impossible. People cannot commune in a cake, for instance, because the only way to share it is to divide it … In a family or a group of friends, on the other hand, people can commune in the pleasure they take in eating a delicious cake together: all share the same delectation, but without having to divide it up![28]

The community of people who commune in Jesus Christ has been called 'Christendom', a term that can have some unfortunate political overtones. However, Jesus himself said: 'My kingdom is not of this world' (John 18:36; cf. Luke 17:20–21). Jesus is the defining, founding member of Christendom in the apolitical sense of the term; the one in whom the Christian community has its spiritual communion in the Trinitarian love that is God. This communion is a metaphysical reality and it is *not* co-extensive with any particular church or denomination, let alone with any earthly political authority. This metaphysical reality is embodied in the rite of 'communion' inaugurated by Jesus' multiply attested reinterpretation of the (already symbolic) Jewish Passover:

> Is not the cup of thanksgiving for which we give thanks a participation in the blood of Christ? And is not the bread that we break a participation in the body of Christ? ...
>
> For I received from the Lord what I also passed on to you: The Lord Jesus, on the night he was betrayed, took bread, and when he had given thanks, he broke it and said, 'This is my body, which is for you; do this in remembrance of me.' In the same way, after supper he took the cup, saying, 'This cup is the new covenant in my blood; do this, whenever you drink it, in remembrance of me.' For whenever you eat this bread and drink this cup, you proclaim the Lord's death until he comes (1 Corinthians 10:16; 11:23–26; cf. Mark 14:22–24; Matthew 26:26–29; Luke 22:19–20; John 6:54–56).

A positive response to the belief *that* Jesus truly offers a relationship with God in and through his own person constitutes a belief *in* Jesus that baptizes the individual into the communal kingdom spirituality of Christendom, 'the community called by God to love him and to express that love in service to others.'[29] This love isn't a feeling, but a choice to 'humbly and simply devote ourselves under God to the promotion of the goods of human life that come under our influence.'[30]

Utopian dreams

Journalist Tobias Jones spent a year living in different spiritual communities. In his book *Utopian Dreams: In Search of a Better Life* (Faber, 2007) he writes:

> Like Utopia, the ideal community is a receding horizon. Just as you're getting closer it seems to be further from you than ever. But the journey does at least bring into focus, albeit fleetingly, what you are after ... there was, within the Christian communities, both

a rigidity and fluidity ... an immaculate mixture of the traditional and the revolutionary ... Their idealism existed not because they thought they had reached perfection, but because they realised how far short they were ... They weren't ghettos or gated or walled, but actually much more open than the self-proclaimed tolerant society from which they had retreated. Their merit lay in the fact that they were so confident of their role that they would reject no human material, nothing was beyond hope ... They weren't isolationist, but stretched your horizons as far as possible ... The people in these communities ... were writing their lives, as it were, because they believed that authority wasn't authoritarian, but authorising; it was the very thing that allowed them to make sense of their lives ... I had seen, in the 'real world', what a society looked like when it was based on a gathering together of rights; these communities were about almost the opposite: congregating responsibilities.[31]

Discovering freedom through responsibility was central in Jones' experience:

In the perfect community, freedom and obedience become, not mutually excluding opposites, but the consequence of one another ... I felt it again and again: we can only be responsible if we have something – place, context, companions – to which we can respond. In community, everyone is part of the whole, drawn into discovering who they are at the same time as they discover who others are. Responsibility depends upon others, upon a conversation.[32]

The fusion of realism and idealism, of authority and freedom lies at the heart of kingdom spirituality. Hence Paul simultaneously laments and rejoices at his spiritual condition:

I have discovered this principle of life – that when I want to do what is right, I inevitably do what is wrong. I love God's law with all my heart. But there is another power within me that is at war with my mind. This power makes me a slave to the sin that is still within me. Oh, what a miserable person I am! Who will free me from this life that is dominated by sin and death? Thank God! The answer is in Jesus Christ our Lord ... (Romans 7:21–25 [NLT])

By the end of his journey, Jones records a significant reaction to this reality:

> I no longer had an issue with hypocrisy. It's the standard adolescent criticism of any idealism that it's practised by hypocrites. I had rejected idealism as a teenager because idealists were, without fail, disappointing. Let down by the gap between theory and practice, I had rejected the theory as well as the practitioners. Now, though, I realised that there was an ideal which understood that gap, which anticipated it. The inevitable existence of hypocrisy was no longer a reason to throw out idealism, but a reason to investigate it.[33]

The Pilgrim's Spiritual Progress

Any spirituality is more *authentic* and *transformative* when it is *intrinsic* (a matter of self-conscious choice) as opposed to when it is *extrinsic* (i.e. a matter of outward cultural conformity). Indeed, by its very nature as a spiritual proposal, Jesus' kingdom spirituality demands an *intrinsic* personal response. As Robert Winston notes:

> Extrinsic religiosity [is] defined as religious self-centredness. Such a person goes to church ... as a means to an end – for what they can get out of it. They might go to church to be seen, because it is the social norm in their society, conferring respectability or social advancement. Going to church ... becomes a social convention. [The 1950s Harvard psychologist Gordon] Allport thought that intrinsic religiosity was different. He identified a group of people who were intrinsically religious, seeing their religion as an end in itself. They tended to be more deeply committed; religion became the organizing principle of their lives, a central and personal experience. In support of his research, Allport found that prejudice was more common in those individuals who scored highly for extrinsic religion. The evidence generally is that intrinsic religiosity seems to be associated with lower levels of anxiety and stress, freedom from guilt, better adjustment in society and less depression. On the other hand, extrinsic religious feelings – where religion is used as a way to belong to and prosper within a group – seem

to be associated with increased tendencies to guilt, worry and anxiety.[34]

Intrinsic participation in Christendom facilitates spiritual development, which we can define as follows.

- 'Spiritual development' means: *making progress towards the ideal of self-consciously informing all of one's relationships* (with God, oneself, other people and with the world in which you live) *through the wise internalization of true beliefs together with concomitant attitudes and behaviours.*

In concrete terms, faith in Jesus incorporates believers into a spiritual community wherein (in co-operation with the Holy Spirit) they can learn to better love God, self and neighbour with all their mind, heart and strength: 'the fruit of the Spirit is love, joy, peace, patience, kindness, goodness, faithfulness, gentleness and self-control' (Galatians 5:22–23; cf. Titus 3:5). It is crucial to grasp the fact that spiritual development is *not* a precondition of salvation, of communion with Christ, but *a product thereof*: 'Jesus is emphatic that obedience to him will flow out of our love for him. What this does not mean is that we must obey Jesus so that he will love us. Rather, he has loved us by grace apart from anything we have done, and as a result we trust him, which is the essence of faith.'[35] Dallas Willard explains that this process of discipleship involves the whole person:

> When I study anything I take its order and nature into my thoughts, and even into my feelings and actions ... Now disciples of Jesus are people who want to take into their being the order of The Kingdom Among Us ... They devote their attention, their thoughtful inquiry, and their practical experimentation to the order of the Kingdom as seen in Jesus, in the written word of scripture, in others who walk in the way, and, indeed, in every good thing in nature, history, and culture.[36]

Thus Paul advises: 'whatever is true, whatever is noble, whatever is right, whatever is pure, whatever is lovely, whatever is admirable – if anything is excellent or praiseworthy – think about such things' (Philippians 4:8). The result of such attention and thoughtful inquiry is a process of personal (and hence social) transformation:

> *Confidence in and reliance upon Jesus* as 'the Son of Man,' the one appointed to save us ... naturally leads to a *desire to be his apprentice* in living in and from the kingdom of God ... The abundance of life realized through apprenticeship to Jesus, 'continuing in his word', naturally leads to obedience ... Obedience, with the life of discipline it requires, both leads to and, then, issues from the *pervasive inner transformation of the heart and soul.*[37]

Hence theologian Michael Wilkins defines discipleship to Jesus as 'living a fully human life in this world in union with Jesus Christ and His people, growing in conformity to His image, and helping others to know and become like Jesus.'[38]

Contemplating Christ

We have pursued a cumulative case for understanding Jesus in the Christian manner, as deity incarnate, and so for taking seriously the kingdom spirituality into which he calls us all through the offer of divine forgiveness demonstrated on the cross.

We've been careful to note that the reader's response to this case depends in part upon the type and strength of the worldview presuppositions that they brought to the inquiry. Unless each of the five 'ways' of coming to understand Jesus we have examined is entirely vacuous, and unless the reader began with an unfalsifiable precommitment to anti-supernaturalism, they should find themselves better disposed towards the Christian understanding of Jesus than they would be without knowledge of the five ways. Exactly how well disposed towards the Christian understanding of Jesus the readers now find themselves will of course depend upon the epistemic weight they attach to the cumulative evidence of the five 'ways', minus the weight of any prior scepticism on their part.

Readers who find themselves less than convinced by the Christian understanding of Jesus should reflect upon the role played in their doubt by attachment to an incompatible world-view. For most readers in this position the worldview in question is likely to be metaphysical naturalism. I wonder if such readers might agree with the suggestion that if it weren't for the strength of their initial prior commitment to naturalism, then they'd think the cumulative case for the Christian understanding of Jesus sufficient to warrant its acceptance? If so, they will concede that anyone who considered the five ways without the same initial degree of scepticism as they did would be rationally inclined to accept the Christian understanding of Jesus. I hope that readers in this position will be willing to ask themselves if their continued attachment to naturalism is a principled commitment able to weather the growing swell of criticism currently levelled at the matter-first worldview. Readers who cannot in good conscience claim an acquaintance with the best contemporary critiques of naturalism should wonder if the failure of the five ways to convince them isn't a matter of building their own spiritual abode on a foundation of sand instead of rock (cf. Matthew 7:24–27). There's obviously only one way to answer such a question with integrity.[39]

Whilst wishing to highlight the significance of the contemporary revival of 'natural theology' to one's assessment of Jesus, I agree with physicist turned theologian John Polkinghorne when he writes that:

> Appeal to the exercise of reason and the general inspection of the world can only offer limited resources for theological investigation and so it can only lead to limited theological insight. If there is indeed a God who is concerned with individual creatures, that … God can only adequately be known through the particularity of revelatory events and in the experiences of worshipful encounter and obedience. Christian theology can welcome the contemporary revival of natural theology, and benefit from it, but the essential ground of its belief will always lie in the irreplaceable uniqueness of the history of Israel, and the life, death and resurrection of Jesus Christ.[40]

It's worth noting that we have only touched upon the 'Old Testament' revelatory background insofar as it aids our understanding of Jesus' claims and fulfilment of prophecy. There are independent arguments supportive of a theistic worldview to be mounted from a consideration of 'the history of Israel'. I recommend that readers minded to pursue this additional avenue of inquiry should invest in Professor K.A. Kitchen's *On the Reliability of the Old Testament* (Eerdmans, 2003).[41]

Contemplating Faith

> The educated religious person is a person of a reasonable and rational faith.
>
> John Mark Reynolds[42]

Faced with the question 'How should we respond to the spirituality of Jesus?' it's worth bearing in mind Charles Colson's observation that 'something responds not only in your head but in the deeper layers of your being. The process is rational, but it is also aesthetic and emotional.'[43] I imagine that, while our focus has been rational, readers will by now have developed some sense of their moral and aesthetic response to the spirituality of Jesus (these values are in any case inextricably intertwined); and I anticipate that some readers will find themselves in sufficient agreement with the cumulative case for the Christian understanding of Jesus to affirm that this understanding is more rationally plausible than its denial.

Still, as Chad V. Meister points out, 'believing that Jesus is the Messiah and being a follower of Jesus are two very different matters ... a person can believe *that*, without believing *in*.'[44] Belief *that* the Christian understanding of Jesus and the spirituality he calls us to embrace is true is a necessary but insufficient condition of entering into the spirituality of the kingdom. For that, one must combine belief *that* with belief *in*. In other words, to enter into the kingdom of God one must exercise trust by putting your faith *in* Jesus as someone with the divine ability to deliver upon his promises of forgiveness and eternal kingdom life. It is this combination of a sufficiently specific and strong *belief that* with the act of trust or *belief in* Jesus that constitutes Christian faith.

As theologian Austin Farrer wrote, faith 'isn't a choice between following reason and trusting the heart. It is a matter of putting heart into a rational conviction, and bringing mind into the heart's devotion.'[45] Christian faith is emphatically *not* a matter of 'belief in the absence of supportive evidence and even in the light of contrary evidence',[46] as atheist Victor J. Stenger asserts. Nor is it something requiring intellectual certainty or excluding intellectual inquisitiveness. As philosopher John Mark Reynolds explains: 'For Socrates, skepticism was wondering about the wonderful ... Belief combined with wonder allows for faith without foolish certainty. Faith ... retains what is hoped for within the bounds of best reason and experience ... Faith is not certainty but a willingness to follow the argument where it leads.'[47] In this, a Christian's theological beliefs are no different from their scientific beliefs. Scientists haven't yet constructed a comprehensive, problem-free theoretical understanding of the material world. Science is, at best, *a partial success*. But scientists don't allow this fact to drive them into the arms of erroneous conclusions such as 'truth is unknowable', or 'no scientific theory is a better explanation than any of its rivals'. Good scientists follow the evidence where it leads them *on balance*, defending their *best* understanding of material reality against rival theories, whilst recognizing that they have more to learn. And what goes for science goes for the spiritual quest. In both cases, we should *expect* there to be mystery, unanswered questions and instances when we simply misunderstand reality. Hence the mere presence of mystery, unanswered questions and misunderstandings should not, *in either case*, lead us to conclude that 'no belief is better than all the others', or that 'no belief is in the right ballpark'. Indeed, we should be suspicious of any spirituality that *lacked* a measure of mystery, paradox, ignorance and misunderstanding:

> One of the truest clues for finding the most important truths is surprise. The real world is strange, not simple ... As [C.S. Lewis] says in *Surprised by Joy*, if any message from the core of reality were to reach us, we should expect to find in it just that unexpectedness that we find in the Christian faith: the taste of reality, not made by us, but hitting us in the face. In *Mere Christianity*, Lewis says that it's no good asking for a simple religion. After all, real things are

not simple. And besides being complicated, reality is usually very odd: 'it is not neat, not obvious, not what you expect … That is one of the reasons why I believe Christianity. It is a religion you could not have guessed.' It is not the sort of thing anyone would have made up.[48]

The analogy between science and spirituality highlights the importance of distinguishing between reasonable and unreasonable expectations to place upon our understanding of reality. It also highlights the importance of distinguishing between those central beliefs that define which spiritual 'ballpark' we are in, and more or less peripheral beliefs that can be changed without leaving the 'ballpark'.

Swimming in reality

G.K. Chesterton warned against placing an *unreasonable* burden upon human reasoning:

> Poetry is sane because it floats easily in an infinite sea; reason seeks to cross the infinite sea, and so make it finite. The result is mental exhaustion … To accept everything is an exercise, to understand everything a strain. The poet only desires exultation and expansion, a world to stretch himself in. The poet only asks to get his head into the heavens. It is the logician who seeks to get the heavens into his head. And it is his head that splits … And if great reasoners are often maniacal, it is equally true that maniacs are commonly great reasoners … If you argue with a madman, it is extremely probable that you will get the worst of it; for in many ways his mind moves all the quicker for not being delayed by the things that go with good judgement. He is not hampered by a sense of humour or by charity, or by the dumb certainties of experience. He is the more logical for losing certain sane affections. Indeed … The mad man is not the man who has lost his reason. The madman is the man who has lost everything except his reason.[49]

In other words: don't try to fit reality into yourself (it won't fit); but do make *reasonable* efforts to fit yourself into reality. Don't try to swallow the sea (you will drown); but do learn to swim. Don't try to *over*simplify things, lest you end up a lunatic; but do seek the simplest adequate understanding of reality – always remembering William of Occam would urge that explanatory adequacy is more important than theoretical simplicity.

A definite philosophy of life

Chesterton argued for the importance of being dedicated not merely to worldview questions, but to seeking to fasten one's mind upon truths that correctly answer them: 'The human brain is a machine for coming to conclusions; if it cannot come to conclusions it is rusty. When we hear of a man too clever to believe [in God], we are hearing of something having almost the character of a contradiction in terms.'[50] According to Chesterton, a human is an animal that makes 'dogma':

> As he piles … conclusion on conclusion in the formation of some tremendous scheme of philosophy … he is … becoming more and more human. When he drops one doctrine after another in a rarefied scepticism, when he declines to tie himself to a system, when he says that he has outgrown definitions, when he says that he disbelieves in finality, when, in his own imagination, he sits … holding no form of creed but contemplating all, then he is by that very process sinking slowly backwards into the vagueness of the vagrant animals and the unconsciousness of the grass. Trees have no dogmas. Turnips are singularly broad-minded.[51]

Chesterton concluded that if there is to be intellectual advance, it must be 'in the construction of a definite philosophy of life. And that philosophy of life must be right and the other philosophies wrong … no man ought to write at all, or even to speak at all, unless he thinks he is in truth and the other man in error.'[52] Intellectual humility thus demands and justifies faith in a definite philosophy of life into which the intellect can advance.

A Person Who Demands Your Confidence

> Christendom provides a home for both reason and meaning ... It makes love the central motive for human action and a reasonable God the end of that love.
>
> John Mark Reynolds[53]

If the Christian understanding of Jesus is true we are faced not merely with a 'definite philosophy of life', but with the divine *logos* who took the form of a servant, the 'Son of Man' himself. To re-fit some words from C.S. Lewis, whether or not to adopt the Christian understanding of Jesus

> is a speculative question as long as it is a question at all. But once it has been answered in the affirmative, you get quite a new situation ... To believe [the Christian understanding of Jesus] is to believe that you as a person now stand in the presence of [Jesus] as a Person. What would, a moment before, have been variations in opinion, now become variations in your personal attitude to a Person. You are no longer faced with an argument which demands your assent, but with a Person who demands your confidence.[54]

To submit to a God who demands your personal confidence doesn't mean abandoning philosophical reflection upon the object of one's confidence; but it does mean that one can no longer treat the object of one's reflection as a hypothetical or distant 'other'. Seeing this, some may be reluctant to acquiesce, and thus may be reluctant to accept the Christian understanding of Jesus. However, if anyone wants to *rationally* disagree with the conclusion of the arguments we have examined, the onus is on them to show where they go wrong according to the rules of rational inquiry.

Of course, as a self-aware fallible knower committed to *the truth* rather than to *my truth*, I acknowledge the theoretical possibility that *I could be mistaken*. I encourage anyone who disagrees with me, to whatever degree, to adopt the same attitude towards truth. As Kelly James Clark writes: 'Intellectual humility is a virtue that recognizes the limits of human understanding. The corresponding vice is an uncritical dogmatism that is intolerant of alternative beliefs and immune to criticism. We ought to have our settled convictions, but we should be aware of their limitations and remain open to legitimate criticism ...'[55] Nevertheless, it is only a dogmatic dedication to the importance of seeking to conform our beliefs to the objective truth about reality, and to carrying out this project co-operatively with one another in such a way that we stand under the authority of what appears to us to be true (rather than what our peers want us to believe), that can justify and sustain a humble appraisal of the human intellectual condition. Even to recognize the limits of human understanding is to affirm both a truth and our ability to know truth. Having admitted that truth exists and is knowable, we cannot map-out the exact limits of the human intellectual condition *a priori*. We can only pursue truth to the best of our ability and see how far we get.

If, as postmodernists claim, it is not objectively true that we ought to seek a marriage of truth between our beliefs and the rest of reality, then truth has no authority over us. In that case, we may as well let each other get away with believing and doing anything we please, and prevent each other getting away with believing and doing anything we please. However, the fact that the totalitarian arrogance of such postmodern relativism is self-contradictory does *not* mean that truth seekers must embrace a similar arrogance of their own. As C. Stephen Evans explains:

> A religious believer who is convinced that her faith is true is not necessarily arrogant. She can, without giving up her convictions, admit her fallibility and appreciate the perspectives of others. If she is a Christian and holds to her faith on the basis of special revelation, she cannot be arrogant. For she recognizes that the knowledge she has of God is not the result of her own cleverness but is, in fact, made possible through her recognition of her own weakness. And if she feels compelled to share her faith with others, it may not be a sign of arrogant pride or imperialism but rather the result of a humble desire for others to know the truth.[56]

It is the humble desire to understand the truth (i.e. to stand under the authority of truth) that undergirds both the dogmatic assertion that *we can know truth*, and the equally dogmatic assertion that *we can fail to know truth*. As Regis Jolivet notes: 'all metaphysical reasoning, even when the conclusion is reached, leaves a fear that we may be deceived, or at least that we may not have examined everything.'[57] However, to let this fear paralyze us as knowers would be to give our fear sway over our knowledge that it is reasonable to claim to know *when we have made responsible efforts to conduct ourselves in obedience to our intellectual duties.* Giving in to the paralyzing fear of being wrong involves accepting a self-defeating misplacing of the burden of proof, and is just as much a mistake as thinking that one is omniscient! A belief may be 'accepted not because it is necessarily undeniably demonstrated, but because it has the capability of explaining known facts and sufficient evidence to give it preference over alternative explanations.'[58] It is in this sense that I believe Christians can and should claim to be able to show that their understanding of Jesus is true. As William A. Dembski comments:

> No one is denying that humans make mistakes. Indeed, as a general rule it is healthy to regard all our claims as potentially fallible in the sense that they can always be scrutinized, criticized and overturned in the light of new evidence. But the mere possibility of being wrong neither precludes the possibility of being right nor the possibility that we can be thoroughly justified in thinking we are right and will continue to be right.[59]

Making a positive response to a person in whose existence you believe on the basis of intuition, trusting testimony, inference from historical evidence, and so forth, my seem like a 'leap of faith' akin to agreeing to go on a date with someone you've met online. And so it is (although it's worth noting that in such a situation one does of course take a risk in saying 'no' as well as in saying 'yes'). Indeed, it isn't hard to think of perfectly sensible *human* relationships with far shakier epistemological foundations than faith in Jesus! In both cases, one makes a 'leap of faith' that is neither blind on the one hand nor indubitable on the other. In both cases one takes a calculated risk that involves one's whole being. In both cases one can proceed one step at a time, building trust through experience, until it seems natural that our thoughts turn to a more permanent and spiritually binding arrangement. All relationships require a step of rational faith, that is, an act of *warranted trust* (in the other person and in ourselves) that commits us to work at the relationship:

Armed with the hypothesis of Christian theism and all the weighty accumulated evidence in its favour, the would-be believer engages in an experiment. This person considers what it would mean, in terms of practical decisions and activities, for him or her to be a true believer. The person then seeks to orient his or her life in that way. The example and assistance of true believers will be a great aid at this stage. There's much to say in favour of this notion and about how to conduct such an experiment. The main thing to observe … is that such a practice often leads to *bona fide* belief [i.e. faith] in God. Sometimes it does so without fanfare. Sometimes the experiment culminates in a belief that is attended by a dramatic religious experience of some sort. In any case, there is often an experimental component that signals the achievement of reconciliation with God … but for many Westerners today, both the opportunity and the need for prior preparation is very real.[60]

Supposing you make such a step of commitment to Jesus; does that mean you are expected to stop thinking, to stifle all future questions and doubts, or never even to have such questions and doubts? Not at all, for as C.S. Lewis advised: 'If ours is an examined faith, we should be unafraid to doubt. If doubt is eventually justified, we were believing what clearly was not worth believing. But if doubt is answered, our faith has grown stronger. It knows God more certainly and it can enjoy God more deeply.'[61] Michael J. Langford wisely considers how the committed Christian should handle spiritual questions and doubts:

We are never asked to smother our intellectual curiosity, and therefore, almost invariably, Christians will have periods of doubt or uncertainty, but if they continue … to live through this period *as if* they were convinced of the reality of God, then this is a continuation of the life of faith. This involves no dishonesty, unless one claims a certainty that one does not possess … If I promise to follow the leader of an expedition into the unknown and to trust him when there is a crisis, I am not promising never to have doubts. I am promising to follow in spite of any doubts that may arise along the way. Similarly, the thoughtful Christian knows he is likely to have periods of doubt in which acts of will and determination will have to carry him through. But what if the doubts persist

... can there still be a viable Christian faith? There can be no simple answer here for each person's own story is different. Undoubtedly, there can come a point where honesty should compel the searcher to say, 'I am no longer a Christian, I am an agnostic', but there are many kinds of persistent doubt where this step is not called for ... doubt is not the opposite of faith. The opposite of faith is faithlessness.[62]

As fallible beings one of the things that we *know* is that we cannot expect to have all the answers! Since philosophy and theology are human attempts to understand an independent reality that far outstrips us, our only reasonable course of action is to seek an understanding of reality that, to the best of our knowledge, raises *the least-serious set of intellectual problems*. Since one can't believe in nothing, choosing one's spirituality is an intrinsically *comparative* exercise. The aim of the exercise is to adopt *the best understanding of reality currently available to us*.

Putting the Pieces Together

> Faith is not certainty but a willingness to follow the argument where it leads.
>
> John Mark Reynolds[63]

Searching for true spirituality is a bit like doing a jigsaw puzzle without having the picture on the box. Suppose you are in the process of doing a jigsaw, and you have in place most of the really crucial 'frame' of pieces (i.e. data) all around the picture's edge, and a fair chuck of the detail of the picture as well, so much so that you are confident that you know what the puzzle you are constructing depicts (at least in general terms). Nevertheless, you still have a pile of unused pieces, and some of those pieces are proving resistant to being slotted into place. Would you look at the unused pieces and conclude that you just don't know what the picture is of after all? Or would you assume that you simply hadn't discovered how to integrate all of the pieces yet? Your grasp of the big picture, based on the pieces you have slotted together, coupled with experience of making progress with previously un-placed pieces, would obviously make the latter assumption far more reasonable than the former.

Even a few really stubborn pieces refusing to fit wouldn't be enough to overturn your confidence in the picture. After all, if you've got enough of the picture to make it reasonable to think that certain pieces really are 'hard to place pieces', rather than pieces simply awaiting developments that will see them finding a home with ease, then you must already have a pretty complete picture before you! So perhaps that detail you assumed was part of a telegraph pole is in fact part of a tree (perhaps you are working under a false methodological assumption). Perhaps you've a piece upside down somewhere (perhaps you've got an inadequate grasp of some particular truth). Perhaps a jigsaw piece from another puzzle has strayed into your pile of pieces (perhaps your understanding of this or that fact is simply wrong for some reason).

Moreover, your confidence that the puzzle depicted the face of Christ, for example, would be increased if: a) most other people working with identical puzzle pieces were making the same picture, and if b) the people who insisted that the picture was actually a still-life all seemed to have made pictures with corners missing and pieces forced together without regard for their natural shape. And so it is with seeking a true spirituality in comparison with other spiritualities. I have many questions about my Christian faith; but I cannot contemplate these questions without taking into consideration both the evidence that warrants the Christian understanding of Jesus on the one hand, or the *even bigger questions* I have about alternative spiritualities on the other hand. Hence I join the apostle after whom I was named in saying: 'Lord, there is no one else that we can go to! Your words give eternal life.' (John 6:68 [CEV])

Conclusion

> Here I am! I stand at the door and knock. If anyone hears my voice and opens the door, I will come in and eat with them, and they with me.
>
> (Revelation 3:20)

True spiritual enlightenment is found in Jesus Christ. As Isaiah foretold:

> on those living in the land of deep darkness
> a light has dawned (Isaiah 9:2).

Introducing his gospel, John joins his own eyewitness testimony to that of John the Baptizer in declaring that through Jesus the prophesied new age of enlightenment has begun:

In the beginning was the Word [*logos*], and the Word was with God, and the Word was God. He was with God in the beginning. Through him all things were made; without him nothing was made that has been made. In him was life, and that life was the light of all people. The light shines in the darkness, and the darkness has not [mastered] it.

There was a man sent from God whose name was John. He came as a witness to testify concerning that light, so that through him all might believe. He himself was not the light; he came only as a witness to the light.

The true light that gives light to everyone was coming into the world. He was in the world, and though the world was made through him, the world did not recognize him. He came to that which was his own, but his own did not receive him. Yet to all who did receive him, to those who believed in his name, he gave the right to become children of God – children born not of natural descent, nor of human decision or a husband's will, but born of God.

The Word became flesh and made his dwelling among us. We have seen his glory, the glory of the one and only [Son], who came from the Father, full of grace and truth.

(John testified concerning him. He cried out, saying, 'This is he of whom I said, "He who comes after me has surpassed me because he was before me."') Out of his fullness we have all received grace in place of grace already given. For the law was given through Moses; grace and truth came through Jesus Christ. No one has ever seen God, but the one and only [Son], who is himself God and is in closest relationship with the Father, has made him known (John 1:1–18).

Enlightenment is the leitmotif of John's gospel, where Jesus announces 'I have come into the world as a light, so that no one who believes in me should stay in darkness' (John 12:46) and proclaims 'I am the light of the world. Whoever follows me will never walk in darkness, but will have the light of life' (John 8:12; cf. John 9:5). Paul uses the same imagery when he recounts how 'God, who said, "Let light shine out of darkness," [Genesis 1:3] made his light shine in our hearts to give us the light of the knowledge of the glory of God in the face of Christ' (2 Corinthians 4:6 [NIV]). On the basis of their knowledge of this divine revelation, Jesus' followers participate in a spiritual community whose duty and joy it is to lovingly propagate the spiritual enlightenment he embodied: 'You are the light of the world. A city on a hill cannot be hidden. Neither do people light a lamp and put it under a bowl. Instead they put it on its stand, and it gives light to everyone in the house' (Matthew 5:14–15; cf. Luke 11:33).

Jesus wants to give us the best quality of relationship (love) with the greatest possible, maximally beautiful being (God). This relationship, founded upon divine forgiveness received through an ongoing spiritual orientation of repentance (*metanoia*) and faith (trust) in response to the life, death and resurrection of Jesus, naturally results in a personally transformative spirituality that is characterized by a developing desire and capacity to love God (and thus both self and neighbour) with all one's mind, heart and strength (cf. Mark 12:33; Acts 3:37; 1 Peter 3:15; Colossians 3:14–17). This authentic, intrinsic form of spirituality organically incorporates the believer into a spiritual community with the highest proximate purpose and the greatest ultimate destiny. This is the spirituality of Jesus, and it isn't a thing to be entered into lightly (cf. Luke 9:62; 14:27–29). True spirituality isn't a bed of roses. It's not a socially comfortable or fashionable lifestyle choice; nor, as the continued persecution and martyrdom of Christians makes clear,[64] is it necessarily a physically safe option. However, it is true, it is good, and it is beautiful.[65]

In light of everything we've investigated about the one who claimed to be the light of the world, I close by relaying Jesus' own invitation to 'the life that is truly life' (1 Timothy 6:19) through humbly understanding who he is:

Ask and it will be given to you; seek and you will find; knock and
the door will be opened to you. For everyone who asks receives;
those who seek find; and to those who knock, the door will be
opened ...

No one knows the Father except the Son and those to whom the
Son chooses to reveal him ...

Come to me, all you who are weary and burdened, and I will
give you rest. Take my yoke upon you and learn from me, for I
am gentle and humble in heart, and you will find rest for your
souls. For my yoke is easy and my burden is light (Matthew 7:7–8,
11:27–30; cf. Luke 11:9–13).

Recommended Resources

Video

Warren, Rick. 'What Does It Mean to Be a Follower of Jesus Christ?'
http://www.leestrobel.com/videoserver/video.php?clip=
strobelT1235 (a useful video for anyone who wants to become a
Christian).

Audio

Moreland, J.P. 'Addiction to Happiness' http://www.okbu.edu/
news/2010-02-22/moreland-unveils-secret-to-happiness.
Transatlantic. *The Whirlwind* (Insideout, 2009).
Willard, Dallas. 'The Need for Spiritual Formation' http://www.bethink-
ing.org/spirituality/intermediate/1-spiritual-formation-the-need-
for-spiritual-formation.htm.

Books

Colson, Charles and Nancy Pearcy. *How Now Shall We Live?* (London:
Marshall Pickering, 1999).
Jones, Tobias. *Utopian Dreams: A Search for a Better Life* (London: Faber,
2007).
Kreeft, Peter. *Christianity for Modern Pagans: Pascal's Pensées Edited, Out-
lined and Explained* (San Francisco: Ignatius, 1993).

— *Heaven: The Heart's Deepest Longing* (San Francisco: Ignatius, 1989).

Lewis, C.S. *The Problem of Pain* (London: Fount, 2002).

— *Surprised by Joy* (London: Fount, 1998).

Moreland, J.P. *The God Question: An Invitation to a Life of Meaning* (Eugene, OR: Harvest House, 2009).

— *Kingdom Triangle* (Grand Rapids, MI: Zondervan, 2007).

— and Klaus Issler. *In Search of a Confident Faith: Overcoming Barriers to Trusting God* (Downers Grove, IL: IVP, 2008).

— and Klaus Issler. *The Lost Virtue of Happiness: Discovering the Disciplines of the Good Life* (Colorado Springs: NavPress, 2006).

Orr-Ewing, Amy and Frog. *Deep: Passion, Character, Community* (Milton Keynes: Authentic, 2008).

Ortberg, John. *The Life You've Always Wanted: Spiritual Disciplines for Ordinary People* (Grand Rapids, MI: Zondervan, 2002).

Steve and Lois Rabey, eds. *Side by Side: Disciple-Making for a New Century – A Handbook* (Colorado Springs: NavPress, 2000).

Sanders, John. *No Other Name: Can Only Christians Be Saved?* (London: SPCK, 1994).

Walls, Jerry L. *Heaven: The Logic of Eternal Joy* (Oxford University Press, 2002).

Ward, Keith. *What the Bible Really Teaches: A Challenge for Fundamentalists* (London: SPCK, 2004).

Willard, Dallas. *The Divine Conspiracy: Rediscovering Our Hidden Life in God* (London: Fount, 1998).

— *Hearing God: Developing a Conversational Relationship with God* (Downers Grove, IL: IVP, 1999).

— *Knowing Christ Today: Why We Can Trust Spiritual Knowledge* (New York: HarperOne, 2009).

— *Renovation of the Heart: Putting On the Character of Christ* (Colorado Springs: NavPress, 2002).

Wright, Tom. *Virtue Reborn* (London: SPCK, 2010).

Wurmbrand, Richard. *Tortured for Christ* (London: Hodder & Stoughton, 2004).

Recommended Resources

Online Appendix

Peter S. Williams. 'Archaeology and the Historical Reliability of the New Testament' http://www.bethinking.org/bible-jesus/advanced/archaeology-and-the-historical-reliability-of-the.htm.

Peter S. Williams

ARN Featured Author http://www.arn.org/authors/williams.html.
Damaris Speaker Page http://www.damaris.org/cm/church/peter williams.
Evangelical Philosophical Society Profile http://www.epsociety.org/library/authors.asp?mode=profile&pid=37.
ID.Plus Blog http://idpluspeterswilliams.blogspot.com.
Peter S. Williams' Podcast Channel http://www.damaris.org/cm/podcasts/category/peterswilliams.

Websites

Apologetics 315 http://apologetics315.blogspot.com.
Biblical Archaeology Review http://www.bib-arch.org.
Paul Copan http://www.paulcopan.com.
William Lane Craig: Reasonable Faith http://www.reasonablefaith.org.

Gary R. Habermas http://www.garyhabermas.com.

John Lennox http://www.johnlennox.org.

Michael Licona http://www.risenjesus.com.

J.P. Moreland http://www.jpmoreland.com.

Alvin Plantinga: The Analytic Theist http://philofreligion.homestead.com/plantingapage.html.

Last Seminary http://www.lastseminary.com.

Lee Strobel http://www.leestrobel.com.

Dallas Willard http://www.dwillard.org.

Podcasts

Apologetics 315 Interviews http://itunes.apple.com/podcast/apologetics-315-interviews/id351907712.

William Lane Craig, *Reasonable Faith* http://itunes.apple.com/podcast/reasonable-faith-podcast/id252618197.

Peter S. Williams' Podcast Channel http://www.damaris.org/cm/podcasts/category/peterswilliams.

Video

Lee Strobel, *The Case for Christ* http://video.google.com/videoplay?docid=844253338346122878#docid=-3473983875617762630.

The Bible

Mounce, William D. and Robert H. Mounce, ed. *The Zondervan Greek and English Interlinear New Testament – TNIV/NLT* (Grand Rapids, MI: Zondervan, 2008).

New International Version Archaeological Study Bible: An Illustrated Walk through Biblical History and Culture (Grand Rapids, MI: Zondervan, 2005).

NIV – The Case for Christ Study Bible: Investigating The Evidence For Belief (ed. Lee Strobel; Grand Rapids, MI: Zondervan, 2009).

TNIV – The Message / Remix Parallel Bible (Grand Rapids, MI: Zondervan, 2005).

Other Books

Arnold, Clinton E., ed. *Zondervan Illustrated Bible Backgrounds Commentary* (Grand Rapids, MI: Zondervan, 2002).

Barnett, Paul. *Finding the Historical Christ* (Grand Rapids, MI: Eerdmans, 2009).

— *Messiah: Jesus – the Evidence of History* (Nottingham: IVP, 2009).

— *Is the New Testament Reliable?* (Downers Grove, IL: IVP, rev. edn, 2003).

Bauckham, Richard. *Jesus and the Eyewitnesses: The Gospels as Eyewitness Testimony* (Grand Rapids, MI: Eerdmans, 2006).

Beckwith, Francis J., ed. *To Everyone an Answer: A Case for the Christian Worldview* (Downers Grove, IL: IVP, 2004).

Bielby, James K., ed. *For Faith and Clarity: Philosophical Contributions to Christian Theology* (Grand Rapids, MI: Baker, 2006).

Blomberg, Craig L. *The Historical Reliability of the Gospels* (Downers Grove, IL: IVP, 2008).

Bock, Darrell L. and Daniel B. Wallace. *Dethroning Jesus: Exposing Popular Culture's Quest to Unseat the Biblical Christ* (Nashville, TN: Thomas Nelson, 2007).

Bowman, Robert and Ed Komoszewski. *Putting Jesus in His Place: The Case for the Deity of Christ* (Grand Rapids, MI: Kregel, 2007).

Boyd, Gregory A. and Paul R. Eddy. *Lord or Legend? Wrestling with the Jesus Dilemma* (Grand Rapids, MI: Baker, 2007).

Bruce, F.F. *The Hard Sayings of Jesus* (London: Hodder & Stoughton, 1998).

Colson, Charles and Nancy Pearcey. *How Now Shall We Live?* (London: Marshall Pickering, 1999).

Copan, Paul, ed. *Will the Real Jesus Please Stand Up? A Debate between William Lane Craig and John Dominic Crossan* (Grand Rapids, MI: Baker, 1998).

— and Paul K. Moser, eds. *The Rationality of Theism* (London: Routledge, 2003).

Craig, William Lane. *On Guard: Defending Your Faith with Reason and Precision* (Wheaton, IL: David C. Cook, 2010).

— *The Son Rises* (Eugene, OR: Wipf & Stock, 2000).

— and J.P. Moreland, eds. *The Blackwell Companion to Natural Theology* (Oxford: Wiley-Blackwell, 2009).

— — eds. *Naturalism: A Critical Analysis* (London: Routledge, 2001).

Davis, Stephen T. *Risen Indeed: Making Sense of the Resurrection* (London: SPCK, 1993).

Earman, John. *Hume's Abject Failure: The Argument against Miracles* (Oxford University Press, 2000).

Evans, Craig A. *Fabricating Jesus: How Modern Scholars Distort the Gospels* (Downers Grove, IL: IVP, 2007).

Evans, C. Stephen. *Why Believe? Reason and Mystery as Pointers to God* (Downers Grove, IL: IVP, 1996).

Foster, Charles. *The Christmas Mystery* (Milton Keynes: Authentic, 2007).

Geivett, R. Douglas and Gary R. Habermas, ed. *In Defence of Miracles: A Comprehensive Case for God's Action in History* (Leicester: Apollos, 1997).

Michael Green, ed. *The Truth of God Incarnate* (London: Hodder, 1977).

Inwagen, Peter van. *God, Knowledge and Mystery: Essays in Philosophical Theology* (Cornell University Press, 1995).

Kitchen, K.A. *On the Reliability of the Old Testament* (Grand Rapids, MI: Eerdmans, 2003).

Kreeft, Peter. *Christianity for Modern Pagans: Pascal's Pensées Edited, Outlined and Explained* (San Francisco: Ignatius, 1993).

— *Heaven: The Heart's Deepest Longing* (San Francisco: Ignatius, 1989).

Lennox, John C. *God's Undertaker: Has Science Buried God?* (Oxford: Lion, 2nd edn, 2009).

Lewis, C.S. *Miracles* (London: Fount, 1998).

— *The Problem of Pain* (London: Fount, 1977).

Marston, Paul and Roger Forster. *God's Strategy in Human History*, (Eugene, OR: Wipf & Stock, 2nd edn, 2000).

McRay, John. *Archaeology and the New Testament* (Grand Rapids, MI: Baker Academic, 1991).

Meister, Chad V. *Building Belief: Constructing Faith from the Ground Up* (Eugene, OR: Wipf & Stock, 2009).

Molnar, Michael R. *The Star of Bethlehem: The Legacy of the Magi* (Rutgers University Press, 2000).

Moreland, J.P. *The God Question: An Invitation to a Life of Meaning* (Eugene, OR: Harvest House, 2009).

— *Kingdom Triangle* (Grand Rapids, MI: Zondervan, 2007).

— *Love Your God with All Your Mind: The Role of Reason in the Life of the Soul* (Colorado Springs: NavPress, 1997).

— *Scaling the Secular City: A Defense of Christianity* (Grand Rapids, MI: Baker, 1987).

Morris, Thomas V. *Making Sense of It All: Pascal and the Meaning of Life* (Grand Rapids, MI: Eerdmans, 1998).

Orr-Ewing, Amy. *Why Trust the Bible? Answers to 10 Tough Questions* (Leicester: IVP, 2005).

Owen, Huw Parri. *Christian Theism: A Study in its Basic Principles* (Edinburgh: T&T Clark, 1984).

Pinnock, Clark H., ed. *The Grace of God and the Will of Man* (Eugene, OR: Bethany House, 1995).

Plantinga, Alvin. *Warranted Christian Belief* (Oxford University Press, 2000).

Price, Randall. *The Stones Cry Out: What Archaeology Reveals about the Truth of the Bible* (Eugene, OR: Harvest House, 1997).

Purtill, Richard. *C.S. Lewis' Case for the Christian Faith* (San Francisco: Ignatius, 2004).

Quarles, Charles L., ed. *Buried Hope or Risen Savior? The Search for the Jesus Tomb* (Nashville, TN: B&H Academic, 2008).

Sanders, John. *No Other Name: Can Only Christians Be Saved?* (London: SPCK, 1994).

Sennett, James F. and Douglas Groothuis, eds. *In Defense of Natural Theology* (Downers Grove, IL: IVP, 2005).

Sherry, Patrick. *Spirit and Beauty* (London: SCM, 2nd edn, 2002).

Spencer, Robert. *Religion of Peace? Why Christianity Is and Islam Isn't* (Washington: Regnery, 2007).

Stevenson, Kenneth E. *Image of the Risen Christ: Remarkable New Evidence about the Shroud* (Toronto, Ontario: Frontier Research, 1999).

Strauss, Mark L. *Four Portraits, One Jesus: An Introduction to Jesus and the Gospels* (Grand Rapids, MI: Zondervan, 2007).

Strobel, Lee. *The Case for the Real Jesus* (Grand Rapids, MI: Zondervan, 2007).

Swinburne, Richard. *Was Jesus God?* (Oxford University Press, 2008).

— *The Resurrection of God Incarnate* (Oxford: Clarendon Press, 2003).

Taylor, James E. *Introducing Apologetics: Cultivating Christian Commitment* (Grand Rapids, MI: Baker Academic, 2006).

Walls, Jerry L. *Heaven: The Logic of Eternal Joy* (Oxford University Press, 2002).

Wilkins, Michael J. and J.P. Moreland, eds. *Jesus under Fire: Modern Scholarship Reinvents the Historical Jesus* (Grand Rapids, MI: Zondervan, 1995).

Willard, Dallas. *Knowing Christ Today: Why We Can Trust Spiritual Knowledge* (New York: HarperOne, 2009).

Williams, Peter S. *A Sceptic's Guide to Atheism: God Is Not Dead* (Carlisle: Paternoster, 2009).

— *I Wish I Could Believe in Meaning: A Response to Nihilism* (Southampton: Damaris, 2004).

— *The Case for Angels* (Carlisle: Paternoster, 2002).

Wright, N.T. *The Resurrection of the Son of God* (London: SPCK, 2003).

Zacharias, Ravi. *Can Man Live without God?* (Milton Keynes: W Publishing Group, 2004).

Endnotes

Author's Preface

[1] Bernard Brandon Scott, cited by James K. Beilby and Paul Rhodes Eddy, 'The Quest for the Historical Jesus: An Introduction', in *The Historical Jesus: Five Views* (ed. James K. Beilby and Paul Rhodes Eddy; London: SPCK, 2010), p. 41.
[2] Beilby and Eddy, op. cit.
[3] ibid.
[4] Stuart C. Hackett, *The Reconstruction of the Christian Revelation Claim* (Eugene, OR: Wipf & Stock, 2008), p. 197.

1 – Five Ways to Understanding Jesus

[1] Immanuel Kant, 'What Is Enlightenment?' http://www.english. upenn.edu/~mgamer/Etexts/kant.html.
[2] Leigh Churchill, *The Blood of Martyrs: The History of the Christian Church from Pentecost to the Age of Theodosius* (Milton Keynes: Paternoster, 2005), p. 59.
[3] Origen, *Against Celsus* and Minucius Felix, *Octavius*, quoted by John Drane, *Introducing the New Testament* (Oxford: Lion, rev. edn, 1999), p. 14.
[4] Minucius Felix, *Octavius* 9:6, quoted by Drane, *Introducing the New Testament* (Oxford: Lion, rev. edn, 1999), p. 14; cf. 'Minucius Felix', *Internet Encyclopedia of Philosophy* http://www.iep.utm.edu/minucius.
[5] Churchill, op. cit., p. 59.

[6] ibid., p. 60.

[7] ibid.

[8] ibid.

[9] Ignatius, Henry Bettenson, trans. and ed., *The Early Christian Fathers* (OUP, 1969), p. 41.

[10] ibid.

[11] ibid., p. 42.

[12] ibid., p. 44.

[13] ibid., pp. 48–9.

[14] C. FitzSimons Allison, 'Modernity or Christianity? John Spong's Culture of Disbelief', in *Can a Bishop Be Wrong? Ten Scholars Challenge John Shelby Spong* (ed. Peter C. Moore; Harrisburg: Morehouse, 1998), p. 41.

[15] cf. 'Polycarp', *Catholic Encyclopedia* http://www.newadvent.org/cathen/12219b.htm; Churchill, op. cit., pp. 77–82.

[16] Irenaeus, *Against Heresies* 3.3.4.

[17] Irenaeus, *Letter to Florinus*, Eusebius, quoted by Richard Bauckham, *Jesus and the Eyewitnesses* (Cambridge: Eerdmans, 2006), p. 35.

[18] Paul Barnett, *Finding the Historical Christ* (Cambridge: Eerdmans, 2009), pp. 77–8.

[19] cf. http://www.newadvent.org/fathers/0125.htm.

[20] *The Martyrdom of Ignatius* http://www.mb-soft.com/believe/txv/ignatiuc.htm.

[21] Eusebius, *Ecclesiastical History* 3.36.1.

[22] Theodoret of Cyrrhus, *Dial. Immutab.* I.iv.33a.

[23] Edwin M. Yamauchi in Lee Strobel, *The Case for Christ* (Grand Rapids, MI: Zondervan, 1998), p. 89.

[24] Paul Foster, 'The Epistles of Ignatius of Antioch', in *The Writings of the Apostolic Fathers* (ed. Paul Foster; London: T&T Clark, 2007), p. 107.

[25] Ignatius, Bettenson, op. cit., p. 46.

[26] cf.http://ancienthistory.about.com/library/bl/bl_text_plinyltrstrajan.htm.

[27] cf.http://ancienthistory.about.com/library/bl/bl_text_plinyltrstrajan.htm.

[28] Gary R. Habermas, *The Historical Jesus: Ancient Evidence for the Life of Christ* (Joplin, MO: College Press, 2001), pp. 201, 223.

[29] Stephen Neill, 'Jesus and History', in *The Truth of God Incarnate* (ed. Michael Green; London: Hodder & Stoughton, 1977), p. 76.

30 Richard Dawkins, *The God Delusion* (London: Black Swan, 2007), p. 5.

31 Richard Dawkins, *The Selfish Gene* (Oxford Paperbacks, 2nd edn, 1989), p. 198.

32 Dawkins, *The God Delusion*, op. cit., p. 122.

33 Victor J. Stenger, *The New Atheism: Taking a Stand for Science and Reason* (New York: Prometheus, 2009), p. 58.

34 Luke Timothy Johnson, *The Real Jesus* (New York: HarperOne, 1997), pp. 123, 126.

35 Geza Vermes, *The Resurrection* (London: Penguin, 2008), p. 1.

36 Paul L. Maier, 'Did Jesus Really Exist?', in *Evidence for God* (ed. William A. Dembski and Michael R. Licona; Grand Rapids, MI: Baker, 2010), p. 143.

37 Graham Stanton, *The Gospels and Jesus* (OUP, 2nd edn, 2002), p. 145. cf. Gary R. Habermas, 'A Summary Critique: Questioning the Existence of Jesus' http://www.garyhabermas.com/articles/crj_summary critique/crj_summarycritique.htm.

38 Dawkins, *The God Delusion* (London: Bantam, 2006), p. 122.

39 ibid., pp. 118, 121, 122–3.

40 N.T. Wright, *Judas and the Gospel of Jesus* (London: SPCK, 2006), p. 30.

41 cf. Richard Dawkins, 'Theology Has No Place in a University' http://www.richarddawkins.net/articles/1698 and 'The Emptiness of Theology' http://www.richarddawkins.net/articles/88.

42 Thomas R. Yoder Neufeld, *Recovering Jesus: The Witness of the New Testament* (Grand Rapids, MI: Brazos, 2007), pp. 15–16. On the development of 'the quest for the historical Jesus' cf. Darrell L. Bock, *Studying the Historical Jesus: A Guide to Sources and Methods* (Grand Rapids, MI: Baker Academic, 2002), ch. 5 and Mark L. Strauss, *Four Portraits, One Jesus* (Grand Rapids, MI: Zondervan, 2007), ch. 11. For an in-depth review of the 'third quest' cf. Ben Witherington III, *The Jesus Quest: The Third Search for the Jew of Nazareth* (Downers Grove, IL: IVP, 1997).

43 Habermas, *The Historical Jesus*, op. cit., p. 24.

44 Craig L. Blomberg, *Making Sense of the New Testament* (Leicester: IVP, 2003), p. 19.

45 William Lane Craig, *Reasonable Faith: Christian Truth and Apologetics* (Wheaton, IL: Crossway, 3rd edn, 2009), p. 18.

46 Darrell L. Bock, *Studying the Historical Jesus: A Guide to Sources and Methods* (Grand Rapids, MI: Baker Academic, 2002), p. 147.

[47] ibid., pp. 147–8.

[48] Josh McDowell and Bill Wilson, *He Walked among Us: Evidence for the Historical Jesus* (Carlisle: Alpha, 2000), p. 72.

[49] Richard Dawkins, *The Greatest Show on Earth: The Evidence for Evolution* (London: Bantam Press, 2009), p. 3.

[50] ibid., p. 4.

[51] cf. http://www.dissentfromdarwin.org.

[52] Dawkins, op. cit., p. 6.

[53] Peter S. Williams, 'A Rough Guide to Creation and Evolution' http://www.arn.org/docs/williams/pw_roughguidetocreationand evolution.htm.

[54] Dawkins, op. cit., p. 7.

[55] cf. *Reasons to Believe* http://www.reasons.org.

[56] cf. William A. Dembski, *The Design Revolution: Answering the Toughest Questions about Intelligent Design* (Downers Grove, IL: IVP, 2004); Bradley Monton, *Seeking God in Science: An Atheist Defends Intelligent Design* (Toronto: Broadview, 2009); Peter S. Williams, 'The Design Inference from Specified Complexity Defended by Scholars Outside the Intelligent Design Movement: A Critical Review', *Philosophia Christi* 9:2 http://www.epsociety.org/library/articles.asp?pid=54; Peter S. Williams, 'Atheists Against Darwinism: Johnson's "Wedge" Breaks Through' http://www.epsociety.org/library/articles.asp?pid=66; Peter S. Williams, 'Intelligent Designs on Science: A Surreply to Alexander's Critique of Intelligent Design Theory' http://www.arn.org/docs/williams/pw_designsonscience.htm.

[57] cf. David Berlinski, *The Deniable Darwin and Other Essays* (Seattle: Discovery Institute, 2010); David Berlinski, *The Devil's Delusion: Atheism and Its Scientific Pretensions* (New York: Crown Forum, 2008); Michael Denton, *Evolution: A Theory in Crisis* (Bethesda, MD: Adler & Adler, 1986); James Le Fanu, *Why Us? How Science Rediscovered the Mystery of Ourselves* (London: Harper, 2009); Jerry Fodor and Massimo Piattelli-Palmarini, *What Darwin Got Wrong* (London: Profile, 2010); Steve Fuller, *Dissent over Descent: Intelligent Design's Challenge to Darwinism* (Cambridge: Icon, 2008).

[58] Dawkins, op. cit., p. 8.

[59] Mark Allan Powell, *The Jesus Debate: Modern Historians Investigate the Life of Jesus* (Oxford: Lion, 1998), p. 180.

[60] Paul Barnett, *Messiah: Jesus – the Evidence of History* (Nottingham: IVP, 2009), p. 11.

61 Mark Vernon, Humanism (London: Teach Yourself/Hodder Education, 2008), p. 55.

62 Paul Guyer, 'Kant, Immanuel', in *Routledge Encyclopedia of Philosophy* (ed. E. Craig; London: Routledge, 2004) http://www.rep.routledge.com/article/DB047.

63 Kant, op. cit.

64 Daniel Dennett, 'Is Religion a Threat to Rationality and Science?' http://www.richarddawkins.net/article,2498,Is-religion-a-threat-to-rationality-and-science,Dan-Dennett-Lord-Winston.

65 Terry Eagleton, *Reason, Faith, and Revolution: Reflections on the God Debate* (Yale University Press, 2009), p. 68.

66 cf. Helena Rosenblatt, 'The Christian Enlightenment', in *Enlightenment, Reawakening and Revolution 1660–1815* (ed. Stewart J. Brown and Timothy Tackett; CUP, 2006). cf. http://www.histories.cambridge.org/extract?id=chol9780521816052_CHOL9780521816052A017.

67 Antony Flew with Roy Abraham Varghese, *There Is a God* (New York: HarperOne, 2009), pp. 185–6.

68 Antony Flew in David Baggett, ed., *Did the Resurrection Happen?* (Downers Grove, IL: IVP, 2009), p. 57.

69 Ivor Bulmer-Thomas, 'St Paul the Missionary', in *St Paul: Teacher and Traveller* (ed. Ivor Bulmer-Thomas; Leighton Buzzard: The Faith Press, 1975), p. 50.

70 J. Daryl Charles, 'Engaging the (Neo)Pagan Mind: Paul's Encounter with Athenian Culture as a Model for Cultural Apologetics (Acts 17:16–34)', *TJ* 16:1 (Spring 1995): p. 50. http://www.biblicalstudies.org.uk/pdf/athenian_charles.pdf.

71 Francis Clark, 'St Paul the Man', in *St Paul*, op. cit., p. 19.

72 Charles, op. cit., p. 60.

73 Peter May, 'What Is Apologetics?' http://www.bethinking.org/what-is-apologetics/what-isapologetics.htm.

74 Kant, op. cit.

75 Vernon, op. cit., p. 75.

76 Immanuel Kant, *Religion within the Limits of Reason Alone*, quoted by Charlotte Allen, *The Human Christ: The Search for the Historical Jesus* (Oxford: Lion, 1998), p. 123.

77 Kant, 'What Is Enlightenment?', op. cit.

78 Dennett, op. cit.

79 Tom Price, 'Loving Logical Faith' http://www.abetterhope.blogspot.com/2010/01/loving-logical-faith.html.

80 Tom Morris, Foreword, in *C.S. Lewis as Philosopher: Truth, Goodness and Beauty* (ed. David Baggett, Gary R. Habermas and Jerry L. Walls; Downers Grove, IL: IVP, 2008), p. 10.

81 Paul Copan, *Loving Wisdom: Christian Philosophy of Religion* (St Louis, MO: Chalice Press, 2007), pp. 3–4.

82 John Polkinghorne, 'Faith in God the Creator', in *Belief: Readings on the Reason for Faith* (ed. Francis S. Collins; New York: HarperOne, 2010), p. 200.

83 Charles Colson and Nancy Pearcey, *Developing a Christian Worldview of Science and Evolution* (Wheaton, IL: Tyndale, 2001), pp. xi, xiii.

84 http://www.rcpsych.ac.uk/mentalhealthinformation/therapies/cognitivebehaviouraltherapy.aspx cf. Lawrence J. Crabb, *Effective Biblical Counselling: How to Become a Capable Counsellor* (London: Marshall Pickering, 1990), esp. ch. 5.

85 Glen Schultz, *Kingdom Education* (Nashville, TN: LifeWay Press, 1998), p. 39.

86 Bill Smith, 'Blazing the North–South Trail', *Just Thinking* (Winter 2001): p. 11.

87 cf. Peter May, 'Testing the Golden Rule' http://www.bethinking.org/bible-jesus/introductory/testing-the-golden-rule.htm.

88 Douglas Groothuis, *On Pascal* (London: Thompson Wadsworth, 2003), p. 41.

89 Norman L. Geisler and Patrick Zukeran, *The Apologetics of Jesus* (Grand Rapids, MI: Baker, 2009), pp. 11–12, 25.

90 C.E.M. Joad, *The Recovery of Belief* (London: Faber, 1952), pp. 16–17.

91 On the transcendentals, cf. John Cottingham, 'Philosophers Are Finding Fresh Meanings in Truth, Goodness and Beauty', *The Times* (17 June 2006). http://www.timesonline.co.uk/tol/comment/faith/article675598.ece; Steven B. Cowan and James S. Spiegel, *The Love of Wisdom: A Christian Introduction to Philosophy* (Nashville, TN: B&H, 2009); Thomas Dubay, *The Evidential Power of Beauty: Science and Theology Meet* (San Francisco: Ignatius, 1999); Douglas Groothuis, *Truth Decay: Defending Christianity against the Challenges of Postmodernism* (Leicester: IVP, 2000); Peter Kreeft, 'The True, the Good and the Beautiful' http://www.peterkreeft.com/audio/27_good-true-beautiful.htm and 'Lewis' Philosophy of Truth, Goodness And Beauty', in *C.S. Lewis as Philosopher: Truth, Goodness and Beauty* (Downers Grove, IL: IVP, 2008); C.S. Lewis, *The Abolition of Man* (London: Fount, 1999); Peter S. Williams, *I Wish I Could Believe in Meaning: A Response to Nihilism* (Southampton: Damaris, 2004).

[92] Phillip E. Johnson, Foreword to Thomas Woodward, *Doubts about Darwin: A History of Intelligent Design* (Grand Rapids, MI: Baker, 2003), p. 7.

[93] Aristotle, *The Art of Rhetoric* (trans. H.C. Lawson-Tancred; London: Penguin Classics, 2004), p. 70.

[94] ibid., p. 80.

[95] ibid., p. 74.

[96] Paul K. Moser, *Jesus and Philosophy: New Essays* (CUP, 2009), Introduction, p. 20.

[97] Thomas Aquinas, *Summa Contra Gentiles, Book One: God*, trans. Anton C. Pegis (University of Notre Dame Press, 2005), pp. 60–61.

[98] Antony Flew, 'Exclusive Flew Interview' http://www.tothesource. org/10_30_2007/10_30_2007.htm.

[99] Craig J. Hazen, 'My Pilgrimage from Atheism to Theism: An Exclusive Interview with Former British Atheist Professor Antony Flew' http:// www.biola.edu/antonyflew/flew-interview.pdf.

[100] Flew, op. cit.

[101] ibid.

[102] Stephen Hawking, 'The Grand Design', in *Eureka / The Times*, September 2010, p. 25.

[103] *The Times*, Thursday 2 September 2010, front page headline.

[104] Hawking, 'The Grand Design', op. cit., p. 18.

[105] Chris Isham in *The Times*, Friday 3 September 2010, p. 8.

[106] John Lennox, 'Stephen Hawking and God: A Response' http://www.johnlennox.org/index.php/en/resource/stephen_ hawking_and_god.

[107] George Ellis in *The Times*, op. cit.

[108] Rowan Williams, ibid., p. 9. cf. William Lane Craig, 'Greg Koukl Interviews William Lane Craig about Hawking's New Book' http://www. rfmedia.org/av/audio/stephen-hawkings-new-book-str-interview/; William Lane Craig, 'Lawrence Krauss on Creation out of Nothing' http://www.reasonablefaith.org/site/News2?page=NewsArticle& id=5887; William Lane Craig, 'Why Does Anything at All Exist?' http:// www.rfmedia.org/av/video/why-does-anything-at-all-exist-wake- forest/.

[109] cf. William Lane Craig, *Reasonable Faith: Christian Truth and Apologetics* (Wheaton, IL: Crossway, 3rd edn, 2008); William Lane Craig and J.P. Moreland, eds, *The Blackwell Companion to Natural Theology* (Oxford: Wiley-Blackwell, 2009); Dean L. Overman, *A Case for the Existence of*

God (Plymouth: Rowman & Littlefield, 2009); Robert J. Spitzer, *New Proofs for the Existence of God: Contributions of Contemporary Physics and Philosophy* (Grand Rapids, MI: Eerdmans, 2010).

[110] Robert C. Koons, 'Science and Theism: Concord, Not Conflict', in *The Rationality of Theism* (ed. Paul Copan and Paul K. Moser; London: Routledge, 2003), p. 73.

[111] Edward Feser, *The Last Superstition* (South Bend, Indiana: St Augustine's Press, 2008), p. viii.

[112] ibid., p. 4.

[113] Michael Ruse, *Isis* (December 2007).

[114] Paul Copan, 'Interview with Paul Copan: Is Yahweh a Moral Monster?' http://www.epsociety.org/blog/2008/04/interview-with-paul-copan-is-yahweh.asp.

[115] See also Peter S. Williams, 'The Emperor's New Clothes: Pointing the Finger at Dawkins' Atheism', *Think* 9:24 (Spring 2010): pp. 29–33 http://www.journals.cambridge.org/action/displayFulltext?type=1&pdftype=1&fid=7191812&jid=THI&volumeId=9&issueId=24&aid=7191804 Other excellent responses to the new atheism are provided by William Lane Craig and Chad Meister, eds, *God Is Good, God Is Great* (Downers Grove, IL: IVP, 2009); Gregory E. Ganssle, *A Reasonable God: Engaging the New Face of Atheism* (Baylor University Press, 2009) and Keith Ward, *Why There Almost Certainly Is a God: Doubting Dawkins* (Oxford: Lion, 2008).

[116] Gary R. Habermas, 'Do You Commit Intellectual Suicide When You Become a Christian?' *Pulse: The Zacharias Trust Magazine* 4 (RZIM, 2010): p. 17.

[117] Robert C. Koons and George Bealer, eds, *The Waning of Materialism* (OUP, 2010), pp. ix, xvii, xx.

[118] Alvin Plantinga, 'Evolution vs. Naturalism', in *Belief: Readings on the Reasons for Faith* (ed. Francis Collins; New York: HarperOne, 2010), p. 300.

[119] David Baggett, *Did the Resurrection Happen? A Conversation with Gary Habermas and Antony Flew* (Downers Grove, IL: IVP, 2009) pp. 137–8. On matters of qualia, consciousness, freedom and rationality cf. Edward Feser, *Philosophy of Mind: A Short Introduction* (Oxford: OneWorld, 2005); Stewart Goetz and Charles Taliaferro, *Naturalism* (Grand Rapids, MI: Eerdmans, 2008); William Hasker, *The Emergent Self* (Cornell University Press, 1999); Robert C. Koons and George Bealer, eds, *The Waning of Materialism* (OUP, 2010); Angus Menuge, *Agents*

under Fire: Materialism and the Rationality of Science (Oxford: Rowman & Littlefield, 2004); J.P. Moreland, *Consciousness and the Existence of God: A Theistic Argument* (London: Routledge, 2008); J.P. Moreland, *The Recalcitrant Imago Dei: Human Persons and the Failure of Naturalism* (London: SCM, 2009); Alvin Plantinga and Michael Tooley, *Knowledge of God* (Oxford: Blackwell, 2008) and Victor Reppert, *C.S. Lewis' Dangerous Idea: In Defense of the Argument from Reason* (Downers Grove, IL: IVP, 2003). On the emergence of life from non-life cf. John C. Lennox, *God's Undertaker: Has Science Buried God?* (Oxford: Lion, 2nd edn, 2009) and Stephen C. Meyer, *Signature in the Cell: DNA and the Evidence for Intelligent Design* (New York: HarperOne, 2010). On the origin of the universe, cf. J.P. Moreland, *Scaling the Secular City: A Defense of Christianity* (Grand Rapids, MI: Baker, 1987). On moral rights and obligations, cf. Robert K. Garcia and Nathan L. King, eds, *Is Goodness without God Good Enough? A Debate on Faith, Secularism and Ethics* (Oxford: Rowman & Littlefield, 2009) and J.P. Moreland, *Scaling the Secular City: A Defense of Christianity* (Grand Rapids, MI: Baker, 1987).

[120] See also: Paul Copan and Paul K. Moser, eds, *The Rationality of Theism* (London: Routledge, 2003); William Lane Craig, *Reasonable Faith: Christian Truth and Apologetics* (Wheaton, IL: Crossway, 3rd edn, 2008); William Lane Craig, ed., *Philosophy of Religion: A Reader and Guide* (Edinburgh University Press, 2002); J.P. Moreland, *Scaling the Secular City* (Grand Rapids, MI: Baker, 1987); J.P. Moreland and William Lane Craig, *Philosophical Foundations for a Christian Worldview* (Downers Grove, IL: IVP, 2003); Alvin Plantinga, *Warranted Christian Belief* (OUP, 2000); Alvin Plantinga and Michael Tooley, *Knowledge of God* (Oxford: Blackwell, 2008); James F. Sennett and Douglas Groothuis, eds, *In Defense of Natural Theology* (Downers Grove, IL: IVP, 2005); J.J.C. Smart and J.J. Haldane, *Atheism and Theism* (Oxford: Blackwell, 2nd edn, 2003) and Stan W. Wallace, ed., *Does God Exist? The Craig–Flew Debate* (Aldershot: Ashgate, 2003).

[121] John Perry and Michael Bratman, *Introduction to Philosophy: Classical and Contemporary Readings* (OUP, 1998).

[122] David Hume, *Natural History of Religion*, quoted by Dave Armstrong, 'Was Skeptical Philosopher David Hume an Atheist?' http://www.ic.net/~erasmus/RAZ515.HTM.

[123] Flew, 'Exclusive Flew Interview', op. cit.

[124] Flew, *There Is a God*, op. cit., p. 185.

[125] ibid.

Endnotes

325

[126] ibid., p. 213.

[127] ibid., p. 187.

[128] David Hume, *Dialogues Concerning Natural Religion* (ed. Norman Kemp Smith; Indianapolis: Bobbs-Merrill, 1947), p. 227.

[129] Bradley Monton, *Seeking God in Science: An Atheist Defends Intelligent Design* (Peterborough, Ontario: Broadview Press, 2009), p. 71.

[130] Peter van Inwagen, *God, Knowledge and Mystery: Essays in Philosophical Theology* (Cornell University Press, 1995), p. 221.

[131] Peter Kreeft, *Because God Is Real: Sixteen Questions, One Answer* (San Francisco: Ignatius, 2008), p. 86.

[132] On the philosophical theology of the Incarnation and the Trinity, see also: Paul Copan, 'Is the Trinity a Logical Blunder? God as Three-in-One'http://www.paulcopan.com/articles/pdf/is-the-Trinity-a-logical-blunder_God-as-three-and-one.pdf; William Lane Craig, ed., *Philosophy of Religion: A Reader and Guide* (Edinburgh University Press, 2002); Thomas V. Morris, *The Logic of God Incarnate* (Eugene, OR: Wipf & Stock, 2001); Michael J. Murray and Michael Rea, *An Introduction to the Philosophy of Religion* (CUP, 2008); Thomas D. Senor, 'The Incarnation and the Trinity', in *Reason for the Hope Within* (ed. Michael J. Murray; Grand Rapids, MI: Eerdmans, 1999) and Richard Swinburne, *The Christian God* (Oxford: Clarendon Press, 1994).

[133] cf. James W. Sire, *Why Should Anyone Believe Anything at All?* (Downers Grove: IVP, 1994), p. 22.

[134] Gordon R. Lewis, 'Criteria for Discerning Spirits', in *Demon Possession* (ed. John Warwick Montgomery; Minneapolis, MN: Bethany House, 1976), p. 348.

[135] Richard Purtill, *Reason to Believe: Why Faith Makes Sense* (San Francisco: Ignatius, 2009), p. 89. cf. William Lane Craig, 'Are There Objective Truths about God?' http://www.rfmedia.org/RF_audio_video/Other_clips/William_Lane_Craig-Are_There_Objective_Truths-2004-06-08-Liszt-1930.mp3

[136] cf. http://www.newadvent.org/summa/1002.htm.

[137] Antony Flew, *God and Philosophy* (London: Hutchinson, 1974), p. 141.

[138] John Polkinghorne and Nicholas Beale, *Questions of Truth* (Louisville, KY: Westminster John Knox Press, 2009), p. 3.

[139] Dawkins, *The God Delusion*, op. cit., p. 73.

[140] ibid.

[141] ibid.

[142] ibid.

[143] 0 and 1 thus operate as boundary conditions that an inferential case may continuously approach but never attain.

[144] ibid., p. 74.

[145] ibid.

[146] Christopher Hitchens in 'Does Atheism Poison Everything?' http://www.c-spanvideo.org/program/id/232872

[147] R. George Wright, 'Cumulative Case Legal Arguments and the Justification of Academic Affirmative Action' http://www.digitalcommons.pace.edu/cgi/viewcontent.cgi?article=1496&context=lawrev.

[148] Timothy and Linda McGrew, 'The Argument from Miracles: A Cumulative Case for the Resurrection of Jesus of Nazareth' http://www.lydiamcgrew.com/Resurrectionarticlesinglefile.pdf.

2 – Trusting the Biblical Testimony to the Historical Jesus

[1] Richard Bauckham, *Jesus and the Eyewitnesses: The Gospels as Eyewitness Testimony* (Cambridge: Eerdmans, 2006), p. 5.

[2] Craig J. Hazen, 'Ever Hearing but Never Understanding: A Response to Mark Hutchins's Critique of John Warwick Montgomery's Historical Apologetics', in *Tough-Minded Christianity: Honoring the Legacy of John Warwick Montgomery* (ed. William Dembski and Thomas Schirrmacher; Nashville, TN: B&H, 2008), p. 29.

[3] Bauckham, op. cit., p. 5.

[4] David Wenham and Steve Walton, *Exploring the New Testament, vol. 1: A Guide to the Gospels and Acts* (Downers Grove, IL: IVP, 2001), p. 139.

[5] Robert Audi, 'Testimony, Credulity, and Veracity', in *The Epistemology of Testimony* (ed. Jennifer Lackey and Ernest Sosa; Oxford: Clarendon Press, 2006), p. 25.

[6] ibid., p. 36.

[7] ibid., p. 26.

[8] Thomas Reid, *Essays on the Intellectual Powers*, quoted by Audi, ibid., p. 33.

[9] ibid.

[10] Richard Swinburne, 'The Existence of God' http://www.users.ox.ac.uk/~orie0087/framesetpdfs.shtml

[11] Iain W. Provan, 'Knowing and Believing: Faith in the Past', in *Behind the Text: Historical and Biblical Interpretation* (ed. Craig Bartholomew,

C. Stephen Evans, Mary Healy and Murray Rea; Grand Rapids, MI: Zondervan, 2003), p. 250.

12 Audi, op. cit., p. 27.

13 ibid.

14 ibid., p. 28.

15 John Warwick Montgomery, *History and Christianity* (Downers Grove, IL: IVP, 1971), p. 29.

16 Hugh Montefiore, *The Miracles of Jesus* (London: SPCK, 2005), p. 20.

17 Peter Graham, 'Liberal Fundamentalism and Its Rivals', in *The Epistemology of Testimony*, op. cit., pp. 104–5.

18 Audi, op. cit., p. 26.

19 Julie Wheldon, 'The Blind's "Sixth Sense"', *Daily Mail*, Tuesday 1 November 2005, p. 3.

20 ibid.

21 ibid.

22 Malcolm Gladwell, *Blink* (London: Penguin, 2005), pp. 9–10.

23 ibid.

24 cf. J.B. Phillips, *The New Testament in Modern English* (London: Fount, 1972).

25 J.B. Phillips, *Ring of Truth* (Basingstoke: Lakeland, 1984), p. 20.

26 ibid., p. 27.

27 ibid., pp. 123–4.

28 Roy Williams, *God, Actually* (Oxford: Monarch, 2009), p. 165.

29 Elizabeth Fricker, 'Testimony and Epistemic Authority', in *The Epistemology of Testimony*, op. cit., p. 237.

30 C.S. Lewis, 'God in the Dock', in *God in the Dock* (ed. Walter Hooper; London: Fount, 1979), p. 82.

31 C.S. Lewis, 'Fern-seed and Elephants', in *Fern-seed and Elephants: And Other Essays on Christianity* (ed. Walter Hooper; Glasgow: Fount, 1975), pp. 106–7, 108.

32 ibid., p. 108.

33 Victor J. Stenger, *The New Atheism: Taking a Stand for Science and Reason* (New York: Prometheus Books, 2009), p. 53. For example, Richard Dawkins asserts that 'Dan Brown's novel *The Da Vinci Code* … is indeed fabricated from start to finish: invented, made-up fiction. In this respect, it is exactly like the gospels.' – *The God Delusion* (London: Black Swan, 2006), p. 123.

34 John Dickson and Greg Clarke, *Life of Jesus* (Sydney: CPX, 2009), p. 138.

[35] William Lane Craig, *On Guard: Defending Your Faith with Reason and Precision* (Colorado Springs: David C. Cook, 2010), p. 183.

[36] Richard Swinburne, *Was Jesus God?* (OUP, 2008), p. 99.

[37] Ernest Sosa, 'Knowledge: Instrumental and Testimonial', in *The Epistemology of Testimony*, op. cit., p. 116.

[38] Richard Dawkins, *The God Delusion* (London: Black Swan, 2006), p. 118.

[39] ibid.

[40] Philip W. Comfort and Jason Driesbach, *The Many Gospels of Jesus: Sorting out the Story of the Life of Jesus* (Carol Stream, IL: Tyndale, 2008), p. 2.

[41] Mark L. Strauss, *Four Portraits, One Jesus: An Introduction to Jesus and the Gospels* (Grand Rapids, MI: Zondervan, 2007), p. 44.

[42] Graham Stanton, *The Gospels and Jesus* (OUP, 1993), p. 35.

[43] Strauss, op. cit., p. 53.

[44] Norman L. Geisler, *Christian Apologetics* (Grand Rapids, MI: Baker, 1995), p. 313.

[45] Craig L. Blomberg, *Making Sense of the New Testament* (Leicester: IVP, 2003), p. 27.

[46] John Dickson, *Investigating Jesus: An Historian's Quest* (Oxford: Lion, 2010), p. 118.

[47] Paul Barnett, *The Birth of Christianity: The First Twenty Years* (Cambridge: Eerdmans, 2005), p. 147.

[48] ibid., p. 125.

[49] Gregory A. Boyd and Paul Rhodes Eddy, *Lord or Legend? Wrestling with the Jesus Dilemma* (Grand Rapids, MI: Baker, 2007), p. 92.

[50] ibid.

[51] ibid., pp. 69–70.

[52] ibid., p. 70.

[53] Bauckham, op. cit., p. 8.

[54] Boyd and Eddy, op. cit., pp. 92–3.

[55] ibid., p. 93.

[56] Paul Rhodes Eddy and Gregory A. Boyd, *The Jesus Legend: A Case for the Historical Reliability of the Synoptic Jesus Tradition* (Grand Rapids, MI: Baker Academic, 2007), p. 395.

[57] J.P. Moreland, *Scaling the Secular City* (Grand Rapids, MI: Baker, 1987), p. 156.

[58] William P. Alston, 'Historical Criticism of the Synoptic Gospels', in *Behind the Text*, op. cit., p. 167.

[59] Paul Copan, *'True for You, but Not for Me': Defeating the Slogans That Leave Christians Speechless* (Eugene, OR: Bethany House, 1998), p. 103.

[60] Stephen T. Davis, 'Should We Believe the Jesus Seminar?', in *Disputed Issues: Contending for Christian Faith in Today's Academic Setting* (Baylor University Press, 2009), p. 12.

[61] Moreland, op. cit., p. 137.

[62] Eddy and Boyd, op. cit., p. 73.

[63] Bauckham, op. cit., p. 39.

[64] Dawkins, op. cit., p. 122.

[65] Mark D. Roberts, *Can We Trust the Gospels? Investigating the Reliability of Matthew, Mark, Luke and John* (Wheaton, IL: Crossway, 2007), p. 49.

[66] Craig L. Blomberg, *Jesus and the Gospels* (Leicester: Apollos, 1997), p. 365.

[67] Timothy Paul Jones, *Misquoting Truth: A Guide to the Fallacies of Bart Ehrman's* Misquoting Jesus (Downers Grove, IL: IVP, 2007), p. 119.

[68] R.T. France, *The Evidence for Jesus* (London: Hodder & Stoughton, 1986), pp. 122, 124.

[69] Craig L. Blomberg, 'Where Do We Start Studying Jesus?', in *Jesus under Fire* (ed. Michael J. Wilkins and J.P. Moreland; Carlisle: Paternoster, 1995), p. 28.

[70] Blomberg, *Making Sense of the New Testament*, op. cit., p. 24.

[71] Craig, *On Guard*, op. cit., p. 191.

[72] Williams, op. cit., pp. 161–2.

[73] F.F. Bruce, *The New Testament Documents: Are They Reliable?* (Downers Grove, IL: IVP, 2006), p. 17.

[74] Moreland, op. cit., p. 151.

[75] Carsten Peter Thiede, *Jesus: Life or Legend?* (Oxford: Lion, 1990), p. 9.

[76] Paul Barnett, *Finding the Historical Christ* (Grand Rapids, MI: Eerdmans, 2009), p. 45.

[77] Paul Barnett, *The Truth about Jesus: The Challenge of the Evidence* (Sydney: Aquila Press, 2004), p. 50.

[78] Barnett, *Finding the Historical Christ*, op. cit., p. 14.

[79] ibid., p. 16.

[80] ibid.

[81] Blomberg, *Jesus and the Gospels*, op. cit., p. 123.

[82] Papias, quoted by Eusebius, *Ecclesiastical History* 3:39.15, cited in Blomberg, *Jesus and the Gospels*, op. cit., p. 123.

[83] Blomberg, op. cit., p. 125.

[84] Simon Greenleaf, *The Testimony of the Evangelists: The Gospels Examined by the Rules of Evidence* (Grand Rapids, MI: Kregel Classics, 1995), p. 23.

[85] Wenham and Walton, op. cit., p. 205.

[86] David Winter, *The Search for the Real Jesus* (London: Hodder & Stoughton, 1982), p. 29.

[87] Thiede, op. cit., p. 44.

[88] cf. Peter S. Williams, *The Case for Angels* (Carlisle: Paternoster, 2002), pp. 127–9.

[89] Thiede, op. cit., p. 44.

[90] ibid., p. 46.

[91] ibid.

[92] Ben Witherington III, 'Christianity in the Making', in *Memories of Jesus: A Critical Appraisal of James D.G. Dunn's Jesus Remembered* (ed. Robert B. Stewart and Gary R. Habermas; B&H Academic, 2010), p. 223.

[93] Thiede, op. cit., pp. 48–9.

[94] ibid., p. 49.

[95] ibid.

[96] John A.T. Robinson, *Can We Trust the New Testament?* (London; Mowbray, 1977), p. 73.

[97] Thiede, op. cit., p. 51.

[98] Craig, op. cit.

[99] Paul Barnett, *Is the New Testament Reliable?* (Downers Grove, IL: IVP, rev. edn, 2003), p. 75.

[100] Boyd and Eddy, op. cit., pp. 68–9.

[101] Michael Green, *The Books the Church Suppressed: What* The Da Vinci Code *Doesn't Tell You* (Oxford: Monarch, 2005), p. 32.

[102] Barnett, op. cit., p. 92.

[103] Strauss, op. cit., p. 252.

[104] James D.G. Dunn, 'Remembering Jesus: How the Quest for the Historical Jesus Lost Its Way', in *The Historical Jesus: Five Views* (ed. James K. Beilby and Paul R. Eddy; London: SPCK, 2010), p. 205.

[105] ibid., p. 209.

[106] Timothy Paul Jones in *Why Trust the Bible?* (Torrance, CA: Rose, 2008), p. 72.

[107] Thiede, op. cit., p. 56.

[108] James D.G. Dunn, 'The New Testament as History', in *Different Gospels: Modern Orthodoxy and Modern Theologies* (ed. Andrew Walker; London: SPCK, 1993), p. 51.

[109] Barnett, *Finding the Historical Christ*, op. cit., p. 114.

[110] ibid., p. 112.

111 Green, op. cit., p. 33.

112 Gregory A. Boyd, *Letters from a Skeptic* (Downers Grove, IL: IVP, 2000), p. 95.

113 Dean L. Overman, *A Case for the Divinity of Jesus: Examining the Ancient Evidence* (Plymouth: Rowman and Littlefield, 2009), pp. 92–3.

114 Norman L. Geisler and Peter Bocchino, *Unshakeable Foundations* (Minneapolis, MN: Bethany House, 2001), p. 121.

115 Green, op. cit., p. 39.

116 ibid.

117 Blomberg, op. cit., p. 170.

118 Data for figures 11 and 12 was sourced from John Warwick Montgomery, ed., *Evidence for Faith* (Dallas: Probe, 1991).

119 Michael Green, *Lies, Lies, Lies! Exposing Myths about the Real Jesus* (Nottingham: IVP, 2009), p. 79.

120 Philip W. Comfort and Jason Driesbach, *The Many Gospels of Jesus: Sorting out the Story of the Life of Jesus* (Carol Stream, IL: Tyndale, 2008), p. 11.

121 Charlotte Allen, *The Human Christ: The Search for the Historical Jesus* (Oxford: Lion, 1998), pp. 80–81.

122 Dawkins, op. cit., p. 121.

123 Barnett, *Finding the Historical Christ*, op. cit., p. 12.

124 Dawkins, op. cit., p. 121.

125 Jones, *Misquoting Truth*, op. cit., p. 134.

126 Dickson, op. cit., p. 46.

127 Comfort and Driesbach, op. cit., pp. xii, xvi.

128 Craig A. Evans, *Fabricating Jesus: How Modern Scholars Distort the Gospels* (Downers Grove, IL: IVP, 2006), p. 99.

129 Darrell L. Bock and Daniel B. Wallace, *Dethroning Jesus: Exposing Popular Culture's Quest to Unseat the Biblical Christ* (Nashville, TN: Thomas Nelson, 2007), p. 48.

130 Winfried Corduan, *No Doubt about It* (Nashville, TN: Broadman & Holman, 1997), p. 193.

131 Geisler and Bocchino, op. cit., p. 257.

132 cf. http://www.en.wikipedia.org/wiki/Codex_Vaticanus.

133 cf. http://www.itsee.bham.ac.uk/projects/sinaiticus/.

134 cf. http://www.en.wikipedia.org/wiki/Codex_Ephraemi_Rescriptus.

135 cf. http://www.en.wikipedia.org/wiki/Chester_Beatty_Papyri.

136 cf. http://www.en.wikipedia.org/wiki/Bodmer_Papyri.

137 cf. http://www.en.wikipedia.org/wiki/Papyrus_52.

[138] Antony Flew in *Did Jesus Rise from the Dead? The Resurrection Debate* (ed. Terry L. Miethe; Eugene, OR: Wipf & Stock, 2003), p. 66.

[139] cf. Ralph O. Muncaster, *Examine the Evidence: Exploring the Case for Christianity* (Eugene, OR: Harvest House, 2004), p. 226.

[140] ibid.

[141] N.T. Wright, Foreword to F.F. Bruce, *The New Testament Documents: Are They Reliable?* (Grand Rapids, MI: Eerdmans, 2000), p. x.

[142] Norman L. Geisler and Frank Turek, *I Don't Have Enough Faith to Be an Atheist* (Wheaton, IL: Crossway, 2004), p. 225.

[143] Ed Turner, 'Peter S. Williams Up Close – Part II' http://www.ed themanicstreetpreacher.wordpress.com/2009/03/07/peter-s-williams-up-close-—part-ii.

[144] Jones, op. cit., pp. 42, 43, 44.

[145] Roberts, op. cit., p. 37.

[146] Blomberg, *The Historical Reliability of the Gospels*, op. cit., p. 381.

[147] Moreland, op. cit., p. 148.

[148] Alister McGrath, *Jesus: Who He Is and Why He Matters* (Leicester: IVP, 1994), p. 69.

[149] Luke Timothy Johnson, *The Real Jesus* (New York: HarperOne, 1997), p. 87.

[150] Paul Barnett, *Paul: Missionary of Jesus* (Cambridge: Eerdmans, 2008), p. 3.

[151] Moreland, op. cit., p. 148.

[152] ibid., pp. 148–9.

[153] ibid., p. 149.

[154] Michel Onfray, *In Defence of Atheism: The Case against Christianity, Judaism and Islam* (London: Serpent's Tail, 2007), p. 115.

[155] Gary R. Habermas, 'Why I Believe the New Testament Is Historically Reliable' http://www.apologetics.com/index.php?option=com_content&view=article&id=165:why-i-believe-the-new-testament-is-historically-reliable&catid=39:historical-apologetics&Itemid=54.

[156] Geisler and Turek, op. cit., p. 223.

[157] Blomberg, op. cit., p. 251.

[158] Blomberg, *Making Sense of the New Testament*, op. cit., p. 53.

[159] Peter S. Williams, 'Archaeology and the Historical Reliability of the New Testament' http://www.bethinking.org/bible-jesus/advanced/archaeology-and-the-historical-reliability-of-the-new-testament.htm; see also (Audio) Peter S. Williams, 'New Testament Archaeology' http://www.damaris.org/cm/podcasts/215.

[160] Darrell L. Bock, *Studying the Historical Jesus: A Guide to Sources and Methods* (Leicester: Apollos, 2007), p. 215.

[161] C. Stephen Evans, 'Tradition, Biblical Interpretation and Historical Truth', in *Behind the Text: Historical and Biblical Interpretation*, op. cit., p. 320.

[162] R.T. France, 'The Gospels as Historical Sources for Jesus, the Founder of Christianity', *Truth* 1 (1985): p. 86.

3 – The First Way – Jesus' Self-Centred Teaching

[1] Darrell L. Bock, *Studying the Historical Jesus: A Guide to Sources and Methods* (Leicester: Apollos, 2002), p 199.

[2] ibid.

[3] David Wenham and Steve Walton, *Exploring the New Testament, vol. 1: A Guide to the Gospels and Acts* (Downers Grove, IL: IVP, 2001), p. 139.

[4] William Lane Craig, *Reasonable Faith: Christian Truth and Apologetics* (Wheaton, IL: Crossway, 3rd edn, 2008), p. 298.

[5] Bock, op. cit., pp. 202–3.

[6] ibid.

[7] Darrell L. Bock, 'The Words of Jesus in the Gospels: Live, Jive, or Memorex?', in *Jesus under Fire: Modern Scholarship Reinvents the Historical Jesus* (Grand Rapids, MI: Zondervan, 1995), p. 90.

[8] John Dickson, *Investigating Jesus: An Historian's Quest* (Oxford: Lion, 2010), p. 124.

[9] Wenham and Walton, op. cit., p. 135.

[10] ibid., p. 136.

[11] ibid., pp. 136–7.

[12] Bock, op. cit., p. 92.

[13] Craig L. Blomberg, *Jesus and the Gospels* (Leicester: Apollos, 1997), p. 186.

[14] Thomas R. Yoder Neufeld, *Recovering Jesus: The Witness of the New Testament* (Grand Rapids, MI: SPCK, 2007), p. 44.

[15] Craig A. Evans, *Fabricating Jesus: How Modern Scholars Distort the Gospels* (Downers Grove, IL: IVP, 2006), p. 140.

[16] Mark L. Strauss, *Four Portraits, One Jesus* (Grand Rapids, MI: Zondervan, 2007), p. 361.

[17] Wenham and Walton, op. cit., p. 138.

[18] Bock, *Studying the Historical Jesus*, op. cit., p. 200.

[19] Neufeld, *Recovering Jesus*, op. cit., p. 44.

[20] Wenham and Walton, op. cit., p. 138.

[21] Bock, op. cit., p. 202.

[22] ibid., p. 201.

[23] Dickson, op. cit., p. 143.

[24] ibid., p. 144.

[25] Neufeld, op. cit., p. 45.

[26] Wenham and Walton, op. cit., p. 139.

[27] Bock, 'The Words of Jesus in the Gospels: Live, Jive, or Memorex?', op. cit., p. 93.

[28] Wenham and Walton, op. cit.

[29] Tom Wright, *Simply Christian* (London: SPCK, 2006), p. 101.

[30] James D.G. Dunn, 'Remembering Jesus: How the Quest for the Historical Jesus Lost Its Way', in *The Historical Jesus: Five Views* (ed. James B. Beilby and Paul R. Eddy; London: SPCK, 2010), p. 204.

[31] Robert W. Funk, *Honest to Jesus* (New York: HarperSanFrancisco, 1996), pp. 279–96.

[32] John W. Loftus, *Why I Became an Atheist: A Former Preacher Rejects Christianity* (New York: Prometheus Books, 2008), p. 329.

[33] ibid., p. 330.

[34] Michael Green, 'Jesus in the New Testament', in *The Truth of God Incarnate* (ed. Michael Green; London: Hodder & Stoughton, 1977), p. 24.

[35] Larry W. Hurtado, *Lord Jesus Christ: Devotion to Jesus in Earliest Christianity* (Grand Rapids, MI: Eerdmans, 2003), pp. 2–3, my italics.

[36] Paul Copan, *'True for You, but Not for Me': Overcoming Objections to Christian Faith* (Minneapolis, MN: Bethany House, rev. edn, 2009), p. 167.

[37] J. Ed Komoszewski, M. James Sawyer and Daniel B. Wallace, *Reinventing Jesus: How Contemporary Skeptics Miss the Real Jesus and Mislead Popular Culture* (Grand Rapids, MI: Kregel, 2006), p. 169.

[38] Paul Barnett, *Messiah: Jesus – the Evidence of History* (Nottingham: IVP, 2009), p. 119.

[39] ibid., p. 120.

[40] J.P. Moreland, *Scaling the Secular City* (Grand Rapids, MI: Baker, 1987), pp. 149–50.

[41] N.T. Wright, *Surprised by Hope* (London: SPCK, 2007), p. 146.

[42] Barnett, op. cit., pp. 43, 104.

[43] ibid., p. 40.

[44] Dean L. Overman, *A Case for the Divinity of Jesus: Examining the Earliest Evidence* (Plymouth: Rowman & Littlefield, 2009), p. 26.

[45] Barnett, op. cit., p. 105.

46 ibid., p. 40.
47 Paul Barnett, *The Birth of Christianity: The First Twenty Years* (Grand Rapids, MI: Eerdmans, 2005), p. 26.
48 Larry W. Hurtado, *How on Earth Did Jesus Become a God? Historical Questions about Earliest Devotion to Jesus* (Grand Rapids, MI: Eerdmans, 2005), p. 33.
49 Barnett, *Messiah*, op. cit., pp. 40–41.
50 Overman, op. cit., p. 22.
51 ibid., pp. 21–2.
52 cf. Overman, op. cit., p. 22.
53 ibid., p. 23.
54 ibid., p. 24.
55 Larry W. Hurtado, 'The Origins of Jesus-Devotion: A Response to Crispin Fletcher-Louis', *Tyndale Bulletin* 61:1 (2010): p. 13.
56 Komoszewski, Sawyer and Wallace, op. cit., p. 172.
57 Green, op. cit., p. 40.
58 ibid., p. 40.
59 Overman, op. cit., pp. 3, 4.
60 ibid., p. 20.
61 Michael F. Bird in *How Did Christianity Begin? A Believer and Non-believer Examine the Evidence* (London: SPCK, 2008), p. 162.
62 Hurtado, *How on Earth Did Jesus Become a God?* op. cit., p. 25.
63 Anthony O'Hear, *Jesus for Beginners* (London: Icon, 1993), p. 84.
64 Norman L. Geisler, *Christian Apologetics* (Grand Rapids, MI: Baker, 1996), pp. 337–8.
65 Richard Bauckham, *God Crucified: Monotheism and Christology in the New Testament* (Grand Rapids, MI: Eerdmans, 1999), p. 26.
66 James E. Taylor, *Introducing Apologetics: Cultivating Christian Commitment* (Grand Rapids, MI: Baker Academic, 2006), pp. 180–81.
67 Craig A. Evans, 'The Historical Jesus and the Deified Christ: How Did the One Lead to the Other?', in *The Nature of Religious Language: A Colloquium* (ed. Stanley E. Porter; Sheffield: Sheffield Academic Press, 1996), p. 67.
68 Peter Zaas in *Who Was Jesus? A Jewish–Christian Dialogue* (ed. Paul Copan and Craig A. Evans; London: WJK, 2001), p. 40.
69 Craig A. Evans, 'The Jesus of History and the Christ of Faith', ibid., p. 66.
70 Peter Kreeft, 'Why I Believe Jesus is the Messiah and Son of God', in *Why I Am a Christian* (ed. Norman L. Geisler and Paul K. Hoffman; Grand Rapids, MI: Baker, rev. edn, 2006), p. 250.

[71] Michel Onfray, *In Defence of Atheism: The Case against Christianity, Judaism and Islam* (London: Serpent's Tail, 2007), p. 125.

[72] ibid., p. 126.

[73] Richard Dawkins, *The God Delusion* (London: Black Swan, 2006), p. 117.

[74] Taylor, op. cit., p. 181.

[75] Mark L. Strauss, *Four Portraits, One Jesus* (Grand Rapids, MI: Zondervan, 2007), p. 365.

[76] Craig L. Blomberg, *Jesus and the Gospels* (Leicester: Apollos, 1997), p. 384.

[77] Dallas Willard, *The Divine Conspiracy: Rediscovering Our Hidden Life in God* (London: Fount, 1998), p. 29.

[78] Neufeld, op. cit., pp. 137–8.

[79] Bird, op. cit., p. 25.

[80] Barnett, op. cit., p. 32.

[81] ibid., pp. 32–3.

[82] ibid., p. 35.

[83] Blomberg, op cit., p. 384.

[84] Barnett, op, cit., p. 36.

[85] N.T. Wright, *Jesus and the Victory of God* (London: SPCK, 1996), p. 176.

[86] Barnett, op. cit., p. 37.

[87] Dunn, 'Remembering Jesus: How the Quest for the Historical Jesus Lost Its Way', op. cit., p. 223.

[88] ibid.

[89] Luke Timothy Johnson in Beilby and Eddy, eds, *The Historical Jesus*, op. cit., p. 174.

[90] Norman L. Geisler and Peter Bocchino, *Unshakeable Foundations* (Minneapolis, MN: Bethany House, 2001), p. 328.

[91] Darrell L. Bock in *The Historical Jesus*, op. cit., pp. 196–7.

[92] William Lane Craig, *Reasonable Faith: Christian Truth and Apologetics* (Wheaton, IL: Crossway, 3rd edn, 2008), pp. 319, 323.

[93] Peter Kreeft, *Between Heaven and Hell* (Downers Grove, IL: IVP, 1982), p. 44.

[94] Donald Guthrie, *New Testament Theology* (Downers Grove, IL: IVP, 1981), p. 280.

[95] Oscar Cullmann, *The Christology of the New Testament* (Philadelphia: Westminster Press, 1966), p. 282.

[96] Michael Green, *Lies, Lies, Lies!* (Nottingham: IVP, 2009), p. 18.

[97] James G. Crossley in *How Did Christianity Begin?* op. cit., p. 1.

[98] Scott McKnight, 'Who Is Jesus? An Introduction to Jesus Studies', in Michael J. Wilkins and J.P. Moreland, eds, *Jesus under Fire: Modern Scholarship Reinvents the Historical Jesus* (Grand Rapids, MI: Zondervan, 1995), p. 67.

[99] Bird, op. cit., p. 29.

[100] William Lane Craig, 'Jesus the Son of God' http://www.reasonable-faith.org/site/News2?page=NewsArticle&id=6247.

[101] ibid., p. 26.

[102] Wenham and Walton, op. cit., p. 184.

[103] Quoted by Terry L. Miethe and Gary R. Habermas, *Why Believe? God Exists!* (Joplin, MO: College Press, 1999), pp. 278, 280.

[104] Robert H. Stein, 'Criteria for the Gospel's Authenticity', in *Contending with Christianity's Critics: Answering New Atheists and Other Objectors* (ed. Paul Copan and William Lane Craig; Nashville, TN: B&H Academic, 2009), p. 95.

[105] Craig, *Reasonable Faith*, op. cit., p. 307.

[106] Robert M. Bowman and J. Ed Komoszewski, *Putting Jesus in His Place: The Case for the Deity of Christ* (Grand Rapids, MI: Kregel, 2007), p. 244.

[107] Komoszewski, Sawyer and Wallace, *Reinventing Jesus*, op. cit., p. 179.

[108] ibid.

[109] Bird, op. cit., p. 27.

[110] Geisler, *Christian Apologetics*, op. cit., pp. 332–3.

[111] Overman, op. cit., p. 59.

[112] Craig, op. cit., p. 317.

[113] Craig A. Evans, 'The Jesus of History of the Christ of Faith', in *Who Was Jesus? A Jewish–Christian Dialogue* (ed. Paul Copan and Craig A. Evans; London: Westminster John Knox Press, 2001), p. 66.

[114] Donald A. Carson, *The Gospel According to John* (Grand Rapids, MI: Eerdmans, 1991), p. 587.

[115] *Archaeological Study Bible: An Illustrated Walk through Biblical History and Culture* (Grand Rapids, MI: Zondervan, 2005), p. 1714.

[116] Josh McDowell and Bill Wilson, *He Walked among Us* (Carlisle: Alpha, 2000), p. 334.

[117] J.P. Moreland, *The God Question: An Invitation to a Life of Meaning* (Eugene, OR: Harvest House, 2009), p. 111.

[118] Carsten Peter Thiede, *Jesus, Man or Myth?* (Oxford: Lion, 2005), p. 136.

[119] G.K. Chesterton, *The Everlasting Man* (London: Hodder & Stoughton, 1927), p. 237.

120 John Rist, 'Where Else?', in *Philosophers Who Believe* (Downers Grove, IL: IVP, 1993), pp. 100–01.

121 John Duncan http://www.en.wikipedia.org/wiki/Lewis%27s_trilemma#cite_note-1.

122 C.S. Lewis, *Mere Christianity* (London: Collins, 1952), pp. 54–6.

123 Josh McDowell, 'The Trilemma, Lord, Lunatic or Liar?' http://www.greatcom.org/resources/areadydefense/ch21/default.htm.

124 Craig, op. cit., p. 299.

125 ibid., pp. 313, 323.

126 Quoted by Craig, ibid., p. 327.

127 William Paley, *Evidences of Christianity* (Charleston, SC: BiblioBazaar, 2007), pp. 256–7, cf. http://www.ccel.org/ccel/paley/evidence.iv.v.html.

128 Taylor, op. cit., p. 183.

129 Peter Kreeft, 'The Divinity of Christ' http://www.catholiceducation.org/articles/religion/re0020.html.

130 Peter Kreeft and Ronald Tacelli, *Handbook of Christian Apologetics* (Downers Grove, IL: IVP, 1994), p. 159.

131 G.K. Chesterton, *The Everlasting Man* (London: Hodder & Stoughton, 1927), pp. 235–7.

132 David A. Horner, '*Aut Deus aut Malus Homo*: A Defense of C.S. Lewis' "Shocking Alternative"', in *C.S. Lewis as Philosopher: Truth, Goodness and Beauty* (ed. David Baggett, Gary R. Habermas and Jerry L. Walls; Downers Grove, IL: IVP Academic, 2008), p. 73.

133 Taylor, op. cit., pp. 182–3.

134 Dawkins, op. cit., p. 284.

135 ibid., pp. 283–4.

136 Richard Dawkins, 'Atheists for Jesus' http://www.richarddawkins.net/articles/20.

137 ibid.

138 Taylor, op. cit., p. 183.

139 Kreeft, 'The Divinity of Christ', op. cit.

140 ibid.

141 cf. 'Richard Dawkins on Studio 4 in Vancouver – Part 3 of 5' http://www.youtube.com/watch?v=XwWQamTzjA0&feature=related.

142 Dawkins, *The God Delusion*, op. cit., p. 117.

143 Chesterton, op. cit., pp. 229–30.

144 Nicky Gumbel, *Is God a Delusion?* (London: Alpha, 2008), p. 80.

[145] Stephen T. Davis, 'The Mad/Bad/God Trilemma: A Reply to Daniel Howard Snyder' http://www.lastseminary.com/trilemma.

[146] Mike King, *The God Delusion Revisited* (Lulu, 2007), p. 63.

[147] Richard Purtill, *Reason to Believe: Why Faith Makes Sense* (San Francisco: Ignatius, 2009), p. 138.

[148] Michael Green, 'Jesus and Historical Scepticism', in *The Truth of God Incarnate* (ed. Michael Green; London: Hodder, 1977).

[149] Craig, op. cit., p. 328.

[150] Chesterton, op. cit., p. 215.

4 – The Second Way – Jesus' Dynamic Deeds

[1] G.E.M. Anscombe, *Intention* (Cambridge, MA: Harvard University Press, 2000), p. 8.

[2] William Lane Craig, *On Guard: Defending Your Faith with Reason and Precision* (Colorado Springs: David C. Cook, 2010), p. 213.

[3] Michael Green, 'Jesus in the New Testament', in *The Truth of God Incarnate* (ed. Michael Green; London: Hodder & Stoughton, 1977), p. 46.

[4] T.C. Hammond, *Reasoning Faith: An Introduction to Christian Apologetics* (London: Inter-Varsity Fellowship, 1943), pp. 216–17.

[5] C.S. Lewis, *Miracles* (London: Fount, 1998), p. 99.

[6] C.S. Lewis, *Studies in Words* (CUP, 2nd edn, 1967), p. 24.

[7] ibid., p. 25.

[8] ibid., p. 45.

[9] cf. William A. Dembski, 'The Incompleteness of Scientific Naturalism' http://www.leaderu.com/orgs/fte/darwinism/chapter7.html; Bradley Monton, *Seeking God in Science: An Atheist Defends Intelligent Design* (Ontario: Broadview, 2009), pp. 51–2.

[10] Lewis, op. cit., pp. 35–8.

[11] ibid., p. 38.

[12] ibid., p. 39.

[13] John Cottingham, *Why Believe?* (London: Continuum, 2009), p. 94.

[14] Peter Kreeft and Ronald Tacelli, *Handbook of Christian Apologetics* (Crowborough: Monarch, 1999), p. 110.

[15] David Baggett, *Did the Resurrection Happen?* (Downers Grove, IL: IVP, 2009), pp. 140–41.

[16] Norman L. Geisler and Frank Turek, *I Don't Have Enough Faith to Be an Atheist* (Wheaton, IL: Crossway, 2004), p. 209.

17 Christopher Hitchens, *God Is Not Great* (London: Atlantic Books, 2007), p. 141.

18 David Hume, 'Of Miracles', in *An Enquiry Concerning Human Understanding* 114:143.

19 ibid., f.n. 115:154.

20 Richard Dawkins, *A Devil's Chaplain* (London: Weidenfeld & Nicolson, 2003), p. 150.

21 Richard Dawkins, 'Is Science a Religion?', quoted by Dinesh D'Souza, *What's So Great about Christianity?* (Washington: Regnery, 2007), p. 180.

22 J.A. Cover, 'Miracles and Christian Theism', in *Reason for the Hope Within* (ed. Michael J. Murray; Cambridge: Eerdmans, 1999), p. 362.

23 David Hume, 'Of Miracles', in *The Portable Atheist* (ed. Christopher Hitchens; London: Da Capo, 2007), p. 34, my italics.

24 Michael Peterson, William Hasker, Bruce Reichenback and David Basinger, *Reason and Religious Belief* (OUP, 1991), pp. 158–9.

25 C. Stephen Evans, *Philosophy of Religion: Thinking about Faith* (Leicester: IVP, 1982), pp. 108–9.

26 J.P. Moreland and William Lane Craig, *Philosophical Foundations for a Christian Worldview* (Downers Grove, IL: IVP, 2003), p. 568.

27 Winfried Corduan, *No Doubt about It* (Nashville, TN: Broadman, Holman & Hunt, 1997), p. 157.

28 cf. Colin J. Humphreys, *The Miracles of Exodus* (London: Continuum, 2004), ch. 2.

29 Michael Poole, *Miracles: Science, the Bible and Experience* (London: Scripture Union, 1992), p. 32.

30 Moreland and Craig, op. cit., p. 568.

31 ibid.

32 Kreeft and Tacelli, op. cit., p. 114.

33 James E. Taylor, *Introducing Apologetics: Cultivating Christian Commitment* (Grand Rapids, MI: Baker Academic, 2006), pp. 188–9.

34 Norman L. Geisler, *Baker Encyclopedia of Christian Apologetics* (Grand Rapids, MI: Baker Academic, 1998), p. 570.

35 R.T. France, *The Evidence for Jesus* (London: Hodder & Stoughton, 1986), p. 167.

36 William P. Alston, 'Biblical Criticism and the Resurrection', in *The Resurrection* (ed. Stephen Davis, Daniel Kendall and Gerald O'Collins; OUP, 1998), p. 182.

[37] William Lane Craig, 'A Classical Apologist's Response', in *Five Views on Apologetics* (ed. Steven B. Cowen; Grand Rapids, MI: Zondervan, 2000), p. 124.

[38] Albert Schweitzer, *The Quest of the Historical Jesus*, trans. W. Montgomery (London: Adam & Charles Black, 3rd edn, 1954), pp. 110–11.

[39] cf. William Lane Craig, 'Christ and Miracles', in *To Everyone an Answer: A Case for the Christian Worldview* (ed. Francis J. Beckwith, William Lane Craig and J.P. Moreland; Downers Grove, IL: IVP, 2004), pp. 139–43; William Lane Craig, 'Rediscovering the Historical Jesus: Presuppositions and Pretensions of the Jesus Seminar' http://www.leaderu.com/offices/billcraig/docs/rediscover1.html; Michael J. Wilkins and J.P. Moreland, eds, *Jesus under Fire: Modern Scholarship Reinvents the Historical Jesus* (Grand Rapids, MI: Zondervan, 1995).

[40] ibid., pp. 2–3.

[41] William Lane Craig, 'Rediscovering the Historical Jesus: Presuppositions and Pretensions of the Jesus Seminar' http://www.leaderu.com/offices/billcraig/docs/rediscover1.html.

[42] Garrett J. DeWeese and J.P Moreland, *Philosophy Made Slightly Less Difficult* (Downers Grove, IL: IVP, 2005), p. 146.

[43] Michael Ruse, *Can a Darwinian Be a Christian?* (CUP, 2004), p. 101.

[44] Stephen C. Meyer, 'The Methodological Equivalence of Design and Descent', in *The Creation Hypothesis* (ed. J.P. Moreland; Downers Grove, IL: IVP, 1994), p. 97.

[45] Del Ratzsch, *Science and Its Limits: The Natural Sciences in Christian Perspective* (Leicester: Apollos, 2000), pp. 123–4.

[46] Bradley Monton, 'Is Intelligent Design Science? Dissecting the Dover Decision' http://www.philsci-archive.pitt.edu/archive/00002592/01/Methodological_Naturalism_Dover_3.doc.

[47] Taylor, op. cit., p. 190.

[48] Tom Wright, *Simply Christian* (London: SPCK, 2006), p. 98.

[49] Hume, *An Enquiry Concerning Human Understanding* 10.1.118.

[50] Kreeft and Tacelli, op. cit.

[51] ibid.

[52] Stephen T. Davis, *Risen Indeed: Making Sense of the Resurrection* (London: SPCK, 1993), p. 4.

[53] ibid.

[54] Hume, op. cit.

[55] Lewis, *Miracles*, op. cit., p. 106.

[56] ibid., p. 111.

[57] Norman L. Geisler, 'Miracles and the Modern Mind', in *In Defence of Miracles* (ed. R. Douglas Geivett and Gary R. Habermas; Leicester: Apollos, 1997), p. 75.

[58] ibid., p. 76.

[59] Corduan, op. cit., p. 172.

[60] John Earman, *Hume's Abject Failure* (OUP, 2000), p. 4.

[61] Geisler, op. cit., p. 79.

[62] Charles Taliaferro and Anders Hendrickson, 'Hume's Racism and His Case against the Miraculous', *Philosophia Christi* 4:2 (2002): p. 428.

[63] ibid., p. 437.

[64] J. Huston, *Reported Miracles* (CUP, 2007), pp. 134, 162, 166.

[65] Geisler, op. cit.

[66] Moreland and Craig, op. cit., p. 570.

[67] Francis J. Beckwith, 'Theism, Miracles, and the Modern Mind', in *The Rationality of Theism* (ed. Paul Copan and Paul K. Moser; London: Routledge, 2003), p. 231.

[68] Baggett, op. cit., p. 140.

[69] Geisler, op. cit., pp. 79, 85.

[70] William Lane Craig, *Reasonable Faith: Christian Truth and Apologetics* (Crossway, 3rd edn, 2008), p. 276.

[71] John Earman, *Hume's Abject Failure* (OUP, 2000), p. 71.

[72] Keith Ward, *The Big Questions in Science and Religion* (West Conshohocken, PA: Templeton, 2008), p. 93.

[73] ibid., p. 106.

[74] Davies, op. cit., pp. 5, 19.

[75] Evans, op. cit., p. 117.

[76] Kreeft and Tacelli, op. cit., p. 109.

[77] J.P. Moreland, *Christianity and the Nature of Science* (Grand Rapids, MI: Baker, 1998), p. 226.

[78] Alan Richardson, *Christian Apologetics* (London: SCM, 1948), p. 171.

[79] Anthony Ernest Harvey, *Jesus and the Constraints of History* (Philadelphia: Westminster Press, 1982), p. 6.

[80] Marcus J. Borg, *Jesus, A New Vision: Spirit, Culture, and the Life of Discipleship* (San Francisco: Harper, 1991), p. 61.

[81] J. Jeremias, *New Testament Theology, vol. 1* (London: SCM, 1971), p. 92.

[82] John Dominic Crossan, *The Historical Jesus: The Life of a Mediterranean Jewish Peasant* (New York: HarperSanFrancisco, 1992), pp. 310–11.

83 Daniel Morias and Michael Gleghorn, 'Did Jesus Really Perform Miracles?' http://www.probe.org/site/c.fdKEIMNsEoG/b.4227257/k.3E6C/Did_Jesus_Really_Perform_Miracles.htm.

84 Barnett, *Messiah*, op. cit., p. 89.

85 cf. Douglas Groothuis, *On Jesus* (London: Thomson Wadsworth, 2003), p. 32.

86 Robert H. Stein, 'Criteria for the Gospel's Authenticity', in *Contending with Christianity's Critics: Answering New Atheists and Other Objectors* (ed. Paul Copan and William Lane Craig; Nashville, TN: B&H Academic, 2009), p. 103.

87 John P. Meier, *A Marginal Jew* (4 vols; Yale University Press, 2007), 2:619.

88 Barnett, op. cit., pp. 86–7.

89 B.L. Blackburn, 'The Miracles of Jesus', in *Studying the Historical Jesus: Evaluations of the State of Current Research* (ed. Chilton and Evans; *Leiden:* Brill, 1993), pp. 356–7.

90 John Meier, quoted by Mark Allan Powell, *The Jesus Debate: Modern Historians Investigate the Life of Jesus* (Oxford: Lion, 1998), p. 150.

91 Barnett, op. cit., p. 90.

92 cf. http://www.christian-thinktank.com/mqx.html.

93 Paula Fredriksen, *Jesus of Nazareth, King of the Jews* (Vintage, 2002), p. 114.

94 Quadratus, quoted by John Woolmer, *Healing and Deliverance* (Crowborough: Monarch, 1999), p. 159.

95 Gary R. Habermas, 'Why I Believe the Miracles of Jesus Actually Happened', in *Why I Am a Christian* (Grand Rapids, MI: Baker, 2006), p. 123.

96 N.T. Wright, *Jesus and the Victory of God* (*Augsburg:* Fortress Press, 1996), p. 187.

97 Richardson, op. cit., p. 170.

98 Christopher Price, 'The Miracles of Jesus: A Historical Inquiry' http://www.christianorigins.com/miracles.html.

99 Wright, op. cit., p. 188.

100 Josephus, *Antiquities*, Book 18, my italics.

101 Babylonian Talmud, *Sanhedrin* 43a, my italics.

102 Geza Vermes, *The Resurrection* (London: Penguin, 2008), p. 160.

103 Celsus, as quoted by Origen, *Contra Celsum* 1.6, my italics.

104 Craig A. Evans, *Fabricating Jesus: How Modern Scholars Distort the Gospels* (Downers Grove, IL: IVP, 2006), pp. 156–7.

[105] David Instone-Brewer, 'Jesus and the Psychiatrists', in *The Unseen World* (ed. Anthony N.S. Lane; Carlisle: Paternoster, 1996), p. 147.

[106] John Drane, *Introducing the New Testament* (Oxford: Lion, rev. edn, 1999), p. 148.

[107] Evans, op. cit., p. 141.

[108] Raymond Brown, *An Introduction to New Testament Christology* (London: Geoffrey Chapman, 1994), p. 63.

[109] Keith Warrington, *Jesus the Healer* (Carlisle: Paternoster, 2000), p. 104.

[110] Price, op. cit., my italics.

[111] Hugh Montefiore, *The Miracles of Jesus* (London: SPCK, 2005), p. 48.

[112] Paul Rhodes Eddy and Gregory A. Boyd, *The Jesus Legend* (Grand Rapids, MI: Baker Academic, 2007), p. 83.

[113] Paul Rhodes Eddy and James K. Beilby, 'The Quest for the Historical Jesus: An Introduction', in *The Historical Jesus: Five Views* (London: SPCK, 2010), pp. 38–9.

[114] Gary R. Habermas, 'Why I Believe the Miracles of Jesus Actually Happened', in *Why I Am a Christian* (ed. Norman L. Geisler and Paul K. Hoffman; Grand Rapids, MI: Baker, 2006), p. 123.

[115] cf. Mortimer J. Adler, *The Angels and Us* (London: Collier, 1982); Peter Kreeft, *Angels and Demons: What Do We Really Know about Them?* (San Francisco: Ignatius, 1995); Phillip H. Wiebe, *God and Other Spirits: Intimations of Transcendence in Christian Experience* (OUP, 2004); Peter S. Williams, *The Case for Angels* (Carlisle: Paternoster, 2002).

[116] Craig, *Reasonable Faith*, op. cit., p. 322.

[117] Michael Symmons Roberts, *The Miracles of Jesus* (Oxford: Lion, 2006), p. 97.

[118] Roy Williams, *God, Actually* (Oxford: Monarch, 2009), p. 170.

[119] Richard Purtill, 'Miracles: What If They Happen?', in *Miracles* (ed. Richard Swinburne; New York: Macmillan, 1989), p. 203.

[120] Graham Stanton, *The Gospels and Jesus* (OUP, 2nd edn, 2002), p. 235.

[121] Graham Stanton, 'Message and Miracles', in *The Cambridge Companion to Jesus* (ed. Markus Bockmuehl; CUP, 2001), p. 67.

[122] Mark L. Strauss, *Four Portraits, One Jesus: An Introduction to Jesus and the Gospels* (Grand Rapids, MI: Zondervan, 2007), p. 458.

[123] Graham Twelftree, *Christ Triumphant* (London: Hodder & Stoughton, 1985), p. 169.

[124] ibid.

[125] Warrington, op. cit., p. 45.

126 Michael Perry, ed. *Deliverance* (London: SPCK, 1996), p. 146.

127 ibid.

128 Ernest Lucas, ed., *Christian Healing* (London: Lynx, 1997), p. 148.

129 M. Scott Peck, *People of the Lie* (London: Arrow, 1990), p. 219.

130 David Instone-Brewer, 'Jesus and the Psychiatrists', in *The Unseen World*, op. cit., p. 135.

131 ibid., p. 138.

132 Warrington, op. cit., p. 45.

133 Gregory A. Boyd, *God at War* (Leicester: IVP, 1997), p. 198.

134 cf. Paul Rhodes Eddy and Gregory A. Boyd, *The Jesus Legend* (Grand Rapids, MI: Baker Academic, 2007), p. 448.

135 Taylor, op. cit., pp. 194, 195, 196.

136 B.D. Chilton and C.A. Evans, eds, *Authenticating the Activities of Jesus* (NTTS 28:2; Leiden: E.J. Brill, 1998), pp. 11–12.

137 Steven B. Cowan, 'Discerning the Voice of God: The Apologetic Function of Miracles', in *Areopagus Journal* (March/April 2008): p. 11.

138 Barnett, op. cit., p. 87.

5 – The Third Way – Jesus' Resurrection

1 David Winter, *Where Do We Go from Here? The Case for Life Beyond Death* (London: Hodder & Stoughton, 1996), p. 47.

2 N.T. Wright, *The Resurrection of the Son of God* (London: SPCK, 2003), p. 685.

3 Lucian of Samosata, *The Passing of Peregrinus*, quoted by Charlotte Allen, *The Human Christ: The Search for the Historical Jesus* (Oxford: Lion, 1998), p. 46.

4 Bart Ehrman in 'Is There Historical Evidence for the Resurrection of Jesus?' (Dr Ehrman's Opening Statement) http://www.reasonablefaith. org/site/DocServer/resurrection-debate-transcript.pdf?docID=621.

5 John W. Loftus, *Why I Became an Atheist: A Former Preacher Rejects Christianity* (New York: Prometheus, 2008), p. 363.

6 N.T. Wright, *Surprised by Hope* (London: SPCK, 2007), p. 55.

7 cf. Michael Licona, 'Paul and the Nature of the Resurrection Body', in *Buried Hope or Risen Savior? The Search for the Jesus Tomb* (ed. Charles L. Quarles; Nashville, TN: Holman, 2008); Stephen T. Davis, 'James D.G. Dunn on the Resurrection of Jesus', in *Memories of Jesus: A Critical Appraisal of James D.G. Dunn's Jesus Remembered* (ed. Robert B. Stewart

and Gary R. Habermas; B&H Academic, 2010); N.T. Wright, *Surprised by Hope* (London: SPCK, 2007).

8 William Lane Craig, 'The Bodily Resurrection of Jesus' http://www.leaderu.com/offices/billcraig/docs/bodily.html.

9 cf. John W. Cooper, *Body, Soul and Life Everlasting: Biblical Anthropology and the Monism–Dualism Debate* (Leicester: Apollos, 1989).

10 cf. John Polkinghorne, *The God of Hope and the End of the World* (London: SPCK, 2002).

11 Markus Bockmuehl, 'Resurrection', in *The Cambridge Companion to Jesus* (ed. Markus Bockmuehl; CUP, 2001), p. 111.

12 Bart Ehrman, *Jesus: Apocalyptic Prophet of the Millennium* (OUP, 1999), p. 231.

13 Francis Watson, 'The Quest for the Real Jesus', in *The Cambridge Companion to Jesus*, op. cit., p. 159.

14 Mark Allan Powell, *The Jesus Debate: Modern Historians Investigate the Life of Christ* (Oxford: Lion, 1998), p. 106.

15 Wright, op. cit., p. 68.

16 William Lane Craig and Walter Sinnot-Armstrong, *God? A Debate between a Christian and an Atheist* (OUP, 2004), p. 37.

17 Stephen T. Davis, '"Seeing" the Risen Jesus', in *The Resurrection* (ed. Stephen T. Davis, Daniel Kendall and Gerald O'Collins; OUP, 1998), p. 136.

18 Marguerite Shuster, 'The Preaching of the Resurrection of Christ in Augustine, Luther, Barth, and Thielicke', ibid., p. 308.

19 John Drane, *Jesus and the Four Gospels: The Real Evidence* (Tring: Lion, 1979), p. 71.

20 Geza Vermes, *The Resurrection* (London: Penguin, 2008), p. 116.

21 ibid., pp. 65–6.

22 N.T. Wright, *The Resurrection of the Son of God* (London: SPCK, 2003), p. 611.

23 cf. John Wenham, *Easter Enigma: Are the Resurrection Accounts in Conflict?* (Carlisle: Paternoster Press, 2nd edn, 1992); Peter Walker, *The Weekend That Changed the World* (London: Marshall Pickering, 1999).

24 Murray J. Harris, *Raised Immortal: Resurrection and Immortality in the New Testament* (Grand Rapids, MI: Eerdmans, 1985), p. 68.

25 Loftus, op. cit., p. 363.

26 Gary R. Habermas in *Five Views on Apologetics* (Grand Rapids, MI: Zondervan), pp. 100, 115.

[27] Terry L. Miethe and Gary R. Habermas, *Why Believe? God Exists!* (Joplin, MO: College Press, 1998), pp. 273–4.

[28] William Lane Craig, 'Qualms about the Resurrection of Jesus' http://www.reasonablefaith.org/site/News2?page=NewsArticle&id=6503.

[29] William Lane Craig, *Reasonable Faith: Christian Truth and Apologetics* (Crossway, 3rd edn, 2008), p. 350.

[30] John Dickson and Greg Clarke, *Life of Jesus* (Sydney: CPX, 2009), p. 116.

[31] Gary R. Habermas, 'The Resurrection and Agnosticism', in *Reasons for Faith* (ed. Norman L. Geisler and Chad V. Meister; Wheaton, IL: Crossway, 2007), pp. 281–2.

[32] Craig, op. cit., p. 360.

[33] Charles Foster, *The Jesus Inquest: The Case for and against the Resurrection of the Christ* (Oxford: Monarch, 2006), p. 220.

[34] Gary R. Habermas, *Did the Resurrection Happen? A Conversation with Gary Habermas and Antony Flew* (ed. David Baggett; Downers Grove, IL: IVP, 2009), p. 26.

[35] Graham Stanton, *The Gospels and Jesus* (OUP, 2002), p. 175.

[36] In a lecture in Michaelmas term entitled 'Reliability of the Gospels', given in Wycliffe Hall, Oxford, 2006.

[37] Gerd Theissen and Annette Merz, *The Historical Jesus: A Comprehensive Guide* (Fortress, 1998), p. 94, quoted by John Dickson, *Life of Jesus: Who He Is and Why He Matters* (Grand Rapids, MI: Zondervan, 2010), p. 39.

[38] Tom Powers, BARev (July/August 2003): p. 51.

[39] Alexander Metherell in Lee Strobel, *The Case for Christ* (Grand Rapids, MI: Zondervan, 1998), pp. 198–9.

[40] Ronald H. Nash, *World-Views in Conflict: Choosing Christianity in a World of Ideas* (Grand Rapids, MI: Zondervan, 1992), p. 158.

[41] Peter Kreeft and Ronald Tacelli, *Handbook of Christian Apologetics* (Crowborough: Monarch, 1999), p. 183.

[42] A. Rendle Short, *Why Believe?* (London: Inter-Varsity Fellowship, 1962), pp. 48–9.

[43] C. Truman Davies, 'The Crucifixion of Jesus – A Medical Account', *Arizona Medicine* (March 1965): p. 186.

[44] William D. Edwards et al., 'On the Physical Death of Jesus Christ' http://www.godandscience.org/apologetics/deathjesus.pdf.

[45] Geza Vermes, op. cit., p. 22.

[46] John Robinson, *The Human Face of God* (London: Westminster Press, 1973), p. 131.

[47] Gerd Ludemann, *Jesus' Resurrection: Fact or Figment?* (Downers Grove, IL: IVP, 2000), p. 52.

[48] Quoted by William Lane Craig, *Jesus' Resurrection: Fact or Figment?* (ed. Paul Copan and Ronald K. Tacelli; Downers Grove, IL: IVP, 2000), p. 35.

[49] William Lane Craig, *The Son Rises* (Eugene, OR: Wipf & Stock, 2000), p. 53.

[50] Raymond Brown, *The Death of the Messiah* (London: Bantam/Doubleday, 1999).

[51] Wolfgang Trilling, *Fragen zur Geschichtlichkeit Jesu* (Patmos Verlag, 1966), p. 157.

[52] Dickson, op. cit., p. 117.

[53] Alister McGrath, *Jesus: Who He Is and Why He Matters* (Leicester: IVP, 1994), p. 89.

[54] J.P. Moreland, *Scaling the Secular City* (Grand Rapids, MI: Baker Books, 1987), p. 163.

[55] N.T. Wright, *Surprised by Hope* (London: SPCK, 2007), p. 73.

[56] Moreland, op. cit., p. 161.

[57] cf. Doug Powell, 'Do the Accounts of the Women at the Empty Tomb Contradict Each Other?' http://www.selflessdefense.doug powell.com/index.php?option=com_content&view=article&id= 10:do-the-accounts-of-the-women-at-the-empty-tomb-contradict-each-other&catid=4:articles&Itemid=3.

[58] *Mishnah Shabout* 4.1, quoted by John Dickson, *Investigating Jesus: An Historian's Quest* (Oxford: Lion, 2010), p. 130.

[59] Vermes, op. cit., p. 142.

[60] William Lane Craig and Walter Sinnot-Armstrong, *God? A Debate between a Christian and an Atheist* (OUP, 2004), p. 23.

[61] Craig A. Evans, 'Who Was Jesus? A Christian Perspective', in *Who Was Jesus? A Jewish–Christian Dialogue* (ed. Paul Copan and Craig A. Evans; Louisville, KY: Westminster John Knox Press, 2001), p. 25.

[62] Antony Flew in *Did the Resurrection Happen?* op. cit., p. 28.

[63] William Lane Craig, *Jesus' Resurrection: Fact or Figment?* op. cit., p. 182.

[64] Craig and Sinnot-Armstrong, op. cit., p. 23.

[65] Jake O'Connell, 'Jesus' Resurrection and Collective Hallucinations', *Tyndale Bulletin* 60:1 (2009): p. 75.

[66] Robert L. Reymond, *Faith's Reasons for Believing* (Fearn, Ross-shire: Mentor, 2008), p. 149.

67 James G. Crossley in *How Did Christianity Begin?* (London: SPCK, 2008), p. 52.

68 Habermas in Baggett, ed., op. cit., p. 56.

69 Reymond, op. cit., p. 149.

70 James G.D. Dunn, *Christianity in the Making, vol. 1: Jesus Remembered* (Grand Rapids, MI: Eerdmans, 2003), p. 825.

71 Pinchas Lapide, *The Resurrection of Jesus: A Jewish Perspective* (Minneapolis, MN: Augsburg, 1983), p. 99.

72 Moreland, op. cit., p. 179.

73 Flew in Baggett, op. cit., p. 57.

74 Craig, *The Son Rises*, op. cit., p. 108.

75 Antony Flew in *Did Jesus Rise from the Dead?* (ed. Terry L. Miethe; Eugene, OR: Wipf & Stock, 2003), p. 79.

76 Reginald H. Fuller, *The Foundations of New Testament Christology* (New York: Scribner, 1965).

77 Vermes, op. cit., p. 149.

78 James G. Crossley in *How Did Christianity Begin?* (London: SPCK, 2008), p. 52.

79 E.P. Sanders, *The Historical Figure of Jesus* (London: Penguin, 1993), p. 280.

80 N.T. Wright, 'Jesus' Resurrection and Christian Origins', in *Passionate Conviction: Contemporary Discourses on Christian Apologetics* (ed. Paul Copan and William Lane Craig; Nashville, TN: B&H Academic, 2007), p. 136.

81 Bart Ehrman in 'Is There Historical Evidence for the Resurrection of Jesus?' (Ehrman's Second Rebuttal) http://www.reasonablefaith.org/site/DocServer/resurrection-debate-transcript.pdf?docID=621.

82 Gary R. Habermas, 'Did Jesus Perform Miracles?', in *Jesus under Fire* (ed. Michael J. Wilkins and J.P. Moreland; Carlisle: Paternoster, 1996), p. 126.

83 Kreeft and Tacelli, op. cit., p. 182.

84 ibid.

85 Michael Green, 'Jesus in the New Testament', in *The Truth of God Incarnate* (London: Hodder & Stoughton, 1977), pp. 36–8.

86 Craig, *Reasonable Faith*, op. cit., p. 391.

87 Gerald O'Collins, 'The Resurrection: The State of the Question', in *The Resurrection* (ed. Stephen T. Davis et al., OUP, 1998), p. 18.

88 Michael Green, 'Jesus and Historical Scepticism', in *The Truth of God Incarnate*, op. cit., p. 128, my italics.

89 Gary R. Habermas, *The Historical Jesus: Ancient Evidence for the Life of Christ* (Joplin, MO: College Press, 2001), p. 281.

90 Craig L. Blomberg, *The Historical Reliability of the Gospels* (Leicester: Apollos, 2007), p. 101.

91 J.N.D. Anderson, *Christianity: The Witness of History* (Tyndale Press, 1969), p. 91; cf. Alister McGrath, 'Resurrection and Incarnation', in *Different Gospels* (ed. Andrew Walker; London: SPCK, 1993).

92 Carl Braaten, *New Directions in Theology Today, vol. 2: History and Hermeneutics* (ed. William Horden; Philadelphia: Westminster Press, 1966), p. 78.

93 Kai Nielsen, 'An Atheist's Rebuttal', in *Does God Exist? The Debate between Theists and Atheists* (Amherst, NY: Prometheus, 1993), p. 66.

94 Vermes, op. cit., p. 145.

95 ibid., p. 144.

96 Richard Purtill, 'Miracles: What If They Happen?', in *Miracles* (ed. Richard Swinburne; New York: Macmillan, 1989), p. 196.

97 William Paley, *A View of the Evidences of Christianity* (2 vols; Westmead, 5th edn, 1970), 1:327–8.

98 Angela Tilby, *Son of God* (London: Hodder & Stoughton, 2001), p. 161.

99 Craig and Sinnott-Armstrong, op. cit., p. 24.

100 Thomas D. Sullivan and Sandra Menssen, 'Revelation and Miracles', in *Christian Philosophical Theology* (ed. Charles Taliaferro and Chad Meister; CUP, 2010), p. 215.

101 Kreeft and Tacelli, op. cit., pp. 184–5.

102 Flew, *Did Jesus Rise from the Dead?* op. cit., p. 79.

103 David Hume, 'Of Miracles', in *The Portable Atheist* (ed. Christopher Hitchens; London: Da Capo, 2007), p. 36.

104 Craig, *Reasonable Faith*, op. cit., pp. 371, 373.

105 The 'Shroud of Turin' – which bears a superficial, photographically negative image of a flogged and crucified man (an image that also contains three-dimensional information) – was formerly dismissed by many on the basis of 1988 carbon dating tests giving a medieval date. However, recent peer-reviewed scientific findings show that the carbon dating was unreliable, while a mass of historical and forensic evidence points towards a first-century date for the Shroud. cf. Raymond N. Rogers, 'Studies on the Radiocarbon Sample from the Shroud of Turin', *Thermochimica Acta* 425: pp. 189–94 http://www.shroud.it/ROGERS-3.PDF; Raymond N. Rogers and Anna Arnoldi, 'The Shroud of Turin: An Amino-Carbonyl Reaction (Maillard

Reaction) May Explain the Image Formation', *Melanoidins* 4 (ed. J.M. Ames; Luxembourg: Office for Official Publications of the European Communities, 2003): pp. 106–13 http://shroud.com/pdfs/rogers7. pdf; John L. Brown, 'Microscopial Investigation of Selected Raes Threads from the Shroud of Turin' http://www.shroud.com/pdfs/ brown1.pdf; Peter S. Williams, 'The Shroud of Turin: A Cumulative Case for Authenticity' http://www.case.edu.au/images/uploads/03 _pdfs/williams-shroud-turin.pdf.

106 cf. William Lane Craig, 'The Guard on the Tomb' http://www.reasonablefaith.org/site/News2?page=NewsArticle&id=5211.

107 Lee Strobel, *The Case for Christ* (Grand Rapids, MI: Zondervan, 1998), p. 192.

108 Foster, op. cit., p. 72.

109 ibid.

110 David Strauss, *A New Life of Jesus* (2 vols; Edinburgh: Williams and Norgate, 2nd edn, 1879), 1:412.

111 Kreeft and Tacelli, op. cit., p. 184.

112 O'Connell, op. cit., p. 85.

113 cf. Michael R. Lincona, 'Were the Resurrection Appearances of Jesus Hallucinations?', in *Evidence for God* (ed. William A. Dembski and Michael R. Licona; Grand Rapids, MI: Baker, 2010), p. 177.

114 Kreeft and Tacelli, op. cit., p. 120.

115 Winfried Corduan, *No Doubt about It: The Case for Christianity* (Nashville, TN: Broadman & Holman, 1997).

116 Craig, op. cit., p. 114.

117 C.S. Lewis, *Miracles* (London: Fount, 1998), p. 156.

118 O'Connell, op. cit., p. 105.

119 ibid., p. 84.

120 ibid., p. 85.

121 ibid.

122 ibid., p. 86.

123 ibid., p. 87–8.

124 ibid., p. 88.

125 Robert H. Gundry in *Jesus' Resurrection: Fact or Figment?* op. cit., p. 109.

126 Wright, *Surprised by Hope*, op. cit., p. 69.

127 James D.G. Dunn, 'In Grateful Dialogue', in *Memories of Jesus*, op. cit., pp. 321–2.

128 Vermes, op. cit., p. 86.

[129] Kreeft and Tacelli, op. cit., pp. 187–8.

[130] Antony O'Hear, *Jesus for Beginners* (Cambridge: Icon, 1993), p. 97.

[131] Kreeft and Tacelli, op. cit., p. 188.

[132] Dallas Willard, *Knowing Christ Today* (New York: HarperOne, 2009), p. 134.

[133] William Lane Craig, 'Contemporary Scholarship and the Historical Resurrection of Jesus Christ' http://www.leaderu.com/truth/1truth22.html.

[134] Stephen T. Davis, *Risen Indeed* (London: SPCK, 1993), pp. 180–81.

[135] Antony Flew in *Resurrected? An Atheist and Theist Dialogue* (ed. John F. Ankerberg; Oxford: Rowman & Littlefield, 2005), p. 29.

[136] Charles Hartshorne in *Did Jesus Rise from the Dead?* op. cit., p. 137.

[137] F.F. Bruce, *The New Testament Documents: Are They Reliable?* (Leicester: IVP, 1981), p. 64.

[138] William Lane Craig, 'The Resurrection of Jesus' ww.reasonablefaith.org/site/News2?page=NewsArticle&id=5351.

[139] N.T. Wright, 'Jesus' Resurrection and Christian Origins', in *Passionate Conviction*, op. cit., pp. 136–7.

[140] Wright, *The Resurrection of the Son of God*, op. cit., p. 654.

[141] Stephen T. Davis in *Jesus' Resurrection: Fact or Figment?* (Leicester: IVP, 2000).

[142] Richard Swinburne, 'Evidence for the Resurrection', in *The Resurrection*, op. cit., p. 207.

[143] Clark H. Pinnock, *Reason Enough: A Case for the Christian Faith* (Carlisle: Paternoster, 1980), p. 88.

[144] R. Douglas Geivett, 'The Epistemology of Resurrection Belief', in *The Resurrection of Jesus* (ed. Robert B. Stewart; London: SPCK, 2006), p. 96.

[145] Baggett, op. cit., p. 128.

[146] Michael R. Licona, 'The Evidence for Jesus' Resurrection', in *The Big Argument: Does God Exist?* (ed. John Ashton and Michael Westacott; Green Forest, AR: Master Books, 2006), p. 372.

[147] William Lane Craig, 'The Craig–Pigliucci Debate: Does God Exist?' http://www.reasonablefaith.org/site/News2?page=NewsArticle&id=5303.

6 – The Fourth Way – Jesus and Fulfilled Prophecy

[1] cf. Carsten Peter Thiede, *The Emmaus Mystery: Discovering Evidence for the Risen Christ* (London: Continuum, 2005).

[2] Craig L. Blomberg, *The Historical Reliability of the Gospels* (Leicester: Apollos, 2008), p. 51.

[3] Alan Richardson, *Christian Apologetics* (London: SCM, 1948), pp. 200–01.

[4] ibid., p. 198.

[5] Norman L. Geisler in Lee Strobel, *The Case for Faith* (Grand Rapids, MI: Zondervan, 2000), p. 132.

[6] Richardson, op. cit., p. 199.

[7] Victor J. Stenger, *The New Atheism: Taking a Stand for Science and Reason* (New York: Prometheus, 2009), p. 181.

[8] Thomas V. Morris, *Making Sense of It All: Pascal and the Meaning of Life* (Grand Rapids, MI: Eerdmans, 1992), p. 165.

[9] William A. Dembski, 'Another Way to Detect Design?' http://www.arn.org/docs/dembski/wd_responsetowiscu.htm.

[10] cf. William A. Dembski, 'The Logical Underpinnings of Intelligent Design', in William A. Dembski and Michael Ruse, eds, *Debating Design: From Darwin to DNA* (CUP, 2004); William A. Dembski, 'Reinstating Design within Science', in *Darwinism, Design, and Public Education* (East Lansing: Michigan State University Press, 2003); William A. Dembski, 'Naturalism and Design', in William Lane Craig and J.P. Moreland, eds, *Naturalism: A Critical Analysis* (London: Routledge, 2000).

[11] cf. Peter S. Williams, 'The Design Inference from Specified Complexity Defended by Scholars Outside the Intelligent Design Movement: A Critical Review', *Philosophia Christi* 9:2 http://www.epsociety.org/library/articles.asp?pid=54.

[12] Richard Dawkins, *The Blind Watchmaker* (London: Penguin, 1990), p. 9.

[13] Richard Dawkins, *Climbing Mount Improbable* (London: Viking, 1996), p. 4.

[14] ibid., p. 3.

[15] ibid.

[16] ibid.

[17] ibid.

[18] ibid.

[19] ibid.

[20] ibid.

[21] Richard Dawkins, op-ed, *Free Inquiry* 24:6 (October/November 2004): pp. 11–12.

[22] William Dembski, 'The Act of Creation: Bridging Transcendence and Immanence' http://www.arn.org/docs/dembski/wd_actofcreation.

htm cf: Robert C. Newman, 'Fulfilled Prophecy as Miracle', in *In Defence of Miracles* (ed. Douglas R. Geivett and Gary R. Habermas; Leicester: Apollos, 1997).

[23] Robert C. Newman, 'Fulfilled Prophecy as Miracle', in *In Defence of Miracles* (ed. Douglas R. Geivett and Gary R. Habermas; Leicester: Apollos, 1997), p. 214.

[24] Charles Foster, *The Christmas Mystery: What on Earth Happened at Bethlehem?* (Milton Keynes: Authentic, 2007); Michael R. Molnar, *The Star of Bethlehem: The Legacy of the Magi* (Rutgers University Press, 2000).

[25] Josephus, *Jewish War* 6.5.4.

[26] cf. Stephen E. Jones, 'Daniel's 70 "Weeks": Proof That Naturalism Is False and Christianity Is True' http://creationevolutiondesign.blog spot.com/2005/07/daniels-70-weeks-proof-that-naturalism.html.

[27] Newman, op. cit., p. 224.

[28] For ease of calculation I have assumed that all twelve tribes were of the same size.

[29] Bethlehem was 1 out of 204 towns in Israel – a number reported by Josephus; and while the chances of being born in a bigger settlement are higher than the chances of being born in a smaller settlement (like Bethlehem), I've been conservative in simply ignoring this factor here.

[30] Although the application of Deuteronomy 18:15 to Jesus may appear to be typological, this OT passage was the basis of a first-century Jewish expectation, formed independently of Jesus' own reputation, that the Messiah would be a prophet. Peter E. Cousins comments: 'By NT times, [Deuteronomy 18:15] was understood as a precursor of the Messiah or of the Messiah himself (Jn 1:21, 45; 6:14; 6:40; Ac 3:20–22; 7:37, etc.).' – 'Deuteronomy', in *Zondervan Bible Commentary: One-Volume Illustrated Edition* (ed. F.F. Bruce; Grand Rapids, MI: Zondervan, 2008), p. 205. This expectation was maintained by the medieval Jewish philosopher Moses Maimonides, who stated: 'The Messiah will be a very great Prophet ...' cf. Josh McDowell, *The New Evidence That Demands a Verdict* (Nashville, TN: Thomas Nelson, 1999), p. 177.

[31] Graham Stanton notes that reports of miracle workers in Jesus' day 'are not common' and that besides Jesus they 'do not include cures of the deaf, the dumb and the lame.' – 'Message and Miracles', in *The Cambridge Companion to Jesus* (ed. Markus Bockmuehl; CUP, 2001), p. 111.

³² Roy Williams, *God, Actually* (Oxford: Monarch, 2009), p. 208.

³³ Geisler in Strobel, op. cit., p. 132.

³⁴ Angela Tilby, *Son of God* (London: Hodder & Stoughton, 2001), p. 157.

³⁵ Norman L. Geisler and Frank Turek, *I Don't Have Enough Faith to Be an Atheist* (Wheaton, IL: Crossway, 2004), p. 339.

³⁶ 'Flogging was a legal preliminary to every Roman execution, and only women and Roman senators or soldiers (except in cases of desertion) were exempt.' – William D. Edwards, Wesley J. Gabel, Floyd E. Hosmer, 'On the Physical Death of Jesus Christ', in JAMA 11 (21 March 1986), pp. 1457–8.

³⁷ John is the only gospel to reference Psalm 22. It also goes into greater detail here than the synoptic gospels, in line with the hypothesis that John was an eyewitness. The Roman legal *Digesta* 48:20.1 reads: 'The Divine Hadrian stated in a Rescript to Aquilius Bradua: "It is evident that, by the name itself, one ought to understand what is meant by 'clothing.' For no one can reasonably say that under this term is included the property of persons who have been condemned, for if anyone is wearing a girdle, no one should claim it on this ground [i.e. one can't claim 'property' that isn't 'clothing']; but any clothing which he wears, or any small sums of money which he may have in his possession for the purpose of living, or any light rings, that is to say, any which are not worth more than five aurei, can be demanded [one can demand 'clothing']. Otherwise, if the convicted person should have on his finger a sardonyx, or any other precious stone of great value, or have in his possession any note calling for a large sum of money, this [i.e. this 'property'] can, by no right, be retained as part of his clothing [i.e. things that *do* come under the definition of 'clothing' *can* be retained by right]." Clothing of which a man can be stripped are those things which he brought with him when he was placed in prison, and with which he is attired when he is conducted to punishment, as the name itself indicates. Hence, neither the executioners nor their assistants can claim these things [i.e. 'possessions' that don't come under the definition of 'clothing'] as spoils at the moment when the culprit is executed [note that the soldiers take the 'clothing' of the culprit when they execute him]. Governors should not appropriate these articles [i.e. 'property'] for their own benefit, or suffer assistants or jailors to profit by this money, but they ought to preserve it [i.e. 'property'] for expenditures which Governors have the right to make; as, for instance, for paper for the use of certain officials; or as donations for soldiers who

have distinguished themselves by their courage; or to be presented to barbarians belonging to an embassy; or for some other purpose. Frequently, moreover, Governors have paid into the Treasury sums of money which they had collected, which is a manifestation of too great diligence, as it will be sufficient if they do not appropriate it to their own use, but permit it to be employed for the benefit of their office.' – cf. The Same, On the Duties of Proconsul, Book X http://www.constitution.org/sps/sps11.htm (my italics and brackets).

[38] Specifically, 1 in 1,073,741,824.

[39] cf. http://www.newton.dep.anl.gov/askasci/ast99/ast99215.htm.

[40] Mark L. Strauss, *Four Portraits, One Jesus: An Introduction to Jesus and the Gospels* (Grand Rapids, MI: Zondervan, 2007), pp. 504–5.

[41] Alister E. McGrath, *Making Sense of the Cross* (Leicester: IVP, 1992), p. 43.

[42] C. Stephen Evans, *Why Believe? Reason and Mystery as Pointers to God* (Leicester: IVP, rev. edn, 1996), pp. 130–31.

[43] Evans, op. cit., p. 131.

[44] Richard Purtill, *Reason to Believe: Why Faith Makes Sense* (San Francisco: Ignatius, 2009), p. 196.

[45] Joel B. Green and Mark D. Baker, *Recovering the Scandal of the Cross: Atonement In New Testament and Contemporary Contexts* (Carlisle: Paternoster, 2000), p. 51.

[46] cf. ibid., pp. 56–7.

[47] Keith Ward, *What the Bible Really Teaches: A Challenge for Fundamentalists* (London: SPCK, 2004), pp. 109–10.

[48] Evans, op. cit., pp. 131–2.

[49] Tim Bayne and Greg Restall, 'A Participatory Model of the Atonement' http://www.consequently.org/papers/pa.pdf cf. Stuart C. Hackett, *The Reconstruction of the Christian Revelation Claim* (Eugene, OR: Wipf & Stock, 2008), pp. 198–200.

[50] Evans, op. cit., p. 133.

[51] Williams, op. cit., p. 209.

[52] Ian Wilson, *The Bible Is History* (London: Weidenfeld & Nicolson, 1999), p. 238.

[53] William Shea, 'Amazing Biblical Prophecies that Came to Pass', in *The Big Argument: Does God Exist?* (ed. John Ashton and Michael Westacott; Portland, OR: Master Books, 2006), p. 333.

[54] F.F. Bruce, *The Hard Sayings of Jesus* (London: Hodder & Stoughton, 1998), pp. 229–30.

[55] David Winter, *The Search for the Real Jesus* (London: Hodder & Stoughton, 1982), p. 102.

[56] ibid.

[57] Geza Vermes, *The Changing Faces of Jesus* (London: Penguin Books, 2000), p. 69.

[58] N.T. Wright, *What Saint Paul Really Said: Was Paul of Tarsus the Real Founder of Christianity?* (Grand Rapids, MI: Eerdmans, 1997), pp. 36–7.

[59] cf. 'Was Jesus Mistaken about His Second Coming?' http://www.christian-thinktank.com/qaim.html.

[60] A.B. Bruce, *Apologetics or Christianity Defensively Stated* (1892), p. 376, quoted by T.C. Hammond, *Reasoning Faith: An Introduction to Christian Apologetics* (London: IVP, 1943), p. 213.

[61] Craig L. Blomberg, *The Historical Reliability of John's Gospel: Issues and Commentary* (Leicester: Apollos, 2001), p. 251.

[62] Stuart C. Hackett, *The Reconstruction of the Christian Revelation Claim* (Eugene, OR: Wipf & Stock, 2008), p. 325.

[63] ibid., p. 214.

[64] Stephen T. Davis, 'Should We Believe the Jesus Seminar?', in *Disputed Issues: Contending for Christian Faith in Today's Academic Setting* (Waco, TX: Baylor University Press, 2009), p. 12.

[65] cf. Paul Barnett, *Jesus and the Rise of Early Christianity* (Downers Grove, IL: IVP, 1999), pp. 303–7; E.M.B. Green, '2 Peter Reconsidered' http://www.biblicalstudies.org.uk/pdf/2peter_green.pdf; David F. Payne, '2 Peter', in *Zondervan Bible Commentary* (ed. F.F. Bruce; Grand Rapids, MI: Zondervan, 2008); Ben Witherington III, 'A Petrine Source in 2 Peter', *Society of Biblical Literature Seminar Papers* (1985), pp. 187–92.

[66] Norman L. Geisler, *Christian Apologetics* (Grand Rapids, MI: Baker, 1979), p. 343.

[67] ibid.

[68] H.P. Owen, *Christian Theism: A Study in Its Basic Principles* (Edinburgh: T&T Clark, 1984), p. 117.

[69] Paul Marston and Roger Forster, *God's Strategy in Human History* (Eugene, OR: Wipf & Stock, 2000), pp. 131, 296, 305.

[70] Irenaeus, *Against Heresies*, quoted by Marston and Forster, ibid., p. 298.

[71] Paul Copan, *That's Just Your Interpretation* (Grand Rapids, MI: Baker, 2001), p. 78.

[72] ibid.

[73] Peter Cave, *This Sentence Is False: An Introduction to Philosophical Paradoxes* (London: Continuum, 2010), p. 133.

[74] Copan, op. cit., p. 80.

[75] Hackett, op. cit., p. 329.

[76] Robert D. Culver, 'Were the Old Testament Prophecies Really Prophetic?', in Howard F. Vos, ed., *Can I Trust the Bible?* (Chicago: Moody Press, 1963), pp. 115–16.

[77] Stephen C. Meyer in *The Creation Hypothesis* (ed. J.P. Moreland; Downers Grove, IL: IVP, 1994), p. 97.

[78] Morris, op. cit., p. 166.

7 – The Fifth Way – Jesus and Contemporary Experience

[1] Peter Kreeft, *Christianity for Modern Pagans* (San Francisco: Ignatius, 1993), p. 325.

[2] Dallas Willard, *Knowing Christ Today* (New York: HarperOne, 2009), pp. 139, 152.

[3] ibid., pp. 141–2.

[4] Amy Orr-Ewing, *But Is It Real? Answering 10 Common Objections to the Christian Faith* (Nottingham: IVP, 2008), p. 23.

[5] Basil Mitchell, *The Justification of Religious Belief* (London: Macmillan, 1973), p. 108.

[6] Niles Eldredge, *The Triumph of Evolution and the Failure of Creationism* (New York: Freeman, 2000), p. 13.

[7] Richard Dawkins, *The God Delusion* (London: Bantam, 2006), p. 90.

[8] ibid., p. 92.

[9] Luke Timothy Johnson, *The Real Jesus* (New York: HarperOne, 1997), p. 122.

[10] Clive Calver, *The Holy Spirit* (Bletchley: Scripture Union, 2001), p. 124.

[11] J.P. Moreland, 'On the Gift of Prophecy' http://www.jpmoreland.com/media/on-the-gift-of-prophecy.

[12] Peter Kreeft, *Angels and Demons* (San Francisco: Ignatius, 1995), p. 102.

[13] Kenneth D. Boa and Robert M. Bowman Jr, *Sense and Nonsense about Angels and Demons* (Grand Rapids, MI: Zondervan, 2007), p. 96.

[14] ibid., pp. 96–7.

[15] Phillip H. Wiebe, *God and Other Spirits: Intimations of Transcendence in Christian Experience* (Oxford University Press, 2004), p. 8.

[16] ibid., p. 7.

[17] ibid.

[18] ibid., p. 190.

[19] ibid., pp. 159–61.

[20] ibid., pp. 11–12.

[21] ibid., p. 13.

[22] David Instone-Brewer, 'Jesus and the Psychiatrists', in *The Unseen World: Christian Reflections on Angels, Demons and the Heavenly Realm* (ed. Anthony N.S. Lane; Carlisle: Paternoster, 1996).

[23] ibid., p. 140.

[24] ibid., pp. 142–3.

[25] ibid., p. 143.

[26] M. Scott Peck, *Glimpses of the Devil* (New York: Free Press, 2005), p. 11.

[27] M. Scott Peck, *People of the Lie* (London: Arrow, 1983), p. 208.

[28] ibid., pp. 208–9.

[29] ibid., pp. 209, 224.

[30] ibid., p. 219.

[31] ibid., pp. 217, 225.

[32] ibid., p. 227.

[33] Billy Graham, *Angels* (London: Hodder & Stoughton, 2004), p. 15.

[34] Wiebe, op. cit., p. 75.

[35] Emma Heathcote-James, *Seeing Angels: True Contemporary Accounts of Hundreds of Angelic Experiences* (London: John Blake, 2001), pp. 237–8.

[36] ibid., p. 247.

[37] ibid., p. 15.

[38] Dawkins, op. cit., p. 65.

[39] ibid., pp. 65–6.

[40] cf. BBC News, 'Heart Patients "Benefit from Prayer"' http://www.news.bbc.co.uk/1/hi/health/1627662.stm.

[41] Phyllis McIntosh, 'Faith Is Powerful Medicine', in *Reader's Digest* (May 2000); cf. R.C. Byrd, 'Positive Therapeutic Effects of Intercessory Prayer in a Coronary Care Unit Population', *SMJ* 81 (1988): pp. 826–9.

[42] Charles Colson and Nancy Pearcey, *How Now Shall We Live?* (London: Marshall Pickering, 2000), p. 313.

[43] J.A. Astin, E. Harkness and E. Ernst MD, 'The Efficacy of "Distant Healing": A Systematic Review of Randomized Trials', *Ann Intern Med* 132 (2000): pp. 903–10.

[44] 'Does God Answer Prayer? ASU Research Says "Yes"' http://www.physorg.com/news93105311.html.

[45] David R. Hodge, quoted in 'Does God Answer Prayer? ASU Research Says "Yes"' http://www.physorg.com/news93105311.html.

[46] Gary R. Habermas, 'Our Personal God: God Interacts with Us' http://www.garyhabermas.com/books/why_believe/whybelieve.htm#ch29.

[47] J.P. Moreland, *Kingdom Triangle* (Grand Rapids, MI: Zondervan, 2007), p. 198.

[48] J.P. Moreland http://preachingtoday.com/illustrations/article_print.html?id=51862.

[49] Michael Poole, *Miracles: Science, the Bible and Experience* (London: Scripture Union, 1992), p. 7.

[50] ibid., p. 8.

[51] ibid., pp. 9–10.

[52] ibid., p. 10.

[53] Bill Lees, 'Are People Healed Today?', in *Christian Healing: What Can We Believe?* (ed. Ernest Lucas; London: Lynx, 1997), pp. 11–12.

[54] *The Independent on Sunday*, 7 January 2007, p. 15.

[55] ibid.

[56] J.P. Moreland and Klaus Issler, *In Search of a Confident Faith: Overcoming Barriers to Trusting in God* (Nottingham: IVP, 2008), p. 149.

[57] Andrew Wilson, *Deluded by Dawkins? A Christian Response to* The God Delusion (Eastbourne: Kingsway, 2007), p. 47.

[58] ibid., pp. 47–8.

[59] Richard Swinburne, *The Existence of God* (Oxford: Clarendon, 1991) pp. 273–4.

[60] H.H. Price, quoted by Charles Taliaferro, *Contemporary Philosophy of Religion* (Oxford: Blackwell, 2001), p. 272.

[61] William P. Alston, *Perceiving God: The Epistemology of Religious Experience* (Cornell University Press, 1991), p. 280.

[62] Paul D. Feinberg, *Five Views on Apologetics* (ed. Steven B. Cowan; Grand Rapids, MI: Zondervan, 2000), p. 161.

[63] Joshua Hoffman and Gary S. Rosenkrantz, *Substance: Its Nature and Existence* (London: Routledge, 1997), p. 7.

[64] Norman L. Geisler and Winfried Corduan, *Philosophy of Religion* (Eugene, OR: Wipf & Stock, 2nd edn, 1988), p. 76.

[65] J.P. Moreland, *Scaling the Secular City* (Grand Rapids, MI: Baker, 1987), p. 235.

[66] ibid., p. 240.

[67] Alston, op. cit., p. 146.

68 ibid., p. 149.

69 ibid., p. 153.

70 ibid., pp. 183, 225.

71 ibid., p. 195.

72 Taliaferro, op. cit., p. 274.

73 Alston, op. cit., pp. 198–9.

74 ibid., p. 67.

75 ibid., p. 33.

76 Moreland, op. cit., p. 238.

77 Taliaferro, op. cit., p. 274.

78 Alston, op. cit., p. 201.

79 C. Stephen Layman, *Letters to Doubting Thomas: A Case for the Existence of God* (OUP, 2007), p. 61.

80 Alston, op. cit., pp. 170–71.

81 ibid., p. 171.

82 ibid., p. 52.

83 ibid., p. 61.

84 ibid.

85 Keith E. Yandell, quoted by Taliaferro, op. cit., p. 267.

86 William P. Alston, 'Why Should There *Not* Be Experience of God?', in *Philosophy of Religion: A Guide and Anthology* (ed. Brian Davies; Oxford, 2000), p. 386.

87 Moreland, op. cit., p. 227.

88 R. Douglas Geivett, 'The Evidential Value of Religious Experience', in *The Rationality of Theism* (ed. Paul Copan and Paul K. Moser; London: Routledge, 2003), p. 183.

89 Alston, *Perceiving God*, op. cit., p. 304.

90 Moreland, op. cit.

91 Alston, op. cit., p. 35.

92 Basil Mitchell, *The Justification of Religious Belief* (London: Macmillan, 1973), p. 42.

93 William Lane Craig, in Lee Strobel, *The Case for Faith* (Grand Rapids, MI: Zondervan, 2000), p. 86.

94 John Dickson, *Life of Christ: Who He Is and Why He Matters* (Grand Rapids, MI: Zondervan, 2010), p. 30.

95 Strobel, op. cit., p. 259.

96 J.P. Moreland in *Does God Exist? The Debate between Theists and Atheists* (New York: Prometheus, 1993), p. 74.

97 Moreland, op. cit., p. 232.

⁹⁸ ibid., pp. 233–4.
⁹⁹ Tom Wright, *Simply Christian* (London: SPCK, 2006), p. 81.

8 – Understanding the Spirituality of Jesus

¹ Douglas Groothuis, *On Pascal* (London: Thompson Wadsworth, 2003), p. 41.
² David Hume, *Dialogues Concerning Natural Religion* (ed. Norman Kemp Smith; Indianapolis: Bobbs-Merrill, 1947), p. 227.
³ Dallas Willard, *The Divine Conspiracy: Rediscovering Our Hidden Life in God* (London: Fount, 1998), p. 2.
⁴ Michael Green, *Lies, Lies, Lies!* (Nottingham: IVP, 2009), p. 18.
⁵ Darrell L. Bock in *The Historical Jesus: Five Views* (ed. James B. Beilby and Paul R. Eddy; London: SPCK, 2010), pp. 196–7.
⁶ Darrell L. Bock, *Jesus According to Scripture: Restoring the Portrait from the Gospels* (Grand Rapids, MI: Baker Academic, 2002), pp. 636–7.
⁷ Perry G. Downs, *Teaching for Spiritual Growth: An Introduction to Christian Education* (Grand Rapids, MI: Zondervan, 1994), p. 18.
⁸ ibid., p. 19.
⁹ Marcus Borg, *Jesus: A New Vision*, p. 17, quoted by Luke Timothy Johnson, *The Real Jesus* (New York: HarperOne, 1997), p. 41.
¹⁰ Peter Kreeft, *Christianity for Modern Pagans* (San Francisco: Ignatius, 1993), p. 147.
¹¹ Bock, op. cit., p. 646.
¹² Charles Colson, *Against the Night: Living in the New Dark Ages* (Ann Arbor, MI: Servant, 1999), p. 140.
¹³ Dallas Willard, *Knowing Christ Today: Why We Can Trust Spiritual Knowledge* (New York: HarperOne, 2009), p. 152.
¹⁴ N.T. Wright, *Surprised by Hope* (London: SPCK, 2007), p. 241–2.
¹⁵ Charles Colson and Nancy Pearcey, *How Now Shall We Live?* (London: Marshall Pickering, 1999), p. 193.
¹⁶ Downs, op. cit., p. 19.
¹⁷ Peter Kreeft, *Heaven: The Heart's Deepest Longing* (San Francisco: Ignatius, 1989), pp. 19–20.
¹⁸ Kreeft, *Christianity for Modern Pagans*, op. cit., p. 31.
¹⁹ David Burnett, *Clash of Worlds* (Mill Hill, London: Monarch, 2002), p. 13.
²⁰ W. Jay Wood, *Epistemology: Becoming Intellectually Virtuous* (Leicester: Apollos, 1998), p. 20.

21 C. Stephen Evans, *Philosophy of Religion: Thinking about Faith* (Leicester: IVP, 1982), p. 166.

22 Philip Yancey, quoted by Tim Chester and Steve Timmis in *Total Church: A Radical Reshaping around Gospel and Community* (Nottingham: IVP, 2007), p. 111.

23 Colson, op. cit., p. 95.

24 Chester and Timmis, op. cit., p. 41.

25 Mark Driscoll and Gerry Breshears, *Vintage Church* (Wheaton, IL: Crossway, 2008), p. 191.

26 Keith Ward, *Christianity: A Short Introduction* (Oxford: OneWorld, 2000), pp. 92–3.

27 Andre Comte-Sponville, *The Book of Atheist Spirituality: An Elegant Argument for Spirituality without God* (London: Bantam Press, 2007), pp. 14–15.

28 ibid., p. 15.

29 ibid., p. 130.

30 Willard, op. cit., p. 155.

31 Tobias Jones, *Utopian Dreams: A Search for a Better Life* (London: Faber, 2007), pp. 155, 197–8.

32 ibid., pp. 155, 198–9.

33 ibid., p. 199.

34 Robert Winston, 'Why Do We Believe in God?' http://www.guardian.co.uk/g2/story/0,,1590776,00.html; cf. B.A. Robinson, 'The Relationship Between Church Membership and Prejudice' http://www.religioustolerance.org/chr_prej.htm.

35 Driscoll and Breshears, op. cit., p. 97.

36 Willard, *The Divine Conspiracy*, op. cit., pp. 395–6.

37 ibid., pp. 402–3.

38 Michael Wilkins in Steve and Lois Rabey, eds, *Side By Side: Disciple-Making for a New Century – A Handbook* (Colorado Springs: NavPress, 2000), p. 217.

39 Readers who want to take up this challenge are directed to the following sources: Paul Copan and Paul K. Moser, eds, *The Rationality of Theism* (London: Routledge, 2003); William Lane Craig and J.P. Moreland, eds, *The Blackwell Companion to Natural Theology* (Oxford: Wiley-Blackwell, 2009); William Lane Craig and J.P. Moreland, eds, *Naturalism: A Critical Analysis* (London: Routledge, 2001); James F. Sennett and Douglas Groothuis, eds, *In Defense of Natural Theology: A Post Humean Assessment* (Downers Grove, IL: IVP, 2005); Peter S. Williams, *I Wish I Could*

Believe in Meaning: A Response to Nihilism (Southampton: Damaris, 2004).

[40] John Polkinghorne, 'Where Is Natural Theology Today?', *Science and Christian Belief* 18:2 (2006): p. 172.

[41] See also: Ellis R. Brotzman, *Old Testament Textual Criticism: A Practical Introduction* (Grand Rapids, MI: Baker, 2002); Brian Edwards and Clive Anderson, *Through the British Museum – with the Bible* (Leominster: Day One, 2004); James K. Hoffmeier, *Israel in Egypt: The Evidence for the Authenticity of the Exodus Tradition* (OUP, 1996); Alfred J. Hoerth, *Archaeology and the Old Testament* (Grand Rapids, MI: Baker Academic, 1998); David M. Howard Jr and Michael A. Grisanti, eds, *Giving Sense: Understanding and Using Old Testament Historical Texts* (Leicester: Apollos, 2003); Colin J. Humphreys, *The Miracles of Exodus: A Scientist's Discovery of the Extraordinary Natural Causes of the Biblical Stories* (London: Continuum, 2003); Walter C. Kaiser Jr, *The Old Testament Documents: Are They Reliable and Relevant?* (Nottingham: IVP Academic, 2001); Randall Price, *The Stones Cry Out: What Archaeology Reveals about the Truth of the Bible* (Eugene, OR: Harvest House, 1997); Jeffery L. Sheler, *Is the Bible True? How Modern Debates and Discoveries Affirm the Essence of the Scriptures* (London: HarperCollins, 2000).

[42] John Mark Reynolds, *Against All Gods: What's Right and Wrong about the New Atheism* (Downers Grove, IL: IVP, 2010), p. 89.

[43] Colson, op. cit., p. 172.

[44] Chad V. Meister, *Building Belief: Constructing Faith from the Ground Up* (Eugene, OR: Wipf & Stock, 2009), p. 178.

[45] Austin Farrer, *A Science of God?* (London: SPCK, 2009), p. 70.

[46] Victor J. Stenger, *The New Atheism: Taking a Stand for Science and Reason* (New York: Prometheus, 2009), p. 45.

[47] Reynolds, op. cit., pp. 88–9, 93.

[48] Peter Kreeft, 'Lewis' Philosophy of Truth, Goodness and Beauty', in *C.S. Lewis as Philosopher: Truth, Goodness and Beauty* (ed. David Baggett, Gary R. Habermas and Jerry L. Walls; Downers Grove, IL: IVP, 2008), p. 32.

[49] G.K. Chesterton, *Orthodoxy* (London: Hodder & Stoughton, 1999), p. 14ff.

[50] G.K. Chesterton, *Heretics* (London: House of Stratus, 2001), p. 125.

[51] ibid., pp. 125–6.

[52] ibid., p. 126.

[53] Reynolds, op. cit., p. 103.

54 C.S. Lewis, 'On Obstinacy in Belief', in *The World's Last Night and Other Essays* (London: Fount, 1973), p. 26.

55 Kelly James Clark, *When Faith Is Not Enough* (Grand Rapids, MI: Eerdmans, 1997), p. 32.

56 Evans, op. cit., p. 184.

57 Regis Jolivet, *The God of Reason* (London: Burns & Oates, 1958), p. 119.

58 Eric S. Waterhouse, *The Philosophical Approach to Religion* (London: Epworth Press, 1933), pp. 76–7.

59 William A. Dembski, 'The Task of Apologetics', in *Unapologetic Apologetics: Meeting the Challenge of Theological Studies* (ed. William A. Dembski and Jay Wesley Richards; Downers Grove, IL: IVP, 2001), p. 34.

60 R. Douglas Geivett, 'David Hume and a Cumulative Case Argument', in *In Defense of Natural Theology: A Post Humean Assessment* (ed. James F. Sennett and Douglas Groothuis; Downers Grove, IL: IVP, 2005), pp. 313–14.

61 C.S. Lewis, quoted by James A. Fowler, 'Doubt' http://www.christinyou.net/pages/doubt.html.

62 Michael J. Langford, *Unblind Faith* (London: SCM, 1982), pp. 6, 8.

63 Reynolds, op. cit., p. 93.

64 cf. 'Martyrs of the Modern Era' http://news.bbc.co.uk/1/hi/uk/129587.stm.

65 The goodness and coherent beauty of Christian spirituality are themselves indicators of the truth of the Christian understanding of Jesus that lies at its core.